LEADING With
COMMUNICATION

A **Practical Approach** to **Leadership Communication**

For Lindsay and Matthew, our children,
for optimistically leading us into the 21st century. Their ability to
laugh at themselves (and sometimes at us) helps us keep things in perspective.

LEADING With COMMUNICATION

A **Practical Approach** to **Leadership Communication**

Teri Kwal Gamble | Michael W. Gamble

College of New Rochelle *New York Institute of Technology*

Los Angeles | London | New Delhi
Singapore | Washington DC

Los Angeles | London | New Delhi
Singapore | Washington DC

FOR INFORMATION:

SAGE Publications, Inc.
2455 Teller Road
Thousand Oaks, California 91320
E-mail: order@sagepub.com

SAGE Publications Ltd.
1 Oliver's Yard
55 City Road
London EC1Y 1SP
United Kingdom

SAGE Publications India Pvt. Ltd.
B 1/I 1 Mohan Cooperative Industrial Area
Mathura Road, New Delhi 110 044
India

SAGE Publications Asia-Pacific Pte. Ltd.
3 Church Street
#10-04 Samsung Hub
Singapore 049483

Acquisitions Editor: Matthew Byrnie
Editorial Assistant: Stephanie Palermini
Production Editor: Astrid Virding
Copy Editor: Mark Bast
Typesetter: C&M Digitals (P) Ltd.
Proofreader: Dennis W. Webb
Indexer: William Ragsdale
Cover Designer: Karine Hovsepian
Marketing Manager: Liz Thornton
Permissions Editor: Karen Ehrmann

Printed in the United States of America

Library of Congress Cataloging-in-Publication Data

Gamble, Teri Kwal.

Leading with communication : a practical approach to leadership communication / Teri Kwal Gamble, Michael W. Gamble.

p. cm.

Includes index.

ISBN 978-1-4129-9426-2 (pbk.)

1. Leadership—Psychological aspects. 2. Leadership—Moral and ethical aspects. 3. Business communication. I. Gamble, Michael, 1943- II. Title.

HD57.7.G356 2013
658.4'5—dc23   2012016291

This book is printed on acid-free paper.

12 13 14 15 16 10 9 8 7 6 5 4 3 2 1

LEADING With COMMUNICATION

A **Practical Approach** to **Leadership Communication**

Teri Kwal Gamble | Michael W. Gamble
College of New Rochelle | *New York Institute of Technology*

Los Angeles | London | New Delhi
Singapore | Washington DC

Los Angeles | London | New Delhi
Singapore | Washington DC

FOR INFORMATION:

SAGE Publications, Inc.
2455 Teller Road
Thousand Oaks, California 91320
E-mail: order@sagepub.com

SAGE Publications Ltd.
1 Oliver's Yard
55 City Road
London EC1Y 1SP
United Kingdom

SAGE Publications India Pvt. Ltd.
B 1/I 1 Mohan Cooperative Industrial Area
Mathura Road, New Delhi 110 044
India

SAGE Publications Asia-Pacific Pte. Ltd.
3 Church Street
#10-04 Samsung Hub
Singapore 049483

Acquisitions Editor: Matthew Byrnie
Editorial Assistant: Stephanie Palermini
Production Editor: Astrid Virding
Copy Editor: Mark Bast
Typesetter: C&M Digitals (P) Ltd.
Proofreader: Dennis W. Webb
Indexer: William Ragsdale
Cover Designer: Karine Hovsepian
Marketing Manager: Liz Thornton
Permissions Editor: Karen Ehrmann

Copyright © 2013 by SAGE Publications, Inc.

Printed in the United States of America

Library of Congress Cataloging-in-Publication Data

Gamble, Teri Kwal.

Leading with communication : a practical approach to leadership communication / Teri Kwal Gamble, Michael W. Gamble.

p. cm.

Includes index.

ISBN 978-1-4129-9426-2 (pbk.)

1. Leadership—Psychological aspects. 2. Leadership—Moral and ethical aspects. 3. Business communication. I. Gamble, Michael, 1943- II. Title.

HD57.7.G356 2013
658.4'5—dc23   2012016291

This book is printed on acid-free paper.

12 13 14 15 16 10 9 8 7 6 5 4 3 2 1

BRIEF CONTENTS

Detailed Contents

PREFACE

What is the greatest challenge students face when taking a course? Many report that it's actually taking the time to read and make it through the text. We wrote *Leading With Communication* to help meet this challenge by providing a core introductory text on leadership that offers a communication focus and facilitates the kind of personal leadership journey students taking a first course in leadership should not only have but also *enjoy*.

Leading With Communication offers a four-part emphasis on theory, skill acquisition, skill application, and skill enhancement to meet three primary leadership challenges: the development of a global perspective, the aptitude to think and act like a leader to foster the leading of change and innovation, and the ability to use technology to lead from a distance, enhance leader visibility, and demonstrate leader credibility.

Our goal is to give students a head start on realizing their leadership potential at the same time that we bring to the forefront interesting and pertinent materials that make the study of leadership relevant, involving, and personal. Students enrolled in a first leadership course will benefit from an approach that blends theory, skill development, and skill application. For that reason, this text offers an array of experiential vehicles, an ethical focus, and pedagogical aids designed to promote both content and skill mastery, providing multiple points of entrance, access, and engagement so that users are motivated to process, internalize, and demonstrate the understandings of leadership highlighted in each chapter.

Leading With Communication addresses leadership from a 21st-century perspective, one that not only demonstrates how social-networking tools can be used to build effective teams, but also explores the interconnectivity of people in globally focused organizations. Given the integration of experiences and lifestyles that business travel and overseas assignments provide the members of our contemporary workforce, students hoping to serve as either leaders or valued team members need to hone their abilities to relate with persons of different cultural and ethnic backgrounds. Making clear the connections between theory, ethics, and real-life applications is essential, as is helping students see themselves as actual and potential leaders in different contexts. Being able to "exercise ethical leadership" and not just serve in leadership roles will enrich the future.

To that end, this text facilitates recall of key concepts about effective leadership communication, integrates "best practices" of effective leaders together with a consideration of leadership's darker side, nurtures an attitude designed to promote a desire for lifelong learning about leadership, and helps prepare users for their professional futures.

Leading With Communication provides an understanding of the leadership concepts and team-building strategies that business and professional communicators working and interacting in 21st-century organizations need to master. The text's skills emphasis, and the recognition it gives to developing the global and technological competencies that support the enactment of leadership, is designed to promote the ability to think critically, ethically, and imaginatively and communicate effectively along with learning how to inspire confidence, foster innovation, and build effective teams.

In effect, *Leading With Communication* functions as an active and experiential vehicle for self-discovery, facilitating the ability to express oneself; engage in visioning; build on glocal, global, and technological experiences; and work collaboratively and creatively. In the process, it also instills fresh perspectives on how best to integrate skills and knowledge, build trust, and elevate the personal performance of leadership, together with how to nurture leadership and teambuilding talents in others.

Because we want *Leading With Communication* to be your leadership resource for communication issues, we also offer the following in-text and online features:

Post It: Imagineering a Better Way

This boxed series contains two types of ideas and innovations: (a) those that experts in leadership judge worthy of trying or implementing and (b) those that students create because they believe them good enough to want to try out or implement for themselves.

Self-Reflection: Looking In and Out

This boxed series contains self-assessment and self-diagnosis opportunities designed to help students think critically about skills, identify personal leadership and teambuilding strengths and challenges, analyze the unanticipated or unintended consequences of leadership blindness, and bridge the gap between how they think they perform and how they actually do.

Observation: Watch and Learn

This boxed series contains assignments designed to help students observe others in action, process the observed behavior to illustrate outcomes and effects, and identify and explain best strategies and practices.

Working It Out: Alone or Together

This series of activities focusing on leadership, team building, and communication challenges helps explore the ethical, cultural, and technological issues that could affect the ability to work collaboratively.

Theory Into Practice

This series highlights the role theory plays in the exercise of leadership. By highlighting research contributions to the field, it engages students in considering the applications and implications of research.

Reel Leadership (Online)

This series points to examples of leadership in popular culture. Through an exploration and analysis of film clips and excerpted leadership dialogues and monologues, this series lets users experience the performance of leadership vicariously.

Instructor's Manual and Test Guide (Online)

In addition, an online instructor's manual and test guide, as well as a syllabus and activities for an online version of the course, are offered.

Also of note, the text's graphically alive format contains photographs and cartoons designed to help the concepts contained in it come to life.

We had fun writing this text. We hope you have fun reading and using it!

ACKNOWLEDGMENTS

We offer our heartfelt gratitude to the extremely dedicated and talented people we have had the good fortune to meet and work with at SAGE. We had a great time working with our acquisitions editor Matthew Byrnie and his team,

Nathan Davidson and Stephanie Palermini. Matt's understanding of and commitment to this project allowed us to turn our goals into reality. We value the relationship we have built. We want to thank project editor Astrid Virding for her creativity and attention to detail, copy editor Mark Bast for his skillful and painstakingly careful reading of the manuscript, assistant editor Terri Accomazzo for the crucial attention paid to ancillaries, Liz Thorton for using her marketing expertise to support our efforts so effectively, permissions editor Karen Ehrmann for her thoroughness, and designer Karina Hovsepian for the text's visual appeal.

We are especially appreciative for our reviewers who so generously shared with us their knowledge, experiences teaching the course, and suggestions for making the text one we are proud to have written—to them we owe our book's fresh approach:

Lori Britt, James Madison University – Harrisonburg
Leonard Edmonds, Arizona State University-Tempe – Tempe
Janie Harden Fritz, Duquesne University – Pittsburgh
Lance Lippert, Illinois State University – Normal
George Nagel, Ferris State University – Big Rapids
Paul Sandin, Butler University – Indianapolis
Sherianne Shuler, Creighton University – Omaha
Peter Smudde, Illinois State University – Normal
Ronald Valenti, St. John Fisher – Rochester
Leah Wyman, California State University-Los Angeles – Los Angeles

PART I

UNDERSTANDING LEADERSHIP

Jupiterimages/Comstock/Thinkstock

Is there a leader in you?
Will you look ahead
When everyone wants to look back?
Do you dream of tomorrow
When others want it now?

UNDERSTANDING THE LEADER IN YOU

Diane, the chief operating officer, was walking toward company headquarters when she saw Danny, one of the company's newly appointed team **leaders**. As they made their way toward the office together, Danny looked at the large number of employees going into the main entrance, some peering at their PDAs, others texting, and still others talking on their cell phones. Few even acknowledged, let alone talked to, each other.

Danny turned to Diane, noting, "I see our people find it tough to disconnect from personal concerns when they come to work. I wonder how we can help them make that transition more easily. I'm also concerned that they rarely work for more than a half hour without some kind of outside interruption." Diane smiled. "That's a good observation, Danny," she said. "You're thinking like a leader. The question of how we can help our people feel more connected to each other so they willingly disconnect from other concerns beyond the office is critical. We want our employees to be able to function as a team, not merely as individuals in a group. I'm glad you're focused on that. That's why I picked you to be a team leader!"

Can you learn to think like a leader? Can you learn to act like a leader? The answer is yes. By learning to communicate effectively, you can accomplish both! There is a kind of **communication intelligence** associated with effective **leadership**. Effective leaders use critical-thinking and reasoning skills in concert with emotional intelligence to solve problems, negotiate solutions, and shape the perceptions and behaviors of others in support of their goals. By learning to think and act like a leader—that is, *by learning to communicate like a leader*—and collaborate effectively with others, you can help find solutions to some of the serious challenges and troubling problems of our day.[1]

Whether we're concerned about the limits of privacy, the health care crisis, corporate greed, social networking, sustainability, the global marketplace, safety at home and abroad, government regulation or deregulation, or satisfying employment, we need leaders who are able to focus on the big picture, see the opportunities in the challenges before them, inspire and mobilize others in gathering information and assessing opportunities, take calculated risks considering fully chain-of-decision options and consequences, and persuade others to join with them in shaping the future.

LEADING QUESTIONS ABOUT LEADERSHIP

What is leadership? Who is a leader? Do you have what it takes to be a leader?

Though questions like these are asked over and over again, many of us remain confused about leadership's nature and our own potential for leadership. For example, where do you stand when it comes to answering this question:

Can we all exercise leadership, or is it reserved only for those "special" persons at an organization's top?

Because of our society's "culture of celebrity" many of us regard leaders as being special people—extremely attractive, charismatic, and personable individuals whom others find themselves attracted to and decide to follow. Such a perception makes Ashton Kutcher and Lady Gaga leaders. After all, millions of people have chosen to follow each of them on Twitter. We need only point to the number of citizens who vote for candidates they believe are good looking and who they would like to be friends with rather than supporting various candidates because they approve of their policies and believe they will change things for the better as proof of the culture of celebrity in action.

Focusing on just an individual, however, while ignoring the social process of leadership can blind us to the roles we play. While one person may possess the formal authority and even pretend to know all the answers, many people need to contribute leadership if the formal leader and his or her followers and organization are to succeed.[2] Thus, leadership depends on communication and interaction between leaders and followers. So, do you want others just to follow you, or are you ready to work with them to help drive change? We hope you choose the latter. To see if you are up to the challenges the latter choice presents, read on.

WHEN CALLED ON TO LEAD, CAN YOU . . .

Focus on the big picture

Identify opportunities

Mobilize followers

Gather information

Consider options and consequences

Work collaboratively to shape the future

What Are Leadership's Challenges?

In all sectors of society, people talk about the need to find leaders who are up to meeting the complex challenges currently facing society and all its public and private institutions. To be sure, we need leaders, but what types of leaders should we be seeking? Is there a set of communication skills and understandings you should possess that would prepare you to be up to performing the leader's role? There is, and our goal is to help you identify and master those skills and underandings.

Let's start with the understanding that leadership, as we just noted, does not reside in a single individual; in fact, we view leadership as *a shared and collaborative effort.* When considered from this perspective, people who may not be in positions of authority can also exert leadership, much as Martin Luther King did in the civil rights movement and Mohandas Gandhi did in India. Neither King nor Gandhi was the head of a nation, but nonetheless each succeeded in mobilizing others to confront and change the future in new and exciting ways. Though perhaps not on so grand a scale, you can do the same.

While often there may be one person in charge, the results ultimately achieved are likely to depend on the efforts and abilities of an entire team. In that sense, *leaders are mobilizers,* not the sole actors.[3] Do you see yourself as a mobilizer? Do you know anyone who is a mobilizer? Maybe that person is a parent, a religious leader, the head of a group you belong to, or a politician. What does she or he do to mobilize the efforts of others? Think about it. It is the abilities of many people exerting leadership that makes the biggest difference.

Sometimes leaders need to be directive, and sometimes they need to be team builders. Sometimes they need to describe their visions by telling others what to do, and sometimes they need to cultivate support, engaging and empowering others to consider how best to move forward—effectively turning leadership into a much more collaborative enterprise. Given specific sets of circumstances, leaders need to be able to assess what is needed and adapt their style of leading to meet the demands of each situation, what some theorists such as Anthony J. Mayo and Nitin Nohira call **situational leadership**.[4]

Thus, being able to exert effective leadership depends on your being able to meet five key challenges, demonstrating that you have the following:

(1) The ability to identify and confront a problem

(2) The ability to turn the problem into an opportunity by communicating a compelling vision—one that sets the problem in a context that others are able to visualize

(3) The ability to align people in support of that vision

(4) The ability to motivate or mobilize others to take action

(5) The willingness to work persistently and collaboratively alongside others until the problem is solved

Your role as a leader is to harness the insights and strengths, what you might call the **collective intelligence** of many individuals who together will orchestrate their walk into a new future. When it comes to leading, your communication skills and understandings become your natural ally.

WHAT DO YOU THINK ABOUT LEADING?

If you are contemplating leadership you also need to learn about yourself and your communication strengths and weaknesses. As you step up the career ladder, having the ability to communicate effectively increases in importance. Leaders lead because they know how to share ideas, respond calmly to the emotions and stresses that new ideas may trigger in others, and interact with others in ways that foster a climate conducive to both creative and critical thinking. As we have noted, we believe that each and every one of you has leadership potential.[5] Your chance of fulfilling that potential, however, depends on three requisites: (1) understanding yourself and others, (2) internalizing sound communication principles, and (3) enacting communication behaviors designed to get results by getting others onboard.

Exploring leadership is not kid's play. Leaders both good and bad affect all our lives in myriad ways, making leadership a very serious business indeed. From the boardroom to the classroom, from the political arena to the religious pulpit, from government chambers to hospital halls, from the battlefield to the playing field, how the leader thinks, what the leader says, what the leader does, what the leader expects of followers, and how the leader behaves when alone and in the company of others makes a difference. Is there a leader in you? We think so!

Self-Reflection: Looking In and Out

1. Identify 10 people who come to mind when you hear the word *leader*. Then answer these questions about the people on your list:

   A. What do these individuals have in common with one another?

   B. How do their experiences differ?

   C. In what ways has each person influenced or touched you? Describe specifically how each leader impacted your life.

2. Generate a list of thoughts that come to mind when you hear the word *leadership*. Explore your list. How many of your thoughts would you classify as positive and how many as negative?

3. Create a collage representing your personal leadership strengths and weaknesses. How might you capitalize on your strengths? What might you do to overcome your weaknesses?

LEADERS GET OTHERS FROM WONDERING WHICH WAY TO GO? TO APPLAUDING THE WAY TO GO!

Question: Who are the persons responsible for figuring out which way to go or what needs to be done?

Answer: Leaders.

> *Question:* Who are the persons who identify what needs to change, whose cooperation is needed to avoid or defuse a crisis, how best to solve a problem, and how to get closer to or reach a goal?
>
> *Answer:* Leaders.

Since at one time or another, we have all faced a "need to fix it" moment, more than likely we have also been among the persons responsible for identifying "the way out," "the way up," or "the way to go." Every group, every team, and every social institution and organization requires that one or more individuals exert leadership—take initiative in setting a path—identifying *the way to go*—

> **Leaders identify the way to go, establishing a path forward.**

and then translate that path, that road map, into a vision others will share, eliciting a cry from the followers they mobilize of *way to go!* So answering the "What is the *way to go?*" question and getting others on board to support the given answer, thereby supplying the *way to go!* or push forward, are both leader responsibilities.

As we see, we can read the words *way to go* either as a question requiring an answer by supplying a specific direction or focus or as an exclamatory—a congratulatory accolade—a recognition of those social qualities an individual possesses that result in others desiring to join with her or him to accomplish a specific task or bring about a needed change. Determining the *way to go* and finding others who will travel that new path because you influence them to believe it to be the *way to go* are prerequisites for leadership.

Now, let us delve more deeply into leadership's nature.

WHAT IS A LEADER? WHAT IS LEADERSHIP?

A *leader* is a person who produces change. Thus, an individual who exerts influence, establishing the path forward—what we referred to as *the way to go*—is a leader. The leader makes a difference in the road others choose to travel. The leader influences others to take one path rather than another, prodding others to work toward achieving a particular goal by convincing them that reaching this goal will make the future better, and, for that reason, it is worthy of their time and attention.

We identify those who join with the leader by applauding his or her efforts and supplying the needed *way to go!* support as followers.

As we will see, both leaders and followers are necessary actors in the leadership process. We define *leadership* as *an interactive process during which one or more individuals use symbols to influence other individuals to join with them in accomplishing change and realizing a shared objective.*

When we say *leaders use symbols to influence* we mean that leaders rely on language, both verbal and nonverbal, to communicate their vision to followers and accomplish their goals. The language leaders use determines if, and to what extent, they will succeed in rallying others to support their goals.

When we say *leadership accomplishes change and realizes a shared objective* we mean that leading involves influencing others to join with the leader in altering the status quo in pursuit of a mutual goal.

What does the cartoon tell you about the coach's view of leadership? To what extent do you agree or disagree with the sentiments expressed?

"And the way you kids kick ass today will speak volumes about the leaders of tomorrow you will be."

Michael Crawford/The New Yorker Collection/www.cartoonbank.com

WHY LEADING IS COMMUNICATING

Communication is the primary tool leaders use to bring people together to affect the performance of a group or an organization. By communicating about the past and identifying problematic present-day situations (*why the status quo must go*), leaders engage us in envisioning a better future. Thus, leaders *bind time* by linking the past, present, and future. In the process, they exhibit the ongoing, complex, and irreversible nature of communication. There is nothing static about communication. If we conceive of present communication experiences as points of arrival from past experiences and also as points of departure for future ones, then we understand that events, while interconnected, are also unrepeatable. As the Chinese proverb reveals, "Even the emperor cannot buy back one single day." Neither can leaders.

Leaders Depend on Communication Skills

Effective leaders enact superior communication skills, demonstrating what we call the performance of **communication competence.** Distinguished by their ability to open people's minds to ideas they might otherwise not be open to, superior leaders also are particularly adept at sharing meaning that elicits desired emotional, cognitive, or behavioral changes in others, contributing to others feeling, thinking, or doing something differently.

What leadership qualities precipitate this? First, effective leaders develop *self-awareness*—the understanding and insight of how they themselves affect others, facilitating their ability to work well with them. Second, leaders *self-regulate*. They have the ability to control or redirect impulses and moods that are disruptive, and they wisely engage in serious thinking before they act. Third, leaders are *self-motivated*. They work because of their passion to pursue goals, not merely because of money. Fourth, leaders have *empathy.* Their understanding of others' needs and what is important to them enables them to build more meaningful relationships. Finally, leaders possess *social skills* that let them build rapport and find common ground with others while concurrently revealing what they themselves stand for and value in the process.[6]

For example, Amy Schulman, the executive vice president and general counsel at Pfizer, tells real-life anecdotes about herself to help her convey her leadership style to the company's employees. The following story about the first time she took a client's deposition helps her show those who work for her that she's not afraid to laugh at herself:

> I thought that the most important thing was to control the witness. I didn't realize that the way you control somebody is not by inimidating them. But I adjusted my chair so that I'd be really tall, and could look

down imposingly on the witness. But I raised it so high that as soon as I sat down, I toppled over and fell backward.[7]

Leaders Develop an Understanding of Self and Others

Effective leaders understand themselves. Because their self-concept enables them to think of themselves as leaders, they also develop their leadership identity and interact with others from that perspective. They are in touch with the cognitive abilities and emotional intelligences a leader requires. They have insight into their analytical, emotional, social, and contextual strengths and weaknesses. Sensitive to constraints that may be placed on them, they can lead from either out front or behind. They know what they do not know, and recognizing the limitations that may be placed on their powers, they continuously work on self-improvement, consciously trying to create a world that others would like to be part of; in effect, finding ways to motivate others to join with them in taking action.[8]

Effective leaders also understand those they seek to lead. Among a leader's myriad constituencies are groups of followers, typically comprised of various stakeholder groups or publics including, but not limited to, employees, stockholders, and members of the community (local, national, and global). The ability of any leader to influence followers depends on how willing followers perceive the leader is to interact with them, as well as on how effective the leader is at influencing their behavior. As the saying goes, "You have to be in it to win it!" By performing an array of communication activities designed to foster connections with followers, the leader exhibits adaptive communication skills and enhances his or her credibility.

Leaders are Adept at Framing and Sharing Narratives

Additionally, how effective a leader is at framing interactions influences his or her realization of desired outcomes. Leaders who are adept at shaping narratives—and telling their stories—tend to develop more emotional and lasting connections with supporters.[9]

In what contexts is the telling of stories appropriate? Any context! We tell stories over coffee, during presentations we give, and in virtually any social or business situation. The contents and tone of the stories we tell reveals who we are, informs others about the values we hold, and describes the object(s) of our focus. Those who respond to a particular story line tend to develop a meaningful emotional relationship with the storyteller—in this case, the leader—becoming collaborators in the leader's story, extending its reach, and helping the leader realize his or her goal(s) in the process.

Observation: Watch and Learn

The Apprentice

Watch any segment of the reality television program *The Apprentice*.

First, describe the task facing each of the teams, the members on each team, and the ways in which each task leader's understanding of self and others, or the lack thereof, contributed to the team's success or failure.

Second, compile a list of communication activities used by the leader in pursuit of the team's goal.

Third, identify how the leader's interaction with team members and others influenced each team's outcome.

Finally, answer these questions:

Do you believe that a leader needs to be hypercompetitive for the team to succeed?

What did we learn about the personal code of ethics of both the leader and followers on each team? For example, did any of the team leaders or members exhibit a "do anything to win" attitude?

To what extent would you have acted similarly or differently if placed in each team leader's position?

ASKING AND ANSWERING MORE QUESTIONS ABOUT LEADERSHIP

Are some of us born leaders while others of us don't stand a chance of ever leading anyone? Can we be taught how to lead? Is it possible not to be appointed as the leader but to emerge as a leader nonetheless? How we answer these questions can positively or negatively shape our beliefs about our leadership potential. Let us address each of these questions now.

> Leading is a shared and collaborative effort. Many contribute leadership for the leader to succeed.

Do You Have to Have Certain Traits to Lead?

Those who adhere to the **trait theory of leadership** believe that some people possess unique inborn characteristics or talents that destine them for leadership roles.[10] Some of the traits attributed to leaders are physical ones; for example, leaders are taller and more attractive than others. Some of the traits are psychological; for instance, leaders are more intelligent and verbally fluent than others or more extroverted and likeable than those not in leadership positions. And some traits are sociological, with the leader having more status and upward mobility than others. Do you know any leaders who possess the physical, psychological, or sociological characteristics mentioned here? What about yourself?

Over time, the trait theory morphed from one highly focused on identifying qualities great leaders had in common to a consideration of the characteristics shared by charismatic and visionary leaders. The theory has produced a seemingly endless list of traits that people perceived leaders to possess. What it does not focus on, however, is the situation facing the leader. In other words, the traits useful in one situation may not be the traits required to meet the demands of another situation.

Can You Learn to Lead?

In contrast to those who believe leaders are born to lead are others who view leadership as a *learnable relational process*—an outcome dependent on what happens when individuals—potential leaders and followers—interact with one another. Thus, adherents of this perspective believe that leaders are not born but made. If we are taught leadership, they argue, we can learn to lead.[11] They point to leaders who learned who they were, what they wanted to achieve, and why they wanted to achieve it and thus were able to gain the support of others.[12] Do you know any leaders who learned to lead others? What did they do to develop into leaders?

Must a Leader Be Appointed?

You know from experience that sometimes an individual is the *appointed leader*—the person assigned to the leadership role—perhaps because of the formal position he or she serves in the organization. The appointed leader may, for example, function as a department head, office manager, or in some other administrative role. But when his or her group or team is faced with solving a particular problem, because of the way others respond to the appointed leader, a completely different person may emerge as the group or team leader. So we ask, in what ways do appointed leadership and **emergent leadership** differ from each other? Unlike appointed leadership, *emergent leadership* is not title dependent. Rather, it results from others accepting and supporting a person's communicative efforts. Others respond to his or her behavior. Who do you believe tends to be more effective at performing leadership responsibilities, the appointed or the emergent leader? Why?

Leaders can exist at any level of the organization chart. Self-directed work teams have leaders, as do unions, protest groups, and student groups.

LEADING AND MANAGING: SIMILARITIES AND DIFFERENCES

How Are Leaders Different From Managers?

LEADERS	MANAGERS
FOSTER AND PRODUCE CHANGE	MAINTAIN STABILITY
DEVELOP A VISION FOR THE FUTURE	PLAN, BUDGET, AND IMPLEMENT VISION
ALIGN PEOPLE INTO TEAMS AND COLLABORATIONS	ORGANIZE AND STAFF
MOTIVATE AND INSPIRE	CONTROL FOR PREDICTABILITY AND CONSISTENCY
MOVE PEOPLE IN A NEW DIRECTION	MAINTAIN POSITION
FOCUS ON THE BIG PICTURE	FOCUS ON DETAILS

Is every leader a manager? Is every manager a leader?

Leading and managing do share much in common. For example, both leading and managing involve working with and influencing others. They both are concerned with the effectiveness of their respective groups. And they both are focused on goal attainment. These similarities contribute to some believing that leading and managing are one and the same thing. Research, however, reveals the expectations we have for leaders and managers are considerably different and so are their responsibilities.

According to leadership theorists James Kouzes and Barry Posner we associate leading with fostering change, paving the way for innovation, and the overcoming of crises, while we associate managing more with maintaining stability, promoting efficiency, and the preservation of order.[13] How do the activities of leaders and managers underscore their apparently different priorities? We rely on leaders to master and change the contexts of our lives—to see into the horizon and create a viable future for us. We rely on managers to keep the organization on the track set by the leader, to implement the leader's vision. Or as Warren Bennis and Ivan Goldsmith note, "A manager does things right. A leader does the right things."[14] The manager believes that "if it ain't broke, don't fix it." The leader believes otherwise. From the leader's vantage point, "When it ain't broke may be the only time you can fix it."[15] Who do you know that is a better manager than leader? Who do you believe to be a better leader than manager? What about yourself?

Leadership scholar John Kotter observes that managers engage in planning and budgeting while leaders develop a vision of the future. Managers organize and staff, finding individuals who are right for a job, while leaders create teams and collaborations composed of people who understand and support the leader's vision. Managers plan and organize to solve problems while leaders motivate and inspire others to overcome barriers to change. Managers exhibit predictability, demonstrating consistent behavior yielding results stakeholders expect, while leaders innovate and foster change by taking followers into the future. In effect, managers are detail oriented and seek to eliminate chaos from organizational life, while leaders clarify the big picture and formulate visions for change.[16]

Thus, while the manager's focus on order and consistency has him or her planning and budgeting, the leader is committed to tolerating and coping with chaos to produce change and movement. Where the manager organizes and staffs, the leader aligns people into teams. As the manager exerts control, the leader motivates and inspires, energizing team members not by pushing them but by satisfying their basic human needs. In other words, managers maintain position; leaders, in contrast, influence people—moving them in new directions.

When combined together, strong management and leadership characterize a successful organization, while the absence of one or both contributes to an organization's diminished effectiveness. Thus, when we talk about the importance of leadership to an organization's future, we are neither denigrating nor diminishing the function of managing.

Working It Out: Alone or Together

Identify the management and leadership skills needed to run and staff a workshop on either of the following topics: ethics in business or sustainability in business. Be specific in describing the character traits, functions, philosophies, and expected results of the persons managing and leading this workshop.

ACTING TO CONTROL OTHERS' IMPRESSIONS: HOW WOULD YOU ACT IF THE LEADER?

How do leaders get people to work together? What influences the leader's ability to recruit others to follow their lead so that people collaborate with one another, and the leader can direct them towards a goal?

Can You Perform Leadership?

Sociologist Erving Goffman's dramaturgical approach to human interaction can help us understand how the skillful enacting of **impression management** plays a critical role in the performance of leadership.[17]

If we consider social interaction as a performance, and the setting(s) in which interaction occurs as the stage, then the actors (the persons on the stage) play their parts to manage the impressions of others sharing the stage with them so they may achieve their goals or objectives. The more skillful the actors, the more effective they are at convincing others that they are knowledgeable, trustworthy, and possess a charisma or dynamism that makes them a person to follow. What dramatic elements do they rely on to accomplish this?

First, leaders use **framing**, specifically defining a scene or situation in a way that helps others interpret its meaning in the way the leader desires. For example, a CEO might explain that by temporarily eliminating the corporate contribution to the pension the leader is taking steps to ensure the long-term health of the company. By framing an action in a specific way the leader hopes to give followers a reason to offer him or her their support.

Leaders also use **scripting**, the identification of each actor's role in the scene—particularly the role of the leader and the leader's supporters or followers. In effect, the leader convinces others on the stage that the leader needs them to play their roles as assigned so they can achieve the desired outcome.

Of course, leaders use **engaging dialogue**—storytelling together with colorful and descriptive language and effective use of nonverbal cues—to guide the response of the other players.

Together, these elements underlie the leader's **performance**. When engaged in performing, a leader makes a number of choices. For example, the leader can opt to use the technique of **exemplification**—serving as an example or acting as a role model for others to follow—or **promotion**—elucidating personal skills and accomplishments and/or a particular vision for others to value. The leader can engage in **face-work**—protecting his or her image by reducing the negative aspects of himself or herself visible to others—or practice ingratiation—using techniques of agreement that make others believe the leader to be more attractive and likeable and less threatening, harmful, or pernicious.

What kind of leadership performance do you tend to respond to most and least favorably? Why?

Do the Right Goals Motivate Your Performance?

As the financial crisis and resulting recession that occurred toward the end of the first decade of the 21st century revealed, some people performing leadership are motivated by greed rather than by the desire to improve things to benefit followers and the public good.

The motivations of some leaders make them toxic. While knowing the risks their actions create, they instead create illusions of safety and pretend absolute certainty in the effort to improve their personal positions, resulting in their harming society and those whom their performance affects. Using only their raw charisma, they solicit the blind trust of followers.

In contrast are leaders who are competent and genuinely care about the lives of their followers, who use knowledge and charisma to build trust and empower others to join them, who demonstrate values congruent with their behavior, and who make a real effort to overcome obstacles and discover solutions to pressing problems. (We will discuss the leader's ethics in greater detail in the next chapter.)

Post It: Imagineering a Better Way

According to a Civility in America 2011 poll, 43% of Americans say they have experienced incivility at work, and another 38% feel the workplace is increasingly disrespectful. When asked who is to blame for workplace incivility (violations of respectful workplace norms including rudeness and insults), workers say the leader is responsible.[18]

Given this new reality, your task is to start a program in civility at your college or university. What aspects of Goffman's dramaturgical approach could you use in support of your goal? Describe how you would enact them. Are there any parts of the process outlined earlier that you would refrain from using? Why? What techniques might you substitute in their place?

GOALS AND OPPORTUNITIES

Our goals in writing this book are to provide you with insights into the meaning and practice of leadership and to help you develop the communication skills and understandings you need to have to lead. In effect, we want to facilitate your personal leadership journey.

In coming chapters we will explore what you can do to enhance your leadership skills, how to practice leadership strategically, how to cultivate followers, and how to exercise leadership responsibly so you deliver on the promises you make. As we investigate the purposes and nature of leadership together, we will focus not only on developing your emotional and social intelligence and an understanding of how others perceive you, but will also help you learn how to mobilize others to confront challenges and increase your understanding of global leadership and technological tools. The importance of being knowledgeable about what is going on around the world and the advantages that come with effectively using social networking and virtual leadership in support of your efforts are undeniable leadership assets.

As you see from the in-chapter exercises contained in this chapter, you will also have abundant opportunities to work on a series of tasks that address the complexities and basics of leadership and that when completed will enhance your insight into what it means to be a leader and to lead. In the process, we hope to also help you develop the imaginative spirit of creative inquiry that effective leaders possess. Our journey into leading with communication has just begun. Come with us as we explore its many dimensions.

Theory Into Practice

A Leader's Lament Versus a Leader's Legacy

Why do some leaders initiate policies that are detrimental to the interests of their followers and organizations while others leave legacies that those who come after them will continue?

Historical research is rich in answers to this question. For example, in this next passage, historian Barbara Tuchman asks a series of questions designed to expose the foolishness of leaders through time:

> Why did the Trojan rulers drag that suspicious-looking wooden horse inside their walls despite every reason to suspect a Greek trick? Why did successive ministries of George III insist on coercing rather than conciliating the American colonies, though repeatedly advised by many counselors that the harm done must be greater than any possible gain? Why did Charles XII and Napoleon and successively Hitler

invade Russia despite the disasters incurred by each predecessor? Why did Montezuma, master of fierce and eager armies and a city of 300,000, succumb passively to a party of several hundred alien invaders, even after they had shown themselves as all too obviously human beings, not gods? . . . Why does American business insist on "growth" when it is demonstrably using up the three basics of life on our planet—land, water, and unpolluted air?"[19]

To be sure, arrogance, loss of focus, or weak character can cause a leader's downfall. When a leader pays scant attention to others' warnings; becomes overly complacent, failing in his or her responsibility to adapt and keep pace with change; or lacks a moral center, seeking personal enrichment at others' expense; the leader is likely to sacrifice his or her legacy.

Over a half century ago, when writing about the importance of one leader's legacy, another social commentator, Walter Lippmann, wrote these thoughts in the *New York Herald Tribune:*

The final test of a leader is that he leaves behind him the conviction and will to carry on. The genius of a good leader is to leave behind him a situation which common sense, without the grace of genius, can deal with successfully.[20]

We test a leader's legacy by its durability and the change the leader fostered. If the leader's ideas and values survive the leader, then chances are that the leader's contribution will contribute to an organization or movement's longevity.

Based on both of these assessments, identify a present-day leader whom you believe faltered and another whom you believe will leave a lasting legacy.

LOOK BACK

Reread this chapter's opening poem. Based on what you now understand about leadership and your leadership potential, why do you believe the speaker asked each of the poem's questions? How would you answer each of these questions now?

Key Terms

Appointed leader (13)

Communication intelligence (4)

Collective intelligence (6)

Emergent leadership (13)

Communication competence (10)

Engaging dialogue (16)

Exemplification (16)

Face-work (16)

Follower (11)

Framing (16)

Impression management (16)

Ingratiation (17)

Leader (3)

Leadership (4)

Learnable relational process (13)

Performance (16)

Promotion (16)

Scripting (16)

Situational leadership (6)

Stakeholder (11)

Trait theory of leadership (12)

Notes

1. Boris Groysberg, *Chasing Stars: The Myth of Talent and the Portability of Performance* (Princeton, NJ: Princeton University Press, 2010).

2. See, for example, R. Bolden, B. Hawkins, J. Gosling, and S. Taylor, *Exploring Leadership: Individual, Organizational and Societal Perspectives* (New York: Oxford University Press, 2011).

3. See, for example, Ronald Heifetz, *Leadership Without Easy Answers* (Cambridge, MA: Harvard University Press, 1998).

4. See, for example, A. J. Mayo and N. Nohira, *In Their Time: The Greatest Business Leaders of the Twentieth Century* (Boston: Harvard Business School Press, 2005).

5. Warren Bennis, *On Becoming a Leader* (Reading, MA: Addison-Wesley, 1989).

6. For a discussion of emotional intelligence, see Daniel Goleman, *Emotional Intelligence* (New York: Bantam, 1995) and *Working With Emotional Intelligence* (New York: Bantam, 1998).

7. Adam Bryant, "Corner Office: Amy Schulman," *New York Times* (December 11, 2011): 2 BU.

8. See, for example, Nitin Nohria and Rakesh Khurana, "Advancing Leadership Theory and Practice," in N. Nohria and Khurana, R. *Handbook of Leadership Theory and Practice* (Boston: Harvard Business Press, 2010), 3–25.

9. Jonah Lehrer, "Why You Just Shared That Baby Video: The Internet Shows Our Deep Preference for Emotional Arousal Over Bare Facts," *Wall Street Journal* (July 23–24, 2011): C12.

10. R. M. Stogdill, "Personal Factors Associated with Leadership: A Survey of the Literature," *Journal of Psychology* 25: 35–71.

11. See, for example, M. D. Mumford, S. J. Zaccaro, M. S. Connelly, and M. A. Marks, "Leadership Skills: Conclusions and Future Directions," *Leadership Quarterly* 11(1): 155–70; and T. V. Mumford, M. A. Campion, and F. P. Morgeson,

"The Leadership Skills Strataplex: Leadership Skill Requirements Across Organization Levels," *Leadership Quarterly* 18 (2007): 154–66.

12. W. Bennis and J. Goldsmith, *Learning to Lead: A Workbook on Becoming a Leader* (New York: Perseus Book Group, 2010), 1–4.

13. J. M. Kouzes and B. Z. Posner, *The Leadership Challenge: How to Get Extraordinary Things Done in Organizations* (San Francisco: Jossey-Bass, 1987), 31–32.

14. Bennis and Goldsmith, *Learning to Lead*, 31.

15. Abraham Zaleznik, "Managers and Leaders: Are They Different?" in *Leadership Insights* (1992): 18. Harvard Business Review, 2010.

16. J. P. Kotter, *A Force for Change: How Leadership Differs From Management* (New York: Free Press, 1990).

17. E. Goffman, *The Presentation of Self in Everyday Life* (Garden City, NY: Doubleday, 1959).

18. Sharon Jason, "At Work, No More Mr. Nice Guy," *USA Today* (August 8, 2011): 1A.

19. Barbara W. Tuchman, *The March of Folly: From Troy to Vietnam* (Ballentine Books, 1984).

20. Walter Lippmann, "Roosevelt Is Gone," *New York Herald Tribune* (April 14, 1945).

Comstock Images/Comstock/Thinkstock

Do you know the consequences of your lie?

Or do you see only its end results?

Do you tell yourself it's for a good purpose,

Or do you actually believe it's fair?

And how will your lie affect me in the end?

Have you considered that?

And when the veneer of your lie cracks

And I see into the mirror

What will I think of you?

2

UNDERSTANDING THE LEADER'S ETHICAL RESPONSIBILITIES

I n July 2011, the following statement appeared in a *News of the World* editorial, a tabloid paper that was part of Rupert Murdoch's news empire until he ordered it shut down: "Quite simply, we lost our way. Phones were hacked, and for that this newspaper is truly sorry."[1]

The scandal that caused the demise of the *News of the World* brought to public attention the fact that some journalists had been offering illegal bribes in exchange for access and information and in an effort to silence investigators had also threatened to expose personal aspects of their private lives if they continued to pursue their investigations aggressively.[2] Such activities led some to question if the cozy relationship between British politicians, Scotland Yard, and the press was ethical.

Certainly, there are lessons leaders can derive from this affair. Though the newspapers were accused of committing criminal acts, there are also ethical issues and concerns raised by such behavior. Critics observe that Murdoch had created a "kill or be killed" culture and stripped people of their conscience, never understanding that there were lines one should not cross.[3]

ETHICAL MATTERS: THINKING ABOUT YOUR ROLE

What role do you believe ethics play in leading? How would you balance the need to achieve results with human values—both of which are leadership imperatives?[4] If adhering to ethical principles is an integral part of any leader's responsibilities, then what is the recourse if a leader or the people who work with a leader "go rogue" engaging in the performance of unethical behavior?

Self-Reflection: Looking In and Out

To aid you in considering the issues discussed in this chapter, compose answers to the following questions, being certain to fully explain each of your responses.

1. Can you give an example of behavior that is legal but unethical? Could you imagine a situation that would find you engaging in such unethical behavior?
2. Would you ever use information that you or a colleague obtained fraudulently?
3. In your opinion, is exaggeration lying?
4. In your opinion, is lying ever justifiable?
5. What actions might cause people to lose trust in a leader?
6. What are you willing to do to get ahead or come out on top?
7. How do you decide where to draw the line between what you believe to be right and wrong?
8. Would you rather fail than compromise your values?
9. Is there any such thing as an acceptable ethical lapse?
10. Is willful blindness—telling those who work for you to not reveal to you questionable actions so that you can claim no knowledge of them—excusable?
11. Should every organization have an ethics code? If you answer yes, what would you put in it? If you answer no, why do you believe such a code to be unnecessary?

Examine your responses. Do any surprise you?

What Role Does Character Play?

What about character? According to Nitin Nohria, dean of the Harvard Business School, character is something each of us has to work at forming and developing over the course of our lives. Like good judgment, character is not something we either possess or don't have.[5] It, too, needs training. Affirming the importance of character, Warren Bennis and Burt Nanus assert that character is what leadership is all about. For them, becoming a leader is akin to becoming an integrated person.[6] Leaders come to understand not only what to do, but also how to be true to themselves.

> The leader sets the ethical standard. Can you withstand the pressures of leading?

We make decisions based on our moral principles every day. For example, many of us expect others to act with integrity, be honest in their dealings with us, treat us with dignity, and be fair. Should we not expect companies and their leaders to do the same? Leaders set the ethical tone for their organizations and have a significant impact on how followers and other stakeholders perform. Often they are the most important source of information and the person to whom others look for guidance.[7]

What Happens When Leaders Fall Short?

There have been too many instances when leaders of companies have fallen short. We need only point to a few examples—Enron (the company that hid debt from its books in order to artificially inflate its value to shareholders), WorldCom (the company that used deceptive accounting to grossly inflate profits, only to go bankrupt), Halliburton (the company accused of overcharging the government), Tyco (the company accused of failure to make accurate financial disclosures, misrepresenting the company's financial condition, and making inappropriate loans), and the mortgage meltdown that precipitated the financial crisis—that have had devastating effects.

What role did the leaders of organizations play in these scandals? What principles, if any, did the leaders hold themselves accountable to, or what principles did others hold them accountable to? How could talented, creative leaders lose their way? What happened to corporate integrity and social responsibility? What happened to the ability to determine what is and is not ethical—the ability to judge right from wrong?

How would you describe the ethical practices of the leader in this cartoon? Are there any parallels in contemporary society?

"*Congratulations, sire—your financial reforms have been successful!*"

David Sipress/The New Yorker Collection/www.cartoonbank.com

Some leaders fail to develop the ability to withstand the pressures of their positions. Instead of such pressures bringing out the best in them, they bring out their worst selves. The leaders then cave into these pressures, knowingly or unwittingly promoting wrongdoing in themselves or others, usually to achieve short-term gains.[8]

IT'S A QUESTION OF VALUE

Milton Rokeach, an expert on human values, defined a value as "an enduring belief about the way things should be done or about the ends we desire."[9] Rokeach identified two value categories: terminal values, which refer to desirable end states of existence or the goals we would like to achieve during our lifetime, and instrumental values, which refer to the means we prefer to use to attain our terminal values or goals.

Look at each of the following lists containing some of the values Rokeach identified. Which value on each list do you believe to be the most important and why? Keep in mind that your values guide your decision making.

Among Terminal Values Are the Following:

True friendship

Self-respect

Happiness

Equality

Freedom

Social recognition

A sense of accomplishment

Security

A comfortable life

An exciting life

Among Instrumental Values Are the Following:

Ambition

Self-control

Capability

Courage

Honesty

Imagination

Independence

Broadmindedness

Obedience

Responsibility

Now, consider how your values will affect you as a leader. Do you think others share your values? Will you be able to use your values to build your credibility?

POSITIONS MATTER: QUESTIONS TO CONSIDER

The following are questions that once answered provide clues to the nature of a leader's character and an organization's decision making.

How Are Privilege and Power Handled?

Leaders often reap social and monetary rewards. A *New York Times* commissioned study of America's top executives, for example, revealed that the average annual salary of a top executive was about $10 million and increasing at a rate of 12% a year—during a time when millions of Americans were experiencing high unemployment, stuck wages, and an unparalleled economic crisis—causing some to question these leaders' belief in fairness and reciprocity, their capacity for empathy and impulse control, or their willingness to work cooperatively for the common good.[10] We expect leaders to take responsibility for the impact their strategies have on others. We expect them to be up to the ethical challenges of their jobs, not just the tasks. Leaders need to think about their power and privileges and how these affect how they approach their responsibilities if they are to earn the trust and loyalty of their followers.

The rank and privileges of a leader raise other concerns as well. Are power and prestige corrupting influences? How much personal power and prestige equal too much power and prestige? Should a leader feed his or her coffers at the expense of followers and supporters? Should he or she attempt to realize personal agendas in addition to or at the expense of business agendas? And what happens if the leader violates the public trust as has happened with far too many community, corporate, and political leaders such as New York's Charles Rangel, who was admonished on the floor of the House for ethics violations; Chicago's former governor Rod Blagojevich, who was convicted of attempting to sell the Senate seat once held by President Barack Obama; or Tyco's Dennis Kozlowski, who was convicted of looting millions of dollars from his company. Does the leader have a moral obligation to himself or herself, or is the leader's moral obligation primarily to followers?[11] And what if a follower objects to what the leader asks him or her to do? How should the leader respond?

Are Lies Ever Told to Control Information?

One of the charges leveled against the big banks involved in the mortgage debacle is that they sought to control information by causing others to believe what they themselves did not believe. They practiced deception on a grand scale.

They told and released information containing lies. Can you imagine being in their position? What would you have done? Do you think lying is always wrong?

What Kind of Lie Is Told?

What is a lie? A lie is the deliberate presentation of information you know is untrue. Like all of us, leaders can lie by omission or commission.

When a lie is based on omission, the leader deliberately withholds relevant information, thereby causing partners, peers, followers, or others to draw an erroneous conclusion. Leaders sometimes decide to withhold or conceal the truth—not revealing information they possess. For example, drug companies have been known not to release all the information about their drugs' harmful effects to the FDA. When this happens, the public suffers because withholding such information could cause harm, and the lie likely was told for the drug company's selfish reasons. But scientists in the drug company probably suffer as well because they may have been instructed to withhold the information from those who had a legitimate right to be informed.

> **Deception has costs! Who trusts a liar?**

When a lie is based on commission, the leader makes a statement that he or she knows is false. Thus, lies do not merely involve the delivery of information that is wrong; rather, they involve the act of intentionally seeking to deceive one or more persons.

Sissela Bok, the author of *Lying: Moral Choice in Public and Private Life*, says that when we lie, it is both our hope and our expectation that we will succeed in making the target of our lie(s) believe information we do not. Bok also notes that liars rarely tell only a single lie because once you lie, there is typically more mending to do.[12] In effect, a lie becomes a tangled web.[13] Thus, liars are in the information distortion business. Information, however, is what we need to make sound decisions. Thus, by corrupting the information people rely on, lying adversely impacts decision making as well.[14]

Have You Told Either Type of Lie?

Lie of Omission	The liar withholds relevant information.
Lie of Commission	The liar makes a statement she or he knows is false.

What Happens When Trust in Information Disappears?

How do lies affect the liar and the lied to once they are uncovered? Rightly, people lose trust in the liar. They will likely doubt whatever information the liar passes on to them in the future. They will also question the liar's expression of feelings. Suspicions and resentments will linger. They are likely to think about other information the liar has previously given to them and question it as well. The relationship between the liar and the lied to, which may have once been strong, weakens. Quite simply, lies are fundamentally destructive to all relationships—including business relationships. Once employees discover that they have been lied to, in addition to destroying trust, both their job performance and satisfaction decline.

What Happens When Information Is Obtained in Questionable Ways?

In the *News of the World* case we spoke of at the outset of this chapter, the press was criticized for obtaining information via hacking, bribery, and trickery. Executives are known to use questionable tactics to come by the information they want. Some, for example, obtain it by reading employee e-mails or eavesdropping on their conversations. Sometimes "nannycams" or spyware are placed in offices, enabling employers to observe and monitor worker performance. When discovered, this too causes workers to question the leader's intentions—especially if their privacy rights have been violated in the process, as happened when Murdoch's newspersons hacked into the contents of private cell phones.

HOW IS RESPONSIBILITY DISTRIBUTED?

When Murdoch was asked if he considered himself responsible for the hacking that his employees had committed, he simply answered, "No." He passed the buck to his managers or the people who worked for them. In contrast, a sign on the desk of a past president of the United States read, "The buck stops here." Leaders need to hold themselves accountable for the actions of their followers. After all, they create the organizational culture and set its ethical framework—formulating the code of ethics that guides its actions.

The heads of MBA programs have observed that they need to do a better job of preparing leaders to pay attention to ethics—acknowledging the need for leaders to believe that ethics trump profit; that leaders have obligations to followers, stakeholder groups, and the public; and that the needs of others need to be put before the leader's personal needs—teachings that leaders need to learn if future ethical meltdowns or crises are to be avoided.

What About the International Scene?

Business ethicist Thomas Donaldson asks, "When we leave home and cross our nation's boundaries, moral clarity often blurs. Without a backdrop of shared attitudes, and without familiar laws, and judicial procedures that define standards of ethical conduct, certainty is elusive."[15] How does a leader maintain integrity in the global arena? Should he or she do business with countries that violate civil and political rights? Should moral and cultural relativism rule, or should a leader adhere to the concept of moral universalism—that we can define basic truths about right and wrong objectively? What guiding principles would you adhere to if demonstrating respect for cultural differences was also a priority?

Leading With Moral Decision Making

Consult your conscience by asking what is right.
Determine if you can achieve the goals without raising ethical issues.
Identify how actions taken will affect others.

Observation: Watch and Learn

Rule 1: Don't lie. Rule 2: Don't cheat. Rule 3: Don't steal. Though these appear to be three simple rules, leaders are known to have violated them—some with irreverent regularity.

Identify a crisis in leadership that can be attributed to the leader's violation of one of the preceding rules. Describe the leader's ethical misstep by identifying the

(Continued)

(Continued)

situation in detail. Include a description of the culture in force during the leader's tenure; a rationale for the leader's actions; an analysis of how the leader's violation of an understood standard of conduct impacted others (for example, the effect of the ethical lapse on employees, shareholders, customers, competitors, and the community); the consequences, if any, experienced by the leader and the organization as a result of the leader's actions; and what advice you would have given the leader prior to his or her choosing to behave unethically and subsequent to the unethical act's commission.

DO YOU KNOW UNETHICAL BEHAVIOR WHEN YOU SEE IT?

Would you knowingly sell shoddy merchandise or equipment to consumers? Would you inflate income figures to make them look better to investors? When faced with such dilemmas, how would you make a choice? If ethics enter into the equation, then your thinking is based on principles of justice, fairness, the expression of values, and your respect for those whom your decision will affect. Certainly, taking a shortcut, such as claiming credit for another person's work, can be tempting, especially if a big payoff is the result. However, if an offender believes that he or she will be punished for the ethical violation, then taking such a shortcut could become less appealing.

Certainly, to behave ethically you need to be able to distinguish right from wrong, as well as be able to assess how the choice you make will impact others. Empathy and perspective taking can be your allies in developing sensitivity to the consequences of your actions. Actions ought to be answerable to ethical principles. Being able to imagine how others will view what you do, not just what you stand to gain or lose, helps you focus on the ethical implications of behavior.

According to Sissela Bok's **model of ethical decision making,** we should use three steps to analyze ethical questions. First, we ought to consult our conscience to see how we feel about the action—its rightness. Second, we ought to determine if we might use another way to achieve our goal that would not raise ethical issues. And third, we should determine how our actions could affect others by consulting the parties involved.[16] Bok's model ensures that you consider alternatives, rather than making a decision prematurely—usually sound advice.

How can ethical behavior and professional ethical standards be encouraged? How can we shore up values of responsibility and trust? At our college, for example, all students are expected to engage in service, not for a grade but because it is the right thing to do. To promote the college's ethically rewarding environment, it gives out service awards in addition to academic awards. It also punishes unethical behavior such as plagiarism with possible expulsion. Which do you personally find more effective in promoting ethical behavior—the reward or the punishment?

Working It Out: Alone or Together

1. Identify the personal standards of conduct you try to live by. Next, identify a time when you faced an ethical dilemma and felt you were in danger of violating one or more of the standards on your list. Finally, describe how you responded and the impact it had. To what extent did your resolution align or conflict with your standards?

2. Examine the standards of conduct used to govern business decisions and actions in an organization of your choosing. Then develop a document that your college or university might incorporate into an ethics and compliance program. Describe the similarities and differences between the document you created and the one used by the organization you researched.

APPROACHING ETHICS: ANALYZING RATIONALES

Philosophers advance a variety of rationales for ethical behavior. Some of the theories focus primarily on the leader's conduct while others delve into his or her character. After reading a summary of each theory, ask yourself which ethical stance you find most reflective of your thinking.

Kant's Categorical Imperative

Immanuel Kant, a German philosopher of the 18th century, contended that people ought to behave morally without exception. For Kant and other proponents of this perspective, choice reflects our human duty to adhere to universal truths. As Kant saw it, behavior was morally justified only if performed from a sense of duty. He insisted that its universality—whether it applied to everyone—was the test of a moral act. For Kant, if we could answer the question, "Would we want everyone to make the same decision we did?" with a yes, then the choice is ethical. If the answer is no, it is unethical. Kant advocated for presenting the truth no matter what the consequences. He believed that respect for people demanded no less.

Utilitarianism

Unlike Kant, early 19th-century British philosophers Jeremy Bentham and John Stuart Mill insisted that a decision's benefits and consequences determined whether or not the decision made was ethical. For Bentham and Stuart then, the best decisions produced the greatest benefits and fewest undesirable consequences for the most people. While utilitarianism appears to be an outcomes-based perspective, sometimes it is difficult to identify accurately all the benefits or costs a decision will precipitate, creating plenty of room for disagreement over whether costs outweigh benefits or benefits outweigh costs.

Ethical Egoism

In contrast to utilitarianism, which seeks to create the most good possible for the largest number of people possible with the fewest costs possible, ethical egoists believe that the best thing a person can do is create good for himself or herself. Operating from this perspective, self-interest becomes the leader's focus. Winning, being the best, and maximizing profits become his or her goals.

Virtue Ethics

We are writing this section midsummer. The fall semester will be here before we know it. Today, a colleague announced that she was leaving the college to take a professorial position at another college. She had known this for some time but kept the decision to herself, when she could have been more considerate and given her employer more notice. Virtue ethics place the responsibility for the ethical decision on the person, not on consequences or principles.

Virtue ethicists believe that people of high moral character are more likely to make sound ethical choices that benefit society as well as the person. Thus, they seek to identify the qualities inherent in the virtuous person, as well as identify what others might do to acquire these virtues. Leaders who consistently act with integrity, who respect followers, who place the interests of others first, who refrain from acting recklessly, who refuse to engage in deceptive behavior, who exercise good judgment, and who display empathy may function as role models for virtue ethics. As they model the behaviors, we learn what justice, respect, compassion, and authenticity are.

WHAT IS ETHICAL? A Summary of Philosophies

Categorical Imperative	The leader has a moral duty to behave ethically.
Utilitarian	The leader weighs benefits and consequences of actions.
Ethical Egoism	The leader focuses on self-interest.
Virtue Ethics	The focus is on the individual responsible.
Altruism	The leader's focus is on concern for others.
Servant Leadership	The leader is the caretaker of followers.

Altruism

For those who believe in altruism, concern for others trumps everything else. Adherents to altruism believe that whether we benefit or not, we ought to help others. Rather than seek personal achievement or control, altruistic leaders seek the best interests of others, aiming for the betterment of individuals, groups, organizations, and society. Their goal is to put into place policies and programs that make things better.

Servant Leadership

Servant leaders focus on what is best for their followers—whom they prefer to perceive and call their partners and whom they empathize with and nurture. The maxim of the servant leader might be "followers first." Servant leaders seek to eliminate social injustices and inequalities, heeding followers' needs and seeking their unconditional acceptance. Servant leaders measure their own success by what happens in the lives of their followers. Were they successful? Did they develop the talents they needed to achieve their goals? Were they provided with needed resources? In many ways, servant leaders see themselves as their followers' caretakers—trusted to act on their behalf.

CHOOSING TO LEAD ETHICALLY

Leaders communicate their ethics through their personal actions and relationships. They create positive environments, ones in which others can develop. Leaders gain credibility and authenticity by serving as role models and engaging in behaviors that others judge to be appropriate and unselfish. Their behavior is transparent, fair, and caring.[17] For example, one New Jersey liberal advocacy group that accepted unlimited and anonymous donations came under fire from Democratic politicians, the people it had been created to help. The politicians asked the organization to disclose the identities of donors. Loretta Weinberg, a New Jersey Democratic state senator, said that keeping donors secret is "completely wrong and should be immediately corrected." She went on to say that "just because" something is "legal, doesn't always make it ethical or in the public interest."[18]

Ethical leaders are honest and show consideration for others, treating them fairly and respectfully. Since we continually assess how leaders perform, if a leader displays ethical qualities at one time but not at another, his or her behavior will be seen as inconsistent, and assessments of inconsistency could interfere with others perceiving the leader as authentic.

Ethical leaders communicate about ethics. Followers and stakeholders find themselves rewarded for behaving ethically and punished for deviating from this norm. The climate the leader creates helps foster conditions conducive to ethical performance. For the leader to maintain his or her credibility, the rewards and punishments must be perceived as fair.

Ethical leaders understand the many directions in which communication flows. Their communication and decision making are transparent. Those in the organization feel free to inform their leaders about ethical issues of which the leader is unaware, and the leader clearly explains to followers the standards all are held accountable to.

Because of the fair treatment they perceive themselves to receive from ethical leaders, employees and other stakeholders are more willing to engage with ethical leaders. They trust them and know the leaders are not likely to seek retribution.[19] They also are more likely to report ethical violations to them. People also express more optimism about the future when working in concert with leaders they rank high in ethical leadership.[20] Things work well when there is no disparity between the leader's words and actions.

Theory Into Practice

The Favorite

Giving preferential treatment to some but not others can cast a pall over the impression a leader makes on followers and on how followers perceive that leader.[21] If followers see the leader doling out rewards to those who do not merit them, acting in an unfriendly manner, tolerating dishonesty or deficient performance in others, or failing to treat everyone fairly, then that leader likely will not have made a good impression, and followers probably will decide that they do not like him or her.

More appropriate behavior for the leader is for him or her to act courteously, warmly, and friendly toward all, fulfill behaviors members expect her or him to perform, and be seen as contributing directly to the organization's success.

How has perceiving a leader to favor someone other than you affected your behavior? When a leader's behavior caused you to doubt his or her honesty or ability to live up to expectations, how did you respond?

JUDGMENT CALLS

Any human can be tempted. It is likely that few of us are immune to the temptations that the desire to accumulate wealth creates. Reining in greed is a challenge of our times, as is the dissolution of ethical standards in general. Dishonesty, confusing the issue, endangering others, wasting resources, favoritism, and a lack of concern for others are just some of the unethical behaviors leaders have been caught engaging in. Because of this, and the ability of leaders to create rationales for having done the wrong thing, we believe that we all need to think seriously about ethics and the need we each have to learn to recognize our ethical responsibilities.

To be sure, what one leader finds ethical another leader may view very differently. In addition, stakeholder and shareholder interests often clash. From a shareholder perspective, decisions made are guided by the need to make the most money possible so that return on investment is maximized. From a stakeholder perspective, consideration is given to the needs and interests of multiple stakeholder groups, not only those with a financial interest. Countless ethical controversies reveal the range and variability of ethical guidelines and reactions.

> Just because it is legal does not make it ethical!

Besides obvious illegal behaviors such as restraint of trade, bribes, and insider trading, ethics are also important because of the impact they have on employee performance, stakeholder confidence, and public perceptions. When, for example, issues arise over conflicts of interest, insider trading, sexual harassment, pay and promotion disparities, the privacy of employees, or an organization's environmental and sustainability record or policies, just to name a few, leaders need to have in place strategies to react to and manage the ethical challenge. Just 46% of Americans surveyed last year said they trusted business. And in increasing numbers, Americans also mistrust the government.[22] We need to motivate ourselves to emulate inspirational leaders with high ethical standards. They are our ticket to a better future.

Post It: Imagineering a Better Way

The organization's culture offers clues to the standards its leaders use to determine the difference between ethical and unethical decision making and behavior. Identify the benefits and/or drawbacks of answering each of the following questions in order to ensure that a decision you are about to make is ethical.

1. Do I truthfully believe in the decision?

2. Can I convince others that my information is true?

3. Is this decision in my best interest?

4. Am I being fair to the people my decision will affect?

5. Is my thinking transparent?

6. Will my decision make the company money?

7. Will my decision give us an advantage over the competition?

8. Will my decision build goodwill?

9. Will my decision benefit the parties involved?

10. Does my decision violate any company policies?

11. How would I feel if people I grew up with and care deeply for find out about my decision?

A compelling reason for leading ethically is how ethical behavior contributes to your reputation as a leader. The choices you make—how you answer the question "What should I do?"—reveal your ethics—for better or worse. While reading this chapter will not guarantee that you will perform ethically as a leader, we hope it provides you with a framework you can use to develop an ethical approach to leading. Remember, the leader sets the ethical tone for an organization. Ethical leaders engender ethical followers. Unethical leaders do the same. Which kind of leader do you imagine you will be?

LOOK BACK

Reread this chapter's opening poem. Based on your personal ethical standards, and using the information in this chapter as background, respond to each of the questions the poem's speaker asks.

Key Terms

Altruism (35)

Character (25)

Ethical egoism (34)

Ethical framework (30)

Ethics (24)

Instrumental values (26)

Kant's categorical imperative (33)

Lie (29)

Model of ethical decision making (32)

Servant leadership (35)

Terminal values (26)

Utilitarianism (34)

Value (26)

Virtue ethics (34)

Notes

1. Cassandra Vinograd, "Murdoch Arrives to Face Fallout," *Record* (July 11, 2011): A9.
2. "Britain's Press Scandal," *New York Times* (July 13, 2011): A26.

3. Joe Nocera, "Murdoch's Fatal Flaw," *New York Times* (July 9, 2011): A19.

4. Jacques P. Thiroux and Keith W. Krasemann, *Ethics Theory and Practice,* 10th ed. (Upper Saddle River, NJ: Prentice Hall, 2009).

5. "Q&A With Nitin Nohria: Looking Ahead Behind the Ivy," in Education Life, *New York Times* (Sunday, July 24, 2011): 14–15.

6. Warren Bennis and Burt Nanus, *Leaders: Strategies for Taking Charge* (New York: HarperBusiness, 1997).

7. Christopher M. Barnes and Joseph Doty, "What Does Contemporary Science Say About Ethical Leadership?" *Army Ethic* (2010): 90–93.

8. "Q&A With Nitin Nohria," *New York Times.*

9. See Milton Rokeach, *The Nature of Human Values* (New York: The Free Press, 1979).

10. Natalie Angier, "Thirst for Fairness May Have Helped Us Survive," *New York Times* (July 5, 2011): D2.

11. See, for example, J. Maner and N. Mead, "The Essential Tension Between Leadership and Power: When Leaders Sacrifice Group Goals for the Sake of Self-Interest," *Journal of Personality and Social Psychology* 99(3) (2010): 482–97.

12. See both Sissela Bok, *Lying: Moral Choice in Public and Private Life* (New York: Pantheon, 1978); and Sissela Bok, *Secrets* (New York: Random House, 1989).

13. James B. Stewart, *Tangled Webs: How False Statements Are Undermining America: From Martha Stewart to Bernie Madoff* (New York: Penguin Press, 2012).

14. See R. B. Cialdini, P. K. Petrova, and N. J. Goldstein, "The Hidden Costs of Organizational Dishonesty," *MIT Sloan Management Review* (Spring 2004): 67–73.

15. Thomas Donaldson, "Values in Tension: Ethics Away From Home," in *Business Ethics: Problems, Principles, Practical Applications,* 2nd ed. (Acton, MA: Copley, 2004), 70.

16. Bok, *Lying,* 1978.

17. M. E. Brown, L. K. Trevino, and D. A. Harrison, "Ethical Leadership: A Social Learning Perspective for Construct Development and Testing," *Organizational Behavior and Human Decision Processes* 97 (2005): 117–34.

18. Chris Megerian, "Dems Want Advocacy Group to List Donors," *Record* (July 28, 2011): A3.

19. K. Credo, A. Armenakis, and R. Young, "Organizational Ethics, Leader-Member Exchange, and Organizational Support: Relationships With Workplace Safety," *Journal of Leadership & Organizational Studies* 17(4) (2009): 325–34.

20. H. B. De Hoogh and D. N. D. Hertog, "Ethical and Despotic Leadership, Relations With Leader's Social Responsibility, Top Management Team Effectiveness, and Subordinates Optimism: A Multi-Method Study," *Leadership Quarterly* 19 (2008): 297–311; and D. M. Mayer, M. Kuenzi, R. Breenbaum, M. Bardes, and R. Salvador,

"How Does Ethical Leadership Flow? Test of a Trickle-Down Model," *Organizational Behavior and Human Decision Processes* 108 (2009): 1–13.

21. R. G. Lord and K. J. Mahar, *Leadership and Information Processing: Linking Perceptions and Performance* (Boston: Unwin Hyman, 1991); and R. J. Hall and R. G. Lord, "Multi-level Information-Processing Explanations of Followers' Leadership Perceptions," in F. Dansereau and F. J. Yammarino, ed., *Leadership: The Multiple-Level Approaches*, vol. 2 (Stamford, CT: Jai Press, 1998), 159–90.

22. Andrew Edgecliffe-Johnson and Francesco Guerrera, "US Public Far Less Trusting of Business," *Financial Times* (January 25, 2011): 2.

LEADERS AND THE PEOPLE AROUND THEM

MATCHING LEADER STYLE TO FOLLOWER
EXPERIENCE AND TASK

PATH-GOAL THEORY

MATCHING LEADERSHIP BEHAVIOR TO
THE SITUATION

## 3

Failure is the basis for success.
Success is the starting point of failure.
Can you have one without the other?

Understanding the Leader/Follower Relationship

Follow the leader. Lead the follower. What exactly is the relationship between leaders and their followers? To be sure, a leader needs followers, and followers need a leader. But who is responsible for and to whom? The answer lies in the nature of leadership itself.

Both roles—leader and follower—are best understood in relationship to the other. Leaders initiate while followers support. But can't followers also initiate? When followers withhold support, doesn't the leader have a problem? Here an analogy can help. Like an elephant and its rider, the followers and their leader need to agree on which way to go because like an unmotivated elephant dooms its rider, unmotivated followers can doom the leader's influence efforts. And just as a stubborn elephant can exhaust its rider, unresponsive followers can frustrate the leader.[1]

What is the leader to do? How can leaders shape an effective path for their followers? For this to happen, leaders need to fulfill twin communication challenges: First, leaders need to offer followers clear direction. Second, they need to make followers feel needed. While accomplishing these two tasks is no easy feat, effective leaders make it easy and natural for followers to follow them. The key lies in the nature of communication leader and followers engage in. Thus, in this chapter, we explore the leader/follower relationship.

LEADERS AND THE PEOPLE AROUND THEM

How much of what leaders accomplish can be attributed to their performance, and how much can be attributed to the people around them?

Leaders' communication can have profound effects on the behavior of the individuals in their circle. How they go about mobilizing followers and/or their ideas to tackle critical challenges reveals a lot about how leaders see their roles and the roles of followers.[2] One of the primary roles of leaders is to develop followers who also lead.

Observation: Watch and Learn

Select a leader portrayed in a popular film of your choosing, for example, Mark Zuckerberg in *The Social Network* or Gene Kranz or Jim Lovell in *Apollo 13*. Based on your viewing of the film, first identify the leadership behaviors exhibited by this person. Next, describe how this leader used and/or failed to use communication to make it easy and natural for followers to listen to and follow his or her lead in pursuit of a goal. Then, discuss how the leader interacted with followers to forge either a productive or unproductive relationship. And, finally, indicate if and to what extent the leader was effective in turning followers into leaders.

Figuring Out the Follower

Offer clear direction. Make followers feel needed.

What are followers like? Certainly, followers are not all the same. Like leaders, followers come in different styles. While some are independent thinkers and take initiative, others prefer to be told what to do and require persistent oversight. While some exhibit active engagement, others appear passive or disengaged.

What kind of follower are you? Do you embody the characteristics of a typical follower, a very good follower, or a follower failure? Let's find out.

Self-Reflection: Looking In and Out

What Style Follower Am I?

For each statement, think of how you would respond when facing a specific "followership" situation.[3] Select a number from 0 to 6 to indicate the extent to which the statement describes you where *0* indicates never applies and *6* indicates virtually always applies.

_____ 1. Does your work help you fulfill some societal goal or personal dream that is important to you?

_____ 2. Are your personal work goals aligned with the organization's priority goals?

_____ 3. Are you highly committed to and energized by your work and organization, giving them your best ideas and performance?

_____ 4. Does your enthusiasm also spread to and energize your coworkers?

_____ 5. Instead of waiting for or merely accepting what the leader tells you, do you personally identify which organizational activities are most critical for achieving the organization's priority goals?

_____ 6. Do you actively develop a distinctive competence in those critical activities so that you become more valuable to the leader and the organization?

_____ 7. When starting a new job or assignment, do you promptly build a record of successes in tasks that are important to the leader?

_____ 8. Can the leader give you a difficult assignment without the benefit of much supervision, knowing that you will meet your deadline with highest-quality work and that you will "fill in the cracks" if need be?

_____ 9. Do you take the initiative to seek out and successfully complete assignments that go above and beyond your job?

(Continued)

(Continued)

_____ 10. When you are not the leader of a group project, do you still contribute at a high level, often doing more than your share?

_____ 11. Do you independently think up and champion new ideas that will contribute significantly to the leader's or the organization's goals?

_____ 12. Do you try to solve the tough problems (technical or organizational), rather than look to the leader to do it for you?

_____ 13. Do you help out other coworkers, making them look good, even when you don't get any credit?

_____ 14. Do you help the leader or group see both the upside potential and downside risks of ideas or plans, playing the devil's advocate if need be?

_____ 15. Do you understand the leader's needs, goals, and constraints and work hard to help meet them?

_____ 16. Do you actively and honestly own up to your strengths and weaknesses rather than put off evaluation?

_____ 17. Do you make a habit of internally questioning the wisdom of the leader's decision rather than just doing what you are told?

_____ 18. When the leader asks you to do something that runs contrary to your professional or personal preferences, do you say no rather than yes?

_____ 19. Do you act on your own ethical standards rather than the leader's or the group's standards?

_____ 20. Do you assert your views on important issues, even though it might mean conflict with your group or reprisals from the leader?

Identifying Your Followership Style

Use the scoring key that follows to indicate your answers to the questions.

Independent-Thinking Items   Active-Engagement Items

Question	Question
1. _____	2. _____
5. _____	3. _____
11. _____	4. _____
12. _____	6. _____

14. _____   7. _____

16. _____   8. _____

17. _____   9. _____

18. _____   10. _____

19. _____   13. _____

20. _____   15. _____

Total Score _____   Total Score _____

Add your scores on the independent-thinking items. Record the total on a vertical axis, as in the graph that follows. Repeat the procedure for the active-engagement items and mark the total on a horizontal axis. Now plot your scores on the graph by drawing perpendicular lines connecting your two scores.

The juxtaposition of these two dimensions forms the basis on which some researchers classify followership styles. See Figure 3.1.

Followership Style	Independent-Thinking Score	Active-Engagement Score
EXEMPLARY	High	High
ALIENATED	High	Low
CONFORMIST	Low	High
PRAGMATIST	Middling	Middling
PASSIVE	Low	Low

To what extent, if any, does where you fall on the graph surprise you? In what ways, if any, does the label accorded your followership style conflict with or confirm your beliefs about yourself?

Source: From THE POWER OF FOLLOWERSHIP by Robert E. Kelley, copyright © 1992 by Consultants to Executives and Organizations, Ltd. Used by permission of Doubleday, a division of Random House, Inc.

According to Kelley, followers fall into one of five followership categories contingent on their scores on the independent-thinking and active-engagement sections of the inventory.[4]

Alienated followers score high in independent thinking. However, because their leaders have either disappointed them or made them feel underappreciated, they expend their energies in opposing rather than supporting the leader's policies. Alienated followers tend to come off as cynics or skeptics. Why do followers become alienated? Followers' alienation may develop in response

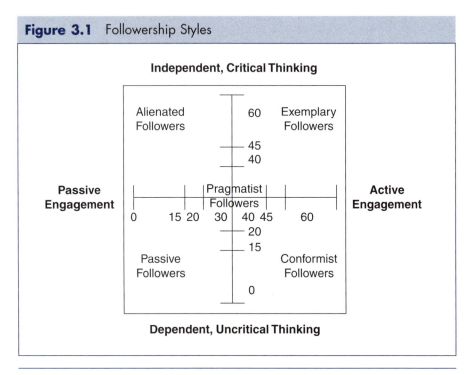

Figure 3.1 Followership Styles

Independent, Critical Thinking

Alienated   60   Exemplary
Followers   Followers

            45
            40

Passive   Pragmatist   **Active**
Engagement   Followers   **Engagement**

0   15 20 30 40 45   60

            20
            15

Passive   Conformist
Followers   Followers

            0

Dependent, Uncritical Thinking

Source: From THE POWER OF FOLLOWERSHIP by Robert E. Kelley, copyright © 1992 by Consultants to Executives and Organizations, Ltd. Used by permission of Doubleday, a division of Random House, Inc.

to any of these factors: a leader's cynicism, being criticized unfairly by the leader, because of their dislike for the leader, or because they feel their efforts go unrecognized. Whatever the reason for their alienation, the fact is that they do not see the environment as fostering their talents.

In comparison to alienated followers, **conformists** are committed to the leader or organization's goals but do little thinking on their own, preferring to defer to the leader's authority. This category of followers comes off as "yes men and women," assenting even when they disagree.

Pragmatists, in contrast, are moderately independent and engaged. While they do just enough to retain their jobs, they do not go "above and beyond" in either thinking or commitment.

On the other hand, **passive followers** score low in both independent thinking and commitment. Either because of a lack of skill or the authoritarian nature of the leader, they do the minimum amount of work they can get away with.

In contrast, **exemplary followers** excel at both critical thinking and commitment, contributing ideas freely to the leader and the organization as they help both attain their goals, building strong relationships in the process.[5]

Theory Into Practice

How Is the Line Between Leader and Follower Drawn?

In her book *Followership,* Barbara Kellerman offers an in-depth consideration of the interaction between leaders and followers. An alternative to Kelley's classification system (discussed earlier in this chapter), Kellerman distinguishes five different categories of followers based on the followers' level of engagement: *isolates* (people who are detached and keep a low profile, preferring to stay out of the way), *bystanders* (people who follow passively, preferring to observe from the sidelines), *participants* (people who are engaged, supporting or opposing the leader; caring enough to try to have an impact), *activists* (people who feel strongly, either engaging with or, if they don't like what they see, trying to remove the leader), and *die-hards* (people who are devoted, either giving their all or seeking to destroy the leader).[6] Thus, Kellerman believes followers respond based on how they view the situation in relationship to the leader.

When followers refuse to go along, leaders can't lead. Believing that followers and leaders share an inseparable relationship, according to Kellerman, followers have dual powers: they may resist or lead, no matter their rank in the organization. They may stand around and do nothing or they can function as change agents, as, for example, whistle-blowers sometimes do. The kind of power leaders exert on followers similarly depends on the intensity of the follower's position. Kellerman observes that in years past, some researchers and practitioners had such a dislike for the word *follower* that they would not even use it, opting to substitute the word *constituent* in place of *follower.*

What would you as a leader do to foster good followership?

Whether followers and leaders acknowledge it or not, followers' preferred style may well be influenced by the leader and the leadership environment in which they find themselves operating. Indeed, at times, leaders function as the catalyst for the behavior of followers.

MATCHING LEADER STYLE TO FOLLOWER EXPERIENCE AND TASK

What a leader thinks about followers affects the leader's behavior as well. If, for example, the leader sees followers as incapable or incompetent, she or he is more apt to model an authoritarian leadership style, strictly supervising and monitoring them. If, in contrast, the leader believes that followers work best when they like the leader, the leader may well exhibit a relationally

> If you're a "yes man" or "yes woman," you are a conformist. Does it make you happy?

oriented leadership style and work to establish a positive emotional relationship with his or her followers. Leaders who have developed a fuller understanding of followership are better able to shift or modify their leadership styles to match their followers' needs. For followers to be successful, leaders need to communicate their expectations clearly and demonstrate the rewards followers will achieve once a goal is realized.

PATH-GOAL THEORY

According to **path-goal theory,** both the nature of the task and the experience and motivation levels of followers interact to determine which leadership style is most appropriate.[7] Robert House and Terrence Mitchell believe that a leader has four communication styles to choose among depending on the environment and followers' needs: (1) **directive leadership** (focused on procedural communication including planning and organizing, task coordination, and policy setting); (2) **supportive leadership** (focused on interpersonal communication including expressing concern for meeting the needs and securing the well-being of followers and fostering a climate conducive to interaction); (3) **participative leadership** (focused on communication designed to involve followers in decision making by eliciting their opinions and ideas; and (4) **achievement-oriented leadership** (focused on goal-oriented communication, emphasizing the rewards of goal attainment and the abilities of followers to achieve their goals).

House and his team assert that the leader enacts a leadership style based on his or her assessment of the skill set followers possess and the leader's determination of whether a task is structured or unstructured. They contend that directive leadership is *most* effective when followers are inexperienced or the task is unstructured. Because of the followers' lack of confidence in their ability to perform satisfactorily, both their motivation and their satisfaction diminish, making it advisable for the leader to direct their performance. In contrast, directive leadership will be *least* effective when followers are competent and behavioral expectations are explicit. Such followers don't need or want **helicopter leaders** hovering over their shoulders shadowing their actions.

On the other hand, when followers are skilled but are lacking in confidence or commitment, their low self-expectations may precipitate poor performance. To combat this, path-goal theory asserts that if the leader delivers supportive communication, recognizing the followers' efforts and bolstering their confidence and commitment, followers will find the tasks facing them less tedious, frustrating, or stressful. In comparison, if followers already perceive tasks to be energizing and fun, supportive communication is unnecessary.

When tasks are unstructured and expectations unclear, according to path-goal theory the leader should engage in participative communication. When followers are involved in problem solving, they begin to think critically about the task facing them. Critical thinking stimulates understanding and motivation. When facing a highly structured task, however, and well aware of the expectations others have, the effects of participative leadership are likely to be minimal.

When the task is challenging and unstructured but followers possess the skills necessary to complete it, if the leader engages in achievement-oriented communication, she or he can help foster positive performance expectations in followers. This outcome is less likely to occur, however, if the task is highly structured (see Table 3.1).

Working It Out: Alone or Together

First, explain how two different leaders you have worked with influenced your followership style. Describe in detail how each leader's communication affected your performance as a follower. Be specific in describing what the leader did and said.

Next, interview or gather research on a leader whose organization and leadership style interests you. Either ask the leader for or discover examples of how this leader's approach to leadership and perceptions of his or her team influence those who work with him or her.

Finally, based on your interview with or research about this leader, explain how you imagine you would fare were you to follow this leader.

Table 3.1 Path-Goal Theory

Leadership Styles	Communication Focus
Directive	Procedures
Supportive	Needs
Participative	Decision making
Achievement	Goals

How do you imagine the disagreement illustrated in this cartoon will affect followers?

MATCHING LEADERSHIP BEHAVIOR TO THE SITUATION

How much does the situation affect the choice of leader or influence the leader's approach? What aspects of the situation deserve our attention? Should leaders be able to read the needs of followers and adapt their behavior to reflect them? Would exhibiting style flexibility give a leader an advantage?

Situational Leadership Theory

Paul Hersey and Kenneth Blanchard's **situational leadership theory** sees the readiness level of followers as dictating the leader's selection of leadership behavior.[8] Believing that leaders should match their leadership style to the ability and willingness of followers, Hersey and Blanchard identify four follower readiness levels:

Readiness Level 1: Low ability and low willingness (The follower possesses neither the skills nor the motivation to succeed.)

Readiness Level 2: Low ability and high willingness (The follower lacks skills but is motivated.)

Readiness Level 3: High ability and low willingness (The follower possesses skills but lacks motivation.)

Readiness Level 4: High ability and high willingness (The follower is both skilled and motivated.)

According to Hersey and Blanchard, R1 followers require very specific guidance from the leader. Interacting with such followers, the leader needs to rely on communication that is high in task direction and low in relationship direction. At this level the leader is telling followers what to do. R2 followers have deficient skills but are motivated. Thus, they too need the leader's direct guidance. However, because they are also willing, followers at this level will also benefit from communication that is supportive. Thus, when interacting with followers at the R2 level, the leader should exhibit communication that is both high task and high relationship, selling the idea that followers can acquire the skills necessary to complete the task. R3 followers have the needed skill set but are lacking in motivation. Thus, for this follower group leaders need to exhibit high relationship communication, promoting participation and encouraging follower involvement in problem solving and decision making. R4 followers are both skilled and motivated. By delegating authority to followers at this level, the leader underscores belief in follower abilities. See Figure 3.2.[9]

Figure 3.2 Leader and Follower Behavior

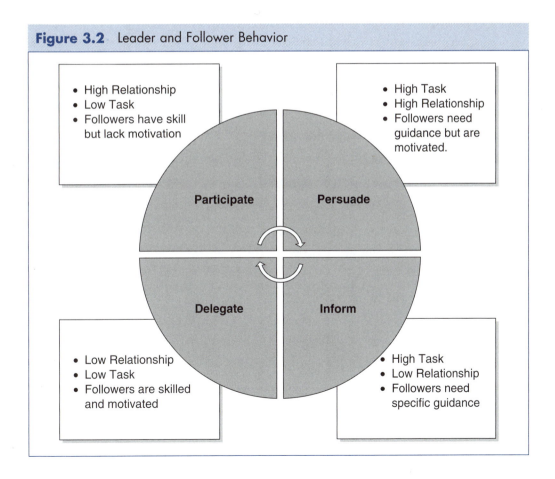

- High Relationship
- Low Task
- Followers have skill but lack motivation

- High Task
- High Relationship
- Followers need guidance but are motivated.

Participate   **Persuade**

Delegate   **Inform**

- Low Relationship
- Low Task
- Followers are skilled and motivated

- High Task
- Low Relationship
- Followers need specific guidance

The Reciprocal Nature of Leader-Follower Relationships: Are Followers In or Out? Are Leaders Liked or Disliked?

Relationships matter. Thus, while the characteristics of leaders and followers can influence the nature of leadership and followership exhibited, so do the relationships leaders and followers share.

Vertical Dyad Linkage Model

"Now you see me, now you don't." That expression may apply to the leader-follower relationship as well. According to George Graen and his associates, developers of **the vertical dyad linkage model (VDL),** leaders distinguish among individual followers, offering differing descriptions of their followers rather than treating them all alike. Acting similarly, individual followers also may offer conflicting descriptions of the same leader.[10] Thus, leaders probably will not use the same leadership style when communicating with followers, leading to the leader having very positive relationships with some followers and less positive relationships with others. In like fashion, some followers will report their relationship with a leader to be very positive, while others will not, perceiving their relationship with the leader as strained or nonrewarding. These differences result in a relationship dichotomy and the creation of an in- and an out-group.

VDL—Are you in or out?

In-group members function as the leader's assistant or advisor, with exchanges between leader and follower exhibiting high levels of trust and support. Just the opposite is true for out-group members, with leader and follower exhibiting a lack of trust and support for one another. Thus, because the leader gives in-group members more responsibility, they are able to exert more influence on the leader. In comparison, out-group members typically find themselves facing a more authoritarian leader and perceive themselves to be the targets of an abundance of task-oriented communication from the leader. Recently, an executive at the Allstate Corporation found out what can go wrong and how quickly one can move from the in-group to the out-group after bad-mouthing his boss and having to abruptly exit the company as a result. The executive had expressed his dissatisfaction with the CEO publicly, delivering a double-barreled pejorative that numerous other employees of the company overheard and reported to the CEO.[11]

So are you in or out? It may well depend on how you negotiate your role and how you perform as a follower. Moving from the out-group to the in-group, while not easy, is possible if the follower volunteers to work more and harder, meeting or surpassing the leader's expectations.

Leader Member Exchange Theory

The vertical dyad linkage model led to the development of **leader member exchange theory (LMX).** Instead of characterizing followers as part of the in-group or the out-group, LMX focuses on the quality of the leader-follower relationship.[12] How would you rate the quality of the relationship you share with a leader of your choice?

> LMX: Do we have a "quality" relationship?

Self-Reflection: Quality Counts

Select a leader you know or have worked with.[13] Picture yourself as a follower of this leader. Rate your relationship with him or her by responding to the following probes:

1. Is where you stand with the leader clear? In other words, how aware are you of how satisfied the leader is with your performance?

   (1) Not at all (2) Not very (3) Somewhat (4) Very (5) Absolutely

2. To what extent, if any, does the leader understand your job-related problems and needs?

   (1) Not at all (2) A little (3) Somewhat (4) A lot (5) Fully

3. To what extent, if any, does the leader recognize your potential?

   (1) Not at all (2) A little (3) Somewhat (4) A lot (5) Fully

4. In your opinion, what are the chances that the leader would use his or her power to help you solve work-related problems?

   (1) 0% (2) 25% (3) 50% (4) 75% (5) 100%

(Continued)

(Continued)

5. In your opinion, what are the chances that the leader would come to your rescue if you needed his or her help?

   (1) 0% (2) 25% (3) 50% (4) 75% (5) 100%

6. What are the chances that you would defend the leader and his or her decisions even if he or she were not present?

   (1) 0% (2) 25% (3) 50% (4) 75% (5) 100%

7. How effective is the working relationship you have with the leader?

   (1) Extremely ineffective

   (2) Very ineffective

   (3) Average in effectiveness

   (4) Very effective

   (5) Extremely effective

Now, how do you imagine a follower would answer these questions were you the selected leader?

Source: Based on Graen & Uhl-Bien (1998). Used by permission.

The higher the LMX score, the better the relationship between leader and follower. Additionally, followers who share a high LMX relationship with a leader tend to produce work of higher quality, demonstrate more commitment to their organizations, are less likely to quit their jobs, are more likely to provide honest feedback, are more apt to go above and beyond the expectations set for them, and are better able to exert influence on the leader and subsequently on the organization—effectively becoming a partner in the exertion of influence and the performance of leadership. When this happens, George Graen and Mary Uhl-Bien assert that the leader-follower relationship forged by quality communication effectively directly contributes to leader making.[14] Thus, improving the quality of the relationship that leader and follower share by effectively deepening its nature appears to empower both the leader and the follower.

Post It: Imagineering A Better Way

Research and evaluate the nature of a challenge your college or university's student body president is currently facing. For example, perhaps your school is contemplating an increase in student fees, the elimination of a department, or the revamping of a program. Identify a past challenge the student body president faced, such as increasing student center programming, for example, and research what the president did that contributed to his or her success or failure.

Based on what you learn from the president or others, what strategies do you recommend the president of the student body use to turn students into exemplary followers? How do you perceive the president's communication style to affect student performance? What followership strengths and weaknesses do you believe that you and other students in your school possess? What recommendations might you make to improve the leader-follower relationship the president and students share?

Effective leaders take responsibility for communicating with followers in ways that are transparent. They think and say *we* rather than *I*. They ensure all involved understand the situation they are facing, paying careful attention to their information needs and the creation of networks of people to support their goals. In effect, followers become leaders as the responsibilities of leadership are shared with newly formed teams.

LOOK BACK

Reread this chapter's opening poem. Based on your understanding of the leader-follower relationship, what do you believe your answer to the question the speaker asks reveals about your views?

Key Terms

Achievement-oriented leadership (50)   Conformists (48)

Alienated followers (47)   Directive leadership (50)

Exemplary followers (48)   Path-goal theory (50)

Helicopter leaders (50)   Pragmatists (48)

Leader member exchange theory   Situational leadership
(LMX) (55)   theory (52)

Participative leadership (50)   Supportive leadership (50)

Passive followers (48)   Vertical dyad linkage model (VDL) (54)

Notes

1. Chip Heath and Dan Heath, *Switch: How to Change Things When Change Is Hard* (New York: Broadway Books, 2010), 8–15.

2. John Kotter, *Leading Change* (Boston: Harvard Business Press, 1995).

3. This questionnaire is from Robert Kelley, *The Power of Followership: How to Create Leaders People Want to Follow and Followers Who Lead Themselves* (New York: Doubleday/Currency, 1992), 89–97.

4. R. Kelley, *The Power of Followership: How to Create Leaders People Want to Follow and Followers Who Lead Themselves* (New York: Doubleday/Currency, 1992).

5. See both R. Kelley, *The Power of Followership: How to Create Leaders People Want to Follow and Followers Who Lead Themselves,* and R. Kelley, "Followership in a Leadership World," in L. C. Spears, ed., *Insights on Leadership: Service Stewardship, Spirit, and Servant-Leadership* (New York: John Wiley & Sons, 1998), 170–84.

6. Barbara Kellerman, *Followership: How Followers Are Creating Change and Changing Leaders* (Boston: Harvard Business School Press, 2008).

7. See, for example, R. J. House, "A Path-Goal Theory of Leader Effectiveness," *Administrative Science Quarterly* 16 (1971): 321–38; and R. J. House and T. R. Mitchell, "Path Goal Theory of Leadership," *Journal of Contemporary Business* 3 (1974): 81–97.

8. P. Hersey, K. H. Blanchard, and D. Johnson, *Management of Organizational Behavior: Leading Human Resources*, 9th ed. (Upper Saddle River, NJ: Prentice Hall, 2008).

9. Center for Leadership Studies, 2006. Reprinted with permission of the Center for Leadership Studies, Inc. Escondido, CA 92025.

10. G. Graen, "Role-Making Processes Within Complex Organizations," in M. D. Dunnette, ed., *Handbook of Industrial Organizational Psychology* (New York: Wiley, 1983), 1201–46; and F. Dansereau, G. Graen, and W. Haga, "A Vertical Dyad Linkage Approach to Leadership in Formal Organizations," *Organizational Behavior and Human Performance* 13 (1975): 46–78.

11. Eric Holm and Joann S. Lublin, "Loose Lips Trip Up Good Hands Executive," *Wall Street Journal* (August 1, 2011): C1, C3.

12. See, for example, M. Uhl-Bien, "Relationship Development as a Key Ingredient for Leadership Development," in S. E. Murphy and R. E. Riggo, eds., *The Future of*

Leadership Development (Mahwah, NJ: Lawrence Erlbaum, 2003), 129–47; and B. H. Mueller and J. Lee, "Leader-Member Exchange and Organizational Communication Satisfaction in Multiple Contexts," *Journal of Business Communication* 39 (2002): 220–44.

13. Based on G. Graen and M. Uhl-Bien, "Relationship-Based Approach to Leadership: Development of Leader-Member Exchange (LMX) Theory of Leadership Over 25 Years: Applying a Multi-Level Multi-Domain Perspective," in F. Danserear and F. J. Yammarino, eds., *Leadership: The Multiple-Level Approaches* vol. 24 (New York: Elsevier, 1998), 123.

14. G. Graen and M. Uhl-Bien, "Relationship-Based Approach to Leadership," 103–58.

PART II

DEVELOPING LEADERSHIP SKILLS

THINKING ABOUT HOW LEADERS THINK

THE LEADER'S THINKING SHAPES AN
ORGANIZATION'S CLIMATE AND CULTURE

LEADERSHIP STYLE AND THE
ORGANIZATIONAL ENVIRONMENT

Do you think when you should feel?
Do you feel when you should think?
Can we separate the two?

4

Thinking Like a Leader

The Power of Thoughtfulness

On September 11, 2001, terrorists bent on attacking the United States hijacked four airplanes. Two of the commandeered planes slammed into the towers of the World Trade Center. A third crashed into the Pentagon. And the fourth aircraft, Flight 93, which experts believe was supposed to have hit the U.S. Capitol, crashed into a Shanksville, Pennsylvania, hillside instead. What happened aboard Flight 93 demonstrates that how a leader thinks and reacts when facing an emergency really matters.

Within minutes of learning of the crisis they were facing, the individuals aboard Flight 93 used their cell phones to gather information about what had been happening on the ground and in the air, discussed what they learned, took a vote, and then acted jointly to bring the airplane they were in down before it was able to reach its target. Their action did not result because of what one person did or believed; it occurred because of the leadership exerted by a number of people who were prepared to think and respond in an emergency.[1]

Had you been on that airplane, do you think you would have been up to the challenge?

Our workplaces are not as scary as those airplanes. But that does not mean that they are not filled with challenges in need of solutions. Contemporary workplace environments are highly competitive, fast-paced, and fast changing. Are you ready to respond to the challenges they present? Leaders who are prepared demonstrate flexibility and balance, thoughtfulness and the ability to think critically, empathy and the willingness to share perspectives, and the ability to choose the right approach and implement it at the right time. But how do leaders prepare themselves for this? They spend time thinking about how effective leaders think.

THINKING ABOUT HOW LEADERS THINK

What does it mean to *think about thinking*, and why would a leader spend time engaged in such an activity?

A leader who thinks about thinking understands that how he or she thinks directly affects the work environment of followers impacting the organization's chances for success. Leaders who think about thinking tend to be thoughtful instead of thoughtless. Thoughtful leaders understand how thinking guides decision making, including options or kinds of alternatives leaders think are available for them to choose among.

Thoughtful leaders display the following five key thinking behaviors:

(1) They avoid thinking about false choices.

(2) They distinguish between unconscious and conscious incompetence and competence.

(3) They recognize the roles doubt and certainty play in decision making.

(4) They embrace a systems orientation.

(5) They ask tough questions.

Replace "or" Thinking With "and" Thinking

It's time to think about thinking!

Thoughtful leaders abandon either-or, all-or-nothing, two-sided thinking and substitute in its place thinking that allows for multiple possibilities, perhaps even the uniting of apparent opposites. For example, in soccer, is it the offense or the defense that wins the game? The truth is that both the offense *and* defense win games.[2] Thus, one of the first steps in improving how a leader thinks is to delete the *or* in thinking and replace it with an *and*.

Differentiate Between Unconscious Competence and Unconscious Incompetence

Thoughtful leaders take steps to become **unconsciously competent**—to make leading seem virtually automatic. Too frequently, leaders *unknowingly* make mistakes—displaying *unconscious incompetence* instead of unconscious competence. The accompanying learning model (see Figure 4.1) illustrates the difference between the two.

Most of us start out **unconsciously incompetent.** Unaware of our lack of knowledge, we do not know what we do not know. When we become aware of what we do not know, real learning begins, and we become consciously incompetent—aware that we are missing knowledge. Once we acquire the missing knowledge, we are able to progress to conscious competence and can apply what we learn as long as we think consciously about doing it. The goal, of course, is to become unconsciously competent—to do the right thing automatically without even having to think about it. What is essential to leadership

Figure 4.1 Model of Learning

	Unconscious	Conscious
Incompetent	I Unconsciously Incompetent	II Consciously Incompetent
Competent	IV Unconsciously Competent	III Consciously Competent

success, however, is that we do not pick up bad habits of thinking and then without thinking base our decisions on them, as too many thoughtless leaders are prone to do.

Thus, to be effective, a leader needs to think effectively, and that means that a leader needs to avoid making mistakes unconsciously. Thus, wise leaders willingly take steps to improve their thinking skills.

Balance Certainty and Uncertainty

Thoughtful leaders know that *doubt* is not a dirty word. In *The Seven Habits of Highly Effective People*, Stephen Covey tells a story, which we paraphrase here, that illustrates this:

It seems that two battleships were on maneuvers in heavy seas. The fog was dense, making visibility poor. The captain of the lead battleship was on watch when the lookout on the bridge warned him, "Light, bearing on the starboard bow." The captain replied, "Is it steady or moving?" The lookout replied, "Steady, Captain." This meant the two battleships were on a collision course. The captain responded, "Signal that ship. Tell them we are on a collision course and to change course 20 degrees." The reply from the other ship followed: "Advise you change course 20 degrees." Not to be one-upped, the captain responded in turn, "Send this message: I am a captain. You change course 20 degrees." In quick order came this response: "I'm a seaman second class. Advise you change course 20 degrees." Really angry, the captain told the lookout to send the following: "Change course 20 degrees. I'm a battleship." This message ended the argument: "I am a lighthouse."[3]

Hubris, or false pride, can keep a leader from blinking, when blinking might be the proper course. Unbridled confidence in decision making can make it difficult for others to challenge leaders' assumptions, making it harder to provide leaders with information that could cause them to adjust their thinking. Certainty is a benefit only when the course set is the right course.

Replace the Concept of Independence With a Systems Orientation

Thoughtful leaders recognize that thinking is not an independent process. They take into account the multiple connected pieces of the organization, from employees to customers, from suppliers to the union. All parts of the organization are interconnected with all the other parts; they do not exist or operate independently or in isolation. The whole is greater than any of its parts. Thus, thoughtful leaders think about the big picture, not merely parts of the picture.

Consider how a change implemented in one part of the organization affects all its other parts. Think about how a change a company made years ago affects how the company runs today. Then consider how making a change in a company today could affect it in the future. For example, consider how thinking about the value employees produce, not merely the hours they put in, could change how things are done in your organization.

Ask Tough Questions

A thinking leader doesn't necessarily have all the answers, but he or she does ask the right questions. What makes a question right? A right question is a tough question. It causes people to pause—to stop and think about why they are or are not taking some action. It engages people in discussion and debate as they confront and seek solutions to the challenges they face.

Thoughtful Leaders

Identify false choices
Are unconsciously competent
Can live with doubt and uncertainty
Embrace a systems orientation
Ask tough questions

By asking questions such as "What have we missed?" "What else should we be thinking about?" or "How could we do this better?" the leader also helps to foster a culture of continuous improvement. Additionally, asking tough questions usually precedes creative thinking because it precipitates the viewing of problems from fresh perspectives, often enabling solutions to be found in the concerns of dissenting voices.[4]

Theory Into Practice

Leading in a Crisis

The organizational world is replete with crises—from environmental disasters to technological failures, from criminal acts to economic threats. How a leader thinks and then reacts when facing such a crisis can contribute to the organization emerging stronger or threaten its survival.[5] Being aware of a problem but taking no action puts the future of an organization in danger as much as does failing to acknowledge responsibility for creating or not planning for the crisis.

Those who emerge stronger from a crisis usually have had a crisis plan in effect; that is, they prepared in advance, were ready when the crisis struck, and thus were able to control the damage done. Being vigilant (for example, being on the lookout for potential errors or enacted biases) and having a workable plan of action, a designated crisis management team (the group assigned to carry out the plan), a single spokesperson or point of contact, a commitment to be available to and work with the media, and a bias for responding honestly and with compassion are key in ensuring the sustainability of the company's name and image.

To see how this works, compare and contrast NASA's responses to and investigations of the disasters that befell both the *Challenger* and *Columbia* spacecrafts. To which crisis do you believe NASA responded more effectively and why?

THE LEADER'S THINKING SHAPES AN ORGANIZATION'S CLIMATE AND CULTURE

Every organization has both a distinctive **climate** and a unique **culture**. And both start with the leader.

Considering Climate

When we speak of an organization's *climate*, we are using a metaphor for the organization's internal environment, that is, how people perceive the nature of the communication practices used in the organization. The kinds of people at the organization's top, the CEO, CFO, COO, etc., tend to define the kinds of people the organization seeks to hire and retain. They also express their relationship to the people who work for them through their communication—effectively creating the organization's climate.

Have you ever worked for a "toxic" leader? What impact did the environment the leader created have on you?

DILBERT © 2010 Scott Adams. Used by permission of UNIVERSAL UCLICK. All rights reserved.

To take the temperature of the climate in your organization, begin by asking yourself some tough questions: How enthusiastic do you feel about going to work? How trusted do you feel? How much do you believe your input is valued? Your response and the response of employees and other stakeholders to questions like these offer clues to the kind of climate that has evolved in your organization.

Self-Reflection: Looking In and Out

Assessing the Leader's Effect on Climate

Using either your workplace, class, or college/university experiences as a point of reference, please respond to the following questions as honestly and candidly as possible, using the following code to interpret the meaning of the numerical symbols:

> 5—Circle the number *5* if you believe the item is a true reflection of your thinking
>
> 4—Circle the number *4* if you believe the item is more true than false as a reflection of your thinking
>
> 3—Circle the number *3* if the item is about a half-true and half-false reflection of your thinking
>
> 2—Circle the number *2* if the item is more false than true as a reflection of your thinking
>
> 1—Circle the number *1* if the item is a false reflection of your thinking

(Continued)

(Continued)

Your responses to the questions that follow should reflect no one's judgment but your own.

1. I think that people naturally commit themselves to high-performance goals.

   5   4   3   2   1

2. I place a great deal of trust in the people I work with.

   5   4   3   2   1

3. I think it is highly important to consult the people who work with me before formulating policies affecting them.

   5   4   3   2   1

4. I think people who work with me generally trust me.

   5   4   3   2   1

5. If I were to receive information from others, I would act on the information I received unless it were demonstrated wrong.

   5   4   3   2   1

6. I tend to communicate candidly with people at all levels of the organization.

   5   4   3   2   1

7. I think people feel free to tell me what's on their minds regardless of their position in the organization.

   5   4   3   2   1

8. My concern for people is equal to my concern for their ability to complete their tasks.

   5   4   3   2   1

9. I think that people throughout the organization listen with open minds to the ideas of others.

   5   4   3   2   1

10. I think that upward communication is equal in importance to downward communication.

    5   4   3   2   1

11. I see to it that personnel receive the information required for them to do their jobs effectively.

    5   4   3   2   1

12. I think it is essential for all organizational personnel to be involved in goal setting and decision making.

    5   4   3   2   1

Analyzing How Communication Affects Climate

1. To compute the overall-climate score, add the responses to the 12 items and divide by 12.

2. To compute the trust score, add the responses to number 2 and number 4 and divide by 2.

3. To compute the participating decision-making score, add the responses to number 3 and number 12 and divide by 2.

4. To get the supportiveness-climate score, add the responses to number 6 and number 7 and divide by 2.

5. To get the openness-in-downward-communication score, add the responses to number 10 and number 11 and divide by 2.

6. To get the listening-in-upward-communication score, add the responses to number 5 and number 9 and divide by 2.

7. To get the concern-for-high-performance-goals score, add the responses to number 1 and number 8 and divide by 2.

What does your self-analysis reveal about your potential to affect organizational climate? In what areas do you think you are most and least effective? How might changing your thoughts about work and the people you work with influence your scores?

Climate affects interaction in all organizations, influencing how people feel about work, how hard they work, what they seek to accomplish, their potential for innovation, and their perceived fit with the organization. By analyzing an organization's climate (even the one in your classroom) we can better understand the thinking that guides the behavior of the organization's leaders including how that thinking affects an organization's members.

Leadership theorist Charles Redding identified the five factors comprising communication climate:

(1) *Supportiveness* (the extent to which members believe their communication relationships with the organization's leaders help them build and maintain their personal worth and importance)

(2) *Participative decision making* (members' perceptions that they are free to communicate upwardly in order to influence decisions made relevant to their positions)

(3) *Trust* (the perception that sources of information and messages are believable and useful)

(4) *Openness and candor* (the belief that leaders communicate honestly with members and that employees can share what they are thinking regarding their position with others)

(5) *High-performance goals* (the clear communication and understanding of and commitment to the organization's objectives)[6]

When these perceptions are realized, the climate becomes more positive. When these expectations go unmet, however, dissatisfaction increases.

In general, if an organization's leaders think employees cannot be trusted, then the climate that develops in that organization is likely to be dehumanizing, one discouraging of both interaction and the formation of employee connections. When a climate is dehumanizing, communication flows predominantly top-down and finds the organization's leadership implementing changes with little, if any, employee input. Often such a noninclusive climate leads to lower levels of production.

At the other extreme, an organization's leaders may pay little attention to the organization's task but focus their thoughts exclusively on the welfare of employees and the obtaining of employee input. Such leaders may obsess with the environment in which employees operate and commit to the idea of having everyone agree on if and when an organizational change should be implemented. This precipitates what we could describe as a "happiness for lunch bunch" climate, a climate that encourages meeting for meetings' sake but is also less than desirable because of its deemphasis on task.

In contrast to these two climates is the *open climate*—a climate that fosters personal growth and achievement but one in which both the organization's personnel and leadership are expected to be task focused, do their jobs, and be accepting of change when it is needed.

Thus, for the organization to have a healthy climate, concern for both task and people need to be integrated, open and accurate communication needs to flow both up and down the organization, a spirit of supportiveness and consultation need to guide thinking, and most importantly, people need to trust one another. Communication practices like these help to enhance relationships benefiting leaders, workers, and the organization. The perceptions employees have relative to relationship quality and communication in the organization, and their involvement and ability to influence the organization, matter. Generally, the more positive an organization's climate is, the more productive are its people.

Considering Culture

While climate measures whether the thoughts people have about what it should be like to work in an organization are being met, the organization's culture describes its inner reality. Culture focuses on the nature of the organization's expectations themselves, as expressed in the organization's business environment, history, values, heroes and heroines, villains, preferred modes of expression, and rites and rituals.

The relationship among who is leading an organization, the organization's members, and the organization's culture is complex. In many ways, every employee of an organization is a reflection in miniature of the culture existing in the organization. How people interact, what they will and will not do, and what they value as being right or wrong speaks volumes. As with climate, how an organization's leaders think, what they think about, and what they communicate to others shape the organization's culture. In time, the evolved culture also influences the actions and behaviors of the organization's leaders and members.[7]

How Do Climate and Culture Differ?

Climate, the internal environment of an organization, is composed of five factors:

1. Supportiveness
2. Participative decision making
3. Trust
4. Openness and candor
5. High-performance goals

Culture, the organization's inner reality, answers this question: How do we do it around here?

Unspoken expectations provide clues to the nature of an organization's culture. For example, the policies, practices, and services that an organization provides usually support the culture created, expressing its values, beliefs, and expected behaviors of people in the organization and creating the organization's "how we do it around here" knowledge base. Different cultures make different outcomes possible. In most circumstances, when the patterns of beliefs and values shared by employees are consistent with the organization's culture, a positive climate results. On the other hand, if the organization's culture and employee values significantly diverge, the climate will more than likely be negative.

Using communication, organizations perform or enact their cultures. If the culture the leaders communicate is strong, employees understand their roles and what is expected of them. If the culture communicated is weak or fragmented, then employee values will be unclear and loyalties sacrificed.

Observation: Watch and Learn

Culture Cues

Use the following questions together with follow-up questions of your own choosing to interview three people who work for one organization, for example, your college or university or an organization in your town. After conducting your interviews, write a paper describing your impression of the nature of the organization's culture.

1. Tell me about the organization you work for and the nature of your job. Which individuals in the organization do you perceive yourself to compete with? Whose support do you count on?

2. Describe your organization's mission. Is it being accomplished? Why or why not?

3. Is there anything unusual about your organization or how it goes about accomplishing its work?

4. How would you describe decision making in your organization?

5. What people in your organization are believed to have contributed in outstanding ways to the organization? What people are believed to have been toxic for the organization, influencing it in negative ways?

6. What rituals or special events does the organization celebrate or hold?

7. If you were to give a presentation about your organization, what stories might you tell to begin and end the speech?

8. If a new employee wanted to be successful working for the organization, what would you tell him or her?

9. If an article about the organization were to appear in a newspaper, what would it be likely to cover?

10. What secrets does your organization have? What would happen if any one of those secrets were leaked?

The pressures an organization faces and how people handle those pressures also offer clues to the nature of the organization's culture and whether when facing such pressures people are able to make sound, ethical decisions.

For example, in 2011 we learned in depth of the scandal at News Corporation involving hacking into private phones and files. But the scandal turned out to be not really new. It was alleged that years earlier George and Richard Rebh, the owners of a small ad firm, Floorgraphics, had been approached by Paul Carlucci, the CEO of a unit of News Corp., who told them that his unit, News America Marketing In-Store Services Inc., was interested in purchasing their firm. The Rebh brothers replied that they weren't interested in selling.

According to a lawsuit the brothers subsequently filed, after that conversation News Corp. opened a "multimillion (dollar) war chest" in an effort to take customers away from Floorgraphics. Floorgraphics accused News Corp. of hacking into its computers and using information found there to lure its clients away. Ultimately, the case went to trial but ended a few days later when News Corp. purchased Floorgraphics for a huge sum of money. The surfacing of this story only raised more questions about the kind of corporate culture that existed at News Corp., an organization in which it appears that unethical behavior was widespread but about which the firm's owners professed their ignorance.

Reports allege that News Corp. paid the legal fees of a convicted felon and paid off victims. And yet it appears that the firm's leaders never intervened to end such behavior. Where was the oversight?[8] While we also refer to this case in our chapter on ethics, the question for you to consider here is how you imagine employees and stakeholders would describe the culture and leadership style at News Corp.

LEADERSHIP STYLE AND THE ORGANIZATIONAL ENVIRONMENT

If given the choice, which one of the following five leadership options would you prefer to enact under most circumstances?

1. I would be the center of direction-giving and decision-making responsibilities.

2. I would share direction-giving and decision-making responsibilities.

3. I would delegate direction-giving and decision-making responsibilities to others.

4. I would persuade others to think and act as I do.

5. I would consult with others before making a decision myself.

Which leadership style does your choice represent? Read on.

Self-Reflection: Looking In and Out

(What's My Style?)

Indicate your level of agreement with each of the following statements:

Statement	Strongly Agree	Agree	Uncertain	Disagree	Strongly Disagree
1. A leader should act independently in making decisions and setting the organization's direction.	1	2	3	4	5
2. A leader should consult with others before making important decisions.	1	2	3	4	5
3. A leader should base decisions on the wishes of others, not his or her own preferences.	1	2	3	4	5

4. A leader should seek input from a committee created for the purpose of giving him or her advice.	1	2	3	4	5
5. A leader should assess the organization's progress single-handedly.	1	2	3	4	5
6. Workers should be able to make decisions without seeking a leader's input or consent.	1	2	3	4	5
7. Employees who break rules should be punished.	1	2	3	4	5
8. Workers should understand the reasons for a leader's decisions.	1	2	3	4	5
9. A leader should be aloof and not bother with monitoring worker progress.	1	2	3	4	5

Directions for scoring: Compute your score on each of the leadership communication styles by recording and then totaling your points in each column.

Authoritarian	Democratic	Laissez-Faire
Question 1 ____	Question 2 ____	Question 3 ____
Question 5 ____	Question 4 ____	Question 6 ____
Question 7 ____	Question 8 ____	Question 9 ____
SCORE:	SCORE:	SCORE:

In which column is your score highest? The higher your score, the more likely it is that you prefer this style of leadership. In which column is your score lowest? This likely represents your least preferred leadership style.

Dominant Styles of Leadership

How a leader expresses and communicates his or her authority is a key indicator of his or her dominant leadership style. Three leadership styles are dominant in the literature:

(1) *The authoritarian/autocratic style.* The leader makes decisions, announcing them to others with the expectation that others will carry them out without dispute. Communication flows in one direction—it is primarily downward and noninteractive.

(2) *The democratic style.* The leader frames the problem but distributes decision-making responsibilities throughout the organization. Communication is multidirectional and highly interactive.

(3) *The laissez-faire style.* The leader cedes all responsibility for making decisions to others in the organization.[9]

Each style influences the leader's relationship to others. For example, **authoritarian/autocratic leaders** emphasize their control position and the belief that unless strictly supervised, people cannot function productively. **Democratic leaders,** in contrast, easily interact with others, encouraging their participation, input, and enthusiasm. **Laissez-faire leaders,** on the other hand, prefer to leave others to fend for themselves.

While some view this last form of leadership as an abdication of leader responsibility, if used appropriately with the right people, it can also result in those left to their own devices rising to the occasion and acting autonomously with the leader not intervening in their work unless consulted.

Leader In Action *Versus* Leader Inaction

Authoritarian	Leader makes decisions.	Leader in action
Democratic	Leader distributes decision-making responsibilities.	Leader in action
Laissez-Faire	Leader cedes responsibility to others.	Leader inaction

Despite the dominance of these three styles, there are actually five prevailing leadership styles used to describe leaders. The remaining two styles are *selling*—closely allied with the autocratic leader; the selling leader makes decisions but does not merely announce them to others, trying instead to persuade others of his or her decision's desirability; communication is primarily downward—and *consultative*—while reserving the right to make the final decision, the consultative leader first seeks advice and input from others, always being clear that the ultimate decision rests in his or her hands; communication is interactive.

Theory-X and Theory-Y Leaders

The leadership style you prefer reveals a lot about how you think about the leader's role and view the people who report to you in the organization. According to leadership expert Douglas McGregor, leaders adhere to one of two different sets of philosophical orientations regarding workers: he dubbed these orientations *theory X* and *theory Y,* representing task-oriented and interpersonally oriented leadership.[10]

The actions of **theory-X leaders** express the following beliefs: (1) most people find work distasteful, (2) most workers prefer to be directed, (3) most people are unmotivated and lacking in ambition, (4) most are unskilled in solving problems creatively, and (5) most need to be tightly controlled. Theory-X leaders naturally migrate to the autocratic or **selling** style of leading. Under this type of leader, communication flows down the organization with decision making concentrated in those who hold power and directions emanating from the top. Upward communication is virtually nonexistent with the exception of systems designed to have employees spy on one another and report infractions to those above them. A theory-X leader generally prefers to communicate in writing and practices a "closed-door" policy; such an orientation typically generates a climate of fear and distrust, limiting peer-to-peer interaction. As we see, theory-X leaders tend to focus primarily on the task or work itself, with little concern being given to workers. Theory-X leaders function more like "bosses" or "enforcers," relying on close supervision, control, and threats of punishment to achieve goals.

In contrast, **theory-Y leaders** internalize and externalize different assumptions about the people working in their organizations. They believe that workers (1) find work as natural as play, (2) are capable of self-direction, (3) have the capacity for creative problem solving, (4) should be involved in decision making, and (5) need self-control as a prerequisite for goal achievement. Theory-Y leaders tend to prefer to use a democratic or **consultative leadership style.** In organizations led by theory-Y leaders, communication flows up, down, and across the organization, decision making is distributed throughout the organization, and people at all organizational levels are consulted and involved. Theory-Y leaders stress the importance of open communication, practicing an "open-door" policy. Because of the frequency and multidirectional nature of honest communication by both leader and workers, theory-Y leaders promote interaction and generate a climate of trust. Theory-Y leaders tend to balance concern for work with concern for the people producing the work.[11] They seek to develop the potential of employees as a means of meeting the organization's goals and function more like mentors or coaches rather than like members of a police force.

Balancing Concern for Task and Workers

We can also differentiate leadership styles based on the leader's concern for task and concern for workers; the degree to which the concerns are balanced divides graphically into an array of contrasting leadership styles[12] (see Figure 4.2).

Figure 4.2   Leadership Styles

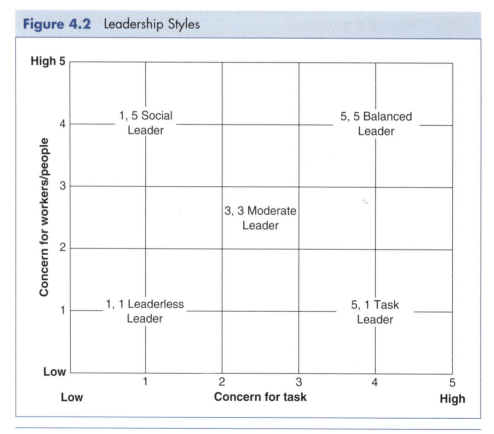

Source: Richmond, Virginia Peck, and McCroskey, James C., *Organizational Communication for Survival: Making Work,* 4th Edition, © 2009. Reprinted by permission of Pearson Education, Inc., Upper Saddle River, NJ.

Social leaders (1, 5) display a high concern for people and a low concern for task. Such leaders enjoy a happy and sociable climate, one in which there is no reason for people to feel disconnected or stressed. As a result, social leaders sometimes find themselves basing decisions on how they will affect the happiness of workers rather than on how they will impact production. Social leaders are also likely to delegate order giving and decision making, preferring not to make the tough calls themselves.

Task leaders (5, 1) display a high concern for task and a low concern for people. They have a machine mentality—with people being seen as replaceable parts. Thus, they have little patience for the personal problems and concerns of workers. As a result, workers perceive them as uninterested, insensitive, and stern.

Balanced leaders (5, 5) have an equally high concern for task and people. Such leaders seek to integrate organizational and employee goals by striving to maintain production at high levels while being sensitive to the needs and concerns of workers. Balanced leaders foster communication at all levels, believing that communication facilitates production.

Laissez-faire or leaderless leaders (1, 1) have a low concern for both task and people. Laissez-faire leaders like to be left alone and their "hands off, don't rock the boat" approach virtually leaves the organization leaderless, with workers dependent on themselves for the organization's maintenance.

Moderate leaders (3, 3) are moderately concerned for both task and people. Falling midway between laissez-faire and balanced leadership, moderate leaders tend to be compromisers in their efforts to meet production and people needs.

Which of these styles most closely exemplifies your approach to leadership? Which do you think represents "the perfect leader"?

Working It Out: Alone or Together

1. First, working individually, examine the list of words below, descriptive of how people might feel and act on the job. Check five words you believe to be representative of your on-the-job behavior.

   _____ acquiescent

   _____ agreeable

   _____ analytical

   (Continued)

(Continued)

_____ assent giving

_____ assertive

_____ avoiding

_____ compliant

_____ conceding

_____ coordinating

_____ critical

_____ debating

_____ directive

_____ disagreeable

_____ energizing

_____ initiating

_____ instructive

_____ judging

_____ leading

_____ resisting

_____ withdrawing

_____ withholding

2. Share the words you checked with two other students or people who know you well. Ask if they perceive you as you perceive yourself or if they see you differently.

3. Consider the following questions: Do the words you checked indicate your general desire to control things yourself or to cede that control to others? Do they signify a desire to be involved with others or to maintain a distance from others? What do the words you selected suggest about the type of leader you would be; particularly, what do they indicate about your leadership style?

Transactional and Transformational Leaders

Researchers similarly differentiate between transactional and transformational leaders.

Transactional leaders are more task oriented while **transformational leaders** are friendlier with followers, fostering warmer interpersonal relationships with them. While the motivational appeals used by the transactional leader are aimed at satisfying basic human needs, the transformational leader motivates followers by appealing to their higher-level or self-actualization needs. According to Abraham Maslow, humans have five levels of needs (see Figure 4.3).[13] In ascending order, they are physiological, safety, belonging and love, self-esteem, and self-actualization. After our first three need levels are met, we can turn our attention to meeting our self-esteem needs—the needs we have to feel good about who we are. Once that need level is also satisfied, we become free to focus on meeting our self-actualization needs.

Thus, in many ways transactional leadership, with its concern for satisfying physiological, safety, and belonging needs, lays the foundation for transformational leadership that focuses on meeting the self-esteem and self-actualization needs of followers. Transformational leaders tend to elicit more follower satisfaction with the leader, enjoy higher degrees of follower commitment, promote more sharing of knowledge, and prepare and empower followers to meet the challenges of change.[14]

Figure 4.3 Maslow's Hierarchy of Needs

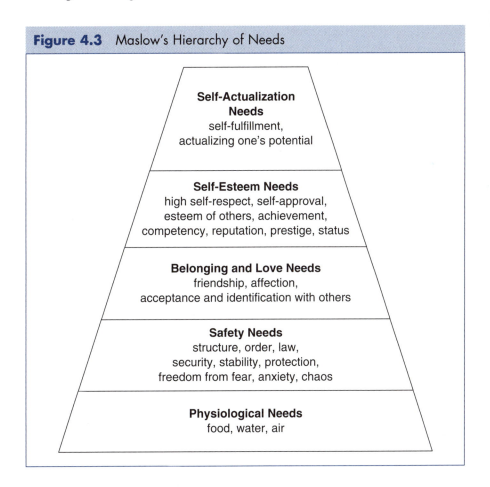

Self-Actualization Needs
self-fulfillment, actualizing one's potential

Self-Esteem Needs
high self-respect, self-approval, esteem of others, achievement, competency, reputation, prestige, status

Belonging and Love Needs
friendship, affection, acceptance and identification with others

Safety Needs
structure, order, law, security, stability, protection, freedom from fear, anxiety, chaos

Physiological Needs
food, water, air

Post It: Imagineering a Better Way

According to Paul Maritz, president and CEO of the software firm VMware, leadership teams need a strategist, a classic manager, a customer champion, and an enforcer.[15] The strategist is the visionary setting the organization's goals; the classic manager is the caretaker of the organization, responsible for making certain everyone knows what he or she needs to do; the customer champion empathizes with and understands what customers will pay for and how they see things; and the enforcer is the person who decides when to halt consideration and make a decision or take action.

Which type of leader do you believe would be best suited to perform each of these roles and why?

Differences in leadership style have an impact on the attitudes and productivity of people. They can make an organization's members more dependent or independent, more or less egocentric, and even increase or decrease their initiative and friendliness. At the risk of oversimplifying theory, by doing things in a positive way, the best leaders are able to get the best out of people.

LOOK BACK

Reread the opening poem. Based on what you have just learned, respond to the speaker's question.

Key Terms

Authoritarian/autocratic leadership style (78)

Balanced leaders (81)

Climate (68)

Consultative leadership style (79)

Culture (68)

Democratic leadership style (78)

Laissez-faire leaders (81)

Laissez-faire leadership style (78)

Moderate leaders (81)

Selling leadership style (79)

Social leaders (81)

Task leaders (81)

Theory-X leaders (79)

Transformational leaders (82)

Theory-Y leaders (79)

Unconsciously competent (65)

Transactional leaders (82)

Unconsciously incompetent (65)

Notes

1. See, for example, Elaine Scarry, *Thinking in an Emergency* (New York: W. W. Norton, 2011).

2. P. S. Pande, *The Six Sigma Leader: How Top Executives Will Prevail in the 21st Century* (New York: McGraw-Hill, 2007), 13–24.

3. S. Covey, *The 7 Habits of Highly Effective People* (New York: Free Press, 2004).

4. See Ellen Langer, *The Power of Mindful Learning* (Cambridge, MA: Perseus Books, 1997).

5. See, for example, I. I. Mitroff, C. M. Pearson, and L. K. Harrington, *The Essential Guide to Managing Corporate Crises: A Step-by-Step Guide for Surviving Major Catastrophes* (New York: Oxford University Press, 1996); and C. M. Pearson and I. I. Mitroff, "From Crisis Prone to Crisis Prepared: A Framework for Crisis Management," *Academy of Management Executive* 7 (February 1993): 48–60.

6. W. C. Redding, *Communication Within the Organization* (New York: Industrial Communication & Purdue University, 1972).

7. E. H. Schein, *Organization Culture and Leadership*, 2nd ed. (San Francisco: Jossey-Bass, 1992).

8. Christina Rexrode and Josh Lederman, "N.J. Firm Accused News Corp. Unit of Hacking in '04," *Record* (July 24, 2011): B1, B6; and "Beware the Veil of Ignorance," *Financial Times* (July 23/24, 2011): 6.

9. K. Lewin, R. Lippitt, and R. K. White, "Patterns of Aggressive Behavior in Experimentally Created 'Social Climates,'" *Journal of Social Psychology* 10 (1939): 271–99.

10. See D. McGregor, *The Human Side of Enterprise* (New York: McGraw-Hill, 1960); and D. McGregor, *The Professional Manager* (New York: McGraw-Hill, 1967).

11. See R. Blake and J. Mouton, *The Managerial Grid* (Houston, TX: Gulf Publishing, 1964).

12. See V. P. Richmond and J. C. McCroskey, *Organizational Communication for Survival: Making Work, Work*, 4th ed. (Boston: Allyn & Bacon, 2009).

13. A. H. Maslow, *Motivation and Personality* (New York: Harper & Row, 1970).

14. E. R. Vires, A. Bakker-Piepr, and W. Aastenveld, "Leadership = Communication? The Relations of Leaders' Communication Styles With Leadership Styles, Knowledge Sharing, and Leadership Outcomes," *Journal of Business and Psychology* 25(3) (2010): 367–80.

15. Bryant, "Does Your Team Have the Four Essential Types?" *New York Times* (October 3, 2010): BU2.

THE LEADER'S /

PERCEPTUAL REALITIES

PERCEPTUAL BARRIERS

PERCEIVING LIKE A LEADER

What is a defining moment?
Is it the moment before
Or the moment after?
Will you know it
When you see it?

PERCEIVING LIKE A LEADER

Paradigm Power

What is the relationship between perception and leadership? Why is it that some leaders are able to look at a problem, deconstruct it, conceive its possible solutions, and then implement the best solution, while others cannot?

Consider this: the Chinese character for *crisis* is the same as the Chinese character for *opportunity*. It's a question of perception. It may well be that one leader's crisis is another leader's opportunity.

As we will see, the leader's ability to perceive—to select, organize, and interpret experience—influences the leader's understanding of situations, followers, and themselves. What the leader perceives and how the leader thinks about what she or he perceives shape his or her understanding of people and events. How a leader interprets experience offers clues to the leader's ideology and the effectiveness of the paradigm the leader employs. For example, when Cathie Black, a journalist and magazine executive but a noneducator, was named as the next chancellor of New York City's public schools, Jeffrey A. Sonnenfeld, founder of the Chief Executive Leadership Institute at Yale University's School of Management, noted that while it was obvious she was not an educator, she had been inspirational, making a difference in the way editors looked at front pages. According to Sonnenfeld, Black had said, "We're going to have women on the front page, not just in the style section, and we're going to have African Americans on our front, not ghettoized in the sports pages," effectively opening the door to a paradigm shift.[1] Unfortunately, Cathie Black did not last more than a scant three months in the role of chancellor. Forced out, her position was ceded to someone who had worked in the New York City school system for years, Dennis Walcott, an educator hailed for being all that Cathie Black wasn't. According to leadership expert Warren Bennis, it appears that a leader has to be good at both shifting and encouraging perspective shifting because shifting stances, whether by the leader or followers, can change everything.[2]

By exploring the *I* behind the leader's eyes, we will come to better understand how the leader's powers of perception influence what the leader thinks is or is not possible. The *I* behind the leader's eyes also influences the frames of reference, perspectives, or paradigms that the leader uses and the extent to which the leader is successful at creating a shared reality, something Cathie Black was not able to do.[3]

THE LEADER'S *I*

Perception provides each of us with a uniquely personal view of the world. Why is this?

Information theorists tell us that our eyes can process about 5 million bits of data per second, but they also tell us that our brains are capable of handling only some 500 bits per second, compelling every one of us to distinguish those stimuli we will attend to or experience from those we will ignore. Leaders are particularly active participants in perceiving, selecting, organizing, and evaluating the multitude of stimuli that are out there competing for attention. And, like every one of us, leaders also practice selective perception, shifting their spotlight of attention from one stimulus to another until one catches their interest and they focus on it. Leaders who have been trained not to make snap judgments regarding what is or could become important have the perceptual advantage because they do not purposefully avoid some stimuli while exposing themselves readily to others. Instead, they take the time they need to learn more about situations and people before filling in any perceptual gaps or drawing any conclusions.

Stages and Frames of Perception

Leaders deconstruct the perceptual process into four stages:

(1) The selecting stage, during which they choose to attend to some stimuli from all those stimuli they are exposed to

(2) The organizing stage, during which they give order to the selected stimuli

(3) The interpreting/evaluating stage, during which they give meaning and draw conclusions about the selected stimuli based on their life experiences

(4) The responding stage, during which they think, say, and/or do something reflective of their perception

Effective leaders develop the ability to change the frames of reference they habitually employ. For example, the renowned composer Gustav Mahler required the members of his symphony orchestra to sit out in the audience periodically to experience how things looked and sounded from the audience's perspective. Changing perspectives changes people. As a result of revisiting and revising their views of the world,

> **When you change perspectives, you change yourself.**

their thoughts about people, and even how they conceive of leadership, leaders may, in time, switch paradigms—the means they use to understand and explain reality—breaking with an ineffective or timeworn way of perceiving things.

While using the wrong paradigm can impede a leader's progress, making the right paradigm shift, one that enables the leader to see a situation in a fresh perspective or totally new light, can open endless possibilities.[4]

Evolving Organizational Paradigms

Leadership expert Stephen Covey identifies four different organizational paradigms: (1) the scientific/authoritarian paradigm, (2) the human relations paradigm, (3) the human resource paradigm, and (4) the principle-centered leadership paradigm. Covey explores how each paradigm affects the leader's perception of people and their role.

A leader who employs the scientific/authoritarian paradigm sees people as economic beings (what Covey calls *stomachs*) and believes his or her role is to motivate them using the "carrot and the stick" technique, effectively manipulating the reward package provided to them.

In contrast, a leader who adopts a human relations paradigm recognizes that people have both economic needs and social needs; in other words, they have hearts in addition to stomachs. They want to be well treated and to feel that they belong. While such a leader still believes he or she is in charge, the leader also tries to develop a harmonious team.

On the other hand, the leader who uses the **human resource paradigm** perceives that people have minds in addition to having hearts and stomachs; that they are psychological beings, not merely economic or social beings. Thus, such a leader seeks to recognize and make better use of the talent, creativity, and resourcefulness of people.

It is, however, the last paradigm that Covey values most because he believes that only a **principle-centered** leader works with the whole person by paying attention to the spiritual needs of people—empowering them with a sense that they are doing something that matters—in addition to meeting their economic, social, and psychological needs.

Covey explains each of the perceptual shifts this way:

> The scientific management (*stomach*) paradigm says, "Pay me well." The human relations (*heart*) paradigm says, "Treat me well." The human resource (*mind*) paradigm suggests, "Use me well." The principle-centered leadership (*whole person*) paradigm says, "Let's talk about vision and mission, roles, and goals. I want to make a meaningful contribution."[5]

Of course, the accuracy and reliability of a leader's perception is equally affected by his or her ability to use a presented opportunity to construct a meaningful frame or mental picture that others will connect with and respond to; it is similarly dependent on a leader's ability to overcome potential perceptual barriers.

Four Organization Paradigms

Scientific/Authoritarian	People are economic beings.	Pay me!
Human Relations	People have economic and social needs.	Treat me well!
Human Resources	People have minds.	Use me well!
Principle-Centered Leadership	People have spiritual needs.	Let me make a meaningful contribution!

Observation: Watch and Learn

Explain how the words and actions of President of the United States Barack Obama can be used to illustrate the four stages of perception, the process of paradigm change, and/or the act of framing when it comes to the handling of the financial crisis or the repeal of the "Don't Ask, Don't Tell" military policy.

PERCEPTUAL REALITIES

To lead effectively, the leader should not assume too much regarding how others see the organization. Leaving things implicit or unspoken also leaves them vulnerable to misinterpretation.

Answer the Big Questions

Instead of leaving followers floundering, leaders need to be able to provide ready answers to the big questions followers—internal and external stakeholders—want answers to on demand. Among the questions leaders need to answer are the following: *Why are we here?* (the mission question), *Where are we headed?* (the vision question), *What do we stand for?* (the values question), and *Who are we really?* (the collective-identity question). The answers leaders give in response to these questions provide clues to the *mental models*, those pictures we hold in our heads of people, events, ourselves, and how the world works, that similarly construct the leader's frame, setting up the persuasive opportunities he or she will use while governing the organization and shaping the leadership context.[6]

By becoming more aware of their mental models, and communicating them to others, leaders also enhance their ability to reframe and adapt their messages when needed. The more awareness leaders develop, and the more they mentally rehearse, the better able they are to provide an effective frame. As Arkadi Kuhlmann, chairman and president of ING Direct USA, says, "You have to understand that everything's being interpreted, and you have to keep thinking in two and three dimensions. People are going to follow you if they have confidence in you. And the No. 1 job of a CEO is to eliminate doubt. My only job, really, is to eliminate doubt in every situation."[7]

The Leadership Perspective Model

The **leadership perspective model** proposed by James M. Kouzes and Barry Z. Posner offers clues to issues about which leader and follower are likely to agree or disagree.[8] Once the leader has an understanding regarding what the points of potential disagreement might be, she or he can prepare to address them.

Kouzes and Posner's model (see Figure 5.1) contains four quadrants: issues of high importance to the leader but of low importance to employees (Quadrant A);

Figure 5.1 The Leadership Perspective Model

A High importance to the leader Low importance to the employee	**B** High importance to the leader High importance to the employee
C Low importance to the leader Low importance to the employee	**D** Low importance to the leader High importance to the employee

Source: Kouzes, Posner, & Biech, *The Leadership Challenge: Activities Book,* © 2010 Pfeiffer. This material is reproduced with permission of John Wiley & Sons, Inc.

issues of high importance to the leader and high importance to employees (Quadrant B); issues of low importance to the leader and low importance to employees (Quadrant C); and issues of low importance to the leader but of high importance to employees (Quadrant D).

The model is of value because if the leader is to understand the perspective of those they lead, then the leader has to focus on how followers perceive things and not just think about her or his own objectives. The model can also help explain why either the leader or followers may refrain from readily accepting certain sources, initiatives, or programs.

Working It Out: Alone or Together

Using Kouzes and Posner's leadership perspective model, identify issues that would fit into each of the model's quadrants. Then, using the issues you identified, analyze the possible rationale for leader and employee perspectives as well as how individual perspectives could affect the presence or absence of enthusiasm. Finally, review your personal experiences dealing with the issues in each quadrant and, in hindsight, how you would now frame them or what you might do differently today.

The Optimism Advantage

In addition to exhibiting confidence (self-efficacy—the belief that you have the abilities needed to complete a task or realize a goal), practicing balanced processing (soliciting and considering viewpoints from those with whom you disagree), and valuing relational transparency (communicating openly and honestly), leaders also give themselves a perceptual advantage if they display *optimism* (demonstrating positive expectations for the future).

Optimism and self-efficacy go hand in hand. Optimistic leaders remain open to perceiving possibilities, believing in their capabilities and what they can achieve. When optimists suffer a defeat they view it as a temporary setback brought about by circumstances, bad luck, or others; they do not view it as a personal failure. Optimists have resilience; they bounce back again and again. Believing in yourself makes it possible for you to accomplish more. In contrast to optimists, pessimists do not believe they can control their destiny. Pessimists think they can't, while optimists think they can.

Psychologist Martin Seligman tells this story: "We tested the swim team at the University of California at Berkely to find out which swimmers were optimists and which were pessimists. To test the effects of attitude, we had the coach "defeat" each one: After a swimmer finished a heat, the coach told him his time—but it wasn't his real time. The coach had falsified it, making it significantly slower. The optimists responded by swimming their next heat faster; the pessimists went slower on their next heat."[9] Having an optimistic outlook gives leaders added strength, making them more resourceful and setting them back on a path to success.[10]

> **Pessimists think they can't. Optimists think they can. What do you think?**

We also see this outlook in the behavior of NFL quarterback Tim Tebow. According to observers, Tebow's optimism is what fires up his teammates. Tebow tells his teammates, "Believe in me" and does so with such persuasive charisma that his teammates renew their belief in themselves—and actually perform better.[11] A leader's optimism can change how others perceive a situation, making a difference.

Theory Into Practice

The Leader as Perception Shaper

Leader theorist Rosabeth Moss Kanter observes that it falls to the leader to use his or her vision to help followers enact the leader's chosen "action possibility"— the particular path the leader perceives the organization should travel to meet individual and collective needs.[12] What is more, the leader needs to believe she or he will be successful. To accomplish this, according to Gail Fairhurst and Robert Starr, the leader needs to manage meaning; that is, the leader needs to encode messages strengthening the extent to which employees identify with the organization by using symbols to imprint the organization's values into the fabric of each employee's experience.

What symbols does your college, organization, or favorite sports team use to create meaning and promote action possibilities among constituents? How do the selected symbols facilitate the development of positive perceptions and behaviors in them?

PERCEPTUAL BARRIERS

While it is important to understand the perceptual perspectives that leaders and followers rely on when interacting about issues of high and low concern to them, it is also important to understand the different paradigms they use when interpreting reality. While we have a variety of paradigms at our disposal, some of the paradigms we adopt can impede decision making by contributing to our perceiving an issue, situation, or people unfairly, inaccurately, or even pessimistically.

The "My Past Holds the Answer" Paradigm

Relying on past learning or experiences to perceive present situations and people may complicate things. Both learning and experience can create expectations, perceptual sets or the readiness to perceive in predetermined ways, influencing the leader's perception of both situations and people. Basing perception only on what was learned or experienced previously can blind a leader to viable alternative interpretations. The reality is that learned perceptions can create biases and blind spots. It is up to the leader not to be controlled by unconscious learning but to gain control of learning by reflecting instead on what it is she or he wants to do. Leaders need to work to escape from limited ways of seeing. As Geoff Vuleta, CEO of Fahrenheit 212, an innovation and consulting firm, notes, "There have been times . . . where I realized I needed to reinvent myself."[13]

The "What I See First Is What I Go With" Paradigm

Should assessments made during the first few minutes influence the leader's judgment? If a leader bases perceptions on an initial assessment, the danger is that the leader will freeze that initial judgment and even if it is wrong, work to make all perceptions conform to it, effectively operating with a closed mind. The effective leader works against making such snap perceptual conclusions.

The "It's Just Like_____," or "You're Just Like _____" Paradigm

If the leader is prone to stereotyping situations and people, carrying with him or her existing impressions or fixed mental images of what to expect, he or she is likely to use broad generalizations to process experience, effectively disregarding information that does not conform to commonly held beliefs. Encouraging pigeonholing by emphasizing similarities is not an effective perceptual practice. Instead of categorizing situations and people, the more effective leader takes the time to distinguish persons and situations from others by noting as many differences as possible. For example, Fahrenheit 212 CEO Geoff Vuleta asks job candidates to reinvent themselves as a beverage. Each candidate presents himself or herself as if in a bottle, explaining his or her personally defining characteristics and traits, bringing his or her individual drink alive for the organization's leader, and pitching why he or she would buy it.[14]

The "I Know It All" Paradigm

No one knows everything there is to know about anything—including leaders. According to *Science and Sanity* author Alfred Korzybski, *allness* refers to the erroneously held belief that any one person can possibly know all there is to know.[15] Wise leaders, therefore, end every assessment they make with the words *et cetera* ("and others"), as a reminder of that fact.

The "Blindering" Paradigm

A leader can blind himself or herself to a problem's solution by defining the problem in a way that imposes restrictions on solutions that do not really exist. Just as blinders placed on a horse limit the number of visual stimuli the horse receives, leaders may don figurative blinders that hinder their ability to look at a problem and come up with a viable solution. Unconsciously adding one or more restrictions that limit perception of the problem impedes discovering a solution and taking appropriate action. We can illustrate blindering's impact with the following exercise: attempt to draw four straight lines that will connect each of the nine dots in Figure 5.2. Do this without lifting your pencil or pen from the page or retracing a line.

Most people find this exercise challenging. Why? Because while the problem imposes only one restriction—that you connect the dots with four straight lines without lifting your pencil or pen from the page or backtracking over a line—most of us add another restriction as well. After looking at the dots, we assume

Figure 5.2

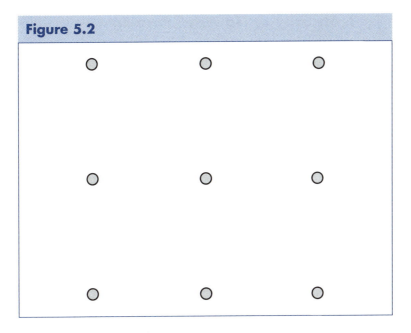

that the figure to be formed must be a square when no such restriction exists. The image of a square limits our perception, blindering us to the problem's solution. (For the solution, see Figure 5.3 at this chapter's end).

The "Fact/Inference Confusion" Paradigm

Like the rest of us, a leader makes numerous inferences every day. The validity or high probability of the inferences the leader makes guides decision making and determines his or her leadership effectiveness. Sometimes, a leader treats as fact that which he or she did not actually observe but which he or she wishes were true. Other times, a leader fails to distinguish between a fact and an inference, treating the inference he or she makes as if it were, in fact, a fact.[16] Facts are not always easy to come by, but it is most important to be able to distinguish between them and inferences. The failure to do so can be dangerous and can cause the leader to jump to a conclusion that contributes to making the wrong decision, taking an inappropriate action, or, at the very least, demonstrating poor judgment.

The "See It My Way or No Way" Paradigm

How would you respond to the leader depicted in this cartoon? What do the leader's words suggest about the paradigm he uses?

"We want to include you in this decision without letting you affect it."

William Haefeli/The New Yorker Collection/www.cartoonbank.com

A leader who fails to experience the world from any perspective but his or her own is egocentric, unaware that other perspectives exist and, as a result, blind to the possibility that the view he or she holds may be incomplete or limited. Such a perspective will likely find the leader failing to promote the mutual understanding necessary for leadership. A perspective, like a paradigm, is a way of viewing the world and one's relation to it. As F. Scott Fitzgerald wrote in *The Crack-Up,* "The test of a first-rate intelligence is the ability to hold two opposed ideas in the mind at the same time, and still retain the ability to function."

Instead of hoping that others see it his or her way or go away, the leader will benefit from developing more comprehensive perception. This is done by putting empathy's three components into practice: (1) **perspective taking**—the ability to assume the viewpoint of others, (2) **emotional understanding**—stepping into the shoes of others and feeling what they feel, and (3) **caring**—being genuinely concerned for the welfare of others. By setting their own opinions aside until they understand those of others, leaders gain an appreciation of what things look like through the eyes of their followers and/or their competitors. This gives them more depth of understanding of others, making them better able to lead.

Since perception is likely to become reality, we should always take time to double-check the accuracy of our perceptions. Consider this story from *Briefings on Talent & Leadership:*

> **Fresh paradigms open endless possibilities.**

A group of settlers in a remote village of Outpost were preparing for winter. The group's leader, unschooled in the old ways, made a guess: the winter was going to be cold and the people should gather firewood. Then one day, he traveled to the nearest town and called the National Weather Service, which confirmed his suspicion: the winter was indeed going to be cold. The leader ordered more firewood to be collected, and checked in with the National Weather Service again a week later, which amended its forecast—not only for a cold winter, but a very cold winter. So the people of Outpost gathered even more wood.

When the leader checked in with the National Weather Service a third time, the prediction was now for a very, very cold winter. Finally, having asked for every branch and twig to be gathered, the leader asked the National Weather Service how they could be so sure. The answer: "The people of Outpost are gathering an awful lot of firewood."[17]

Self-Reflection: Looking In and Out

1. Focus on one of the described perceptual barriers. Describe in detail what you will do to ensure that you do not let this perceptual barrier prevent you from accurately assessing a situation.

2. Select a partner to share your plan with. What feedback can you give your partner that would be helpful? Repeat this step with a minimum of three partners.

3. What did you learn from the sharing of ideas?

PERCEIVING LIKE A LEADER

A major part of leading is making good decisions. Effective leaders automatically weigh and balance evidence and feelings, relying on both analytical (left brain) and intuitive (right brain) thinking in their search to find ways to join reason and emotion. Insightful leaders know when to rely on analytics and when to rely on their gut. They trust their judgment and use their experience—instinctually perceiving whether to forge ahead or take cover because they see possibilities and opportunities where others do not.

The French word for *insight* translates as *penetration*. By penetrating insightfully, that is, perceiving a situation more fully and more clearly, a leader enhances his or her leadership effectiveness. Perception may or may not be reality. While we may know the figures, such as sales volume or market share, we may delude ourselves when it comes to how "on board" people are, how willing they are to embrace an idea, how committed they are to our vision, or how willing they are to go above and beyond. Others may see things differently than we do.

Here are four steps you can take to sharpen your perceptual skills:

1. Get to really know your followers. Understand their perceptions of the organization and you. Watch out for preconceptions on your part or theirs. Listen to opposing viewpoints. Make it your business to uncover hidden problems. Remember, to ensure that the leader and followers do not work at cross-purposes, they need to share congruent, not disparate, perceptions.

2. Make hunting for ideas a habit. By staying up with the research in your field you accumulate the raw material needed to see a problem's parts or develop new associations of thought. Regularly linking two ideas not previously linked to each other enhances your powers of perception.

3. Give yourself permission to think in novel ways—make curiosity and taking mental risks their own reward. Your organization may have a competitive advantage at a point in time, but what is crucial is whether you will have the evolutionary advantage needed over time.[18]

4. Put aside your own concerns long enough to take an active interest in understanding others and their concerns. Take time to learn from others' perspectives.

Working It Out: Alone or Together

According to a very old tale, there was a farmer who lived in an economically depressed country village. Many considered the farmer pretty well off because he owned a horse, using it for transportation and for plowing. One day, the horse took off. The neighbors told the farmer how unfortunate this was. The farmer replied, "Maybe."

Toward the middle of the same week, the horse came back to the farmer, bringing two wild horses along with it. The neighbors celebrated, rejoicing at the farmer's good luck, telling him how fortunate he was. The farmer again replied, "Maybe."

The next day, the farmer's son attempted to mount one of the wild horses, only to break his leg when the horse reared up, throwing him off. The neighbors again told the farmer how bad his luck was. Once more, the farmer replied with a one-word answer: "Maybe."

The following week a platoon of soldiers entered the village with orders to conscript all young men into the army. They did not take the farmer's son, however, because he had a broken leg. The neighbors told the farmer that he was lucky that his son didn't have to go into the army. The farmer replied, "Maybe."

1. What did you learn from the farmer's neighbors? What did you learn from the farmer? How can you apply the lessons learned to your behavior as a leader?

2. Use the story's message to redefine as an opportunity a problem that you, your school, or an organization you work for currently faces. Begin by identifying how the frame applied to the situation from the outset contributed to defining the situation as a problem. Next, consciously change frames. See the problem as an opportunity. Identify the benefits the "new" opportunity presents. Explain how changing frames changes a situation's meaning.

Effective leaders don't let their perceptions box them in or out. Their ability to exercise flexibility instead of perceiving in but one dimension frees leaders to think more creatively. Shifting, and getting others to shift, to a different perspective can make all the difference.

LOOK BACK

Reread the opening poem. How might your paradigm influence your reaction to the speaker's question?

Figure 5.3 In Section on Blindering

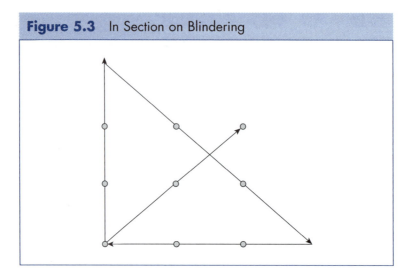

Key Terms

Balanced processing (93)

Caring (99)

Emotional understanding (98)

Human relations paradigm (89)

Human resource paradigm (90)

Leadership perspective model (92)

Perception (87)

Perspective taking (98)

Principle-centered leadership paradigm (90)

Relational transparency (93)

Scientific/authoritarian paradigm (89)

Self-efficacy (93)

Stakeholders (91)

Notes

1. "Experts See a Tough Road for Schools Chief Nominee," *New York Times* (November 28, 2010): 9.

2. W. Bennis, *On Becoming a Leader* (Reading, MA: Addison-Wesley, 1995), 120.

3. G. Fairhurst, *The Power of Framing: Creating the Language of Leadership* (San Francisco: Jossey-Bass, 2011).

4. S. R. Covey, *Principle-Centered Leadership* (New York: Simon & Schuster, 1990), 173–80.

5. Ibid., p. 180.

6. P. Senge, A. Kleiner, C. Roberts, R. Ross, G. Roth, and B. Smith, *The Dance of Change: The Challenges of Sustaining Momentum in Learning Organizations* (New York: Doubleday Currency, 1999).

7. Adam Bryant, "Putting Himself Up for Re-Election (By His Staff)," *New York Times* (October 31, 2010): BU2.

8. J. Kouzes and B. Posner, *The Leadership Challenge Activities Book* (San Francisco: Pfeiffer, 2010).

9. Martin P. Seligman, interview in *Success* (July-August 1994): 41.

10. K. M. Sutcliffe and T. J. Vogus, "Organizing for Resilience," in K. S. Cameron, J. E. Dutton, and R. E. Quinn, eds., *Positive Organizational Scholarship* (San Francisco: Berrett-Koehler, 2003), 94–110.

11. Frank Bruni, "Tim Tebow's Gospel of Optimism," *New York Times* (December 11, 2011): 4 SR.

12. See R. M. Kanter, *The Change Masters: Innovation for Productivity in the American Corporation* (New York: Simon & Schuster, 1983); and G. T. Fairhurst and R. A. Starr, *The Art of Framing: Managing the Language of Leadership* (San Francisco: Jossey-Bass, 1996).

13. Adam Bryant, "Can You Handle the 100-Day To-Do List?" *New York Times* (November 21, 2010): BU2.

14. Ibid.

15. Korzybski, *Science and Sanity,* 4th ed. (San Francisco: International Society for General Semantics, 1980).

16. Sharon Begley, "People Believe a 'Fact' That Fits Their Views Even If It's Clearly False," *Wall Street Journal* (February 4, 2005): B1.

17. Gary Burnison, "Leaving Perceptions Behind," *Briefings on Talent & Leadership* (2011): 5.

18. Gary Hamel, "Management a la Google," *Wall Street Journal* (April 26, 2006): A16.

Comstock Images/Comstock/Thinkstock

I can't hear you.

I'm too busy listening to me.

If I stop listening to me

Will I learn something from you?

How can I be sure?

LISTENING
LIKE A LEADER

Response Power

Famed American author Ernest Hemingway is credited with saying, "I like to listen. I have learned a great deal from listening. Most people never listen." To what extent, if any, do Hemingway's words ring true for you?

While leaders are likely to prepare themselves to speak, few have been taught to listen. Could listening be something that leaders (and followers) take for granted? Would all of us benefit from taking the importance of listening to heart?

The Chinese character for "listening" (see Figure 6.1) combines a number of symbols joining the ears, the eyes, and the heart, suggesting that when listening, listeners should give their undivided attention by using their hearts as well as their eyes and ears. Are you aware of any leaders who follow this advice?

> **Leaders use their ears, eyes, and heart when listening.**

Figure 6.1

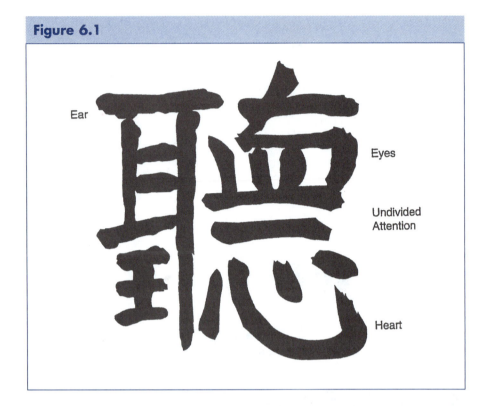

Ear

Eyes

Undivided
Attention

Heart

Working It Out: Alone or Together

Research leadership in action by citing examples of leaders whom you believe listen not only with their ears but also with their eyes and hearts. Identify the words uttered and the behaviors exhibited by the leader that contributed to your judgment. In what ways and to what extent did the leader's words and behaviors affect others? Be specific.

THE LISTENING LEADER

The listening behavior of a leader has an impact on all of the leader's relationships. Unlike hearing, which can be accomplished without a conscious intention, listening is a deliberate process dependent upon a complex set of acquired skills. When part of a problem-solving team, effective listeners are perceived to have the most leadership skills.[1] Peter Drucker, a founder of the leadership development field, noted, "The leader of the past knew how to answer. The leader of the future will know how to ask."[2] Asking only works, however, if the leader is prepared to listen to the answer.

Styles of Listening

Listening is situational. Leaders tend to exhibit one of four listening styles—people centered, action centered, content centered, or time centered—depending on the demands of the listening situation they find themselves in.[3]

The **people-centered listening style** finds the listener using supportive listening skills to focus on the emotions or feelings of others in an effort to find common areas of interest so both parties can relate effectively to one another and, if necessary, a compromise can be reached. A leader who is people centered will quickly pick up on and respond to the moods of others.

The **action-centered listening style** finds listeners using informational listening skills to identify what is important in the message. Because of the emphasis they place on organization and precision, such listeners want speakers to get to the point quickly and easily tire of speakers who appear to be disorganized. A leader who is action centered questions the assumptions speakers make, in effect second-guessing them by proffering alternative explanations.[4]

The **content-centered listening style** finds listeners focusing on a message's facts and details. A content-centered leader likes to be intellectually challenged and to think things through, uses critical listening skills, and enjoys playing devil's advocate, often asking pointed questions and even dismissing information attributed to sources a speaker used that he or she believes to be nonexpert.

The **time-centered listening style** finds listeners advocating for messages to be delivered succinctly. Because they value efficiency and disdain irrelevancy, they want primarily the bullet points. A time-centered leader will often set and enforce a time limit on message delivery, abruptly interrupting the speaker when the allotted time is up. This style is more effective in emergency situations; otherwise, it is generally considered a rather ineffective style.[5]

Type of Listener	Focus
People centered	Emotions and feelings
Action centered	Importance
Content centered	Facts and details
Time centered	Efficiency

Listening researchers Kitty Watson and Larry Barker affirm that approximately 40% of us have one primary listening style—especially when under stress. Another 40% of us are style switchers—we want to listen to content (content centered), but we want what we are listening to to be delivered efficiently (time centered). Some 20% of us have no favored listening style at all—perhaps because of listening apprehension or burnout.[6]

Self-Reflection: Looking In and Out

How do you evaluate your listening skills? Explain your answers to the following questions by supplying supporting examples.

1. How likely are you to interrupt when somebody tries to tell you something?

2. How likely are you to jump to a conclusion before listening to the entire story?

3. How likely are you to signal a lack of interest with nonverbal cues?

4. How likely are you to listen to only what interests you?

5. How likely are you to spend more time talking than listening?

6. How likely are you to daydream while listening?

7. How likely are you to plan your response or rebuttal while another person is speaking?

8. How likely are you to become impatient with a speaker?

9. How likely are you to let yourself become distracted?

10. How likely are you to let your emotional state get the best of you?

Next, select a leader prominent in the public arena or one presented in a film, Miranda Priestly in *The Devil Wears Prada* for example, and answer the same list of questions as if you were that person. Evaluate the selected leader's listening effectiveness.

In his bestselling book *The Seven Habits of Highly Effective People*, author Stephen Covey identifies listening as one of seven key habits, insisting that it is the deep understanding that comes from listening that is critical if leaders are to lead.[7] Do you agree?

> What impact does interrupting or talking over another person's words have on the ability to work together? How would you respond were someone to do that to you?

LISTENING PRACTICES OF LEADERS

A leader's listening behaviors can promote or prevent others from following the leader.

Whether the leader is decentered or egocentric makes a difference.

The Decentered Leader

Using active listening skills gives the leader an advantage. In fact, supporters rate leaders who demonstrate listening skills as more effective. Listening leaders wisely seek to understand and respond to what they hear before expecting others to understand or respond to them. Unfortunately, some leaders expect others to listen to and understand them while ignoring their ethical responsibility to listen to and understand others. By refusing to decenter, that is, refusing to place the focus on others rather than on themselves, they create communication problems that could be avoided. In contrast are leaders who regularly decenter and regularly practice three key types of listening behavior: comprehensive listening (listening to acquire knowledge), critical listening (listening to decide whether to accept or reject a message by weighing its usefulness, soundness, and accuracy), and empathic listening (listening to understand the feelings and perspectives of followers or stakeholders).

Engaging in empathic listening requires that the leader activate three skills that enable him or her to listen from the speaker's perspective: empathic responsiveness (the experiencing of an emotional response that corresponds to the emotions of another person)[8], **perspective taking** (the placing of the self into another person's shoes)[9], and **sympathetic responsiveness** (the expression of compassion and concern for the situation the other person faces). By using all three skills together, the leader enables himself or herself to *feel with* followers or stakeholders.[10]

When practicing empathic listening, the leader also relies on two additional competencies: the ability to read the nonverbal cues of others, including their facial expressions, and the ability to **paraphrase**—restating in the leader's own words what the other person says, feels, and means—a tool of active listening that lets followers know their leader cares enough to listen to what is said and to respond to the feelings expressed. When following the *paraphrasing rule,* the leader restates what the sender says, feels, and means correctly and to the sender's satisfaction before replying.[11] Empathic listeners put themselves in the other's place, being careful not to interrupt speakers by cutting off their words. The reality is that unless leaders understand their followers and stakeholders they can't possibly lead them effectively.

ARE YOU AN EMPATHIC LISTENER?	**YES**	**NO**
Do you display empathic responsiveness?		
Do you engage in perspective taking?		
Do you display sympathetic responsiveness?		

The Egocentric Leader

Leaders who are egocentric are often lazy listeners, believing, in error, that because of their importance others need to understand them, but they don't need to understand others. To this end, they may exhibit one or more of the following unethical listening behaviors.

Fraudulent Listening. Egocentric leaders may be pseudolisteners; they merely pretend to listen while the words of others fall on their hearing, but not listening, ears.

Monopolistic Listening. Intrigued with their own thoughts and ideas, egocentric leaders are also monopolistic listeners, convinced that listening to others would be a waste of their time. Thus, they tend to deliver monologues rather than to engage in dialogue that enables others to feel they have been heard.

Completive Listening. Egocentric leaders think they have all the answers. They become completers, never quite getting the whole story when they listen but certain they can fill in the gaps—though they often make mistakes in doing so. Because we can process ideas much more quickly than people speak, our minds often race ahead and we complete the speaker's thoughts before he or she even speaks them—unfortunately, often erroneously.

Selective Listening. Like a bee to a flower, egocentric leaders are selective listeners, paying attention only to those portions of a speaker's remarks that interest them. In their search for honey, selective listeners often miss the flower.

Avoidant Listening. Egocentric leaders are avoidant listeners. They simply close their ears to information they would rather not deal with.

Defensive Listening. Egocentric leaders are often masking one or more of their insecurities. Because they assume others will criticize or belittle them, they tend to be defensive listeners, interpreting the remarks of others as personal affronts or attacks.

Attackers. Egocentric leaders often lie in wait so they can undercut speakers and challenge them whenever they make a mistake, attacking the speaker in the effort to outdo them.

Unfortunately, too many people fail to listen with the intent to understand, and too many listen only with the intent to reply. When others speak, instead of listening, they focus on preparing to speak. As Covey notes, they are engaging in "collective monologuing," which leads to their never really getting what someone else is thinking or experiencing.[12] Imagine if instead of taking hard-set positions and issuing ultimatums during negotiations to raise the debt ceiling of the United States government, both sides had said something like the following to one another: "We would like you to write the bill the way you want it so that we can ensure our understanding of your needs and concerns. We will respond to those needs and concerns. Then we can talk about solutions." Then imagine the opposition and the president's team saying to one another, "Now

Observation: Watch and Learn

View an interview with a business or political leader that airs on *Meet the Press* or another news/opinion/commentary program of your choosing such as *The Rachel Maddow Show* or *The O'Reilly Factor.* Then follow these steps.

1. Compile a list of the questions the host asked the leader, indicating your assessment of how effectively the leader listened to and answered each of the host's questions.

2. Analyze the overall attitude expressed by both the host's and the leader's nonverbal cues, the extent to which they successfully controlled their emotional state, and how they handled disagreements or hostile questions.

3. Count the number of times the host or the guest used the paraphrase and note its impact on the discussion.

4. Finally, describe any obstacles to listening as well as ineffective examples of listening exhibited by either party.

let's be sure we understand what you've put down here" and actually paraphrasing the opposition's content to be certain they undersood each item as intended, allowing the other side to correct them until they got it right. If this strategy had been adopted, both sides might have been more ready and willing to listen rather than fighting each other. Before you can be understood, you need to understand.

FEEDBACK: THE RESPONSE CONNECTION

What is feedback, and what is its connection to listening? The capacity of people to engage in self-regulating behavior depends on the kinds of information exchanged via feedback. Part of the leader's function is to scan the environment, relate what he or she discovers about the operating norms of the organization, detect deviations from these norms, question each norm's relevance or appropriateness, and respond by initiating corrective action when warranted.[13]

Feedback Defined

The word feedback implies that we are feeding someone by giving something back to him or her. Feedback consists of all the verbal and nonverbal messages that a person consciously or unconsciously sends out in response to another person's communicative behavior. Sometimes feedback is honest; other times it is dishonest but can have an effect nonetheless. Sometimes feedback is interpreted as intended; other times the receiver misses the point or intentionally chooses to misperceive the message sent. What is important is that leaders give feeback as well as seek feedback from others. In many ways, feedback serves as a weathervane of leadership, enabling leaders to share their plans and focus on concerns and reactions of others.

Types of Feedback

Giving feedback about job performance and behavior is one of the leader's responsibilities. Often done face to face, the leader has an array of feedback tools to use when conducting a feedback-focused dialogue. **Evaluative feedback** occurs when an opinion is stated or a positive or negative judgment is made. Given properly, evaluative feedback can help individuals grow and develop. Evaluative feedback can be positive and rewarding or negative and punishing. *Positive evaluative feedback* reinforces behavior, causing it to continue in the direction it is heading, while *negative evaluative feedback,* when accurately perceived, can help extinguish behavior judged to be inappropriate or ineffectual. According to industrial psychologist Don Tosti, positive feedback should be offered immediately while negative feedback is best offered just prior to the opportunity for repeating an undesired behavior. Doing that gives the negative feedback more of a coaching than criticizing character.

What is important is that the deliverer of feedback not accumulate an abundance of wrongdoings and then deliver them all at once, effectively ambushing the receiver. That would likely elicit defensiveness and resentment and put the recipient in a "counterattack" mode.

In contrast to evaluative feedback, **nonevaluative feedback** is nondirective in that no overt attempt is made to direct the behavior of another. Instead, it is designed to help the listener learn more about another person's feelings and thoughts. When offering nonevaluative feedback we simply describe, question, or indicate our interest in the other person's communication. Among the techniques we use to do this are *probing* (asking for additional information), *understanding* (demonstrating comprehension of what the person said, perhaps through the paraphrase), *supporting* (acknowledging the importance of what the other person is sharing), and I *messages* (conveying personal feelings about the situation).

I messages merit special attention. *I* messages indicate that users own the expressed thoughts and feelings and refrain from shifting responsibility from themselves onto another. For example, instead of telling a speaker, "You're not making yourself clear" or "You haven't convinced "me," the user of an *I* message says, "I'm not understanding your point" or "I'm not convinced." Thus, *I*-message users do not place blame but instead acknowledge their role in the interaction, explicitly assuming responsibility for their perceptions and feelings.

I statements are most effective when we can divide them into four parts: the first clarifying your feelings, the second explaining what behavior you believe elicited such feelings, the third defining the behavior you find objectionable or are taking issue with, and the fourth offering your solution to the problem.

1. Start with an "I feel" statement; for example, "I feel unconvinced by the provided argument."

2. Add a "when you" statement; for example, "When you make a claim but fail to offer evidence, I begin to doubt the claim's validity."

3. Add a "because" statement; for example, "Because I doubt the validity of the argument, I have questions about the position taken."

4. End with an "I would appreciate it if" statement; for example, "I would appreciate it if you would research reasons establishing why I should accept your premise."

The four-step approach lets you voice your concerns as well as explain how you would like the other person to change his or her behavior.

After offering feedback, a leader should also solicit input from its recipient. Acknowledging your openness to receiving the individual's interpretation of his or her own behavior can help raise the leader's stature. In addition, when delivering feedback, rely on the *feedforward impulse;* that is, first think through the likely impact your remarks will have on the person receiving them so that you may modify them in advance and enhance their usefulness to the other person.

Leaders receive feedback from both internal and external sources. Internal feedback is feedback the leader gives to herself or himself while monitoring her or his leadership behavior or performance. It is the leader's self-talk. External feedback is feedback the leader receives from others. To be an effective listening leader, you need to be open to both sources of feedback, paying attention not only to your own reactions but also to the reactions of others.

The Significance of the Leader's Response

As we see, a leader may respond both while the speaker is talking and once the speaker stops.

If responding during speech, you want to demonstrate that you are listening and you want to be supportive, perhaps by supplying backchanneling cues with words like *I see* and nonverbal signals like a head nod that are designed to let the other person know you are involved and attentive. Similarly, *paraphrasing the speaker* (repeating in one's own words what the speaker has said), *analyzing* (offering your own slant on what the speaker has said), and *advising* (offering advice to the speaker) demonstrate your active involvement.

Responses following speech include requests for clarification, challenges, indications of *support* (expressing agreement with the speaker), or expressions of *empathy* (expressing that you understand and share the speaker's feelings).

It is when the leader *stonewalls* (stays silent and nonverbally inexpressive), reveals little about his or her response, or seems responsive but in reality never varies the kind of response given that speakers remain uncertain about the impact their words have had.

COACHING APPROACHES AND THE LISTENING LEADER

A leader's listening behavior offers clues to the kind of coach the leader will be. Coaching is a supportive relationship in which leaders help others develop their skills. Ideally coach and coachee determine together how they will interact, how frequently they will meet, and how progress will be assessed.

The two main coaching styles are directive and nondirective coaching.

The Directive Coach

The **directive coach** is ego involved, taking the position that since she or he is the expert, she or he knows what the person being coached needs to do as well as how the individual should do it. Thus, directive coaches tell those they are coaching what they should and should not do. Rather than addressing the needs of the person being coached, the directive coach serves as a model and seeks to have the coachee emulate him or her. While this approach can be a time saver, it tends to be prescriptive and limits coach-coachee interaction.

The Nondirective Coach

In contrast, the **nondirective coach** sees himself or herself as a facilitator of personal growth. Coach and coachee establish a partnership, with the coachee setting a goal and working with the leader/coach to develop skills. Unlike directive coaches, nondirective coaches need to be proficient listeners. Rather than merely give information, they solicit information from the person they are coaching and ask questions rather than giving directions. "Why do you think this is happening?" "What do you hope to achieve?" "If you were to find yourself in this situation again, how might you approach it differently?" and "Who would you like to help you?" are examples of questions nondirective coaches use to facilitate the coachee's development.[14]

> Nondirective coaches are great listeners!

Which kind of coach would you prefer work with you to develop your communication and leadership abilities? Which kind of coach do you think you will be?

LISTENING RULES

By adopting the right attitude, making the effort, and applying the following three rules you can lead by listening.

Resist the Impulse to Talk More Than You Listen

Zeno of Citium said it best: "We have been given two ears and but a single mouth, in order that we may hear more and talk less." While leaders need to share ideas with followers, give feedback to ensure understanding, and seek new information, they also need to value the information they receive by listening. As a Chinese proverb suggests, "To be heard, there are times you need to stay silent."

Resist Technological and Other Distractions

Interruptive calls, texts, or tweets impede effective listening as much as a preoccupation with personal or company problems when interacting with others. Being always *on* is a turnoff. Leaders needs to make eye contact with the people actually present rather than with handheld or other computer screens that keep them from being fully attentive and could contribute to their missing important information that ultimately interferes with their attaining desired results. Getting a sense for another person's emotional reactions can be as important as understanding his or her words.

Resist the Rush-to-Judgment Urge

Don't assume you know what someone means. Commit to understanding an idea before you judge its merit. Snap judgments contribute to tuning out when you should still be tuned in to what others are saying. First listen. Verify understanding. Then assess. When others feel listened to, they have greater confidence in and will make a greater commitment to you.[15]

Theory Into Practice

Perspective Taking and the Listening Leader

Roger Fisher and William Ury, together with associates of Harvard Negotiation Project, advocate the use of a problem-solving negotiation style, also known as the principled negotiation model.[16] The model identifies four steps to implement when negotiating: (1) distinguish the people involved from the problem faced (*don't attack those with whom you disagree; instead, work side by side to resolve the issues*); (2) focus on interests, not individual positions (*there can be multiple ways of meeting needs or interests*); (3) invent options for mutual gain (*brainstorming can result in parties having their needs met by identifying their common interests*); and (4) insist that objective criteria be used (*criteria should favor neither party but reflect widely used norms instead*).

(Continued)

(Continued)

When you understand another's perspective, you become better able to identify expectations and predict goals. By determining if the other person practices a personally oriented (*relationally oriented*), high-task (*getting right down to business*), cooperative (*interest in and concern for others*), or competitive (*interest in and concern for benefiting oneself*) negotiating style, you can identify the most appropriate way to approach the negotiation.

Use these four steps and conflict orientations to analyze either a negotiation situation of your own choosing or to determine how Hamas and the Israelis reached an accord on a prisoner exchange in 2011 that resulted in the freeing of one abducted Israeli soldier, Gilad Shalit, in exchange for more than 1,000 Palestinian prisoners.

Resist Thinking That Members of Different Cultures Listen Similarly to the Members of Your Culture

People from diverse cultures display different listening preferences. Germans, for example, favor an action-oriented approach, asking lots of questions and displaying their keen curiosity. In contrast, the Japanese display an indirect approach, not directly inquiring but inferring from received cues. Americans, in contrast, focus on the time they are spending listening and conversing.[17]

Post It: Imagineering a Better Way

Describe a time when you felt that a leader failed to listen effectively to followers and a time when because of listening effectively a leader was able to avert or better handle a crisis. Then analyze the following with reference to each leader:

1. What was the nature of the circumstances the leader faced?
2. What types of behaviors did the leader exhibit?
3. How did followers respond?

Based on your analysis, what advice, if any, do you believe the successful leader might offer the leader who failed?

Alan Trefler, founder and CEO of Pegasystems, a business technology firm, notes that in his company it is everyone's job to have an informed opinion. He also affirms that to be able to actually hear those opinions, everyone has to be able to listen. Making this happen—ensuring that those who have strong opinions do not drown out the opinions of others—requires conscious thought and discipline.[18]

The former Speaker of the House of Representatives, Dennis Hastert, also understood the value of listening. Describing his leadership role, Speaker Hastert put it this way: "They call me the Speaker, but they ought to call me the Listener."[19]

LOOK BACK

Reread the opening poem. Based on what you now know, what would you tell the speaker?

Key Terms

Action-centered listening style (107)

Avoidant listening (111)

Completive listening (111)

Comprehensive listening (109)

Content-centered listening style (107)

Critical listening (109)

Defensive listening (111)

Directive coach (116)

Empathic listening (109)

Empathic responsiveness (109)

Evaluative feedback (113)

Feedback (113)

Fraudulent listening (110)

Listening (105)

Monopolistic listening (111)

Nondirective coach (116)

Nonevaluative feedback (114)

Paraphrase (110)

People-centered listening style (107)

Perspective taking (110)

Selective listening (111)

Sympathetic responsiveness (110)

Time-centered listening style (107)

Notes

1. S. Johnson and C. Bechler, "Examining the Realtionship Between Listening Effectiveness and Leadership Emergence: Perceptions, Behaviors, and Recall," *Small Group Research* 29 (1998): 452–71.

2. Warren Bennis and Joan Goldsmith, *Learning to Lead: Workbook on Becoming a Leader* (New York: Basic Books, 2010), 129.

3. M. K. Johnston, J. B. Weaver, K. W. Watson, and L. B. Barker, "Listening Styles: Biological or Psychological Differences?" *International Journal of Listening* 14 (2000): 32–46.

4. D. M. Kirtley and J. Honeycutt, "Listening Styles and Their Correspondence with Second-Guessing," *Communication Research Reports* 13 (1996): 1–9.

5. D. Benzel, "Lead Through Listening," *Supervision* 69(6): 14–15.

6. L. L. Barker and K. W. Watson, *Listen Up* (New York: St. Martin's Press, 2000).

7. Stephen Covey, *The Seven Habits of Highly Effective People* (New York: Simon & Schuster, 1989).

8. B. L. Omdahl, *Cognitive Appraisal, Emotion, and Empathy* (Mahwah, NJ: Lawrence Erlbaum, 1995).

9. T. Holtgraves, *Language in Social Action: Social Psychology and Language Use* (Mahwah, NJ: Lawrence Erlbaum, 2002).

10. See, for example, J. B. Weaver III and M. B. Kirtley, "Listening Styles and Empathy," *Southern Communication Journal* 60 (1995): 131–40.

11. D. W. Johnson, "The Effectiveness of Role Reversal: The Actor or the Listener," *Psychological Reports* 28 (1971): 275–82.

12. Covey, *The Seven Habits of Highly Effective People*, 252–56.

13. Gareth Morgan, *Images of Organization,* 2nd ed. (Thousand Oaks, CA: Sage, 1997), 86.

14. See Lois B. Hart and Charlotte S. Waisman, *The Leadership Training Activity Book* (New York: AMACOM, 2005), 241–44.

15. M. Kornacki, "Managers' Communication Skills Put Under Scrutiny by New Research," *TJ Online* (April 20, 2009). Retrieved from www.trainingjournal.com/news/2009–04–20-managers-communication-skills-put-under-scrutiny-by-new-research/.

16. R. Fisher and W. Ury, *Getting to Yes,* 2nd ed. (New York: Penguin Books, 1991); and A. E. Tenbrusel and D. M. Messick, "Power Asymmetries and the Ethical Atmosphere in Negotiations," in J. M. Darley, D. M. Messick, and T. R. Tyler, eds., *Social Influences on Ethical Behavior in Organizations* (Mahwah, NJ: Lawrence Erlbaum, 2001), 201–16.

17. See, for example, C. Kiewitz, J. B. Weaver III, B. Brosius, and G. Weimann, "Cultural Differences in Listening Styles Preferences: A Comparison of Young Adults in Germany, Israel, and the United States," *International Journal of Public Opinion Research* 9 (1997): 233–48.

18. Adam Bryant, "Your Opinions Are Respected (and Required)," *New York Times* (August 7, 2011): BU2.

19. J. Franzen, "The Listener," *New Yorker* (October 6, 2003): 85.

FINDING YOUR VOICE   THE LEADER'S LANGUAGE

THE LEADER'S STORY

Tell me a story.

Not any story.

Tell me the story of your life.

Let me see the person who lives inside

The person you are.

Let me know why I should care.

Why I should follow.

7

STORYTELLING LIKE A LEADER

The Power of Words

Leaders lead using many different voices. The trick is to discover and use your own voice to lead, to know who you are and to share that with others—in other words, above all else, to be an **authentic leader.**[1]

When leaders are authentic, leadership emerges from their life stories. Because **storytelling** is a needed leadership competency, your journey as a leader begins with you understanding the story of your life—your personal narrative. In fact, according to novelist John Barth, "The story of your life is not your life. It is your story."[2]

Just as leaders use different voices to lead, so there are also many different ways to tell stories. Effective leaders tell a full spectrum of stories, some based on difficult experiences and others based on formative ones. Leaders reframe their experiences, learn how to embody and perform them, and then, using stories, articulate powerful inspirational messages that surmount boredom and foster living participation in order to inspire and guide others. The more personal and authentic the story, the more easily receivers identify with and latch on to its common themes, alligning them with their own experiences and knowledge.

Are you prepared to tell stories that pass on understandings and dreams, bridge barriers, take hold of others, engender more positive feelings, bring people closer both physically and psychologically, and help them to adapt and engage?[3] Leaders of movements and organizations change repeatedly. But powerful inspirational stories last.[4] It's time to meet your inner storyteller.

> The leader is the organization's storyteller.

FINDING YOUR VOICE

While we learned in Chapter 6 on listening that effective leaders listen to the words of others, that quality alone does not distinguish them as leaders. Leaders also need to be effective wordsmiths in their own right, adept at using words to tell stories that help make sense of their goals; share the history and motivations of their lives, organizations, or movements; convey their identify and beliefs; and make positive, lasting impressions on followers.[5] Because a prime leadership task is for the leader to instill, describe, and communicate a vision, the leader's success depends upon the ability to use words and tell stories that capture the organization's culture, create meanings, and shape expectations in others, motivating their positive action.

Self-Reflection: Looking In and Out

Using a scale of 1 to 10 with *1* representing *never* and *10* representing *always,* award yourself the number of points you believe you deserve for each of the following statements:

1. I speak like a leader.
2. Most of the time, I tell a story to make my point.
3. People tend to respond favorably to the stories I tell.
4. I find it easy to speak in metaphorical language.
5. I reach people on an emotional level.

6. My words are an apt reflection of me.

7. People remember my words.

8. Others find my words motivating.

9. I repeat what I think is important.

10. When I present ideas, I invite audience interaction.

What do the scores you have given yourself suggest about your readiness to use words to lead?

We are all storytellers. The ability to send and receive messages that create common ground can accelerate the leader's efforts to build meaningful and inclusive relationships with employees and other key stakeholders. If you can use words and narration that resonates with receivers, helping them to imagine new perspectives, then with storytelling you have at the ready a valuable leadership tool, one that lets you personally connect with stakeholders whose support you need.[6]

THE LEADER'S STORY

Every leader has a story to tell because every experience can be turned into one. Whether the leader's goal is to share knowledge or teach a lesson, inspire or motivate, remind followers of the past or prepare them for the future, build credibility by telling his or her own life story, or enhance brand recognition, it is how the leader words and tells that story that determines whether or not it will fulfill its desired outcome.[7] The leader needs to see himself or herself as the organization's voice—its storyteller—prepared to tell the right story at the right time. In fact, storytelling is one of the leader's most significant acts. Being able to translate thoughts and ideas into words that others understand and to which they respond is an essential leadership skill. Through the stories the leader tells, receivers reflect on experiences designed to capture their hearts and minds, or as executive coaches Richard Maxell and Robert Dickman assert, "A story is a fact, wrapped in an emotion that compels us to take an action that transforms our world."[8]

Designed to engage and inspire audiences, stories help leaders shape the reality they want their followers to imagine. Two examples come to mind. First, think of former president George Bush at ground zero soon after the terrorist attacks of 9/11. Having been handed a bullhorn, he stood on a pile of rubble, placed his arm around a fireman, and addressed the crowd. That image is implanted in our minds. It represented the right story at the right time. Next, think of Bush standing on the deck of a navy carrier wearing a flight jacket, declaring our war against Iraq over and claiming victory. While that story was also compelling and has shown its staying power, we learned soon after it was far too early for the leader to be telling it.

We see what gives a story longevity, but what gives it legs? First, the story reflects the leader's passion or a sense of purpose that rallies receivers to participate with the leader in creating a better future. Second, it supplies an antagonist or villain—someone evil or perhaps a problem everyone is able to agree on that threatens the future. Third, it offers up a hero or protagonist who will conquer the villain or offer a solution to the problem. Fourth, it creates an awakening in the hero and receivers—the experiencing of an *aha* moment, an opportunity for learning, and the culmination of what the leader and receivers experience and visualize—one that, once they take it to heart, will make the world a better place. Finally, it reveals a need for change or an opportunity for transformation.

> A good story can transform the world.

When a leader tells the right story at the right time, it's as if the leader's words have magic power: we respond to and follow the leader, taking his or her words to heart. However, when a leader uses the wrong words to tell a story, speaking words that fail to move us, or tells the story at the wrong time, we feel disappointed and often look elsewhere for inspiration. In fact, for many of us, leaders *are* what they say—no more and no less.[9]

Working It Out: Alone or Together

In *Words That Work: It's Not What You Say, It's What People Hear,* author and political consultant Frank Luntz confirms that great quotes are memorable, sticking in our brains, effectively becoming part of our cultural vocabulary, causing us to use and refer to them years after they were first uttered.

Identify a "great quote" by a leader that you believe either had or will have such an impact on society. What was or is it about the quote that you think either led or will lead us to continue using or referring to it? And how do you imagine others will refer to or use the leader's words in years to come?

We said earlier in this section that every leader has a story to tell. But for leaders to find stories to tell, they need to develop an awareness of themselves and others and reflect on the purposes they want their stories to serve—how they want to reach and tap into the experiences of their receivers—building connections that impart information, facilitate learning, and spark insights precipitating action. Storytelling is the leader's sense-making currency, providing connections and delivering to receivers a context for new facts.[10] It may well be true that the shortest distance between leaders and their followers is a story.

Let's try it out. Pick one of the following story starters and use it to tell a story from your experience that you can use to teach others a lesson you learned. Tell us the situation, describe the characters or people involved, explain the conflict, and reveal the solution and the impact it has had.

> Once upon a time . . .
>
> I'll never forget the first time . . .
>
> It was the scariest day of my life . . .
>
> It was the best day of my life . . .
>
> When I was growing up, my (grandma, grandpa, mom, dad, sister, brother, best friend) told me . . .
>
> What if . . . [11]

After telling your story and actively listening to the stories told by others, reflect on how the experience described enhanced your awareness and understanding of self and others. According to Peter Senge, when people understand each other, it is easier for a commonality of direction to emerge. By sharing stories we are able to "look out" through one another's views.[12] As a result, stories help foster trust and collaboration.

What kinds of stories do leaders tell? According to Stephen Denning the stories you tell when leading can be used to spark action, communicate who you are, transmit ideas, communicate who the organization is, share knowledge, and lead people into the future. For example, if your goal were to spark action, the story you tell might describe a successful change, yet leave room for the listener to imagine. Your might even say, "Just imagine . . ." or "What if . . . ?" If your objective was to share knowledge, your story might focus on a mistake made, how it was corrected, and why the solution was effective. Receivers will be helped to think, "We'd better look out for that too."[13] You can tell a story about solving an important problem or about what you did to achieve a milestone. You can tell a story about the stories told to you when you first joined the company. The point is that mastering storytelling can inspire action, motivate change, and transfer knowledge.

Stories Work When They

Reflect the leader's passion

Supply an antagonist or villain

Offer up a hero or protagonist

Create an awakening in receivers

Reveal a need for change or opportunity for transformation

What advice would you give the leader in the cartoon about how to use stories as a motivational tool?

THE LEADER'S LANGUAGE

Authors Warren Bennis and Joan Goldsmith contend, "Leadership is a transaction between leader and follower."[14] When worded effectively, the stories leaders tell help cement the leader-follower connection, but when worded ineffectively, they instead precipitate questions and concerns that threaten to sever those ties. Should this occur, the leader is left to clean up the mess his or her words made.

For followers to perceive a leader as credible, the leader must communicate like a leader. But what exactly does communicating like a leader mean? Leaders who communicate like leaders have a heightened sensitivity to language. They are wordsmiths, choosing words that add vividness and force to their ideas, effectively steering followers toward the leader's goal, strengthening the image followers have of them, and enhancing their ability to inspire.

Observation: Watch and Learn

Begin by recalling a time when you observed a leader recognizing the efforts of a team member who went above and beyond in contributing to a project. What did the leader do to convey the person's contributions to you and others? What techniques did the leader use to paint the scene and tell the story so that you and your fellow receivers found the presentation interesting, memorable, and motivating?

Next, when together with friends or family members, instead of talking about your day, do as leadership theorists James Kouzes and Barry Posner suggest: tell a story about your day.[15] Describe in rich detail what you had hoped to accomplish on the selected day, who you worked with, what you did to motivate or energize them, and how you felt about the results you achieved at day's end.

Language Tools Leaders Use

Language is tied to leader credibility. The words a leader uses can help us to perceive him or her as confident and trustworthy or cause us to question his or her competence and confidence. While there is no set formula we can give you to ensure you will speak like a leader—in other words, we can't tell you to add two similes, one metaphor, a moving illustration, and a startling example to a presentation, and you'll be successful at getting others to follow your lead—we can review some of the language tools available to the leader so that you become very familiar with how effective leaders use words in the stories they tell to their advantage.

Develop Language Sensitivity

Leaders avoid using words or expressions that insult, anger, demean, or devalue others. Calling others derogatory names, intimidating them, or using profanity can produce unwanted negative outcomes. For example, calling environmentalists *tree huggers* or labeling people with conservative social and political values *country club fat cats* could reflect badly on the leader among people who disagree with that assessment, as happened when former vice presidential candidate Sarah Palin accused journalists of "blood libel" for blaming heated political rhetoric for the violence that occurred in 2011 in Tucson, Arizona.

The leader would also be wise to avoid using clichés—words or phrases that at one time were effective but due to overuse have now lost their impact. For example, asking colleagues to "think out of the box" has now become cliché; it would be better to ask them to view the situation from an alternative perspective.

Keep It Simple

According to Albert Einstein, "If you can't explain it simply, you don't understand it well enough." While insecure leaders rely on complex language, the most effective leaders forsake word armor (speech that cloaks thought or appeals to narrow audiences), preferring instead to use focused and slang- and jargon-free language. The sentences they speak are perhaps the length of Twitter posts (140 characters or fewer).

Their speech is also distinguished by their avoidance of words that are confusing and alienating, what some might call *technobabble* or *gobbledygook,* in favor of speech that is direct, concise, and simple. For example, former secretary of defense Donald Rumsfeld is credited with uttering these words: "Reports that say something hasn't happened are always interesting to me. Because as we know, there are known knowns; there are things we know we know. We also know there are known unknowns; that is to say, we know there are some things we do not know. But also unknown unknowns—the ones we don't know we don't know."[16] To be sure, Rumsfeld's message could have been delivered more simply if he had only eliminated a host of unnecessary words. In contrast, look at how simply Jack Welch, former CEO of General Electric, delivered his message: "General Electric will be number one or number two in each of its businesses, and if it can't achieve that position it will fix, close, or sell the business." What an easy-to-understand statement.

Make Strategic Word Choices

The most effective leaders understand that followers are not dictionaries; most will respond to the connotative or subjective meaning of words not their denotative or dictionary meanings. By recognizing and acknowledging the feelings and personal associations that a chosen word might stimulate in their receivers, leaders become better able to control the perceptions, conceptions, and reflections of receivers and steer them toward the response they desire. Their language creates excitement.

Use Word Pictures: Tell Stories Rich in Metaphors and Imagery

Communication scholars use the word narrative to cover what is involved when we describe what people are doing and why. A narrative is an organized story containing a plot or sequence of events, characters or agents, a thesis or theme, and an outcome. Stories enable the leader to personalize a message, providing it with a frame and an outcome, one that may provide the moral—a reasonable or inevitable justification for the action that was taken. Through the stories they tell, leaders announce their perspective. All stories are presentational—presenting events in a way that suits the leader's personal interests. We can learn a lot about a leader by how he or she tells a story.

The most effective leaders understand the power inherent in descriptive or colorful language, and they use it to communicate complex information elegantly and in an emotionally appealing manner. While they can speak the language of logic, they understand that the language of emotion tends to be more motivating and powerful. Thus, they create vision stories—stories that capture and communicate a compelling and specific description of what things will look and feel like when the future is achieved. The stories they tell are filled with sensory language. One theory about how language affects receivers is **framing theory.** According to framing theory, when we compare two unlike things in a figure of speech, the comparison influences us on an unconscious level. In other words, the metaphor we use causes us to make an association. Change the metaphor, and you change the way you think about a subject.[17]

Jesse Jackson in his often-referred-to "Rainbow Coalition" speech used a number of powerful figures of speech including the simile, a direct comparison of dissimilar things usually with the words *like* or *as*. Because the simile explicitly compares things that are essentially different and are not usually paired with each other, it helps receivers retain the message. Here is an excerpt from Jackson's speech:

America is not like a blanket—one piece of unbroken cloth, the same color, the same texture, the same size. America is more like a quilt—many patches, many pieces, many sizes, and woven and held together by a common thread.[18]

Similarly, Chief Seattle, a Native American leader, used effective similes to make his point:

The white people are many. They are like the grass that covers vast prairies. My people are few. They resemble the scattering trees of a storm-swept plain.[19]

Complex metaphors form the basis for narratives or stories. For example, author Gail T. Fairhurst cites one senior executive's complex metaphor for corporate mergers:

Well, it's almost like dating somebody . . . you talk about culture and what you like and don't and how you work and don't, (but) you don't know until you live together, right? You're on your best behavior in merger meetings . . . the ugly isn't coming out. You're not arguing with someone about whether you should have a policy over something or not. You're not doing more high-level kind of due diligence. Whether you have 14 people approving something or one doesn't come out in due diligence. Nobody says in due diligence, "Now how many approvals does it take to give somebody a $500 bonus?" That's not the level of detail you're working at. But when you live together, that's the kind of thing that drives you crazy. Now (their) company says five people have to sign this to give somebody a $1,000 bonus; (ours) says their manager can approve that. So trying to bring that kind of stuff together you would never know that in due diligence. You don't get to that level.[20]

Repeat, Repeat, Repeat

The most effective leaders understand that their ideas are fighting for attention. Rarely do they get through the first time. They rely on restatement and repetition to get their ideas across. The more you repeat it, the more receivers remember it. One of the most famous examples of successful use of repetition is the speech delivered by civil rights leader Martin Luther King Jr. in 1963 at the Lincoln Memorial:

I say to you today, my friends, so even though we face the difficulties of today and tomorrow, I still have a dream. It is a dream deeply rooted in the American dream. I have a dream that one day this nation will rise up, live out the true meaning of its creed: "We hold these truths to be self-evident: that all men are created equal. . . ."

I have a dream that my four little children will one day live in a nation where they will not be judged by the color of their skin but by the content of their character. I have a dream today. . . .

I have a dream that one day every valley shall be exalted, and every hill and mountain shall be made low, the rough places shall be made plain, and the crooked places shall be made straight, and the glory of the Lord will be revealed, and all flesh shall see it together.[21]

Use Both *I* Language and *We* Language

As we noted when we spoke of *I* messages, *I* language finds the leader taking responsibility for or ownership of a message. In effect, the leader assumes responsibility for his or her thoughts, feelings, and actions.

In addition, combining *I* language with *we* language is also a common practice. The leader uses *we* language to indicate that the subject is the concern and responsibility of both the leader and receivers. By using *we* language the leader builds a collaborative climate—a kind of "we're in this together" message. When receivers feel that sentiment, they won't forget it.

Theory Into Practice: Social Movements and Stories

In 2011, a new social movement known as *Occupy* emerged. According to Marshall Ganz, a social movement emerges as a result of the efforts of purposeful actors who assert new public values, form new relationships rooted in those values, and mobilize followers to translate the values into action by telling a new story.[22] Ganz notes that the story contains the following: a plot (comprised of a challenge, a choice, and an outcome that engages interest, causing us to pay attention as the protagonist moves toward the desired goal); a character (someone with whom we can empathically identify); a moral (the story's point that we experience emotionally, causing us to feel we have to act); and a setting (the relational context).

Identify a story told about the Occupy movement or another movement of your choice. Is it a story of *self* (a moment when a member faced a challenge), a story of *us* (a story that expresses the values we share), or a story of *now* (a story articulating an urgent challenge that demands immediate action)? Explain.

Generate Receiver Involvement or Participation

While our brains find it difficult to pay attention to boring speakers, the speaker who creates an emotionally charged event captures our interest. Inviting interaction does just that. Involvement with the leader's message tends to increase receiver agreement with that message. When receivers are able to connect with the leader, they are

> **Stories connect leaders and followers.**

more likely to become involved. Their involvement is also increased when the leader asks them to do something during the presentation itself. For example, here's how one student leader used audience participation to demonstrate the impact of voting rights restrictions:

Voting is something that a lot of us may take for granted. Today, the only requirements for voting are that you are a U.S. citizen aged 18 or older who has lived in the same place for at least 30 days—and that you have registered. But it hasn't always been that way. Americans have had to struggle for the right to vote. I'd like to illustrate this by asking everyone to please stand. I'm going to ask some questions. If you answer no to any question, please sit down.

Do you have five extra dollars in your pocket right now? If not, sit down. Up until 1964, poll taxes existed in many states.

Have you resided at the same address for at least one year? If not, sit down. Residency requirements of more than 20 days weren't abolished until 1970.

Are you white? If not, sit down. The 15th Amendment gave nonwhites the right to vote in 1870, but many states didn't enforce it until the late 1960s.

Are you male? If not, sit down. The 19th Amendment gave women the right to vote only in 1920.

Are you Protestant? If not, sit down. That's right. Religious requirements existed in the early days throughout the country.[23]

What are some of the speeches given by leaders that we remember years after the speech was given? In what ways were these speeches similar to vision statements? For example, we remember and still talk about Franklin Delano Roosevelt's "Declaration of War" speech following the Japanese attack on Pearl Harbor, John F. Kennedy's inaugural address, Martin Luther King Jr.'s "I Have a Dream" speech, and Ronald Reagan's eulogy to the astronauts who perished aboard the doomed *Challenger* spacecraft. What did the speeches of these leaders share in common? What made their speeches memorable? Each speech contained language that was clear, understandable, and rich in imagery. Absent from them was doublespeak, jargon, offensiveness, and convoluted technical language. In their unique ways, these leaders also challenged us to commit ourselves to making their dream of the future come alive.

Post It: Imagineering a Better Way

Suppose you need to give a presentation on what it means for your organization to think globally. First, identify the specific points you want to make in your talk. Next, brainstorm with your team what you might select to serve as your unifying metaphor, and defend your choice by explaining why you believe listeners will relate to it. Finally, demonstrate how you will integrate at least three additional language tools and the five ingredients of a story discussed in this chapter in your presentation.

So, from a leadership perspective, how important are stories? Consider this observation by psychologist Drew Westen, who in 2009 stood with his daughter listening to President Barack Obama's inauguration speech: "I had a feeling of unease. It wasn't just that the man who could be so eloquent had seemingly chosen not to be on this auspicious occasion, although that turned out to be a troubling harbinger of things to come. It was that there was a story the American people were waiting to hear—and needed to hear—but he didn't tell it."[24] Westen reiterates the role stories play in transmitting knowledge and values, asserting that during the financial crisis, Americans had needed Obama to tell them a story—a compelling narrative like the one Franklin D. Roosevelt had offered in 1936—that made sense and demonstrated understanding of what they were feeling, a story that might have gone something like this:

> I know you're scared and angry. Many of you have lost your jobs, your homes, your hope. This was a disaster, but it was not a natural disaster. It was made by Wall Street gamblers who speculated with your lives and futures. It was made by conservative extremists who told us that if we just eliminated regulations and rewarded greed and recklessness, it would all work out. But it didn't work out. And it didn't work out 80 years ago, when the same people sold our grandparents the same bill of goods, with the same results. But we learned something from our grandparents about how to fix it, and we will draw on their wisdom. We will restore business confidence the old-fashioned way: by putting money back in the pockets of working Americans by putting them back to work, and by restoring integrity to our financial markets and demanding it of those who want to run them. I can't promise that we won't make mistakes along the way. But I can promise you that they will be honest mistakes, and that your government has your back again.[25]

But the president did not tell the story.

In summary, Jack Harris, vice president of Eli Lilly & Co. and the CEO of Barnes and Conti Associates, sees leadership storytelling as a means of "communicating a complex idea in a clear and powerful way. Human beings learn from experience—their own and others—through stories. Stories create an indelible message and are a container for important life lessons. As leaders, we learn to use our own stories to communicate important messages to others."[26] Leading with stories can precipitate more active exchanges between the leader and receivers. Leading with stories can set out who the protagonists and villains are. Leading with stories can embolden followers to climb mountains, understand why the goal is worth pursuing, and remember what the mission is all about.

When you are in a leadership role and the chips are down, will there be a storyteller inside you?

LOOK BACK

Reread the opening poem. What story would you tell to answer the speaker's question?

Key Terms

Authentic leader (123)

Connotative (130)

Credibility (125)

Denotative (130)

Framing theory (131)

"I" language (132)

Narrative (130)

Storytelling (123)

"We" language (132)

Notes

1. Bill George, *Authentic Leadership: Rediscovering the Secrets to Creating Lasting Value* (San Francisco: Jossey-Bass, 2003).

2. See Bill George, Peter Sims, Andrew N. McLean, and Diana Mayer, "Discovering Your Authentic Leadership," *Harvard Business Review* (February, 2007), www.HBR.org.

3. T. T. Barker and K. Gower, "Strategic Application of Storytelling in Organizations," *Journal of Business Communication* 47(3) (2010): 295–312.

4. K. W. Parry and H. Hansen, "The Organizational Story as Leadership," *Leadership* 3(3) (August 2007): 281–300.

5. K. B. Boal and P. I. Schultz, "Storytelling, Time, and Evolution: The Role of Strategic Leadership in Complex Adaptive Systems," *Leadership Quarterly* 18(4): 411–28.

6. T. Mohan, H. McGregor, S. Saunders, and R. Archee, *Communicating as Professionals* (Melbourne: Thomson, 2008).

7. S. Denning, "Effective Storytelling: Strategic Business Narrative Techniques," *Strategy and Leadership* 36(1): 42–48.

8. Richard Maxell and Robert Dickman, *The Elements of Persuasion* (New York: HarperCollins, 2007), 5.

9. Steven Pinker, *The Stuff of Thought: Language as a Window Into Human Nature* (New York: Viking, 2007).

10. D. M. Boje, "The Storytelling Organization: A Study of Story Performance in an Office-Supply Firm," *Administrative Science Quarterly* 36(3) (1991): 106–26.

11. C. M. Phoel, "Leading Words: How to Use Stories to Change Minds and Ignite Action," *Harvard Management Communication Letter* 3(2) (Spring 2006): 3–5.

12. P. Senge, *The Fifth Discipline: The Art and Practice of the Learning Organization* (New York: Doubleday, 1990).

13. Stephen Denning, *The Secret Language of Leadership* (San Francisco: Jossey-Bass, 2007); also see Stephen Denning, *The Leader's Guide to Storytelling: Mastering the Art and Discipline of Business Narrative* (San Francisco: Jossey-Bass, 2011).

14. Warren Bennis and Joan Goldsmith, *Learning to Lead: A Workbook on Becoming a Leader* (Reading, MA: Addison-Wesley, 1994), 102.

15. James Kouzes and Barry Posner, *The Leadership Challenge Workbook* (San Francisco: Jossey-Bass, 2003), 103.

16. See Jonathan Pitts, "At a D.C. Workshop, Participants in the Plain Language Conference Plead for End to Convoluted Communication," *Sun* (November 7, 2005): 1C, 6C.

17. See, for example, G. Lakoff, "Framing the Dems," *American Prospect* (August 1, 2003); and G. Lakoff and M. Johnson, *Metaphors We Live By* (Chicago: University of Chicago Press, 1980).

18. Jesse Jackson, "Rainbow Coalition," presented to the Democratic National Convention, July 17, 1984.

19. Chief Seattle, "The Indian's Night Promises to Be Dark," in W. C. Vanderwerth, *Indian Oratory: Famous Speeches by Noted Indian Chieftains* (Norman: University of Oklahoma Press, 1971).

20. Gail T. Fairhurst, *The Power of Framing: Creating the Language of Leadership* (San Francisco: Jossey-Bass, 2011), 95.

21. Martin Luther King, Jr., "I Have a Dream," presented at Lincoln Memorial in Washington, DC, August 28, 1963.

22. Marshall Ganz, "Leading Change: Leadership, Organization, and Social Movements," in Nitin Nohria and Rakesh Khurana, *Handbook of Leadership Theory and Practice* (Boston: Harvard Business Press, 2010), 527–68.

23. From the voter registration project, New York Public Interest Research Group, Brooklyn College chapter, 2004, as reported in Ronald B. Adler and George Rodman, *Understanding Human Communication*, 10th ed. (New York: Oxford University Press, 2009), 367–68.

24. Drew Westen, "What Happened to Obama?" *New York Times* (August 7, 2011): SR1, 6–7.

25. Ibid.

26. J. Harris and B. K. Barnes, "Leadership Storytelling," *Industrial and Commercial Training* 38(7) (2006): 350–53.

Creatas/Creatas/Thinkstock

Do I look strong?

Do I sound strong?

Can I convince you of my strength?

Even if my ideas are weak?

And if my ideas are strong

How do I need to look and sound

For you to believe me?

8

PRESENTING YOURSELF LIKE A LEADER

Understanding the Power of Nonverbal Communication

I f the essence of leadership is influence, then it falls to the leader to demonstrate sufficient influence to elicit commitment from followers. We are more likely to commit to follow someone whom we perceive to be credible. Simply put, credible leaders have more followers because they exert more influence.[1] Can a leader's nonverbal behavior act as a credibility builder? What does it take to convey the look and presence of a leader? And what does it take for the demeanor and behavior you exhibit to measure up to the scrutiny of followers? How can leaders use **nonverbal communication** to achieve communication goals?

Consider this. Writing about Christine Lagarde, the first woman to head the International Monetary Fund, journalist Gillian Tett observed the following:

> Lagarde's footwear was revealing. As she sat on a vast white sofa in the high-ceiling managing director's office in Washington, DC, she was not wearing the clumpy footwear of a woman trying to break into a man's world; nor the sky-high power stilettos seen in New York. Instead, her navy low-heeled court shoes reeked of a self-confident, je ne sais quai French elegance. They were exceedingly feminine but practical and brimming with power.[2]

Would such a description ever be written about a male leader's shoes? However, the very fact that it was written and appeared in the first paragraph of the article about Lagarde demonstrates the attention paid to nonverbal cues and the importance they play in helping the leader send the right message.

> **Words carry only 7% of a message's emotional meaning.**

SETTING NONVERBAL COMMUNICATION GOALS

What are your nonverbal communication goals? What would you do to create a positive first impression? How about being able to more naturally communicate power and influence or the feelings and meanings behind your words? And wouldn't it be helpful to detect when deception is at work? The multidimensional nature of nonverbal communication makes realizing goals like these within your reach.

Self-Reflection: Looking In and Out

Answer the following questions with a *yes, maybe,* or *no:*

1. When addressing followers do you dress like they're dressed?
2. Do you tend to wear neutral colors?
3. Does your posture tend to be open and relaxed?

4. Are you likely to make sustained eye contact when interacting with others?

5. Does your voice sound confident?

6. Is your behavior consistent?

7. Do your words and behavior support each other?

8. Are you able to demonstrate your concern for others?

9. Do you mirror the behavior of those you want to reach?

10. Do you come across as friendly?

Anything less than a *yes* answer to the preceding questions calls into question your influence potential. Nonverbal communication is an important part of communicating leadership.

What happens when words and nonverbal cues conflict? Do you agree with the leader's diagnosis and solution? Do you know any leaders with a problem similar to the one depicted here?

Leaders may not always be able to control events, but they should be able to control the behavior they exhibit when responding to events. This requires that leaders put their verbal and nonverbal communication into perspective. According to communication scholar Albert Mehrabian, approximately 7% of our emotional understanding of others is attributed to their words, while 38% and 55%, respectively, are attributed to their verbal tone and facial expression.[3] Thus, when it comes to leading, we cannot overestimate the power of nonverbal cues. In fact, when a leader's words and nonverbal cues conflict, followers tend to believe the latter. Thus, leaders would be wise to rely on mastering the ability to make their verbal and nonverbal messages congruent if they hope to use nonverbal messages to win adherents. Literally, leaders have to "walk the talk." How you walk into a room, your ability to express appropriate emotion, the way you use your voice, your understanding of how nonverbal communication sends messages about messages (metamessages) that reveal how to interpret what is said, and your facility in detecting when others aren't being sincere are essential skills.

Although nonverbal messages may be sent deliberately or accidentally, their meaning depends on how they are interpreted. Consequently, nonverbal messages fulfill **metacommunicative functions;** that is, they communicate about communication, effectively helping to clarify both the nature of a relationship, and/or the meaning of verbal messages. Based on others' interpretation of the leader's **nonverbal cues,** they may decide they like or dislike the leader, will listen to or reject her or his ideas, or want to sustain or terminate an interaction.

HOW NONVERBAL MESSAGES FUNCTION

With the wink of an eye, a certain facial expression, voice tone, bodily movement, use of space or touch, a leader can change the meaning of his or her words. As the leader's ability to use nonverbal behavior and contextual cues improves, so does the leader's ability to build effective relationships and lead.

Whereas words are best at conveying thoughts or ideas, nonverbal cues are best at conveying information about relational matters such as liking, respect, and social control. To be sure, the meaning of neither the leader's verbal nor nonverbal messages should be interpreted without carefully considering the other. Since the leader's use of nonverbal cues is integral to communication, let us review the functions his or her nonverbal messages serve.

1. Nonverbal cues may *contradict* or *negate* the leader's verbal messages. When this happens what the leader says and does are at odds. Imagine the leader who learns a trusted employee is leaving the company and shouts, "I'm not angry!" The leader's nonverbal message negates his or her words. Such an interaction represents a *double message*—the leader's words say one thing, the nonverbal cues another.

2. Nonverbal cues can *emphasize* or *underscore* a verbal message. For example, by raising or lowering his or her voice or slowing down his or her rate of speech the leader can deliberately stress a series of words, using nonverbal cues to accentuate their importance.

3. Nonverbal cues can *regulate* or *control* interaction. Using nonverbal cues, the leader may establish the rules of order or "turn taking" during meetings. With eye contact, gestures, and voice the leader can control who should speak next and thus directs the flow of verbal exchanges. The leader's regulatory skills influence others' judgments. For example, if an associate feels that talking to the leader is like talking to a wall, or that when she or he tries to comment, she or he can't get a word in edgewise, it may be because the leader is not giving this person the turns or attention that she or he feels is deserved.

4. Nonverbal cues can *complement* a message—as when the leader learns that an employee's child is ill, asks if there is anything he or she can do, and simultaneously puts a hand on the employee's shoulder, demonstrating his or her concern.

> **Aim for channel congruence.**

5. Nonverbal cues may *substitute for* a verbal message. For example, when we don't know what to say to express our sorrow at the death of a coworker, an embrace often suffices. Similarly, when someone asks, "What do you think?" a shrug of the shoulders is sometimes used in place of "I don't know." Often when actions substitute for words, the nonverbal cues function as symbols of the verbal messages because they are widely understood.

CHARACTERISTICS OF NONVERBAL COMMUNICATION

As we noted, nonverbal communication is an essential part of the leadership communication package. When considered from a nonverbal perspective, every leader (and for that matter, every follower) is a lighthouse of information continually sending messages from which others derive meaning. Why is this?

Nonverbal Behavior Has Message Value

While we can refrain ourselves from speaking—we literally can shut our mouths—it is impossible for us to refrain ourselves from behaving. Behavior, whether intentional or unintentional, is ongoing. Thus, leaders (and their followers) continually emit a wealth of nonverbal information.

You cannot stop sending nonverbal messages. As long as another person is aware of your presence and is there to decode your nonverbal communication, it is impossible for you not to communicate. Even if you turn your back on the observer and remove yourself from his or her sight, you are communicating.

With this in mind, if someone were to enter the space in which you are now reading, what messages might he or she derive from your nonverbal demeanor? Are you seated at a desk or reclining on a bed? What does your face suggest regarding your level of interest and degree of understanding? Do you have the demeanor of a leader?

Nonverbal Communication Is Ambiguous

Although nonverbal cues are continuous and frequently involuntary, we can evaluate them in different ways—that is, what we communicate may be ambiguous and subject to misinterpretation. One nonverbal cue can trigger a variety of meanings. For example, wearing jeans can be symbolic of a relaxed mode of dress or it can be construed as a statement of support for the gay community, as when gay organizations without warning surprise blue jean wearers by posting signs that say, "Wear jeans if you advocate gay rights."

Others may derive from the nonverbal cues you send something different from what you think you are conveying. There could be any number of reasons why a person looks at a watch, coughs, or rubs his or her eyes. All nonverbal behavior should be interpreted within a specific context.

Nonverbal Communication Is Primarily Relational

Frequently, it is easier to communicate our emotions and feelings nonverbally than with words. We convey liking, attraction, anger, and respect for authority nonverbally; in fact, our primary means of revealing our inner states that typically are not readily transmitted using words is through nonverbal communication. For example, we usually look to the face to assess emotional state. We look to the mouth to evaluate contempt. We look to the eyes to evaluate dominance and competence. We base our judgments of confidence and relationship closeness on our reading of gestures and posture, and we listen to the voice to help us evaluate both assertiveness and self-confidence.

Frequently we are unaware of the nonverbal cues we send, inadvertently revealing information we would rather conceal. Without intending it, our nonverbal messages let others know how we feel about ourselves and how we feel about them. As our awareness of our nonverbal communication increases, its informational value decreases. In effect, a conscious intention to manage the impression we convey means that we will do our best only to communicate messages that are in our own best interest.

USING NONVERBAL
COMMUNICATION TO PROJECT LEADERSHIP

In January 2011, we saw monologist Colin Quinn's one-person show *A Long Story Short*. One scene in the performance has Quinn telling a story to a supposedly eager receiver who while listening to him continued to stretch and warm up in preparation for a run. What message did the listener's continuing to stretch send? The listener's behavior did not signal a readiness to listen. Because the receiver's verbal and nonverbal messages conflicted, the importance of the relationship between the speaker and the receiver was called into question. And because of channel incongruence, the audience was made to doubt the receiver's sincerity and trustworthiness. The message: recognizing the power of congruence is a first step in being perceived as congruent and is essential for a leader to be perceived as a leader.

Think of people in leadership positions. How do they announce their power? Is it the way they carry themselves? Do their voices announce that they are in command? Could there be a leadership message in their control of space and their environment? Or is it a combination of all their nonverbal cues together? Whether the leader is trying to display confidence, power, or persuade others of the rightness of a position or decision, his or her nonverbal cues will influence others. The nonverbal messages the leader emits, consciously and unconsciously, determine whether followers will judge him or her to be credible, which, in turn, determines whether they will be convinced to follow the leader.

POWER AND APPEARANCE

Although the old maxim "You can't tell a book by its cover" may have been drilled into us when we were young, because of stereotypes appearance plays a role in determining how followers respond to leaders. If a leader looks good, many assume the leader is good. Once we internalize these impressions, they influence subsequent judgments about the leader.

Because we use **appearance** when assessing leaders, leaders work at communicating the image they want others to perceive. Indeed, today in their quest to have others see them as more attractive, leaders may even alter their physical appearance. Unfortunately, the altering of appearance can have a negative impact on the leader's being able to use nonverbal communication to enhance understanding, and what is more, it has also been found to interfere with empathizing abilities. Researchers have investigated, for example, if receiving

Botox injections, which freeze facial movements, might cause people trouble when they try to read the emotions of others. They determined that those individuals treated with Botox had a lower accuracy rate not only in sending emotionally charged messages, but also in interpreting expressed emotions. Tampering with a leader's nonverbal cues apparently can be harmful for authentic communication.[4]

While appearance is related to leadership, it is not the only determiner of who will and will not be an effective leader. Nonetheless, it is helpful for us to explore aspects of nonverbal behavior that leaders use to express and communicate leadership. For example, the leader may communicate power through clothing and physical size. Dressing in high-status clothing, having an individual sense of style, and standing tall can each individually and together help convey the leader's position and dominance. And as we noted, when it comes to leadership, first impressions count. As testimony to this, a few years back, in an effort to manage client impressions, the Swiss bank UBS established a dress code for executives describing how they should use a polished appearance to impress. The code suggested wearing suits in dark gray, black, or navy blue because these colors "symbolize competence, formalism, and sobriety."[5] This, of course, was at a time when the firm was trying to rebuild its tarnished image. Needless to say, attitudes about which clothing conveys leadership keep changing, with leaders sometimes "dressing down"—wearing clothing similar to those worn by the people whose support they seek—in a "just plain folks" leadership moment.

Of note is the fact that leaders tend to engage in self-monitoring; that is, they are aware of their own behavior and how it affects others. As a result, they are better equipped to take steps to adjust their behavior to meet the needs and expectations of others.

THE LEADER'S BODY LANGUAGE: LEADING WITH KINESICS

Kinesics, a Greek word meaning *movement,* is the study of the relationship between body language and communication, including the study of facial expression, posture, and physical gestures.

Faces

Let us start at the top by focusing on the leader's facial expressions. Of all the nonverbal channels the leader has at his or her disposal, the face is the single most important broadcaster of the leader's emotions. To avoid having the face weaken their position with followers, leaders rely on a number of facial management techniques. For example, a leader may intensify or exaggerate a facial expression to match follower expectations, deintensify or deemphasize a facial expression to conform with what others would judge to be more appropriate, or neutralize an expression to display an inner strength or to avoid giving feelings away. In addition to avoiding the display of any emotion, they can also mask an emotion by replacing one emotion with another that they believe is more appropriate and to which others will respond more favorably.

> **What emotions is your face broadcasting right now?**

Eye Contact

The leader's ability to maintain eye contact also enhances leadership. Eye contact opens the communication channel, conveys confidence, and suggests that the leader has nothing to conceal from followers. In addition, receivers tend to interpret what the leader says more positively when the leader makes eye contact with them. Smiling sincerely, similarly, makes the leader seem more approachable. Additionally, leaders use eye contact to enhance and communicate their trustworthiness. Of course, a glare from a leader can also be intimidating. Effective leaders also read the eyes of followers. For example, when individuals are excited or aroused by what the leader says, the pupils of their eyes will dilate.[6]

Working It Out: Alone or Together

From Behind the Leader's Eyes

Using examples found on Hulu or YouTube, report on the eye behavior of Secretary of State Hillary Clinton and that of President Barack Obama. Compare and contrast who engaged in more contact, how often each leader averted his or her gaze, and the extent to which each signaled interest or disinterest with his or her eyes. After getting behind each leader's eyes, identify which leader you believed used eye contact more effectively.

The Smile

What about the smile? Leaders sometimes flash what might be called "a power grin"—raising their chins so they look down at others—in a kind of dominant but false smile. On the other hand, a leader's "social smile" can do a lot to generate a melding of minds with supporters. We typically recognize genuine smiles by mimicking them.[7]

Posture

The face, of course, is not the only nonverbal tool at the leader's disposal. The leader's posture also helps communicate stature. In *Body Politics*, Nancy Henley notes that "the bearing with which one presents oneself proclaims one's position in life."[8] Do you have the bearing of a leader? For example, when in the company of others, do you tend to keep your head raised or lowered? Is your posture straight and erect or do you slouch? Some leaders think that appearing to stand tall helps them appear more powerful, thereby fostering their leadership. One female CEO, for example, persists in wearing stiletto heels even though she is five feet, nine inches tall because she believes they make her seem more intimidating.[9] Another male CEO, six feet, three inches tall, in the midst of heated negotiations puts his hand on the shoulder of those shorter than him, crowding into their personal space, attempting to demonstrate his personal decisiveness and dominance. Another CEO says that he would rather be bald than short.[10] In fact, in *Blink*, author Malcolm Gladwell observed that 30% of Fortune 500 CEOs are at least six feet, two inches tall, versus just 4% of all men and even fewer women.[11]

Body Tension

How comfortable you seem is also communicated. We often look to **tension** or **body relaxation** to reveal who has the power in a relationship, with the person who is the most relaxed in a given situation typically being perceived to have more status.[12] How does the body express tension? Where do you find it? Sometimes what a leader does with his or her lower limbs conveys his or her tension or anxiety. Individuals may try to look relaxed from the waist up, but if their legs are crossed tightly, or one foot is thrust so rigidly in the air that it appears as if it could break off, they are revealing their discomfort.[13]

Gestures

Gestures also communicate leadership. When First Lady Michelle Obama accompanied President Obama to England, she used a gesture that breached British protocol; she placed her arm around the queen, violating the prevailing custom that visitors should not touch the queen unless returning a handshake. Mrs. Obama used the gesture as a sign of friendship. Leaders use a number of such gestures to project their approachability. Consider this description of former president Bill Clinton:

> I've seen him do it a million times, but I can't tell you how he does it. . . . The right-handed part. I can tell you what he does with his left hand. He's a genius with it. He might put that hand on your elbow . . . or your bicep, like he's doing now. Basic move. He's interested in you. He's honored to meet you. But if he gets any higher, if he gets on your shoulder . . . it's not as intimate. He'll share a laugh with you, a light secret. And if he doesn't know you, but wants to share emotion . . . he'll lock you in a two-hander. You'll see when he shakes hands with you.[14]

Leaders similarly use gestures to express confidence and even signal dominance, including the aforementioned hand steeple that signals high confidence in thoughts or a position taken. Juxtaposed to the steeple, hand-wringing signals when the leader is stressed or overly concerned.[15] Similarly, when individuals display their thumbs extended up, this too signals confidence in thoughts and circumstances. Contrast this with individuals who place their thumbs in their pockets, a gesture usually indicative of uncertainty or lack of confidence.[16] Of necessity, leaders learn to control fidgeting or other cues that could betray nervousness and replace them with gestures that convey their control of a situation. A leader's gait, manner of movement, and physical bearing work together to help others perceive the leader as resolute and determined. In addition, when confident of their position, leaders also appear relaxed. In fact, relaxation is a power cue.

Culture and Nonverbal Cues

We should point out that while some nonverbal cues appear to be universal—for example, there is strong agreement across cultures about which facial expressions represent basic emotions such as happiness, sadness, and surprise—the meaning of other nonverbal cues varies from culture to culture. The nod that we interpret as yes, for instance, in other cultures would be interpreted as no, while in still others, it merely means the person understands the question.[17]

Similarly, a gesture we consider friendly may be given an obscene meaning in another culture. For example, during the parade marking his second inauguration, President George W. Bush raised his hand and gave a two-finger "hook 'em horns" gesture as the University of Texas marching band passed by his viewing stand. The Associated Press reported that a Norwegian newspaper had interpreted the gesture as an insult because in Norse culture, it is a sign of the devil.[18]

THE LEADER'S VOICE: LEADING WITH PARALANGUAGE

Paralanguage includes the elements of speech that are not standard words such as pitch (the highness or lowness of a voice), volume (its loudness or softness), tempo (rapid or slow), use of pauses (their frequency and duration), and the presence or absence of disfluencies. Why are these important? Because *how* something is said is often interpreted by receivers as *what* is said. Your voice influences how others see you.

Ideally, the leader's voice conveys control and confidence. Both men and women with deeper voices are perceived as more authoritative and effective. It is doubtful that you can think of a leader whose voice is whiny. Instead, most leaders exhibit voices that announce a powerful, take-charge attitude. We associate higher-pitched voices with helplessness, tenseness, and nervousness. In contrast, we attribute the qualities of strength and maturity to lower-pitched voices.

Leaders also usually display fewer hesitation phenomena or vocal distracters such as filled pauses—the *ums* and *ers* of conversation—instead choosing silence when they need time to reflect; thus, their speech comes across as more fluid and more confident. If you saw the film *The King's Speech*, you understand how hard the titular head of Great Britain during World War II, King George, a man afflicted with a severe stutter, worked to overcome his speech impediment so that he could deliver his words in a way that would inspire his nation. How you speak significantly affects the meaning people give to your words.

Research reveals that receivers are more likely to respond positively to and comply with requests from speakers whose speech rate most closely matches their own.[19]

THE LEADER'S SPACE: LEADING WITH PROXEMICS

Because of their power, leaders use space and distance differently from those who possess less status. Leaders are generally accorded more personal space, carrying with them a larger personal bubble than others, and because they also control the degree of approach, leaders are able to enter or occupy the space of people possessing less status than they have.

The Leader's Office

As the description of the ceiling height in Christine Lagarde's office cited at the outset of this chapter reveals, the leader's office also contains nonverbal cues that frame leader interactions with people who enter his or her space. For example, the leader's office furniture communicates messages about his or her status and power, formality or informality, and approachability in general. If the room contains a conference table, when meeting with others the leader may signal his or her authority by taking the power or head position. In fact, when asked to select a seat conveying leadership or dominance, people chose the end position. Generally, the end (for task-centered leaders) and central positions (for socioemotional-centered leaders) communicate leadership more than less central positions.[20]

Culture and Proxemics

Of course, again, different cultures give different meanings to **proxemic** cues. For example, leaders need to be sensitive to rules for appropriate distance between people, which can differ from culture to culture. To the Japanese, a comfortable distance is 40.2 inches; for a U.S. resident it is 35.4 inches; and to a Venezuelan, it is 32.2 inches. Can you see how not knowing this and failing to adapt could lead to problems for a U.S. leader doing business internationally? The Latin American could conceivably perceive the leader as withdrawn while the Japanese might believe his or her behavior to be too aggressive.[21]

LEADING COLORS

Understanding the impact of color can also give the leader an advantage. Just knowing that color affects people both emotionally and physiologically frees the leader to use color to send a desired message. Over the years, for example, a number of companies have chosen to associate themselves with the color blue as did "Big Blue" (IBM), JetBlue (the airline), Blue Kite (a wireless firm), and Blue Martini (a software company). Affirming these choices, the executive director of the Pantone Color Institute noted, "Blue is invariably connected with sky and water. The sky has never fallen and water has never gone away. It has dependability and constancy."[22]

Color can communicate a company's dependability; it can also convey its concern for the environment. On the other hand, leaders can use the color red to announce their authority and their self-confidence.[23] Of course, color can also be used to stimulate creativity (blue).[24]

Theory Into Practice

Stimulating Creativity

What might a leader do to stimulate creativity in himself or herself and others? According to a study by Mehta and Zhu, one answer may lie in the color of the room in which people work.

In "Blue or Red? Exploring the Effect of Color on Cognitive Task Performance,"[25] the authors report that persons performing tasks against a red background did better on tests dependent on memory such as recalling and attending to details, while persons performing tasks against a blue background did better on tests requiring imagination and invention. Thus, when the leader wants others to engage in a brainstorming session for something like a new product or solution, she or he should get team members together in a blue room. The impact of the contrasting colors may be attributed to the moods they engender. For example, when subjects were questioned regarding how red and blue made them feel, most said that red symbolized caution, danger, or errors, while blue represented peace and openness. It appears that red promotes cautiousness and an orientation for detail. In contrast, blue promotes creativity and positive action.

What the study did not reveal is if members of different cultures would respond to the colors differently. For example, in China red does not signify danger but prosperity and luck.

What color room would you suggest workers meet in to figure out a schedule for launching a new product? What color room would you have them work in to design new packaging for an existing product?

THE LEADER'S USE OF TIME: LEADING WITH CHRONEMICS

Leaders around the world use and structure time differently because of their disparate orientations to it. Individuals belonging to monochronic cultures (North American, German, and Swiss, for example) are schedule driven as was

President George W. Bush. He viewed time as valuable and therefore was obsessive about punctuality—his and others. In contrast, people belonging to polychronic cultures (South American, Mediterranean, Arab) are more flexible, tolerate interruptions, and are not slaves to their timepieces. It is an asset for the leader to understand differences in time orientations. It is equally an asset for those around the leader to respect the leader's orientation to time. Being other-oriented helps both leaders and followers.

In the United States, time is a reflector of status. When negotiating a real estate transaction, a group of Chinese millionaires were more than an hour late for a meeting with Donald Trump. What message do you imagine they were sending him? Status, generally, determines who waits. If we are important, others usually have to make an appointment to see us. Typically, leaders of organizations are seen by appointment only, whereas the leader may, without notice, drop in on people with lesser status.

WHEN EXPECTATIONS ARE VIOLATED

Now and then, we all violate nonverbal expectations. According to **expectancy violations theory,** people develop expectations for appropriate nonverbal behavior based on cultural backgrounds, personal experiences, and their understanding of others. When our expectations are violated, we become more engaged, and how we choose to react depends on our relationship with the other person. Here leaders typically have more leeway because if the violating person is a rewarding communicator—one who has high credibility, status, and attractiveness—we may simply adjust our expectation and perhaps even reciprocate the behavior. In other cases, we use reactive behavior to correct for the violation.[26]

Working It Out: Alone or Together

Tape a news interview of a leader, perhaps a member of Congress, a CEO, or a sports coach. After viewing the interview a number of times, describe in detail the nonverbal cues the leader displayed during the interview.

(Continued)

(Continued)

According to Stanford University professor Lara Tiedens, leaders acquire status by looking directly at others, using an open posture and displaying vigorous gestures. She observes that they also speak loudly and in a deep voice, often interrupting at will and leaning in close to reduce the space of others while expanding their own. Based on her observations, Tiedens recommends that leaders attempt to be seen as taller and louder.[27] To what extent do your observations support this recommendation?

DECEPTION AND IMMEDIACY

While actors are trained and thus quite good at controlling the display of both verbal and nonverbal cues during performances, for nontheatrical folk, nonverbal cues are, in general, the less controllable of the two. While we may "zip our lips" to keep from saying something we might regret, it is often difficult to conceal real feelings. Similarly it is helpful to come off as likeable.

The Truth About Leakage: Leadership Lapses

The betrayal of internal emotion is called **leakage.** A number of leaders, former presidents Richard Nixon and Bill Clinton among them, have suffered leadership lapses, betraying themselves to followers by emitting leakage cues and unintentionally sending nonverbal messages that revealed the deceptiveness of their communication to others.

Leaders use different strategies to deceive. According to **interpersonal deception** theory,[28] when lying, leaders may engage in *falsification* (creating a fiction), *concealment* (not revealing a real reason for an action), or *equivocation* (changing the subject and dodging the issue altogether).

Among the cues that signal when a leader is lying are *nervous displays* (excessive blinking, vocal tension, extraneous fidgeting or posture shifting, a fixated facial expression), *negative emotional signs* (limited eye contact, vocal agitation), and *incompetent communication* (making numerous speaking errors, displaying frozen, rigid posture, using exaggerated gestures, displaying little spontaneity in communication). Researchers have also discovered that when attempting to deceive, individuals may either shift pitch more often or attempt to overcontrol their voices. In addition, they may look away and display fewer hand movements.[29]

When we accuse someone of lying, and then observe his or her nervousness, that could be another story. When it comes to reading deception cues, it is equally important to keep in mind that a person's nervousness may be attributed to his or her being accused of lying rather than a sign that the person is lying.[30]

Immediacy and the Leader: Leadership Opportunities

Immediacy is the degree to which someone appears to be approachable or likeable. One theory of why George W. Bush defeated Al Gore in the 2000 presidential election was because Bush appeared to be more friendly and approachable than Gore. Relations with a leader are likely to be more positive when the leader uses nonverbal immediacy behaviors. Among nonverbal cues related to immediacy are the making of direct eye contact, the maintaining of close physical distance, the exhibiting of natural body movement, smiling, and vocal expressiveness and variety. The degree to which a leader appears to be likable and approachable or distant and standoffish may be the difference between a smile and a frown, making eye contact or looking away, and varying vocal tone or speaking in a monotone.

> **Use nonverbal immediacy to foster positive relationships.**

Post It: Imagineering a Better Way

Consider the behavior of your college or university president when in attendance at public events held on and off campus. Generally, would you describe him or her as coming across as warm and friendly or cool and reserved? How would you describe his or her nonverbal behavior? When addressing the college community, for example, does he or she stand behind the lectern or move toward receivers? Are his or her gestures suggestive of power and presence or uncertainty and confusion? Do the vocal cues he or she uses convey authority or do they weaken his or her presence?

Using a 1-to-10 scale, where *1* represents *never* and *10* represents *always,* rate the president when it comes to the following cues:

1. Using open gestures
2. Displaying a smile

(Continued)

> (Continued)
>
> 3. Using vocal expressiveness
> 4. Appearing warm and approachable
> 5. Making you feel comfortable
>
> What conclusions can you draw regarding whether or not the president possesses "the right amount" of immediacy? What steps would you advise the president take to further enhance her or his leadership presence on and off campus?

A lot of what followers feel and believe about a leader is based on what they observe and hear. Thus, leaders need to focus on mastering nonverbal cues to enhance leadership. When interacting with or addressing receivers, a leader who resembles "a deer in the headlights," and a leader who exhibits evasive behavior such as closing one's eyes, placing one's hands in front of the face, or turning one's feet toward the nearest exit, will have less credibility than a leader who displays high comfort and high confidence.

For a leader, being a skilled user of nonverbal communication is an important part of the job. For that reason, effective leaders are other-oriented. They are proficient self-monitors and observers of others. They seek to take in as many nonverbal cues as possible in attempting to determine if words and nonverbal behavior complement or contradict one another, if emotions are real or masked, and if leakage cues are visible. In addition, they use their nonverbal behavior to promote immediacy and establish connections with others.

LOOK BACK

Reread the opening poem. The speaker asks a number of questions. How would you answer them in reference to yourself?

Key Terms

Appearance (145)

Body tension (148)

Chronemics (152)

Expectancy violations theory (153)

Notes

1. J. M. Kouzes and B. Z. Posner, *Credibility: How Leaders Gain and Lose It, Why People Demand It* (San Francisco: Jossey-Bass, 2003), 22.

2. Gillain Tett, "Power With Grace," *Financial Times* (December 10–11, 2001): 1, 26.

3. A. Mehrabian, *Nonverbal Communication* (Chicago: Aldine-Atherton, 1972).

4. Christopher Shea, "Blinkered by Botox," *Wall Street Journal* (May 14–15, 2011): C4.

5. Elena Berton, "Dress to Impress, UBS Tells Its Staff," *Wall Street Journal* (December 15, 2010): C1, C2.

6. Paul Preston, *Communication for Managers* (Englewood Cliffs, NJ: Prentice Hall, 1979), 161.

7. Carl Zimmer, "More to a Smile Than Lips and Teeth," *New York Times* (January 25, 2011): D1, D4.

8. Nancy Henley, *Body Politics: Power, Sex, and Nonverbal Communication* (New York: Simon & Schuster, 1986).

9. Christina Binkley, "Heelpolitik: The Power of a Pair of Stilettos," *Wall Street Journal* (August 2, 2007): D8.

10. Del Jones, "The Bald Truth About CEOs," *USA Today* (March 14, 2008): 1B, 2B.

11. Malcom Gladwell, *Blink* (New York: Little, Brown, 2005).

12. A. Mehrabian, *Silent Messages* (Belmont, CA: Wadsworth, 1981).

13. Martin Groder, "Incongruous Behavior: How to Read the Signals," *Bottom Line* (March 30, 1983): 13.

14. From the opening scene in the film *Primary Colors*.

15. J. Navarro, *What Every Body Is Saying* (New York: HarperCollins, 2008), 147–50.

16. Ibid., 152–53.

17. P. Ekman, "Cross-Cultural Studies of Facial Expression," in P. Ekman, ed., *Darwin and Facial Expression* (New York: Academic Press, 1973).

18. J. Douglas Jr., "Outside Texas, 'Hook 'em Horns' Gesture Has Different and Unflattering Meanings," *Fort Worth Star-Telegram* (January 23, 2005): 2A.

19. See, for example, D. Buller and K. Aune, "The Effects of Speech Rate Similarity on Compliance: Application of Communication Accommodation Theory," *Western Journal of Communication* 56 (1992): 37–53.

20. C. Ward, "Seating Arrangement and Leadership Emergence in Small Discussion Groups," *Journal of Social Psychology* 74, 83–90; A. Hare and R. Bales, "Seating Position and Small Group Interaction," *Sociometry* 26: 480–86.

21. N. Sussman and H. Rosenfeld, "Influence of Culture, Language and Sex on Conversational Distance," *Journal of Personality and Social Psychology* 42 (1982): 67–74.

22. Susan Carey, "More U.S. Companies Are Blue, and It's Not Just the Stock Market," *Wall Street Journal* (August 30, 2001): A1, A2.

23. Roy A. Smith, "The Color of Confidence," *Wall Street Journal* (September 25–26, 2010): D3.

24. Pam Belluck, "Reinvent Wheel? Blue Room. Defusing a Bomb? Red Room," *New York Times* (February 6, 2009): A1, A15.

25. Ravi Mehta and Rui (Juliet) Zhu, "Blue or Red? Exploring the Effect of Color on Cognitive Task Performance," *Science* 27 (February 2009): 1226–29.

26. See J. K. Burgoon and N. E. Dunbar, "Nonverbal Expressions of Dominance and Power in Human Relationships," in V. Manusov and M. L. Patterson, eds., *The SAGE Handbook of Nonverbal Communication* (Thousand Oaks, CA: Sage, 2006), 279–97.

27. Del Jones, "Does Height Equal Power?" *USA Today* (July 18, 2007): 1B, 2B.

28. David B. Buller and Judee K. Burgoon, "Interpersonal Deception Theory," *Communication Theory* 6 (1996): 203–42.

29. See A. Vrij, L. Akehurst, and P. Morris, "Individual Differences in Hand Movements During Deception," *Journal of Nonverbal Behavior* 21 (1997): 87–102; L. Anolli and R. Ciceri, "The Voice of Deception: Vocal Strategies of Naïve and Able Liars," *Journal of Nonverbal Behavior* 21 (1997): 259–85.

30. P. Ekman, *Telling Lies: Clues to Deceit in the Marketplace, Politics, and Marriage* (New York: Norton, 2001).

PART III

EXERCISING LEADERSHIP

You say, "Yes."
I say, "No."
So how do we get there?

LEADING THE WAY THROUGH CONFLICT

It played to audiences for six months of previews without opening, setting a record. During its six months of previews, five actors were injured falling off the set or crashing from hanging wires. During the lengthy preview period, the Broadway show received a plethora of poor-to-mediocre reviews, the director Julie Taymor was fired, and Bono and the Edge, the two U2 members who composed the songs, hired a team to rewrite the show. Finally, *Spider-Man* officially opened, again to poor-to-mediocre reviews. One can only imagine the conflicts that occurred prior to and after the show's delayed opening. Can you hear the original director, Julie Taymor, refusing to accept offers of outside help and objecting to the focus groups the producers relied on to tell them what worked? Can you hear the production team blaming one another for the production's technical failures? Can you hear the producers and the director engaging in rationalizations instead of confronting the truth about the play's confusing script?

The *Spider-Man* story holds lessons for aspiring leaders. We'll phrase them as questions: Where was the energy to respond quickly to setbacks? What happened to the willingness to change? Where was the spirit of partnership and the understanding that while a single visionary may provide a breakthrough idea or spark, it usually takes a team to yield consistent results? What happened to the ability to make a midcourse correction? What happened to the openness to respond appropriately to feedback without letting ego get in the way? Why was a stonewalling attitude permitted to persist for so long? How was it that infighting was able to replace the notion of "shared responsibility"? Why were disagreements able to elicit unabated tensions? Why was it so hard for those involved to respond to criticism and face the truth about the show? Why was it so difficult for those involved from the outset to see the show's flaws clearly?[1]

THINKING ABOUT CONFLICT

The dictionary defines **conflict** as "disagreement . . . war, battle, and collision." Such a definition suggests that conflict is negative and has undesirable consequences. Growing up, many of us were taught that nice people don't fight, that if we want to be accepted and valued, we have to be nice. We were told that agreement was good, and conflict was bad. Was that your experience?

Negotiating conflict is a necessary leadership competency. It is important to understand that it is not so much conflicts or disagreements that create problems, but the way leaders approach and handle conflict-producing situations. Disagreements are normal, and their presence does not necessarily signal trouble. Rather, how conflict is managed reveals the health of the leader's relationship with those who disagree.

For example, when Governor Chris Christie of New Jersey was challenged by a Garden State resident named Gail who was wondering why Christie, whose children attend a parochial school, felt comfortable cutting funding for public schools, Christie responded, "Hey, Gail, you know what? First off, it's none of your business. I don't ask you where you send your kids to school. Don't bother me about where I send mine."[2]

When interests collide, where perceived scarce resources need to be divided, or when goals are seen as incompatible, the arising conflict tests the relationships a leader shares with others. It becomes incumbent upon the leader to balance and coordinate the emerging competing interests so that they benefit the public, organization, or group as a whole and not the self-serving interests of any one party. The leader's goal is to have those facing a conflict use the conflict as a motivator, a force for stimulating learning and innovation, a means of clarifying problems we did not see or understand before, as well as a means to understand their interdependence.[3]

There are different kinds of conflict the leader needs to be able to handle: personal conflicts, interpersonal conflicts, or conflicts occurring between competing groups, but whatever its nature or source, conflict is likely to pit individuals against each other as they compete for limited resources, power, and position or status. Sometimes these conflicts occur in the open for all to witness and work jointly at resolving; other times, they exist underground or below the surface and are exacerbated by hidden agendas that can be very powerful forces. However, for their differences to be handled effectively, the parties to the conflict need to be ready to discuss and understand them.[4]

Leadership expert Warren Bennis identifies a series of internal conflicts that leaders need to be adept at resolving to lead effectively. He categorizes the conflicts and their resolutions as follows:[5]

Conflicts	Resolutions
Blind Trust vs. Suspicion	Hope
Independence vs. Dependence	Autonomy
Initiative vs. Imitation	Purpose
Industry vs. Inferiority	Competence
Identity vs. Confusion	Integrity
Intimacy vs. Isolation	Empathy
Generosity vs. Selfishness	Maturity
Illusion vs. Delusion	Wisdom

According to Bennis, aspiring leaders need to learn to reflect honestly on their experiences to arrive at these resolutions. With this in mind, let us begin the reflection process.

CONFLICT QUERIES: PERSPECTIVES AND OPPORTUNITIES

How do you behave when embroiled in a conflict? What if the employees who work with you just cannot seem to get along with one another? Do you have the skills required to prevent the conflicts they experience from escalating? And what if you disagree with others? Can you keep the disagreements between you from derailing your ability to work together? Knowing how to handle conflict is a leadership requirement. Without that ability, the problems caused by interpersonal conflict can challenge even the most effective organization.

In almost every meeting room, virtual or real, people find themselves disagreeing with one another. Let's explore your behavior when that happens to you.

Self-Reflection: Looking In and Out

The purpose of this inventory is to help you identify the typical behaviors you exhibit when involved in a conflict.[6] For each question, give yourself a *5* if you always engage in the behavior described, a *4* if you frequently display that behavior, a *3* if you occasionally exhibit the behavior, a *2* if you rarely behave that way, and a *1* if you never engage in the behavior.

_____ 1. When others disagree with me, I expect them to ultimately accept my position.

_____ 2. I feel betrayed when someone I trust disagrees with me.

_____ 3. I believe that people who disagree with me have likely thought their positions through carefully.

_____ 4. When individuals disagree with me, I try to view the situation as they see it.

_____ 5. I try not to work directly with people whom I believe will disagree with me.

_____ 6. When individuals disagree with me, I do my best to learn from them.

_____ 7. When engaged in controversy, my position tends to become more set.

_____ 8. The more someone questions my position, the more hostile I tend to become.

_____ 9. I question the position taken by someone who disagrees with me but never the person's integrity.

_____ 10. When someone disagrees with me, I paraphrase his or her remarks to be certain I understand them.

_____ 11. When someone disagrees with me, I do not respond.

_____ 12. When someone disagrees with me, I like it because it widens my perspective.

_____ 13. When faced with others who question my position, my goal is to prove me right and them wrong.

_____ 14. When you criticize me, I will find a way to diminish you in the eyes of others.

_____ 15. I believe that I can disagree with a person's position but maintain interest in his or her ideas.

_____ 16. During controversy, I focus on the ideas of the person disagreeing with me, not just my position.

_____ 17. If I think others are going to disagree with me, I don't voice my position.

_____ 18. When others challenge my position, I give them a fair hearing and will even alter my position if their arguments are convincing.

_____ 19. I use facts and opinions to vanquish those who disagree with me.

_____ 20. If you don't agree with me, I am less likely to like you.

_____ 21. Even if I criticize and question the stance taken by another person, I still communicate my liking for the individual as a person.

_____ 22. I try to see the situation as the person who disagrees with me sees it; I want to see from behind his or her eyes.

_____ 23. I don't like to argue with anyone, so I don't.

_____ 24. When disagreements occur, my goal is to clarify the differences and commonalities in positions and see if there is a way for us to combine our ideas into one position we can all live with.

_____ 25. When others disagree with my position, I will prove them wrong.

_____ 26. When others disagree with me, I conclude that they reject me.

_____ 27. Even when I oppose the position another takes, I still affirm the person's ability to challenge and improve my thinking.

_____ 28. When I argue with another person, I restate his or her position before offering my own.

_____ 29. After someone challenges my position, I try to avoid interacting with him or her.

_____ 30. When engaged in a controversy, I acknowledge that the goal is to make the best decision possible.

Analyzing The Results

Enter your answer for each question on the accompanying answer sheet. The higher your score in each section, the greater is your tendency to engage in the described behavior.

Win-Lose	Rejection	Comfirmation
___ 1	___ 2	___ 3
___ 7	___ 8	___ 9

(Continued)

(Continued)

___ 13	___ 14	___ 15
___ 19	___ 20	___ 21
___ 25	___ 26	___ 27
_____ Total	_____ Total	_____ Total

Perspective Taking	Avoidance	Problem Solving
___ 4	___ 5	___ 6
___ 10	___ 11	___ 12
___ 16	___ 17	___ 18
___ 22	___ 23	___ 24
___ 28	___ 29	___ 30
_____ Total	_____ Total	_____ Total

When involved in a controversy, engaging in behavior related to problem solving, confirmation, and perspective taking tends to be more productive than exhibiting behaviors associated with win-lose, rejection, or conflict avoidance. If you scored more than 15 points in a category, you are likely to use that approach.

On the whole, how would you assess your orientation to conflict: do the approaches you use tend to be constructive or destructive? If destructive, it is time to think about the steps you can take and the behaviors you need to try on to turn disagreement into a positive force for more effective leadership.

This inventory sets the stage for an examination of the skills you need to work on and use if you are to lead the way in handling and resolving conflict.

Source: Johnson, David W., and Johnson, Frank P., *Joining Together: Group Theory and Group Skills*, 10th Edition, © 2009. Reprinted by permission of Pearson Education, Inc., Upper Saddle River, NJ.

LEADERS NEED TO HANDLE, NOT MANGLE, CONFLICTS

How a leader models the handling of conflicts affects decision making and the satisfaction of those who work with that leader. In most healthy relationships, conflicts occur regularly and are handled effectively. In contrast, poor conflict management mangles and destroys relationships and the emotional health of participants.

Mangling Conflict

A leader mangles the handling of conflict by engaging in one or more of the following destructive behaviors.

• Attacking the other person by making accusations or displaying passive aggression. If the leader's tone becomes negative or sarcastic, or the leader attempts to inflict guilt on the person disagreeing, the leader may actually inflame the conflict.

• Acting defensively. Too often, a leader who feels threatened or attacked adopts a defensive posture to signal his or her displeasure—limiting opportunities for resolution.

• Stonewalling. At times the leader refuses to acknowledge or talk about differences. Such a response can build a relationship wall that becomes more and more difficult to surmount.

• Communicating contempt. Once a leader displays contempt for another person, the relationship enters dangerous territory.

To cement our understanding, we will revisit these resolution inhibitors later in this chapter.

Managing Conflict

Conflict Creators: Which Riles You More?

Attacking
Acting defensively
Stonewalling
Communicating contempt

In contrast, a leader manages conflict skillfully when she or he engages others in dialogue. In other words, in lieu of criticizing or attacking the disagreeing person, the leader opts to speak respectfully and in a nonthreatening manner. Rather than trying to win the conflict, the leader converses to be understood. Recognizing that there are many perspectives, not only two, the leader embarks on an exploration of possible ways to resolve the disagreement constructively. Rather than exhibiting a competitive mind-set—perceiving the conflict situation in all-or-nothing, win-lose terms—the leader adopts a cooperative mind-set, one in which she or he disagrees without becoming disagreeable, as a way is sought to resolve the conflict to each person's mutual satisfaction. Such leaders embrace the moral of the following Aesop's fable, *The Four Oxen and the Lion*:

> A lion used to prowl about a field in which four oxen used to dwell. Many a time he tried to attack them; but whenever he came near, they turned their tails to one another, so that whichever way he approached them he was met by the horns of one of them. At last, however, they fell a-quarreling among themselves, and each went off to pasture alone in a separate corner of the field. Then the lion attacked them one by one and soon made an end to all four.[7]

Is this what happened in the case of *Spider-Man?* Conflict should enrich not destroy. When winning becomes the goal, ego involvement is high, and the conflict becomes a test of personal worth and competence. To attain victory, the "combatants" erroneously believe the opposition must be defeated. Conversely, when the parties to a conflict view it cooperatively, they tend to look for a mutually beneficial way to resolve the disagreement. When this happens, the conflict is defined as a common problem and each person works to understand the position and frame of reference of the other—perhaps through role reversal; that is, acting as if you were the person with whom you are in conflict.

Leaders also need people in their lives who they can count on to tell them the truth, and they need to encourage dissent. Leaders need to be willing to face what is really going on—they need to comprehend fully what the situation is if they are to be able to fix it. If leaders are surrounded by people who let them make mistakes instead of helping them to face reality and correct their courses of action, they become impeders rather than facilitators of effective leadership. Leaders need to be challenged not coddled. They need to have people willing to confront them much like the fools in Shakespeare's plays confronted their masters with painful truths. Thus, disagreement or dissent, and how leaders react to it, reveals much about how leaders see themselves.

Theory Into Practice

Leaders Argue Constructively

Schultz, Infante, and Rancer[8] report that group members who argue, rather than merely accept the ideas of others, position themselves to emerge as group leaders. What is more, groups in which such argumentation occurs usually generate better ideas that enable them to come up with better solutions. As a result, leaders at all organizational levels would do well to rely on argumentation to help them build cases for the positions they take on issues of controversy.

Unfortunately, some leaders believe mistakenly that it is okay to become verbally aggressive when arguing. Verbal aggressiveness, however, is likely to be construed as hostile, while argumentativeness, in contrast, involves a spirited testing of positions. Researchers strongly advise against confusing the two.

The following are among the tactics used by the verbally aggressive that have no place in advancing a leader's argument in behalf of a position taken: personal insults, including attacks on another's character, competence, or appearance; threats or profane remarks; and looks of disgust or aggressive gestures.

When making an argument, the leader simply states his or her position as a proposition—establishing clearly what it is that he or she is asserting, valuing, or recommending as a course of action or departure from the status quo. The leader then develops arguments to support the stance taken. The following are included in a typical argument: *a claim* or conclusion, *supporting evidence* (in the form of statistics, examples or illustrations, testimony), *reasons* (rationales for the position taken), and a *summary statement* (a statement reiterating what the leader is asking for). When necessary, the leader needs to be prepared to deflect opposing arguments by questioning the evidence and reasoning other parties offer when objecting to the leader's approach. The leader may question the accuracy, applicability, reliability, or substance of arguments, as well as poke holes in reasoning errors, exposing fallacious arguments. Others, of course, should be free to do the same for arguments the leader offers.

Identify an argument you engaged in that turned unpleasant. Explain behaviors that you or others enacted that contributed to this turn. Identify steps that could have been taken to keep the argument civil, facilitating successful argumentation, rather than letting the verbally aggressive nature of the interaction interfere with its objectives.

THE CONFLICT GRID: RESPONSE STYLES

Among the most used paradigms or models for representing ways to respond to conflict is Robert Blake and Jane Mouton's **conflict grid** (see Figure 9.1).[9] The grid is composed of two scales. The horizontal scale represents the degree to which a person desires to realize personal goals. The vertical scale represents the degree to which a person expresses concern for others. The interface of the two scales reveals how strongly a person feels about both concerns, that is, how his or her concern for self and others is apportioned.

Both scales range from 1 (low) to 9 (high), representing increasing importance of personal goals ("concern for production of results") and of other people ("concern for people"). Based on this measure, Blake and Mouton have classified five conflict styles. As you review their grid and the following style descriptions, identify which style comes closest to your own.

A person with a 1.1 conflict style is usually described as an **avoider;** typically avoiders view conflict as a punishing experience and one they prefer to do without. Because they have little tolerance for the frustrations conflict produces, they opt instead to physically and/or mentally remove themselves from the conflict situation. They will change the subject rather than confront it, deny a conflict exists, or find a way to sidestep the issue in controversy. Their attitude can be summed up as "lose and walk away." What avoiders usually fail to realize is that this approach can increase tensions.

A person with a 1.9 style is said to be an **accommodator**. How does the accommodator differ from the avoider? Accommodators prefer to "give in and lose." They are nonconfrontational. Because accommodators overvalue the maintenance of relationships and undervalue their own goal achievement, their main concern is to ensure their acceptance by others. Thus, though they may experience conflicts, because of the potential that conflicts have to cause ill feelings, they choose to placate others rather than deal directly with the conflict. The overriding goal of accommodators is to preserve peace and harmony.

A person with a 5.5 style is labeled as a **compromiser.** Compromisers feel a need to "find a middle ground"—their means of permitting each party to the conflict to gain something. Thus compromisers settle for a workable solution, though the one they settle on may not be the best solution. Compromisers come away with half a loaf and feel half satisfied—or half dissatisfied—leaving some to classify this approach to conflict as lose-lose.

A person with a 9.1 style is given the label **competitive forcer.** The holder of a win-lose attitude, the competitive forcer perceives his or her personal goals as of paramount importance. The need to win overwhelms other concerns. Competitive forcers will do battle with and seek to dominate those who stand in their way—whatever the potential cost or harm. Would you

Figure 9.1 Blake and Mouton's Conflict Grid

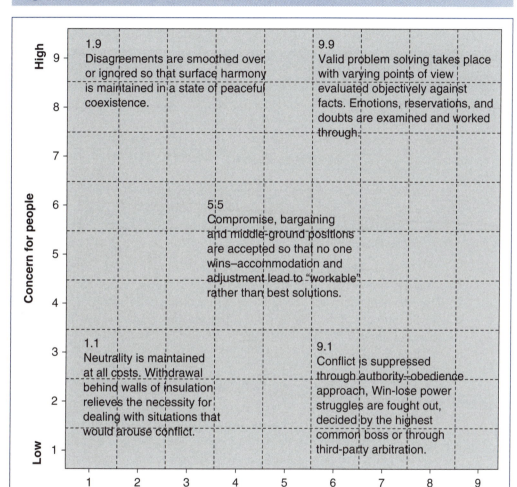

Source: Grid International. "The Fifth Achievement" by Robert Blake and Jane Srgley Mouton, *Journal of Applied Behavioral Science: A Publication of the NTL Institute* 6, no. 4. Published by SAGE Publications on behalf of the NTL Institute for Applied Behavioral Science.

guess this to be Governor Christie's style based on the example offered at the beginning of this chapter?

A person with a 9.9 style has a win-win attitude and is aptly named a **problem-solving collaborator.** Such persons are results and persons oriented and seek to satisfy their own goals while at the same time seeking to satisfy the goals of others. They display respect for opposing opinions and are able and willing to discuss differences without personally attacking others.

Responding to Conflict—Pick Your Favorite

Avoid	Just walk away
Accommodate	Give in
Compromise	Meet in the middle
Force	Win!!!
Collaborate	Problem solve to satisfy yourself and others

All of these styles may be appropriate at one time or another. For example, the leader may opt to exhibit avoidance behavior to buy time. He or she may choose to compete when the other person will take advantage of a noncompetitive approach. When there is not sufficient time to achieve a win-win solution or an impasse has been reached, compromise may be justified. With that said, however, researchers usually find the 9.9 and 1.9 approaches to conflict more effective than 9.1 or 1.1 approaches.[10] Thus, one of the most important challenges facing leaders is the ability to turn conflicts into productive, not destructive, interactions. Rather than reacting automatically and in the same frozen way in all conflict contexts, being able to assess whether to avoid or engage, compete or cooperate, compromise, accommodate, or collaborate is key. Flexibility and adaptability mean that you can alter your behavior in response to the behavior of others.

CONFLICT AND INTERACTION

Unfortunately, conflicts sometimes get out of hand. What begins as disagreement and an exploration of opposing views deteriorates into a hostile exchange of accusations. What causes this to happen? Whether interactions involving conflict are productive or destructive depends on the nature of the communication used. If disagreement is accompanied by shouting and bullying, threat and fear usually permeate interactions. Developing an awareness of options individuals face when engaging in conflict can help prepare us to use communication strategies that defuse rather than escalate the conflict.

First, the critical start-up period of a conflict sets the tone. If criticism is used in the first few minutes that individuals perceive themselves to be in conflict, the mood can quickly become negative. Using *you* statements such as "you always" or "you never" that assign blame typically have a destructive effect. Substituting an *I* statement that describes concern, however, can transform criticism from being perceived as destructive into a constructive complaint.

Second, if defensiveness predominates during a conflict, individuals usually engage in a power struggle. People become defensive when they feel attacked. In contrast, support helps neutralize defensiveness. When the other person feels heard and listened to, that person understands that he or she can disagree but still have your support.

Third, stonewalling, or the desire to remove oneself from a conflict because of anger or because one no longer wants to engage, leads to a participant withdrawing from interacting. Usually, people stonewall and hold back when they sense hostility. By asking others directly what they are thinking, you may be able to pull them back into the discussion.

Fourth, expressing contempt for another usually fosters a spiral of destructive communication. Instead of signaling their contempt for others, people need to learn to voice their concerns.[11]

Consider the four communication modes just identified. Which of these modes have you used on others or have others used on you during a conflict? What precipitated use of the employed approach? How might you have communicated your disagreement or concerns more constructively?[12]

Negative views of conflict keep people from handling conflict-producing situations productively. Approaching a situation rife with conflict positively, however, is desirable. But it requires adopting a problem-solving rather than blaming perspective. When problems are openly addressed, people can solve them. Thus, conflict can be approached like war on a battlefield, as a game of wits, as a balancing act, or it can be cultivated and harvested like a vegetable garden. The choice is yours.

Working It Out: Alone or Together

Use the following conflict metaphors to help you imagine and frame ways to approach conflict: conflict is like war; conflict is like a game of wits; conflict is like a balancing act; and conflict can be cultivated and harvested like a vegetable garden. Then generate two additional conflict metaphors of your own, one reflective of yet another negative view toward conflict and the other reflective of an alternative positive view.

(Continued)

(Continued)

Next, select six recent global events that had world leaders facing complicated conflicts. For each event, focus on one leader connected with the event and explain how that leader's behavior illustrates one or more of the six conflict metaphors in action. Be sure to explain whether the leader's approach exacerbated or eased the way for a resolution to the conflict. Then identify other options the leader might have used to resolve the conflict and discuss your findings.

How would you respond to the request of the leader in this cartoon? What conflict approach do you believe the cartoonist is illustrating?

CAN THERE BE TOO MUCH AGREEMENT? GROUPTHINK AND THE COSTS OF CONCURRENCE SEEKING

Is there such a thing as too much agreement? How you answer this question may reveal your real attitude toward conflict.

The leader's view of conflict permeates his or her team. While repeatedly opting for conflict avoidance is not in the best interests of any organization that hopes to survive, when team members perceive the leader as inhibiting disagreement, they may hop on board with similar behavior. This can lead the organization down a dangerous path with members deliberately avoiding the realistic appraisal of situations and courses of action. Concurrence seeking limits discussion because the concurrence seeker's goal is to avoid arguments. When careful consideration is replaced by automatic consent or even compromise, the leader has made a calculated choice.[13] But remember—compromise also can be viewed as a lose-lose approach. For this reason, opposing opinions should be considered, not shoved under the bus.

Groupthink[14] is a related concept. As with concurrence seekers, the goal of groupthinkers is to preserve a harmonious atmosphere. During

> **Don't use concurrence seeking to cut off discussion.**

groupthink members set aside whatever doubts and misgivings they have about a decision or policy in favor of agreeing with one another and achieving consensus—manufactured though it may be—because, remember, the overriding goal is to avoid conflict. Thus, the outcome of groupthink is conformity—with rationalizations occurring, illusions preventing anyone from questioning or challenging courses of action, and a sense of invulnerability—the unquestioning belief that the ideas individuals are holding are correct and morally right—blinding participants to potential dangers and preventing them from thinking critically. When groupthink is at work, assumed consensus keeps people from voicing any doubts that exist. Instead, efforts are made to protect the leader from receiving information that could impede his or her confidence, and rationalizations rule.

Groupthink is reproduced in countless organizations. It is pointed to as a cause of the failure of the Bay of Pigs invasion, the reason for the *Challenger* shuttle explosion upon takeoff and the disintegration of the *Columbia* space shuttle upon reentry, the corporate culture that led to the Watergate cover-up and the demise of former energy giant Enron, the rationale for the suppression of arguments against the war in Iraq, and even as a reason for the lack of critical analysis that precipitated the subprime mortgage debacle.[15] For example, during this crisis, or what some have called "economic Armageddon," there were a considerable number of doubters who dared to question the policy decisions being made by Wall Street firms and Fannie Mae and Freddie Mac. Their warnings were ignored and dismissively silenced by those who could have halted the fiasco. Instead, Fannie Mae executives assailed them calling them "digit-heads" and "economic pencil brains."[16] In like fashion, groupthink was likely also a contributing factor in the explosion of a West Virginia mine owned by Massey Energy in which 29 miners were killed in 2010. After a year spent reviewing pages and pages of documents and interviewing over 250 people, investigators concluded that a culture of impunity could be blamed for the disaster. Massey managers were pressured to overlook dangerous conditions, and workers who thought about reporting risks were intimated to keep silent.[17] When talking openly and honestly about what is going on is off limits, when facing truths is avoided at all costs, a failure in leadership occurs.[18] Groupthink stifles healthy conflict. Can you see why it falls to leaders to reorient attitudes toward conflict so that dissent is not equated with disloyalty, free discussion is encouraged, and fear of conflict does not lead those involved to avoid the search for alternatives while too easily accepting bad ideas?

In order to combat groupthink, leaders should take the following steps:

1. Encourage disagreement. Demonstrate your openness to dissent.

2. Ask different people to function as critical evaluators so that courses of action are questioned and assessed dispassionately.

3. Remove themselves from some meetings so others who might be reticent to voice concerns in their presence will feel freer to do so.

4. Solicit advice from outside experts. Pay careful attention to the risks they see.

5. Encourage people to turn conflict into a positive force by playing "devil's advocate" and openly challenging others to defend their positions and decisions.

6. Recognize that silence does not connote agreement. Let people voice their thoughts anonymously in writing. Hold secret rather than hand votes.

Observation: Watch and Learn

Use the following symptoms of groupthink to analyze the behaviors exhibited by the people involved in any of the crises mentioned earlier or another groupthink-precipitated crisis of your choosing.

Illusion of invulnerability. Individuals believe they cannot lose because they are invincible. Because they think they can't possibly fail, they take huge risks—even making rash decisions that could cause irreparable harm to the organization or others.

Rationalization. Those involved ignore warnings and negative input by explaining them away or asserting that they are not to be taken seriously because they would never undertake any action that would do damage.

Illusion of morality. Individuals are convinced of their inherent goodness. Since they are good, so are their actions. They brush aside any signs or suggestions that this may not be so.

Stereotyping. Those "on the team" view those not part of the team as "evil" or "lacking in intelligence." Whatever others believe is wrong. Because they divide people into in- or out-groups, and people don't want to become part of the out-group, dissent in labeling rarely occurs.

Peer pressure. When one member perceives another member as wavering, direct pressure is applied to that person in an effort to cut off any disagreement. Team players rule, and if you are a team player, you support the team without question.

Self-censorship. People fail to voice their doubts out of fear of being ostracized or expelled for deviating from the group consensus.

Illusion of unanimity. This is the perception that "all agree" even though it is false. Because people remain silent if they disagree but voice their agreement when they concur, the illusion is that all support the decision.

Mindguarding. Self-appointed "mindguards" literally do just that—protect the leader's mind from coming into contact with anything or anyone that could disrupt his or her thinking or chosen course of action. They protect the leader from learning from others information that runs counter to or might undermine the group's plan. They are the group's filters—letting only supporting information through to the leader.

Take Time to Understand Your DQ (Disagreement Quotient)

Leaders with a high tolerance for disagreement do not let conflict become a negative. Their affinity for having thoughtful, careful colleagues to work with overrides their desire for all to agree. In contrast, leaders with a low tolerance for disagreement discourage critical inquiry by reacting with hostility, including verbal aggressiveness toward those who dissent. However, not having the ability to productively engage in and resolve conflict puts organizations at risk.

> To raise your DQ, increase your tolerance for disagreement.

Your disagreement quotient is also affected by your understanding of diverse attitudes toward conflict due to cultural and gender differences. Cultural values, for example, can affect feelings about how individuals react to being in conflict—even influencing whether they will address the conflict in the open at all. Leaders need to be prepared for and adapt to cultural variations. For example, in collectivist cultures like those in China and Japan, saving face is paramount. Thus, in such cultures before you can resolve the issues in conflict, you need to address the face issues of the parties involved in the conflict first. Confrontation is frowned upon because it can disrupt social harmony, and thus, they aim to resolve disagreements in private. The Chinese and the Japanese will use silence as a means of avoiding direct conflict, relying on nonverbal cues to express their disapproval. In contrast, in individualistic cultures such as the United States, conflict tends to be related to individual goals and is viewed as a part of competition and self-expression. However, when engaged in conflict with collectivists, the advice is to "use deep-level silence, deliberate pauses, and patient conversational turn taking."[19] By separating positions from people, and focusing on issues, you also help preserve face and protect egos.

Similarly, gender can play a role in how individuals approach and resolve disagreements, with men tending to compete and argue and women more comfortable seeking consensus.[20] Yet, overall, men and women in the United States approach conflict more similarly than differently.

Post It: Imagineering a Better Way

How can we use language as an ally in resolving conflicts? The words we use can enhance or impede collaboration. According to conflict theorists William Wilmot and Joyce Hocker the following statements are among collaboration facilitators:

> This is a problem we haven't had to face before. I'm sure we can work it out.
>
> What is it that you were most hoping for?
>
> I want to postpone making a decision until our next meeting. Today I want to explore all the options open to us.
>
> Let's get an example of economic preparedness for an objective source.
>
> I understand why you want to split the difference, but let's try for some creative alternatives.
>
> Your threat tells me how vital this point is to you, but it will work better with me not to threaten. Can we back this up and come at it another way?
>
> I see you think this is the best solution. Let's see if we can each be satisfied with the decision.[21]

Explain how the preceding statements discourage competing while encouraging the search for creative options.

So, healthy relationships, no matter what the status of the people involved, will as a matter of course experience interpersonal conflict. What is important to remember is that conflict and negative emotions are not synonyms. Constructive conflict involves perspective sharing, and perspective sharing promotes problem solving. Dialogue, not monologue, facilitates conflict resolution.[22]

LOOK BACK

Reread the opening poem. How would you now answer the question the speaker asks?

Key Terms

Accommodator (170)

Avoider (170)

Competitive forcer (170)

Compromiser (170)

Concurrence seeking (174)

Conflict (162)

Conflict grid (170)

Groupthink (175)

Problem-solving collaborator (171)

Role reversal (168)

Notes

1. For more information, see John Gapper, "Why Bono Didn't Save Spider-Man," *Financial Times* (June 16, 2011): 11; Patrick Healy, "Taymor Tries to Reclaim a Reputation," *New York Times* (June 20, 2011): C1, C5; and Tim Hartford, *Adapt: Why Success Always Starts With Failure* (New York: Farrar, Straus, and Giroux, 2011).

2. Michael Smerconish, "Christie's Moment to Run for President Is Now," *Record* (June 30, 2011): A21.

3. See, for example, W. W. Wilmot and J. Hocker, *Interpersonal Conflict,* 8th ed. (New York: McGraw-Hill, 2011).

4. See Dudley D. Cahn and Ruth Anna Abigail, *Managing Conflict Through Communication,* 3rd ed. (Boston: Pearson/Allyn & Bacon, 2007).

5. Warren Bennis, *On Becoming a Leader* (Reading, MA: Addison-Wesley, 1989), 119.

6. Adapted from an exercise in David W. Johnson and Frank P. Johnson, *Joining Together,* 10th ed. (Upper Saddle River, NJ: Pearson, 2009), 320–23.

7. Adapted from Aesop's Fables.

8. See B. Schultz, "Argumentativeness: Its Effect in Group Decision Making and its Role in Leadership Perception," *Communication Quarterly* 30 (1982): 368–75; D. Infante, *Arguing Constructively* (Prospect Heights, IL: Waveland Press, 1988); and D. Infante and A. Rancer, "Argumentativeness and Verbal Aggressiveness: A Review of Recent Theory and Research," in B. Burleson, ed., *Communication Yearbook 19* (Thousand Oaks, CA: Sage, 1988), 219–351.

9. Robert Blake and Jane Mouton, "The Fifth Achievement," *Journal of Applied Behavioral Science* 6 (1970): 413–26.

10. See, for example, Alan Filley, *Interpersonal Conflict Resolution* (Glenview, IL: Scott, Foresman, 1975).

11. See, for example, J. M. Gottman, *The Marriage Clinic: A Scientifically Based Marital Therapy* (New York: W.W. Norton, 1999).

12. See, for example, D. M. Smith, *How Great Teams Turn Conflict Into Strength* (New York: Penguin Group, 2008); and John G. Oetzel and Stella Ting-Toomey, eds., *The SAGE Handbook of Conflict Communication* (Thousand Oaks, CA: Sage, 2006).

13. R. Walton, *Managing Conflict* (Reading, MA: Addison-Wesley, 1987).

14. See I. Janis, *Victims of Groupthink* (Boston: Houghton Mifflin, 1972); and I. Janis, *Groupthink* (Boston: Houghton Mifflin, 1982).

15. See, for example, R. Y. Hirokawa, D. S. Gouran, and A. Martz, "Understanding the Sources of Faulty Group Decision Making: A Lesson From the Challenger Disaster," *Small Group Behavior* 19 (1988): 411–33; D. Jehl, "Panel Unanimous: 'Groupthink' Backed Prewar Assumptions, Report Concludes," *New York Times* (July 10, 2004): A1; and *The 9/11 Commission Report: Final Report of the National Commission on Terrorist Attacks Upon the United States* (Washington, DC: National Commission on Terrorist Attacks, 2004).

16. Pam Luecke, "Nation Goes On Its Merry Way to Ruin," *New York Times* (June 28, 2011): C6; and Gretchen Morgenson and Joshua Rosner, *Reckless Endangerment: How Outsized Ambition, Greed, and Corruption Led to Economic Armageddon* (New York: Times Books, 2011).

17. Sabrina Tavernise, "Mine Owners Misled Inspectors Before Blast, Investigators Say," *New York Times* (June 30, 2011): A14.

18. T. Postemes, R. Spears, and S. Cihangir, "Quality of Decision Making and Group Norms," *Journal of Personality and Social Psychology* 80: 918–30.

19. S. Ting-Toomey, "Managing Intercultural Conflicts Effectively," in L. A. Samovar and R. E. Porter, eds., *Intercultural Communication: A Reader,* 9th ed. (Belmont, CA: Wadsworth, 2000).

20. D. Tannen, *You Just Don't Understand: Women and Men in Conversation* (New York: William Morrow, 1990).

21. See William Wilmot and Joyce Hocker, *Interpersonal Conflict,* 8th ed. (New York: McGraw-Hill, 2011), 265–66.

22. S. W. Littlejohn and K. Domenici, *Engaging Communication in Conflict: Systematic Practice* (Thousand Oaks, CA: Sage, 2001), 44–45.

You have power.

I want power.

When I am power-less

You feel power-full

Why are you so power hungry?

10

ESTABLISHING AND SHARING POWER

T his chapter is about **power**—a word that researcher Rosabeth Moss Kanter once said was "America's last dirty word."[1] Kanter believed that Americans found it easier to talk about money and sex than power. But that was over three decades ago, and today things are different. Power, so to speak, is now the name of the game. We have power grabs and power plays, people who are power hungry and people who shirk power. The dynamics of power intrigue us. Whatever your views about power, power helps leaders get things done.

LOOKING FOR POWER

Power, authority, and influence are related. In the armed forces, for example, a common saying is that "rank has its privileges." There are officers' quarters and officers' clubs that are separate and distinct from those frequented by non-commissioned soldiers. A noncommissioned soldier always salutes an officer first. The officer returns the salute.

Similarly, George Orwell in his classic fable *Animal Farm* reveals how even in a system that is supposedly egalitarian and based on the maxim that "all animals are equal," those who assume leadership roles—in Orwell's story, the pigs—are quick to take advantage of the others by assigning animals who are not pigs to complete the hardest chores, while claiming the most comfortable quarters on the farm as the pigs' personal domain. The pigs, to the horror of the other animals, soon reveal that "some animals are more equal than others."

Thus, when you have status and power, it is not long before you believe that you deserve to be treated differently from the rank and file—that your privileged position and its inherent status bring with them the promise of perks or favorable treatment. Is this the story of power? The answer is sometimes, but certainly not always.

Power and leadership appear to be interdependent; that is, they work hand in hand. Some leaders use power for good while others abuse it. To the extent they are able to exert influence followers also can exert power. When this occurs, leaders and followers effectively share leadership. Becoming aware of how influential you can be is important for performing leadership functions, being perceived as demonstrating leadership, and sharing leadership.

In this chapter, we explore the nature and bases of power, its potential to be used constructively and destructively, as well as the effects of altering the balance of power and the dangers inherent in power plays.

> **Power is influence!**

What Is Power?

You may know it when you see it, but can you define power in your own words? Who would you identify as a powerful person? Who would you identify as a powerless person? Which type of person would you like to be?

The renowned sociologist Max Weber defined power as "the probability that one actor within a social relationship will be in a position to carry out his [or her] own will despite resistance."[2] Years later, people perceived power to be the ability to get things done, the ability to harness resources to achieve a goal.[3] Today, we see power as the ability to influence others—to influence their thoughts, values, and/or behavior. There can be no leadership without power because the leader's role is to persuade others to follow so that together, leaders and followers can create and achieve shared goals. Thus, leadership and power are inextricably linked. In fact, it is difficult to think of a leader without also thinking about the leader's power.[4] Let's think about that now.

Self-Reflection: Looking In and Out

This exercise gives you the chance to reflect on power as a leadership competency.

First, what images come to mind when you think of power? Write down each image you come up with. Label each of your images as positive or negative.

Second, compile a list of five people you see as being powerful. What, in your opinion, makes the people on your list powerful? Where do you think their power comes from? Identify how you have seen them use their power, and imagine how each would react were she or he to lose power.

Third, explain how you conceive of power. That is, in your opinion, is power a personal quality, earned, given, or a combination of factors? Also identify when you feel most and least powerful, a time when you used your power in a way you believe appropriate, and a time when you felt that you misused or abused the power you had.

Finally, using a scale of 1 to 10 where *1* represents "having no power at all" and *10* being "all powerful," rate how powerful (or powerless) you currently perceive yourself to be. Explain your reasons for rating yourself as you did.

How do leaders use power to convince others to do what they want? What means do they employ to get others to change? How do leaders persuade people to follow their lead? How have leaders sought to influence you? How did they use their power on you? Certainly, authority legitimizes power. Sometimes those in authority use coercive threats (fear) or inducements (forms of payment) to manipulate others. Adolph Hitler, Jim Jones, David Koresh, and Osama Bin Laden were leaders who used coercive power. Lobbyists, on the other hand, rely on inducements. Other times, leaders issue commands, like those given by generals to the troops. While these may work, what works best is attracting rather than manipulating, getting people to buy into values, rather than commanding them to do so, and getting them to genuinely like and embrace the goals, rather than paying them for their support. Command power coerces us to change what we do, inducement power convinces us to give in for a payoff, while attraction power shapes what others want from us much more subtly. Of course, "in the real world" inducements and attraction may work in concert. For example, the government may try to persuade young people not to take drugs by running ads featuring admired celebrities, but if this fails, they still have the power of the law behind them. Of course, followers have similar options. They can resist, they can lead in a different direction, or they can go along with the leader, effectively empowering him or her.

The Duality of Power

Most of us have dual roles—we are both leaders and followers depending on the situation and the context.[5] We lead and follow in all directions—functioning similar to a compass. Richard Haass put it this way: "North represents those for whom you work. To the south are those who work for you. East stands for colleagues, those in your organization with whom you work. West represents those outside your organization who have the potential to affect matters that affect you."[6]

Leaders need to attract and persuade people all around them and be in tune with their concerns. For example, in June 2011, political aides spoke of President Obama's attitude toward gay marriage as "evolving." Obama was determining where his "followers" were trending and adjusting his attitude accordingly. Thus, followers can often lead the leader. Additionally, in our age of openness, leaders are acknowledging that "the more power you give away, the more power you have." Recognizing the power of followers and sharing information with them grows the leader-follower relationship. [7]

WHERE DOES POWER COME FROM?

People throughout the organization exercise power, not just those at the top of the organizational hierarchy. In other words, leaders do not have to have formal authority to exert power. A classic work on the sources of power is French and Raven's study of the bases of social power.[8] French and Raven conceived of power as emanating from within a dyadic relationship, one composed of an influencer and the person influenced. They identified five power bases: *referent* (power derived from the followers' identification with and liking for the leader), *expert* (power based on the followers' perception of the leader's competence), *legitimate* (power derived from status or position), *reward* (power based on the ability of the leader to give rewards to followers), and *coercive* (power based on the leader's ability to punish followers). Let us explore each of these types in more detail.

Referent Power

This kind of power is a result of others wanting to identify with the person in power. They perceive the individual as attractive and possessing valuable resources or personal qualities. You possess **referent power** if people like you. We give more credence to advice given by persons we admire, identify with, and want to be like. Charismatic individuals have **referent power**; because people are attracted to them, they willingly are led by them.

Type of Power	Where It Comes From
Referent	The ability to attract people
Expert	Knowledge and expertise
Legitimate	Position and role
Reward	Control of resources
Coercive	The ability to threaten or punish

Expert Power

Have you ever heard the line "Knowledge is power"? **Expert power** is a result of others attributing knowledge and expertise to the power source. Expert power rests with a person. Individuals bestow power on this person because they find him or her to be credible, trustworthy, and relevant. In other words, the person has the right credentials, a reputation for honesty, and information that is useful for the situation they are facing. We pay more attention to the knowledgeable person than to those whom we perceive as being less informed. Keep in mind that being an expert is not sufficient; to wield this type of power others must perceive you as one. Over time, people become better at recognizing and yielding to the strengths of different individuals they work with.

Legitimate Power

Legitimate power is akin to authority. It is due to the position or role the person occupies with others feeling obliged to accept and respond to his or her influence. Thus, if someone appoints you to a position, gives you a title, or you are elected to an office, your position gives you the power to influence others. Others will go along with you because of the position you occupy. In other words, they feel duty bound to follow your direction.

Reward Power

This source of power depends on the person in power having the ability and resources to dole out rewards that others place value upon. If you can grant others favors, invest in them, or give other rewards, including social approval or praise, you have more power than people who lack the ability to reward others. Reward power rests on the ability to deliver positive consequences or remove negative ones in response to exhibited behavior. If you can deliver a reward that no one else has the power to deliver, your perceived power rises. But you have to know where to draw the line. When too many rewards are delivered, those receiving them may begin to feel bribed.

Coercive Power

Fear of undesirable consequences is the source of this kind of power. Coercive power gets people to do things against their will. The person who possesses coercive power can inflict punishment and threaten others in order to get them to conform. If you can cut someone's salary, fire them, or force them to do something they prefer not doing, you have coercive power—that is, as long as people believe you will follow through and execute your threat. Otherwise it will not function as a viable power source.

Legitimate, reward, and coercive power are seen as a result of the position power of the leader, while referent power and expert power are perceived to be a result of the leader's personal power, that is, a result of followers liking and perceiving the leader as knowledgeable. Because both leaders and followers use power to promote their goals, the power source and how power is used reveal much about the leader-follower relationship.

Observation: Watch and Learn

Which of the following types of power have you used on others or have others used on you: referent, expert, legitimate, reward, and coercive? Complete the following self-survey for each power type:

Example of _____ power in action:

Effect on self: _____

Effect on others: _____

How might you use this form of power to attain your vision in the future? Which type(s) of power do you use most frequently? Which do you personally find most effective? Which do you find most satisfying? Which do you believe imposes limits on the user? Which do you believe creates the most opportunities for the user?

POWER HAS COSTS AND BENEFITS

According to **social exchange theory,** leaders should seek to maintain good relationships with followers so that they function as their allies.[9] Leaders help foster good relations by using their reward power and their ability to share valuable resources, contributing to others depending on them and wanting to work with or for them. When the leader has something to offer, he or she gains power in others' eyes. Thus, resources and power go together. Leaders also work at cultivating support. They do this, in part, by sharing credit, granting favors, and helping others feel needed and important. When leaders lose the support of followers, however, followers can similarly use their coercive power to play "punish the leader"—perhaps by not volunteering for task forces or voting for their competitor in the case of a politician.

When deciding which "power tool" to use, you need to weigh the advantages of the form of power you

> A wise leader is restrained in using power.

are favoring against it drawbacks. For example, reward power tends to boost performance while typically increasing costs. Legitimate power bows to the organizational hierarchy and is usually effective for eliciting obedience but is likely to decrease both task performance and satisfaction in followers. Expert power, in contrast, tends to increase task performance and satisfaction in followers but is only effective when followers share the leader's goals. Similarly, referent power increases both task performance and satisfaction in followers but becomes less effective if used too frequently plus it can take significant time to develop. The effective use of power requires a delicate balance.

WHEN POWER IS UNEQUAL: THE HIGHS AND LOWS OF POWER

Can individuals have too much power? Does power really corrupt? What are the negatives of power? Considering the differences between high- and low-power people can provide some insight.

High-power people have considerable capacity for affecting the outcomes of others. Low-power people believe themselves to have scant capacity for exerting such influence. Large power differentials, especially when the high-power person believes in a right to power, increase the chances that the use of power will be destructive and contribute to acts of moral hypocrisy. Once you accumulate power and let the feeling of entitlement get to you, immoral behavior may soon follow.[10]

High-power people perceive themselves, situations, and opportunities different from low-power people. They have an inflated opinion of themselves, typically think themselves more capable than they are, and also usually do not have a clear understanding of how low-power people perceive them.[11] They believe low-power people like and admire them and would never hide information from them. When low-power people do not defer to high-power people—daring to question their authority—high-power people are insulted and outraged, believing that deference and reverence are due them. Additionally, high-power people are likely to devalue low-power people; contending that low-power people should "know their place." High-power people tend to try to intimidate low-power people, rejecting requests for change and working to maintain the status quo in order to protect their superior power. Such behavior often leads to the institutionalization of injustices against persons with low power. Being treated as incapable and helpless can make one *feel* incapable and helpless, contributing to the high-power person's continued oppression and dominance over the low-power person.

Bullies and Power Plays

What do you do with the power you have? According to psychologist David McClelland, people with a high need for power can make effective leaders—but there is a caveat: this is so only if they also develop the ability to restrain the use of their power.[12] For example, Ruth J. Simmons, who was the president of Brown University for over a decade, realized that how she sought to solve problems and interact with others got in the way of achieving her goals. Once she realized that she could achieve more by working amiably with people rather than trying to embarrass them by publicly pointing out their deficiencies, she was able to become a more effective leader. According to Simmons, "You can get a lot more done if people have a sense that you respect them, and that you listen to them."[13]

Workplace bullies develop no such restraint. Bullying others—repeatedly attempting to dominate and humiliate them—while a too common human behavior—is usually counterproductive because of its tendency to decrease rather than boost performance.[14] In fact, when entrenched, a culture of bullying can actually destroy a company. According to Daniel Goleman, leaders who are bullies need to reform before their behavior catches up with them.[15]

What would you tell the characters in this cartoon about how to use power? Which character do you believe is the bully? Why?

DILBERT © 2011 Scott Adams. Used by permission of UNIVERSAL UCLICK. All rights reserved.

Workplace bullying is a prime example of misusing power. It is characterized by the persistent intimidation and degradation, or undermining, of one or more persons via hostile and aggressive communication such as making false accusations, harshly criticizing, disregarding a person's feelings, giving the silent treatment, yelling and verbally abusing a person in front of others, misusing confidential information, and sabotaging on-the-job performance. Over 50% of employees surveyed report being affected by workplace bullying either as its perpetrator, the target, or a witness.[16]

Bullies promote their own power at others' expense; they equate power with force, are selfish, and move against others. Their appetite for control is insatiable. The more power they feel they have, the more they want power and the more they seek it. Because they see their targets as subservient to them, bullies tend to incite destructive conflicts, maximizing the power differences between themselves and those they bully and creating enemies in the process.[17] It is also possible, of course, for employees and leaders to bully one of their own. The term *mobbing* connotes a group of coworkers targeting another worker.[18] However, more typically, it is the inequitable power balance between the bully and bullied that increases the potential for the bully to use power destructively.

Theory Into Practice

From the Mouth of Machiavelli

According to Machiavelli, a prince (the person in power) should be *feared* not *loved*. Do you agree?

While some studies have found a negative correlation between manipulation, exploitation, and deceitful behavior (also known as *Machiavellianism*) and leadership outcomes, others have found a positive relationship. Machiavelli treated fear and love as opposites. But are they? They are not. Hatred, not fear, is the opposite of love. And hatred, according to Machiavelli, was not to be viewed as an effective leadership tool. In fact, he advised that leaders should avoid being hated at all costs.

So, how controlling should the leader be?[19] Some leaders throw their weight around relying on coercion, threatening and bullying followers into place and counting on fear and intimidation to help them obtain their objectives. Other leaders, however, see no need to be feared, relying on softer means such as inspiration to attract followers to support them and their goals. Smart power is not merely the use of hard power but an amalgam of hard and soft power, and it appears to work. A wise leader, it seems, twists neither minds nor arms.

Identify a leader who is or was hated. What was she or he able to accomplish? What do you believe his or her legacy to be?

Identify a leader who is or was a bully. What tactics did she or he use? How did others respond?

Identify a leader whom you believe uses smart power. What has she or he been able to accomplish? What do you believe his or her legacy to be?

EMPOWERMENT

Empowerment not only flattens an organization's structure and empowers followers, but indirectly it also enhances the leader's power at the same time that it inhibits the leader's abuse of power. In addition to increasing worker job satisfaction and performance, the sharing of power also goes a long way toward fostering employee cooperation and collaboration. When power is shared with them, the group becomes more than the sum of its parts, actively participating in decision making and achieving more than any one person could on his or her own. Additionally, by facilitating the personal growth and development of employees, the sharing of power also precipitates their innovativeness and makes them less fearful of change because they feel they own it. According to Henry Sims and Charles Manz, leaders who empower others by helping them learn to lead themselves are "super-leaders."[20] Super-leaders foster a climate conducive to independent thought and action.

What kinds of leaders refuse to share power? Those who are so taken with power that they expect others to absolutely obey their every command, as well as those who are so insecure that they feel they have to keep all the power to maintain their position and prestige in the eyes of others, like the bullies we spoke of earlier.

> **Empowering means sharing power.**

SELF-LEADERSHIP

Self-leadership differs from empowerment. In empowerment, the leader is the catalyst; in self-leadership followers learn to lead themselves independently of an authority. Self-leadership requires self-discipline and self-confidence, goal setting and self-talk, and self-monitoring and assessment.

Self-discipline means you know when it is time to work and not play. You know how to create an environment conducive to working. You know how to avoid distractions and what you need to do to produce quality work. One key to self-discipline is passion for the work you need to do—that positive feeling that comes from doing something you genuinely care about and feel is important.

Goal setting is another story. Many of us compose "to do" lists. Others of us participate in the creation of one-, five-, or ten-year plans. Whatever the nature of the project or goal, it becomes easier if we break it down into steps, with each step having a due date and a benchmark to indicate its accomplishment. Self-talk can ease the way. When you face a bump on the way to a goal, don't get down on yourself or become negative. Instead, tell yourself that if you prevail, you will succeed.

People who lead themselves do not require or anticipate feedback from superiors; rather, they assess their own actions, rewarding or withholding a reward from themselves depending on how well they conclude they are doing. Self-leaders do not require others to tell them if they are succeeding. They know and if necessary take corrective action.

Working It Out: Alone or Together

Create four scenarios: the first in which the leader succeeds in empowering followers, the second in which she or he tries but fails to empower them, the third in which the leader chooses to selfishly horde resources so that she or he maintains all power for himself or herself, and the last in which self-leaders use self-leadership strategies.

Some of your scenarios should reveal what leaders do to impede feelings of powerlessness: what they do to prepare and motivate followers and themselves to take a more active role toward their responsibilities, demonstrating their willingness to assume ownership and power. Other scenarios should reveal what leaders do to encourage feelings of powerlessness: how leaders fail in shifting the locus of the decision-making authority, either because they do not provide their workers and themselves with needed emotional support or resources, do not demonstrate their confidence in their workers or themselves, do not model the way effectively, and/or do not structure tasks in ways that ensure their workers' and own success.

Empowering others and developing self-leaders spur the efforts of employees and their loyalty. They are what we call examples of power being used smartly. As we see, power can be expanded and shared. It can be exerted by anyone able to influence others. It need not be conceived as a zero-sum resource, with the more power one party has the less power that is available to others. Nor should it be conceived of as a commodity to be hoarded or employed solely to promote one's own success. Instead, power can promote both the interdependence and independence of individuals and leaders.

Post It: Imagineering a Better Way

Using materials of your own choosing, create a collage representing the way you believe power ought to be used. Create a second collage representing the way high-power people or bullies use power. Finally, create a third collage representing the way you perceive a leader in your college or community to use power. Then identify the differences and similarities in the three collages.

Power gives leaders the potential to affect outcomes. It does the same for followers and other stakeholders. We have power over another to the extent we are able to exert control over consequences we face. Having power, being comfortable with power, and sharing power are not one and the same thing. Power is in all of our hands. We need to find ways to balance it. The leader's responsibility is to use, and get others to use, power wisely. How will you exercise power from here on in?

LOOK BACK

Reread the poem at the opening of this chapter. How would you now answer the question the speaker asks? What advice would you offer to resolve power plays?

Key Terms

Attraction power (185)

Coercive power (185)

Command power (185)

Empowerment (192)

Expert power (187)

Inducement power (185)

Legitimate power (187)

Power (183)

Referent power (187)

Reward power (188)

Self-leadership (193)

Social exchange theory (189)

Workplace bullying (191)

Notes

1. Rosabeth Moss Kanter, "Power Failure in Management Circuits," *Harvard Business Review* (July-August 1979): 65.

2. Max Weber, *The Theory of Social and Economic Organization,* translated and edited by A. M. Henderson and Talcott Parsons (New York: The Free Press, 1947), 152.

3. David Krackhardt, "Assessing the Political Landscape: Structure, Cognition, and Power in Organizations," *Administrative Science Quarterly* 35 (1990): 343.

4. For example, see Joseph S. Nye, Jr., *The Powers to Lead* (New York: Oxford University Press, 2008).

5. Ronald A. Heifetz, *Leadership Without Easy Answers* (Cambridge, MA: Belknap Press of Harvard University Press, 1994); and Robert E. Kelley, *The Power of Followership: How to Create Leaders People Want to Follow, and Followers Who Lead Themselves* (New York: Doubleday/Currency, 1992).

6. Richard N. Haass, *The Bureaucratic Entrepreneur: How to Be Effective in Any Unruly Organization* (Washington, DC: Brookings Institution Press, 1999), 2.

7. Charlene Li, *Open Leadership: How Social Technology Can Transform the Way You Lead* (San Francisco: Jossey-Bass, 2010), 24.

8. J. R. French Jr. and B. Raven, "The Bases of Social Power," in D. Cartwright, ed., *Studies in Social Power* (Ann Arbor, MI: Institute for Social Research, 1959); and J. R. French Jr. and B. Raven, "The Bases of Social Power," in D. Cartwright, ed., *Group Dynamics: Research and Theory* (New York: Harper & Row), 259–69.

9. See J. W. Thibault and H. H. Kelley, *Interpersonal Relations: A Theory of Interdependence* (New York: John Wiley, 1978).

10. See Joris Lammers, Diederik A. Stapel, and Adam D. Galinsky, "Power Increases Hypocrisy: Moralizing in Reasoning, Immorality in Behavior," *Psychological Science* 21(5) (2010): 737–44.

11. See R. Baumeister, L. Smart, and J. Boden, "Relation of Threatened Egotism to Violence and Aggression: The Dark Side of High Self-Esteem," *Psychological Review* 103 (1996): 5–33; and M. Harris and J. Schaubroeck, "A Meta-Analysis of Self-Supervisor, Self-Peer, and Peer-Supervisor Ratings," *Personnel Psychology* 41 (1988): 43–62.

12. David C. McClelland and David H. Burnham, "Power Is the Great Motivator," *Harvard Business Review* 54(2) (March-April, 1976): 100–10.

13. Adam Bryant, "Corner Office: Ruth J. Simmons," *New York Times* (December 4, 2011): BU2.

14. Michael G. Harvey, Joyce T. Heames, R. Glenn Richey, and Nancy Leonard, "Bullying: From the Playground to the Boardroom," *Journal of Leadership and Organizational Studies* 12(4) (2006): 1–11.

15. See Daniel Goleman, Richard Boyatzis, and Annie McKee, *Primal Leadership: Learning to Lead With Emotional Intelligence* (Boston: Harvard Business School Press, 2002), 45.

16. For more information, see the Workplace Bullying Institute and their 2010 Zogby survey: www.workplacebullying.org/wbiresearch/2010-wbi-national-survey/.

17. See David R. Hawkins, *Power vs. Force: The Hidden Determinants of Human Behavior* (Carlsbad, CA: Hay House, 2002), 132–34.

18. *Workplace Bullying and Disruptive Behavior: What Everyone Needs to Know*, Report # 87–2-2011 (Washington State Department of Labor & Industries, April 2011).

19. See Niccolo Machiavelli, *The Prince* (New York: New American Library, 1952); Michael G. Harvey, Joyce T. Heames, R. Glenn Richey, and Nancy Leonard, "Bullying: From the Playground to the Boardroom," *Journal of Leadership and Organizational*

Studies 12(4) (2006): 1–11; Katrina Bedell, Samuel Hunter, Amanda Angie, and Andrew Vert, "A Historiometric Examination of Machiavellianism and a New Taxonomy of Leadership," *Journal of Leadership and Organizational Studies* 12(4) (2006): 50–72; and Ronald J. Deluga, "American Presidential Machiavellianism: Implications for Charismatic Leadership and Rated Performance," *Leadership Quarterly* 12 (2001): 339–63.

20. See, for example, C. C. Manz and H. P. Sims, Jr. *The New Superleadership: Leading Others to Lead Themselves* (San Francisco: Berrett-Hoehler, 2001); and C. C. Manz and C. P. Neck, *Mastering Self-Leadership: Empowering Yourself for Personal Excellence* (Upper Saddle River, NJ: Prentice Hall, 1999).

Stockbyte/Stockbyte/Thinkstock

Do you have a problem?
What? You say it's my problem.
I don't think so.
You're sure, you say.
A problem never belongs
To one person only.

11

PROMOTING COLLABORATIVE PROBLEM SOLVING

In August 2010, the San Jose mine in Chile caved in, trapping 33 men deep underground. Shift foreman Luis Urzua was the group's leader. He and some of the other men scouted the damaged tunnel and confirmed what all feared—there was no way out.

Realizing their survival would depend on their working together as a team, Urzua organized the men into work groups; they established rules, deciding that all their decisions would be made by majority vote. Once engineers on the surface contacted the men, establishing their location, Urzua helped coordinate their rescue efforts. The men remained underground for 70 days before their rescuers succeeded in bringing them up from what could have become their tomb. When Urzua finally emerged from the mine, Luis exclaimed, "It has been a bit of a long shift."[1] The rescue effort had been a collaborative effort of teams working above and below the ground.

The efforts of these teams help illustrate a number of key principles. First, having strong group identification and the recognition that they share a common fate promoted each team's efforts, improving motivation and increasing cooperation. Second, setting and monitoring group norms establishing the appropriateness of member behavior facilitated team member interaction and enhanced their ability to work together.

How do you believe you would have fared were you a member of either the above- or below-ground team?

Generally, how do you feel about working in teams? What teams are you currently a member of? What teams do you aspire to be a member of? What teams would you like to lead? How do you know when a team you are on is effective? Even more importantly, why do some students react negatively when told they will be working in teams? For example, how often do you or someone you know say something like, "I hate working in teams!" Or "Why does this have to be a team project?" What can you do to ensure that you or those with whom you work don't feel this way and that the teams you lead or are a member of excel?

These are some of the questions we explore in this chapter. But first we have to clarify what a team is.

WHAT DO WE MEAN BY *TEAM?*

Teams come in all shapes and sizes. For example, every organization likely has task forces, committees, project teams, quality teams, and improvement teams. To ensure the success of teams we are on, we need to understand their nature. For our purposes, a *team* is a group of behaviorally integrated, interdependent but diverse people who come together for a reasonably sustained period of time to share information, collaborate, make decisions, and problem solve.[2]

Sometimes a leader builds a team by convincing those who may not need or want to work together that all will benefit if they do. Other times, a pressing situation or problem presents the impetus for forming a team. And still other times, organizations simply desire to build collaborative communities charged with focusing on their shared purposes.[3] For example, as a result of their working together on surgical teams, doctors and nurses have succeeded in cutting the death rate from surgery by 18%. Taking their cue from the aviation industry in which airplane crews meet to anticipate and prepare for potential safety risks, surgical teams determined that if they held briefings and debriefings before and after each operation, they better prepared themselves to recognize red flags, challenge each other about safety risks, and develop pre- and postsurgical checklists helping to avoid medical team failures.[4]

As Peter Loscher, the president and chief executive of Siemens, notes, "Business is about lining up a leadership team or a group of people and you rally them behind a course or a certain direction. But the underlying strength is the trust within the team—so that you are no longer just playing individually at your best, but you're also trying to understand what you can do to make the team better."[5]

> **Leaders are team builders.**

Whatever a team's reason for being, in order for a team to maintain itself and realize its goals, the team's members need to agree on how to work together—and for this to occur, they need to figure out how best to relate to one another. For instance, a person used to having others perceive him or her as a "star" may find it difficult to subsume his or her ego and yield or give credit to his or her team members, or as the saying goes, "There is no *I* in team."

Part of the leader's role when it comes to teams is to facilitate their operation by creating conditions and a sense of stability that allows the team's members to work together collaboratively and do great work whatever the task. A prime reason we use teams is to achieve **synergy**—the idea that together a team can produce better results, better solutions, than any person can working alone.

All teams are **groups,** but not all groups are teams. Like groups, teams are composed of people who interact with one another, occupy certain roles with respect to one another, and cooperate to accomplish goals. But by definition, teams also contain individuals who have diverse skills and thus are able to bring different resources to a problem or task. According to Linda Lausell Bryant, executive director of Inwood House in New York, an organization that focuses on the health issues of teenagers, the members of a team also have roles to play, need to perform those roles to the best of their abilities, and at the same time have to understand each other's roles.[6] Thus, it follows that for a team to succeed, its members must pool their abilities, knowledge, and insights to solve problems and make decisions that are better than any single individual on the team could have produced acting independently.

Self-Reflection: Looking In and Out

Use the following inventory to assess your attitude toward teams, your beliefs about your role in them, and your conceptions of how responsible a leader is for a team's success. For each question below, give yourself a score ranging from 1 to 5, with *1* representing *almost never, 2* representing *rarely, 3* representing *sometimes, 4* representing *often,* and *5* representing *almost always.*

Attitude toward team:

1. I'd rather work in concert with others than independently. _____

2. I enjoy working with people whose backgrounds, interests, and experiences are different from my own. _____

3. I like to hear all perspectives before making a decision. _____

4. I believe a team outperforms what I can do on my own. _____

5. A team with a clearly defined goal will outperform other teams. _____

6. Team goals are more important than individual goals. _____

7. Teams need resources to get the job done. _____

Beliefs about my role:

1. I prefer to initiate ideas or actions. _____

2. I facilitate the introduction of information. _____

3. I summarize and pull ideas together. _____

4. I keep the team focused on its goal. _____

5. I seek to determine if the team is making progress. _____

6. I encourage team members, supporting their efforts. _____

7. I diffuse member conflicts. _____

8. I clarify the goal. _____

9. I seek common ground. _____

10. I work to ensure all have a voice and are listened to. _____

11. One person should never be the focus of the group's attention. _____

12. Hostility is an inappropriate response to not getting one's way. _____

13. Disengaging is an inappropriate response to experiencing difficulty. _____

Beliefs about the leader's role:

1. Members can perform team and leadership functions simultaneously. _____

2. Leaders track team performance. _____

3. Leaders may need to intervene to resolve issues. _____

4. Leaders create conditions conducive to teamwork. _____

5. Leaders build team member confidence. _____

6. Leaders set and clarify the team's goals. _____

Use your score in each section as an indication of how highly you value team, individual, and leader performance. The items on which you scored a *1* or a *2* reveal potential areas of concern or weakness. The higher your scores, the more likely it is that you understand the importance of a collaborative work, the kinds of roles you should be prepared to assume, and the part leaders play in ensuring the team's success.

WHY USE A TEAM?

Leaders build teams to facilitate problem solving and decision making. Their goal is to bring together persons who can contribute a range of perspectives and an array of diverse ideas. In order to accomplish this, some leaders are secure enough to place former rivals on their teams like President Obama did when he appointed Hillary Clinton to his cabinet, asked Joe Biden to be his vice president, and named Republican Jon Huntsman Jr. U.S. ambassador to China, knowing full well that Huntsman might run against him in the next election, which Huntsman did when he entered the Republican primary.

Potential Advantages of Using a Team

What are the advantages of the team when it comes to decision making and problem solving?

First, a team makes it possible for people with different information and diverse perspectives to pool their resources—increasing the likelihood that they will produce effective solutions. Putting too many members with homogeneous characteristics and similar backgrounds on a team actually makes coming up with sound solutions less likely. Why? Diversity, not similarity, spurs debate and dialogue.

Second, working on a team increases each individual's motivation to find a solution, and members also display more commitment to the solution once it is agreed to.

Third, it is easier for a team than an individual to identify and filter out errors before they become costly or do harm. When they work well, and team members are unafraid to speak their minds, teams more than individuals are better equipped to predict difficulties, identify weaknesses, assess consequences, and explore possibilities.

Fourth, because a number of people came together and reached one conclusion, the decisions a team produces tend to be better received than they would be if a single individual put them forth. Finally, people generally find it more rewarding to work on teams.

> A team with synergy outperforms its individual members.

Potential Disadvantages of Using a Team

Do not imagine that teams do not present disadvantages, because they do.

First, a team member can shirk his or her responsibilities by ignoring them or trying to pass them off to others. Such "free riders" or "social loafers" can prevent the team from achieving synergy unless others on the team willingly pick up their slack.

Second, the goals of an individual on the team can conflict with the team's goals. By using the team to fulfill self-oriented objectives, an individual can sabotage the team's efforts.

Third, the more forceful or powerful members of the team can dominate discussion. Some members, as we learned in the chapter on power, may hesitate to criticize the contributions of higher-status members. Thus, position and perceived power can influence whose ideas are listened to and accepted.

Fourth, the stubbornness and sense of entitlement higher-status members have can precipitate deadlock. When this occurs, the team is likely to fail in its obligation to use the knowledge and skills of all members.

Fifth, the decisions made by a team after discussion may prove riskier than the decisions any one individual would make. This occurrence is called the

risky shift. Finally, it usually takes more time for a team to reach a decision than for an individual to reach one.

How Do You Know When to Use a Team?

Given the advantages and disadvantages of a team, it makes sense to use a team when you can answer most of the following questions with a yes:

1. Does a complex problem need to be resolved?
2. Does the problem have many parts or facets?
3. Would it be unlikely for a single individual to possess all the information needed to solve the problem?
4. Would problem solving be more effective if the responsibility for problem solving were divided up?
5. Would the problem-solving process benefit from there being many potential solutions to the presented problem and not merely one?
6. Would diverse perspectives improve problem solving?
7. Is it likely that team members will engage in task-related behavior?

TEAMS DEVELOP IN STAGES

Leaders need to coach and mentor teams through their developmental stages. The primary stages of a team's development are (1) forming, (2) storming, (3) norming, (4) performing, and (5) adjourning.[7] How well a leader guides team members through these stages affects the team's effectiveness.

Stages

Forming	Meet and learn about one another
Storming	Determine how to work together
Norming	Create rules
Performing	Problem solve, perform task and maintenance functions
Adjourning	Review and reflect on accomplishments

Forming

When individuals first become members of a team, it is common for them to experience some initial confusion or uncertainty—also known as *primary tensions*. Members may be unsure about how to interact with one another and unclear about their roles on the team. During the team's **forming** stage, the primary objective of team members is to fit in and have others like them. Members make the effort to find out about one another and the group's task. Team members learn about each other, including each person's strengths and weaknesses. Once team members feel valued and accepted, they begin to identify with their team.

Storming

As members figure out how to work together, the team's **storming** stage, it is probable that team members will experience both task and relational conflicts. These conflicts, or *secondary tensions,* result from members' disagreeing or struggling to exert leadership as they try to clarify what the goals of the team are, how the team should go about achieving them, and what roles each member should play in the process. Thus, during this stage, member focus is on expressing ideas and opinions and securing a place in the team's power structure.

Norming

Gradually, members firm up roles, a team leader or leaders emerge, and the rules and structure of the team are revealed. We call this stage the **norming** stage. During the norming stage, team members solidify behavioral norms, particularly those relating to conflict management. They set the ground rules for working together. They decide how to decide. Once the team accomplishes this, it has a sense of identity with members aware of their interdependence and demonstrating more of a willingness to cooperate. When clear standards of excellence guide the team's actions, team functioning improves because members rise to meet the high expectations that are set.

Performing

During a team's **performing** stage, member focus switches to task accomplishment. Members actively problem solve, combining their skills, knowledge, and abilities to overcome obstacles and realize their goals. The ability of members to integrate individual actions and perform roles contributing to their collective success demonstrates their ability to collaborate. The extent to which members enact task- and team-building or maintenance roles, refrain from enacting self-serving (nonfunctional or dysfunctional) roles, and demonstrate the willingness to compensate for each other's weaknesses directly affects whether or not the group succeeds or fails.

Members Perform Roles

Although the role classification model created by Kenneth Benne and Paul Sheats dates back a half century, it is still commonly used to measure team member performance today.[8] The following are among the task-oriented roles members perform to realize team goals: *initiating* (the member defines a problem, suggests methods, and starts the group moving along new paths or in different directions by offering a plan); *information seeking* (the member asks for facts and information, seeking relevant data about the problem from others); *opinion seeking* (the member solicits opinion, expressions of feeling, and value); *information giving* (the member provides ideas and suggestions); *opinion giving* (the member reveals his or her feelings, beliefs, and values); *clarifying* (the member elaborates on others' ideas and tries to increase clarity and decrease confusion); *coordinating* (the member draws contributions together); *evaluating* (the member establishes standards for judging the team's solutions); and *consensus seeking* (the member checks on the state of team member agreement).

Members perform the following maintenance roles to ensure the team's smooth running: *encouraging* (the member is warm, receptive, and responsive to others and their ideas); *gatekeeping* (the member keeps communication channels open, ensuring one or two members do not dominate discussion); *harmonizing* (the member mediates differences between other members and seeks to alleviate member tensions); *compromising* (the member admits error and modifies positions to achieve group progress); and *standard setting* (the members indicates the criteria for evaluating the team's functioning and assesses whether members are satisfied with procedures being used).

In contrast to task and maintenance roles, the following self-serving roles keep the team from performing effectively: *blocking* (the member disagrees and digresses to ensure nothing is accomplished); *aggression* (the member hurls criticisms and blame at other members in an effort to inflate his or her own status); *recognition seeking* (the member boasts of his or her own accomplishments, seeking to become the focus of attention); *withdrawing* (the member daydreams, appears indifferent, or sulks); *dominating* (the member insists on getting his or her own way in an effort to control the team); *joking* (the member engages in horseplay or makes cynical remarks); *self-confessing* (the members uses team members as an audience for personal revelations); and *help seeking* (the member attempts to elicit sympathy or pity from other members).

Performance depends on goal achievement and team maintenance.

Adjourning

Finally, during the team's **adjourning** stage members review and reflect on their accomplishments, as well as where they fell short or failed, and determine how or whether the team should terminate or continue working together.

Observation: Watch and Learn

1. Choose a team you are currently a member of or were once a member of for a sustained period of time. Describes the team's development through each of its life stages, supplying an example of team and member behavior during each stage.

2. Sit in on a meeting of a campus problem-solving team. Identify your perception of the team's goal for the meeting, team norms, and member and leader behaviors that facilitated or impeded the team's progress.

3. Build a team of your own and brainstorm how to improve an aspect of life at your college. Share your plan with the appropriate campus leaders.

THE LEADER'S ROLE IN FOSTERING TEAM DEVELOPMENT

Of course, the leader's role during team development is to facilitate the group's performance strategies, keeping team members connected and helping them overcome shortcomings so that team members can proceed ultimately on a path that will allow them to complete the task and obtain objectives. Leaders facilitate this by ensuring that team members explore a full range of solutions to a problem, that they not come together prematurely when it comes to making a decision or be so focused on their diverging opinions and differences that fault lines form, splintering them into divisive or competing subgroups and ultimately making it impossible for them to come together to collaborate because of the divisions that have been forged. When leaders are alert to dangers like these, if they occur, they can intervene when necessary and work to bring the team back to focus on its task and common goals.[9]

Of course, as we learned in the chapter on conflict, some teams experience just the opposite of coming apart. Rather than falling prey to fault lines, these teams become consumed by the desire to stay together—focusing too much on achieving cohesion and unity—which contributes to their falling prey to a lack of candor and the fallacy of groupthink. Thus, in addition to helping the team bridge fault lines, the leader's task is also to ensure that team members engage in vigorous debate and, while not getting mired in that debate, also do not settle on a solution based on a false consensus. When called for, effective team leadership—including leader interventions—is essential for a team's success.

How well do you imagine the team pictured in the cartoon will function? Have you ever been on a team with members like those depicted here?

CHARACTERISTICS OF SUCCESSFUL TEAMS

When successful teams were studied, results revealed the following characteristics: effective team members, effective team relationships, effective team problem solving, effective team leadership, and an effective organizational environment.[10]

Theory Into Practice

Transitioning From a Working Group Into a Team

A working group is different from a team. While members of working groups meet to share information, discuss situations and goals, coordinate activities, and engage in problem solving and decision making, typically each member is only individually accountable and responsible for his or her individual efforts. Members of teams, in contrast, work together to produce a collective outcome or product, taking initiative in an area of expertise but sharing roles and responsibilities. Katzenback, Smith, and Donnellon are among researchers who have documented the process of transitioning from a working group to a team.[11]

The transition involves a number of stages: (1) *pseudo team* (during which the group is a team in name only, and performance initially declines); (2) *potential team* (during which performance improves due to the group's conscious efforts); (3) *real team* (during which performance continues its acceleration as members commit to being mutually accountable to their common purpose and goals); and eventually arriving at a (4) *high-performance team* (committed to sustaining success and growth).

The following are also identified as critical to a team's effectiveness: identification with the team; realization of its interdependence; minimization of power differences; feelings of closeness to and concern for one another; and a collaborative orientation.

Based on this description, which campus groups do you consider teams and why?

Why Are Some Team Members More Effective Than Others?

The most effective team members are (1) experienced and knowledgeable, (2) have their sights clearly on the task(s) they need to complete to achieve their goal, (3) assist the team in resolving difficulties, (4) promote an open exchange of ideas among team members, (5) are willing to assist others, take initiative, and act, and (6) exhibit personal confidence and engaging interpersonal skills.

Why Are Some Teams More Effective Than Others?

The most effective teams have members with strong interpersonal skills who explain their positions clearly, listen to one another, and give and receive feedback freely while maintaining strong interpersonal relationships. Research also consistently reveals that teams richer in diversity perform better and produce better results than teams not so fortunate. Thus, the leader's ability to bring together people of different cultures, backgrounds, and generations is critical.

According to CEO Bart Becht, "It doesn't matter whether I have a Pakistani, a Chinese person, a Brit, or a Turk, man or woman, sitting in the same room, or whether I have people from sales or something else, so long as I have people with different experiences—because the chance for new ideas is much greater when you have people with different backgrounds. The chance for conflict is also higher—and conflict is good per se, as long as it's constructive and gets us to the best idea."[12] Effective teams are motivated by a goal they consider to be worthwhile and important. They do not let power issues or personal agendas interfere with their focus on their goal.

Why Is Problem Solving More Effecive in Some Teams Than in Others?

Chairman and CEO of Royal Caribbean Cruises, Richard D. Fain, says, "I always find that you learn more by arguing with someone than by just agreeing with them."[13] Problem solving is most effective when members have clear goals, understand their task, work in a healthy climate encouraging of open communication, and employ a systematic, results-driven strategy facilitative of goal attainment, such as the reflective thinking framework proposed by John Dewey.[14]

Use of Reflective Thinking

The reflective-thinking framework suggests that to solve a problem teams approach it by answering the following six questions: (1) What is the problem? (2) What are the facts we know about the situation including its importance, causes, and effects? (3) What criteria must a solution meet? (4) What are possible solutions? (5) Which solution is best? and (6) How can we implement the solution? For the reflective-thinking system to work, team members need to suspend judgment and open themselves to all ideas. They need to emphasize fact finding and inquiry and appraise thoroughly all data and alternative courses of action.

Use of Brainstorming

Brainstorming is also a means teams use to facilitate the search for better ideas and solutions and promote a free flow of ideas. To ensure brainstorming's success, team members follow these guidelines. First, they suspend judgment temporarily—this is perhaps the most important aspect of brainstorming. When a member introduces an idea, others may not evaluate or criticize it. Second, members encourage freewheeling; knowing that it is easier to tame a wild idea than to invigorate an inert idea, they bring all ideas to the table, encouraging a "try anything" attitude. Third, they seek quantity of ideas by prohibiting self- or team censorship from interfering with this goal. Fourth, each team member seeks to build on, improve, or modify the ideas of others. Members mix and match ideas, forming interesting combinations. Fifth, they record all ideas so they can access ideas generated during the brainstorming session. Sixth, once the brainstorming session is completed, team members assess ideas for usefulness and applicability.[15]

> Use brainstorming to promote a free flow of ideas.

Alex Osborne, a proponent of brainstorming, has identified seven ways to look at a problem or challenge creatively. He uses the mnemonic *SCAMPER* to help prod you to remember the following strategies:

S—Substitute
C—Combine
A—Adapt
M—Modify
P—Put to another use
E—Eliminate
R—Rearrange or reverse

Using these strategies should help you think about a subject in different ways. Can you come up with an example of how using one of more of the preceding concepts facilitated the solving of a problem? For example, consider how the DVR replaced the VCR.

Prevention of Groupthink

Effective problem-solving teams also take appropriate actions to prevent groupthink; that is, they take the necessary steps to ensure that they do not place unanimous agreement above all other considerations, knowing the consequences for doing so. They similarly take steps to ensure they do not make a mismanaged decision, that is, a decision in which team members express public support for a decision that they privately oppose but fear to reveal, also known as **the Abilene paradox.**[16] By failing to accurately communicate their doubts and concerns, team members also fail to realize they have company and persist in acting in direct opposition to their beliefs. For example, while the Department of Energy aggressively promoted the idea that natural gas was the fuel of the future and politicked for allies, apparently not everyone in the Department of Energy agreed. Scores of internal e-mails expressed skepticism, even going so far as to claim the industry was setting itself up for failure. Thus, while the Department of Energy was acting on a veneer of agreement, a significant number of those involved apparently had serious hidden doubts.[17]

Why Are Some Team Leaders More Effective Than Others?

The most effective team leaders facilitate the efforts of their team by focusing on the team's goal, framing and interpreting success in terms of the collective—what the team accomplishes as opposed to the individual, encouraging a collaborative climate, building the confidence of team members, being perceived as competent, keeping their priorities straight, managing team performance, and sharing credit for organizational outcomes.

The leader monitors the team's work, in part, to ascertain if members are effectively sharing information and opinions, dealing competently with any relational issues, and

> **Who do you want on your team?**

generally performing in the team's best interests. Thus, the leader's focus is on how effectively members assume task and maintenance roles and the extent to which self-serving roles interfere with these efforts.[18] Sometimes the leader determines that team members lack the skills needed to meet the demands of the task; in this case the leader might provide members with special training. If the leader observes that interpersonal conflict is interfering with the team's functioning, he or she might step in and coach members on how to manage the task. We should note that members on the team also perform these leadership functions.

Why Is the Organizational Environment of Some Teams More Effective Than Others?

Teams work best when both organizational climate and culture create a supportive atmosphere in which trust and cooperation can thrive. They work best when members consider how their decisions and actions will impact others and if they are consistent with the values and principles the organization stands for. Thus, they make decisions in keeping with their organization's character, ones they expect good results will come from. They make decisions and interact in ways they are not embarrassed to make public.

Working It Out: Alone or Together

Decision-making teams are expected to make ethical decisions, but their performance does not necessarily reflect this behavioral standard. For example, the decisions teams of banking and investment professionals made contributed to this country's most recent financial crisis, causing many to wonder if working in teams was the catalyst for risk taking that led to sacrificing ethics for financial gain.

With this in mind, draw up a list of golden rules that you believe teams should use to ensure ethical decision making.

COLLABORATING HAS BENEFITS

As some students have discovered after hesitating to attend a graduate school that emphasized team-based learning, working in teams—particularly diverse teams—enables members to think and look at problems differently, develop new perspectives, and come to grips with the complexity of the world.

Thus, by learning how to work in teams, you equip yourself with the skills needed to help your organizations avoid the decline organizations populated with ineffective teams may suffer. You learn why it is important not to acquiesce in making a decision but instead work together with others to make a decision successful, agreeing not to undermine the decision after the fact. You understand why it is better to share credit than to seek credit for yourself. You develop the ability to argue for a cause, not promote narrow self-interests. You learn to deliver the truth, not shield leaders and others from grim facts. You learn to ask the right questions, rather than just deliver statements. And, most importantly, you also learn to put the right people on your team.[19]

Post It: Imagineering a Better Way

According to Irving Janis, teams can bring out the best and worst in human decision making. In part, this is because teams engineer consensus, making unanimous agreement more important than other considerations (groupthink), or mismanage agreement by supporting decisions they privately oppose (the Abilene paradox).

Compile a list of expert suggestions for bringing out the best. Then add your own suggestion to the list.

At the heart of leadership is the art of working collaboratively with others to solve problems and make good decisions. How you approach this affects your potential for innovation and success as a leader. Leaders work with others to create the innovative ideas that drive organizations forward. Being open to changing perspectives expands possibilities and creates opportunities. Seeing something we weren't able to see before often provides a solution to a problem and sets us on a fresh course. As the ancient Chinese general and philosopher Sun Tzu said, "Change the way you look at things, and things you look at change."

LOOK BACK

Reread the opening poem. Who in your opinion owns a problem? How would you respond to the speaker's contention?

Key Terms

The Abilene paradox (213)   Brainstorming (212)

Adjourning (208)   Forming (206)

Notes

1. Jonathan Franklin, "Luis Urzua, the Foreman Keeping Hope Alive for Chile's Trapped Miners," *Observer* (September 5, 2010): 11.

2. See Richard J. Hackman, *Leading Team: Setting the Stage for Great Performances* (Boston: HBS Press, 2002).

3. Laurence Prusak, "Building a Collaborative Enterprise," *Harvard Business Review* (July-August, 2011): 95–101.

4. Liz Szabo, "Study: Teamwork Makes Surgery Safer," *USA Today* (October 20, 2010): D5.

5. Adam Bryant, "The Trust That Makes a Team Click," *New York Times* (July 31, 2011): BU2.

6. Adam Bryant, "Note to Staff: We're a Team, Not a Family," *New York Times* (May 15, 2011): BU2.

7. B. Tuchman, "Developmental Sequence in Small Groups," *Psychological Bulletin* 63 (1965): 384–99; and S. A. Wheelen and J. M. Hockberger, "Validation Studies of the Group Development Questionnaire," *Small Group Research* 27(1) (1996): 143–70.

8. Kenneth Benne and Paul Sheats, "Functional Roles of Group Members," *Journal of Social Issues* 4 (1948): 41–49.

9. Lynda Gratton, Andreas Vight, and Tamara Erickson, "Bridging Faultlines in Diverse Teams," *MIT Sloan Management Review* 48(4) (2007): 22–29.

10. See F. LaFasto and C. Larson, *When Teams Work Best* (Thousand Oaks, CA: Sage, 2001); and C. E. Larson and F. M. J. LaFasto, *Teamwork: What Must Go Right/ What Can Go Wrong* (Newbury Park, CA: Sage, 1989).

11. J. R. Katzenback and D. K. Smith, "The Discipline of Teams," *Harvard Business Review* (March-April 1993): 111–20; and J. R. Katzenback and D. K. Smith, *The Wisdom of Teams* (Boston: Harvard Business School Press, 1993); and A. Donnellon, *Team Talk: The Power of Language in Team Dynamics* (Boston: Harvard Business School Press, 1996).

12. See Herminia Ibarra and Morton T. Hansen, "Are You a Collaborative Leader?" *Harvard Business Review* (July-August, 2011): 72.

13. Adam Bryant, "Want Clarity? Learn to Play Devil's Advocate," *New York Times* (February 27, 2011): BU2.

14. See John Dewey, *How We Think* (Boston: Heath, 1910).

15. See Alex Osborn, *Applied Imagination* (New York: Scribner, 1957); James Webb Young, *A Technique for Producing Ideas* (New York: McGraw-Hill, 2003); and Kelly K. Spors, "Productive Brainstorms Take the Right Mix of Elements," *Wall Street Journal* (July 24, 2008): B5.

16. J. Harvey, *The Abilene Paradox and Other Meditations on Management* (New York: Simon & Schuster, 1988).

17. Ian Urbina, "Behind Veneer, Doubt on Future of Natural Gas," *New York Times* (June 27, 2011): A1, A12.

18. C. S. Burke, K. C. Stagl, C. Klein, C. G. F. Goodwin, E. Salas, and S. M. Halpin, "What Type of Leadership Behaviors Are Functional in Teams? A Meta-Analysis," *Leadership Quarterly* 17 (2006): 288–307.

19. See Jim Collins, *How the Mighty Fall* (New York: Random House, 2010).

BEYOND POWER:
THE CREDIBILITY FACTOR

ACQUIRING "STAR POWER": ENHANCING
YOUR PERSONAL CREDIBILITY

BEYOND MY WAY:
THE "YOUR WAY" FACTOR

NEGOTIATING TO SUCCEED

LEADERS AND CHARISMA

## 12

Convince me
With kept promises
An extended hand
Found facts.
Reason with me
Don't force me.
Tell me truth
Not fiction.
Help me accept reality
Don't sell me on appearance.

INFLUENCING AND INSPIRING OTHERS

To lead is to influence others. Leaders are persuaders, the users of symbols and language designed to inspire cooperation. Leaders are also attitude and behavior shapers—the sellers of ideas and actions.

What attributes must you have to be able to persuade others to support you? How do leaders elicit compliance from others or gain their commitment? Is it because of what they say or the approaches they use? Is it because of who they are or the positions they occupy? Or could it be the result of their credibility?

To answer these questions and determine how you can become more effective at exerting influence, let's look at a number of influence factors that matter.

> **Credibility is in the eye of the beholder.**

BEYOND POWER: THE CREDIBILITY FACTOR

When we previously spoke about power, we noted that some leaders derive their power from their positions. But while authority may matter, it is not the only persuasive power leaders possess. Whether or not a person is perceived to have credibility also matters.[1] From a leadership perspective, **credibility** is the followers' assessment of the competence, trustworthiness, and dynamism or charisma of the leader.

Credibility is in the eye of the beholder. It exists in the minds of receivers. There is nothing objective about it.[2] Credibility is based on the attitudes of receivers toward a source. For example, if those whom you hope to influence believe you to be knowledgeable, to have a track record of success, to possess valued skills and understandings, to be a consistently reliable and truthful source of information, and to be personable, warm, friendly, likeable, and charismatic, then you are more likely to inspire them, and they are more likely to accept your goals as their own. In effect, leaders do not determine whether they have or do not have credibility; their followers do.

The study of credibility is not new.[3] It dates back to the ancient Greeks who studied the oratorical skills of their leaders and linked their leaders' ability to influence others to members of the public judging them to be of high moral character, intelligent, and skilled at weaving logos, pathos, and ethos into their presentations. In other words, leaders inspired them and gained their cooperation by using logical arguments, emotional appeals, and personal attributes to persuade and educate the members of the public.

This still holds true today—with even more heightened scrutiny, especially when it comes to assessments of the consistency of a leader's behavior in all spheres of his or her life. Perhaps that is why an Internet service, *Reputation.com*, exists to help people defend their reputations. For example, while Representative Anthony Wiener of New York was once perceived to be a rising political leader, an ardent advocate on the floor of the House, and a potential candidate for the mayor of New York City, that image was destroyed when it was learned that though married, he had tweeted inappropriate, sexually revealing pictures of himself to a number of different young women and then, to make matters worse, lied about it, initially denying that he had sent the tweets, insisting instead that his Twitter account had been hacked. Once the lie was revealed, Wiener was compelled to resign. Without credibility it would likely be impossible for him to convince others that his ideas were worth accepting.

Leaders get caught in different kinds of credibility traps. Because they need to appeal to the members of different publics—among them stockholders, employees, members of the community, and customers—leaders need to be sure that what they say or promise to the members of one constituency does not conflict with what they say or promise to the members of other constituencies. We live in an age when the words and presentations of leaders are recorded and broadcast on the Internet for all to listen to and view. Imagine the embarrassment when the leader's words trip him or her up because what the leader told one audience differs significantly from what he or she tells another.

Failures of character and consistency have contributed to the downfall of many leaders, just as evidence of the goodwill and fulfilled promises of leaders have contributed to their being held in high esteem. Expertise and relationships are the foundation of credibility—the glue—that causes supporters to stick to and with a leader.

People are more likely to follow leaders they think know what they are doing and to whom they are attracted.[4] You can enhance perceptions of your credibility by becoming a subject matter expert, earning special certifications, and picking the best team you can—selecting to work alongside individuals who have connections to and the admiration of those whose support you seek. In part, this helps explain why once in office, presidents place past opponents in their cabinet and on their advisory teams.

ACQUIRING "STAR POWER": ENHANCING YOUR PERSONAL CREDIBILITY

Understanding how credible you are in others' eyes can be an eye opener. It can also help you understand the steps you need to take to enhance your credibility—that is, it can clarify what you need to do to help others perceive you as more competent, honest, or dynamic.

Self-Reflection: Looking In and Out

First, use the following series of scales to rate your credibility, marking the line between the two descriptors where you believe you fall. Then, ask a peer (either another student or a coworker) and a supervisor (either a professor or someone you report to) to fill out the same form about you—but keep them unaware of how you rated yourself. Compare and contrast your self-evaluation with the credibility assessments others provided about you. On which credibility aspects did you agree, and on which did your ratings diverge? What steps can you take to narrow the areas of difference?

Assessing Credibility

Competence

Knowledgeable ____ ____ ____ ____ ____ Unknowledgeable
Expert   ____ ____ ____ ____ ____ Novice
Informed   ____ ____ ____ ____ ____ Uninformed

(Continued)

(Continued)

Proficient	____	____	____	____	____ Deficient
Experienced	____	____	____	____	____ Inexperienced

Trustworthiness

Honest	____	____	____	____	____ Dishonest
Reliable	____	____	____	____	____ Unreliable
Consistent	____	____	____	____	____ Inconsistent
Interested in Others	____	____	____	____	____ Self-Serving

Dynamism

Active	____	____	____	____	____ Passive
Charismatic	____	____	____	____	____ Boring
Energetic	____	____	____	____	____ Lethargic
Assertive	____	____	____	____	____ Hesitant
Personable	____	____	____	____	____ Distant

Based on these analyses, identify any dimensions of credibility in need of your attention. Then, suggest specific steps you could take to generate a more favorable impression, build your persuasiveness, and enhance your credibility in others' eyes.

There are a number of actions leaders can take in order to boost perceptions of their credibility. Some involve how leaders present themselves to others, others involve the recognition of shared values and concerns, and yet others speak to leaders' role in communication and enlisting others in support of a shared agenda and vision.

Presenting Yourself to Others

Supporters are most influenced by a leader whom they believe to be qualified. Demonstrate your competence by helping your constituents recognize your knowledge including your range of experiences, educational background, and special credentials. To earn their trust, reveal to them life experiences you have had that they might share and identify with. Acknowledge your ties to other groups they support and distance yourself from those whose behavior they call into question. If they might ever have a valid reason to question your motives, address the issue first before others raise doubts about your trustworthiness of honesty.

When you speak with those whose support you want, dress in a way that demonstrates your respect for them but also enables them to feel comfortable with and respect you. Similarity in dress, like similarity in ideas, can be persuasive. Then walk the walk, and talk the talk. Look them in the eye. Use language that is clear, direct, and devoid of jargon. Communicate your passion, emotional intensity, and commitment not only with your words, but with your nonverbal cues as well. Your voice should convey your confidence. Your posture and gestures should demonstrate your attentiveness and energy. Your demeanor, together with your words, should make it clear that you welcome responses and are open to learning about their ideas and feelings.

Acknowledging and Affirming Receivers

Prove to receivers that you know how to listen by seeking their feedback and responding in kind. Encourage others to voice their values, true feelings, and concerns. By keeping it real for receivers, you demonstrate your respect for diverse perspectives and values. Let them know those viewpoints and values you have in common and explain how projects, policies, and procedures reflect them.

Communicating and Defending
Your Vision—Enacting the Mission

Effective leaders put ideas into action, helping others to appreciate their commitment and optimism. Followers need to see leaders model the way— consistently delivering messages that express common values and goals. Thus, it is important to demonstrate your ability to act on your principles and to reference them when making decisions or putting those decisions into effect. Remind others of your joint purpose and how everyone shares responsibility for the group's direction and outcome.

Leaders need to develop their abilities to serve as advocates and argue for their causes. They have to be adept not only at presenting, but also at defending their stated positions and goals. They also need to prepare themselves for those who may attack their competence, character, or even appearance. In the face of such attacks they need to be able to maintain their composure, restrain the impulse to react defiantly or strike back aggressively, and instead defend themselves and their positions while at the same time preserving interpersonal channels and relations.

Taking the following steps can help you accomplish these leadership goals. First, take time to define the argumentative situation by stating the problem in the form of a claim or proposition of fact, value, or policy. (You will recall that we introduced the role of argumentation in Chapter 9.) **Propositions of fact** focus on what is or is not (e.g., "The federal deficit is a threat to the economic security of the U.S."). **Propositions of value** focus on issues of rightness or wrongness, good or evil (e.g., "The use of bribes to secure business is immoral"). **Propositions of policy** focus on potential courses of action (e.g., "We should invest in alternative fuel sources"). The propositional frame lets you identify and understand the side people support.

Next, examine the proposition and invent arguments in support of or in opposition to it. Look at the nature of the problem, the problem's causes, possible solutions, and potential consequences the potential solutions present.

Finally, communicate and defend your position. Focus on points of controversy and reason ethically. This means you refrain from using faulty reasoning that perverts the argumentation process, such as **name calling** (attacking the person rather than the position); offering a **red herring** (sending receivers on a wild goose chase by causing them to focus on an irrelevant issue); creating a **false division** (compelling receivers to choose between two options when there are many options); identifying a **false cause** (leading receivers to assume mistakenly that one event causes another merely because they occur sequentially); or using a **bandwagon appeal** (that just because many people favor what the leader is advocating, the receivers should too).

During the argumentation period, you also need to maintain your relationships with those who disagree with you. By demonstrating interest in and openness to opposing views, and not becoming verbally aggressive, you can pave the way to understanding and possible agreement or compromise. Defending your vision in a way that influences and inspires others is a prime requisite for leadership.

Theory Into Practice

The Leader's Paradigm

Paradigms, the presentation of ideas, and leading go hand in hand.[5] A perusal of your daily newspaper will likely demonstrate how prevalent presentations are in every leader's life. Hardly a day goes by when a leader does not deliver a presentation of one kind or another to an audience comprised of representative members of one concerned public or another. What is rhetoric's role in helping the leader widen receiver understanding of the leader's paradigm? What do leaders say to humanize their vision, tasks, and roles? Much is revealed by the paradigm a leader adopts. The leader's story, vision, and leadership approach are echoes of it. Thus, understanding the leader's paradigm is key to understanding the leader.

Recognizing that a leader can lead from either the front or from behind, consider the following quotes, the first from a Western perspective and the second from an Eastern perspective, each expressive of a different leadership paradigm: (1) "Leadership involves finding a parade and getting in front of it," and (2) "To lead the people, walk behind them."

Share a presentation by a leader that illustrates either of these two paradigms at work. Which do you suppose is more effective when it comes to mobilizing others, defending a vision, or innovating for survival?

BEYOND MY WAY: THE "YOUR WAY" FACTOR

To build your persuasiveness as a leader, look at your goal from behind the eyes of those you seek to influence. See things from the perspective of your receivers. Frame your message to appeal to their interests by clearly revealing to them what they stand to gain.

Also offer them different kinds of evidence—facts, stories, and analogies. Rely on both reason and emotion to build your case. Find the means to connect with them both intellectually and emotionally.

Once you have a handle on what receivers think and feel about what you are asking them to believe or do, once you understand their experiences, cognitive needs, and emotional states, you will be better able to adopt a strategy that speaks directly to them and facilitates your getting from them the *yes* you seek.

Getting to Yes: Persuasive Power Tools

According to persuasion expert Robert Cialdini, persuaders have six persuasive power tools, what Cialdini calls their "weapons of influence." These tools are also instrumental in helping a leader achieve his or her persuasive objectives. They are **reciprocity, commitment** and **consistency, social proof, liking, authority,** and **scarcity**.

How can you use these tools to your advantage?[6] We explore that next.

What do you imagine the leader depicted in this cartoon would do to influence and inspire others? Would it work? What words would you use to describe his relationship with followers?

"Why is everyone's valuable input so stupid?"

Bruce Kaplan/The New Yorker Collection/www.cartoonbank.com

Reciprocity

Reciprocity gains its power from the simple fact that when someone does us a favor or gives us something, we feel some sense of obligation to repay them. In fact, the saying "much obliged" is another way of saying "thanks." For that reason, we send birthday cards to people who send us cards. We vote for politicians who do good things for the district in which we live. Similarly, lobbyists give money to politicians who support their special interests. When people share resources with us, or provide resources to us, they likely have the expectation that at some point in the future we might do something for or give something back to them.

Giving people something they do not require and have not asked for helps gain their compliance. A gift, though small in cost, can yield a return that far surpasses its worth. Thus, leaders who can grant favors are putting the reciprocity rule into play. By building a reservoir of goodwill, such leaders also build networks of potential allies who, in the future, will more than likely reciprocate.

Commitment and Consistency

We expect others to be consistent in their behavior and not to contradict themselves. We also know that gaining a commitment from others increases their consistency tendencies. In other words, once we make a commitment, we tend to act in accordance with our promise, even if it is not in our own self-interest. If persuaders can get us to make a commitment, the chances are good that we will act to reinforce it. Once we make a commitment, we are more likely to agree with requests in keeping with our prior commitments. Bigger commitments typically follow smaller ones because each small commitment causes people to change the way they look at themselves. People are persuaded slowly; as receivers take small steps forward, the persuader moves closer to the goal.

Persuasion Power Tool	Why It Works
Reciprocity	We feel an obligation to repay.
Commitment and consistency	We feel the need to fulfill a promise.
Social proof	We tend to follow others.
Liking	Attraction increases consent.
Authority	Power increases compliance.
Scarcity	We want what we fear losing.

Social Proof

People are persuaded by one another. In fact, that is the story of fads. People follow others. We look to each other to determine what to think, what to do, and what is right. We follow the lead of those whom we respect. If they say something is right, we follow it. If they wear an item of clothing, we wear it. We figure out how to behave by watching others. As the saying goes, "There is safety in numbers." When we believe others are already complying, our willingness to comply increases.

Liking

We're more persuaded by people whom we like. For this reason, people attempting to persuade us try to increase their attractiveness and likability in our eyes. Additionally, we tend to like people we perceive to be like us, also becoming more likely to consent to their requests. For some of us, just the mention of a friend's name or the name of someone we like is enough for us to comply. What is more, perceived similarity motivates compliance. So do compliments.

Authority

Many of us feel strong pressure to comply with an authority. Thus, being perceived as an authority figure can enhance persuasiveness. Symbols of authority, titles, dress, and the trappings of authority can be used to induce compliance. Sometimes, the authorities we listen to are experts. We should note that the authority figure need not be the leader but might well be an expert the leader has brought in.

Scarcity

The more we think we might lose something, the more we want it. We don't like to be told we can't have something. We want to be able to exercise our free choice. When we believe that we're in danger of having to give something up or surrender a right, we fight to retain it. We want to be special. We don't want to lose opportunities. When we have what we want, we often don't think about losing it, but when wanting replaces having, we then desire what we lack even more. Thus, eliciting the fear of loss is a powerful compliance strategy.

Working It Out: Alone or Together

Select a well-known leader. First, compile examples demonstrating how this person used as many of the preceding persuasive tools as possible in support of his or her leadership agenda. Next, enumerate the costs and benefits of each persuasive strategy the leader used. Then use your insight to identify other ways the leader might have used these tools to sell his or her persuasive goal(s) to others. Finally, suggest guidelines aspiring leaders should follow when it comes to employing these persuasive tactics in pursuit of a goal.

NEGOTIATING TO SUCCEED

According to Harvey Whille, president of Local 1262 of the United Food and Commercial Workers union, "You don't get what you have coming to you. You don't get what you deserve. You don't get what you have earned. You get what you negotiate."[7] When people aren't cooperating with the leader, she or he needs to learn why.

Leading an organization is not a "my way" thing. While pushing for your vision is your role as the leader, you need to never forget that you can't do it alone. Therefore, bringing people together to support your mission is also your role. However, individuals often have competing goals, and because of this the leader also needs to be skilled at negotiating. In fact, negotiating is a critical part of a leader's world.

Whenever interdependent individuals do not share the identical preference, they negotiate to determine what each is to give and take.[8] Instead of framing leadership as a zero-sum game in which the leader always has to win, it helps to frame it in such a way that people will cooperate and collaborate for joint gains and to achieve an optimal outcome.

Again, in order to negotiate effectively you need to understand the underlying needs, interests, and objectives of those you have to negotiate with. You need to understand how they view the world. Effectively, you need to look at the situation from your point of view and theirs and be able to keep both perspectives in mind. You need to understand the big picture before you can enact a scene in it effectively. Brainstorming options in order to identify a mutually beneficial outcome is helpful because for you to succeed, and them to buy in, your goals and their goals need to align.

To accomplish this, a leader actively promotes the sharing of interests. Doing this usually also reveals the motives and personal goals of those involved. The next step is to discuss perceptions. Here, the goal is to find out why those opposed feel the way they do. Then you brainstorm possible agreements. This helps to uncover underlying interests as well as to reveal your differences. Perhaps with this done, you will be able to commit to moving forward together.

Taking the preceding steps will help you avoid the following negotiating pitfalls: (1) judging prematurely, (2) asserting there is a single answer, (3) acting as if the pie to be divided is fixed rather than expandable, (4) being short-sighted in defending partisan positions, or (4) defending the status quo for its own sake.[9]

Another way of conceptualizing the negotiation process is an outgrowth of the Harvard Negotiation Project called *principled negotiation.* Principled negotiation is composed of four basic elements:

(1) *People.* Separate the people from the problem.

(2) *Interests.* Instead of focusing on positions, explore interests.

(3) *Options.* Before making a decision, generate an array of possibilities.

(4) *Criteria.* Decide objective criteria on which to base the result.

The process of principled negotiation turns the leader back into a problem solver rather than an adversary and more easily leads to results that work for all parties.[10]

Observation: Watch and Learn

How a leader negotiates can build or destroy his or her credibility. Words and actions can create trust or cause others to distrust. If a leader makes promises but does not keep them, the leader will have a difficult time convincing others to believe him or her in the future.

Identify a negotiation involving civil rights, worker rights, or a political or military conflict that you believe had a positive outcome because of the leader's credibility. Explain what the leader did or said to facilitate this.

Identify a negotiation in which you believe distrust played a role in producing a less than satisfactory outcome. What do you think a more effective leader might have done to produce a more fruitful outcome?

Negotiating in good faith makes it possible for people to support leaders even when they did not initially support their policies. Being able to convey the compelling vision that guides them confidently and with enthusiasm helps leaders sell their ideas and attract others to work with them. Why do they succeed? Could it be because of their charisma?

LEADERS AND CHARISMA

The late Steve Jobs, the founder of Apple, had been pushed out of the company in the 1970s, only to return to it in 1997 when Apple found itself in danger of failing.

What did Steve Jobs do to turn things around? Jobs offered a compelling new vision—Apple would become a leader in computer design and mobile technology. Jobs emotionally connected the company and its products like the iPad, Airbook, and iPhone with customers. Jobs, the personal face of Apple, put himself front and center on the stage, self-confidently pitching Apple products. When Jobs fell ill and failed to show up for one product launch, it made headlines around the world. People found Jobs inspiring, and he transformed the way we think about Apple.

Remember, charisma is in the eye of the beholder. Supporters attribute it to leaders they judge to be inspiring, leaders who use emotional appeals and put forth bold visions. These leaders get others to feel so dissatisfied with the status quo that they choose to follow as the leaders leap well beyond it, even taking personal risks to do so.

Charismatic leaders capitalize on three core communication strengths:

(1) They know how to build relationships. Being in their presence excites their followers.

(2) They are adept at creating symbolic visions that inspire followers to imagine a more desirable future.

(3) They are skilled agents of influence.

Their confidence, competence, and trustworthiness together with their referent power make it possible for them to attract the support of others and achieve their goals.[11]

However, as we have seen, you may use charisma positively or negatively. You can use it on behalf of others or for your own self-glorification and personal gain. Thus, charisma elicits both positive and negative results.

As we discussed earlier, when a leader uses charisma to persuade followers to devote themselves to the leader rather than to the leader's ideas or mission, the goal of the leader is simply to secure power while weakening his or her followers who look to the leader as an authoritative parent on whom they depend.

In contrast, leaders have positive effects when their goal is to have followers internalize the values inherent in their missions. Such leaders seek to engage followers in decision making with the primary objective being not merely to wield personal power but to imbue followers with a sense of purpose. By not emphasizing the dark side of charisma, leaders stand clear of its dangers—which surface when devotion to the person replaces support for the leader's ideas or strategies.[12]

Charisma sometimes turns leaders into celebrities. Admired leaders frequently pop up on newscasts, and their faces appear in newspapers and even on magazine covers. They become their company's public face. We look at leaders such as Steve Jobs and wonder if Apple would have been able to shine without its superstar visionary.[13]

We sometimes forget that there is also a team behind the leader on which the leader depends. While some may believe there is only one Steve Jobs, not all leaders, to be sure, come off as larger than life. Leaders who are effective at communicating their vision to followers and who share success and decision making with supporters build organizations that should be able to thrive long after they step down.[14]

Post It: Imagineering a Better Way

Transformational leaders appeal to followers to move beyond self-interest in an effort to secure a major change for the common good. When effective, supporters passionately work to achieve the bold vision put forth by the leader. Who, in your eyes, is a contemporary transformational leader? What role, if any, did the person's charisma play in your decision? Explore what experts such as Bernard Bass, Tom Peters, Warren Bennis and Burt Nanus, and James Kouzes and Barry Posner have to say about charisma and transformational leadership.[15]

Based on your research, what advice regarding the use of communication would you offer a leader who wanted to convince others to devote themselves to his or her ideas?

LOOK BACK

Reread the opening poem. How would you respond to the requests of the speaker? If you do as the speaker asks, do you think your ability to influence and inspire will be increased? If so, why? If not, why not?

Key Terms

Authority (225)

Charismatic leaders (231)

Bandwagon appeal (224)

Commitment (225)

Notes

1. M. M. Kouzes and B. Z. Posner, *Credibility: How Leaders Gain and Lose It, Why People Demand It* (San Francisco: Jossey-Bass, 2003), 22.

2. T. Gamble and M. Gamble, *Communication Works,* 10th ed. (New York: McGraw-Hill, 2010), 437–39.

3. See, for example, W. M. Sattler, "Conceptions of Ethos in Ancient Rhetoric," *Speech Monographs* 14 (1947): 55–65.

4. See Jay Lorsch, "A Contingency Theory of Leadership," in Nitin Nohria and Rakesh Khurana, eds., *Handbook of Leadership Theory and Practice* (Boston: Harvard Business Press, 2010), 411–29.

5. See Linda A. Hill, Maurizio Travalgini, Greg Brandeau, and Emily Stecker, "Unlocking the Slices of Genius in Your Organization: Leading for Innovation," in Nitin Nohria and Rakesh Khurana, eds., *Handbook of Leadership Theory and Practice* (Boston: Harvard Business Press, 2010), 611–54; John Pepper, *What Really Matters: Service, Leadership, People and Values* (New Haven, CT: Yale University Press, 2007); Robert Eccles and Nitin Nohria, *Behind the Hype* (Boston: Harvard Business School Press, 1992); and Warren Bennis, Gretchin Spreitzer, and Thomas Cummings, eds., *The Future of Leadership: Today's Top Leadership Thinkers Speak to Tomorrow's Leaders* (San Francisco: Jossey-Bass, 2001).

6. For a comprehensive examination of weapons of influence, see Robert B. Cialdini, *Influence,* 5th ed. (Boston: Allyn & Bacon, 2009).

7. Joan Verdon, "Union Leader Dedicated to Workers' Rights," *Record* (July 3, 2011): B6.

8. Margaret A. Neale and Max H. Bazerman, "Negotiating Rationally the Power and Impact of the Negotiator's Frame," *Academy of Management Executive* (August, 1992): 42.

9. David W. Johnson and Frank P. Johnson, *Joining Together,* 10th ed. (Upper Saddle River, NJ: Merrill, 2009), 403.

10. Roger Fisher and William Ury, *Getting to Yes* (New York: Penguin Books, 1983).

11. See R. J. Richardson and S. K. Thayer, *The Charisma Factor* (Englewood Cliffs, NJ: Prentice Hall, 1993).

12. For a discussion of charisma, see Robert J. House and Jane M. Howell, "Personality and Charismatic Leadership," *Leadership Quarterly* 3(2) (1992): 81–108.

13. Dan Lyons, "Without Jobs in Charge, Can Apple Shine?" *Newsweek* (July 4–11, 2011): 68.

14. James Collins, *Good to Great* (New York: Harper Business, 2001).

15. To begin your investigation, you might look at the following work: James McGregor Burns, *Leadership* (New York: HarperCollins, 1978).

PART IV

MEETING LEADERSHIP CHALLENGES

Thinkstock Images/Comstock/Thinkstock

What does difference look like?

Does it have an odor or an aroma?

Do you wrap yourself around it or push it away?

Have you looked at yourself today?

Someone is answering the same questions with you in mind.

13

VALUING CULTURE AND DIVERSITY

We start this chapter with this premise: diversity *is good*. Why do we draw this conclusion? For one thing, if the leaders of an organization are too alike, then they are likely to look at problems the same way, and as we have seen, too much of the same thinking can mean too little thinking is going on. Instead, the expectation is that diversity will pave the way for new and different ways of thinking, and thinking in new and different ways leads to innovations.

On the other hand, we have also seen that when people have divergent outlooks, they can get bogged down in conflicts that when not handled effectively can block their ability to move forward. Thus, diversity without the skills to harness its strengths could be an impediment rather than an asset to you.

From yet another perspective, our world has become what media theorist and forecaster Marshall McLuhan predicted it would become: a global village.[1] Our interdependence with people next door and around the world makes intercultural communication and cooperation across neighborhoods and national borders necessary. In fact, as companies expand their operations across borders, global experience becomes a leadership prerequisite.[2]

That said, the goal of this chapter is to help you develop the skills and understandings that can unlock diversity's benefits and enable you to work effectively with colleagues who are different from you—who come from different cultures or are of a different ethnicity, race, or gender.[3] Diversity matters. Working with people from many cultures and managing diversity locally and globally are increasingly important leadership functions. Contemporary leaders need to become adept at creating visions that transcend divergent cultures and contrasting worldviews.[4]

GLOCAL AND GLOBAL REALITY: WHAT DIVERSITY IS

We live in the age of globalization. **Globalization,** the increasing economic, political, and cultural integration and interdependence of diverse cultures, increases the probability that leaders of today and tomorrow will be working with people from all over the world. Multinational companies and coproduction agreements are the norm. **Glocalization,** a newer concept, describes how globalization merges with local interests and environments.

Diversity is a result of both forces; it is the recognition and valuing of difference and encompasses such factors as age, gender, race, ethnicity, ability, religion, sexual orientation, and education. By erasing the notion of territorial boundaries between countries, and gradually eroding the idea of the term *nation,* digital technology is also playing a role in accelerating diversity, making it increasingly necessary for leaders to be **multiculturalists**—persons respectful of and actively engaged with their counterparts and supporters who are from distinctively different cultures, but who are linked to them physically or electronically.[5]

TYPES OF DIVERSITY

Identity diversity
Cognitive diversity

When it comes to life in their organizations, leaders need to be equipped to capitalize on two kinds of diversity: **identity diversity**—people who come from different cultures, races, and religions—and **cognitive diversity**—people who have different outlooks and training but who come together to fulfill the organization's purpose. Leaders, who will have increased interaction with persons with whom they differ, need to expand their communication choices and meet these challenges by mastering how to respond appropriately to different cultures and communication styles.

THE CULTURE/COMMUNICATION INTERFACE

What lessons do you need to understand to exert leadership when cultures meet? Culture teaches many lessons including how to say hello and good-bye, when to speak or remain silent, how to act when angry or upset, where to look when speaking or listening, how much to gesture, and how close to stand to another. Sometimes even that is not enough. For example, when Chinese workers were sent to Afghanistan, they reported the following: "It was crucial to understand that you can't hang out on the roof bare-chested to cool down from the heat—the neighbors will shoot you as they think you intend to molest their wives."[6]

When cultures meet, the first need is to recognize and acknowledge differences. It is likely you will be interacting with persons whose behavioral norms and values are different from yours, so those differences ought to be accepted for you to interact meaningfully with one another. While this seems to be a commonsense approach, a number of factors can interfere and complicate things, including ethnocentrism, stereotypes, and prejudice.

Ethnocentrism

Ethnocentrism—the tendency to see your culture as superior to and more natural than all others—is key to having a failed intercultural communication experience.[7] When you are ethnocentric, you lack cultural flexibility and experience anxiety when interacting with persons from different cultures. Ethnocentric individuals fail to recognize the unique perspectives of persons from other cultures, typically believe the members of other cultures to be inferior, and therefore are quick to blame them for problems.

The more ethnocentric persons are, the less tolerant they are of the traditions and cultural practices of persons from other cultures, making it harder for them to interact comfortably with them. In direct opposition to ethnocentrism is an attitude supportive of cultural relativism—the acceptance of other cultural groups as equal in value to your own—the belief that understanding the behavior of other groups is not dependent on your frame of reference but will benefit from an understanding of the context in which the behavior occurs. While remaining true to their own cultural values, skilled leaders support cultural relativism, understanding that its promotion will enrich their organizations.

Stereotypes

Stereotypes—the mental images or pictures we carry around in our heads, the shortcuts we use that guide our reactions to and generate unrealistic pictures of things—can prevent us from distinguishing differences, making it impossible for us to treat a person apart from the group.

Prejudice

Prejudice—a positive or negative prejudgment, usually based on faulty data—can lead us to create in- and out-groups, contributing to our feeling more negatively toward out-group members who become easy targets for our anger. Usually conceived of in a race context, prejudice also applies in gender, age, and sexual-preference contexts.[8] Before they can help others acknowledge and handle their ethnocentric tendencies, stereotyping proclivities, and prejudices, leaders have to acknowledge their own.

Roadblocks in Diversity's Way

Ethnocentrism	Seeing your own culture as superior
Stereotypes	Failing to distinguish differences
Prejudice	Prejudging

We will address these three diversity deterrents again later in this chapter because instead of letting these three barriers get in the way, leaders need to do their part to develop skills and understandings that successfully help themselves and others reduce the strangeness of strangers.

Self-Reflection: Looking In and Out

Label each of the following statements as either *true* or *false.* For each statement, provide an example of one or more behavior(s) you exhibit to explain your rationale for your answer. Be as specific as possible.

1. I would rather interact with someone like myself than with someone who is very different from me.

2. I find it easier to cooperate or collaborate with people similar to me than with people unlike me.

3. I believe it is natural for me to put more trust in people who share my cultural background than in people from another culture.

4. I am less fearful around persons who share my culture than among those who differ from me.

5. I go out of my way to be with people who I believe are just like me.

6. I usually keep my distance from people unlike me.

7. I am more likely to blame people unlike me for creating problems than I am to blame people who are like me.

8. I rely on my frame of reference when judging the behavior of people unlike me.

9. I contend that people different from me are more likely to threaten my ability to succeed than are people like me.

10. I believe that people different from me would benefit from making the effort to become more like me.

To what extent do your answers suggest any feelings of ethnocentrism? To what extent do they suggest you practice cultural relativism? How content are you with your answers? What steps do you believe you or others should take to minimize ethnocentric behavior?

UNDERSTANDING HOW CULTURES DIFFER

A culture is the system of knowledge, beliefs, values, customs, behaviors, and artifacts that members acquire, share, and use during daily living.[9] Researchers describe cultures using the following dialectics: (1) individualism versus collectivism, (2) high-context communication versus low-context communication, (3) high-power distance versus low-power distance, (4) monochronic versus polychronic, and (5) masculine versus feminine.

Understanding these contrasting cultural orientations can help a leader adjust to diversity.

Cultural Dialectics

Individualism versus collectivism

High-context communication versus low-context communication

High-power distance versus low-power distance

Monochronic versus polychronic

Masculine versus feminine

Individualism Versus Collectivism

The **individualism**-versus-**collectivism** dialectic reveals how people define themselves in relationship to others.[10] The United States, France, Great Britain, and Germany are categorized as individualistic cultures while Arab, African, Asian, and Latin American countries are categorized as collectivistic cultures. Members of individualistic cultures give precedence to individual goals because of the value they place upon individual initiative and achievement. Collectivistic culture members give precedence to group goals because of the value they place on nurturing groups rather than developing a sense of self.

Thus, workers from individualistic cultures prefer individual awards, while those from collectivistic cultures prefer team awards. Members from individualistic cultures want self-development opportunities, while in collectivistic cultures, the group is nurtured, not the individual.

High-Context Communication Versus Low-Context Communication

Cultures with **high-context communication systems** are tradition bound.[11] Members of such cultures tend to value thoughtfulness; they reserve reactions and appear to be overly polite and indirect when relating to others. They believe that most messages can be understood if receivers are attuned to nonverbal, contextual information rather than words. Believing that not everything needs to be explained, members of high-context communication cultures, including Japan and China, value silence based on the belief that a person of few words is to be respected and trusted.

In contrast, cultures with low-context communication systems encourage members to communicate more directly. Members of low-context cultures plainly code their messages, even asking people they have just meet for personal background information including where they went to college, for whom they work, and where they live. Members of low-context cultures also rely on verbal interaction for clarity, frequently self-disclosing, a practice usually shunned as socially inappropriate by high-context communication members. Leaders from low-context cultures might also find themselves facing communication hurdles were they to encourage persons from high-context cultures to be forthright in their criticism.

High-Power Distance Versus Low-Power Distance

Power distance measures how willingly a culture's members accept power differences.[12]

Persons from high-power-distance cultures, including Saudi Arabia and India, perceive power as a fact of life and tend to stress its coercive or reference nature. Inequality in high-power-distance cultures is the norm. Followers accede to the wishes and orders of their superiors, who believe they deserve special privileges.

In contrast, persons from low-power-distance cultures such as the United States, Sweden, and Israel believe power should only be used if legitimate. As a result, they promote equal rights, value expert or legitimate power, emphasize the interdependence of leaders and followers, and disagree with one another when necessary. In low-power-distance cultures, those in power may try to appear less powerful than they really are.

How does power distance affect relationships between leaders and their followers? Workers from high-power-distance cultures may be reluctant to participate in decision making, while workers from low-power-distance cultures may be offended when the leader fails to ask for their input, relying on his or her authority to make the decision instead.

Monochronic Versus Polychronic

In some countries such as Kenya and Argentina, activities are conducted at a slower rhythm and without the "get it done now" sense of urgency present in other places like most of Europe and North America. People attuned to **mono-chronic** time carefully schedule their time and events.

In contrast, persons brought up using **polychronic** time readily give in to distractions and interruptions, work on several projects at the same time, and prefer not sticking to a rigid time schedule. As a result, they often show up late, change an appointment at the last minute, or choose not to show up at all—something a monochronic time user would never do willingly.

Masculine Versus Feminine

Cultures display different attitudes toward gender.

High-masculine cultures, for example, place more value on aggressiveness, strength, and symbols of material success. **Masculine cultures** socialize members to be dominant and competitive, to confront conflict head-on, and to aim to win. Females are less likely to emerge as leaders in masculine cultures. Attaining recognition and achievement motivates leaders in masculine cultures.

Highly **feminine cultures** place greater value on relationships, tenderness, and quality of life. Japan, Italy, Germany, Mexico, and Great Britain have masculine cultures, while Sweden, Norway, the Netherlands, Thailand, and Chile have feminine cultures. Feminine cultures socialize members to compromise and negotiate and to see a win-win solution. In feminine cultures, more effort is made to collaborate, communicate interpersonally, and achieve consensus. While masculine cultures value work, feminine cultures value quality of life and work-life balance.

Observation: Watch and Learn

Identify a leader whose cultural background differs substantially from your own. Answer these questions about your selected leader.

1. How would you describe the leader's sense of self?
2. What do you believe the leader values most?
3. What behaviors has this leader exhibited that you applaud?
4. What behaviors has this leader exhibited that you have difficulty with?
5. How do you think this leader feels about competing?

6. How do you think this leader feels about cooperating?

7. Describe the leader's orientation with respect to the following dialectics by supplying examples to validate your perceptions:

Individualism versus collectivism

High-context communication versus low-context communication

High-power distance versus low-power distance

Monochronic versus polychronic

Masculine versus feminine

Based on your answers, what accommodations would you make to establish a meaningful relationship with this leader?

THE GLOBE STUDIES

A series of studies initiated by Robert House and conducted under the auspices of the Global Leadership and Organizational Behavior Effectiveness research initiative have generated significant understandings about the culture-leadership relationship.[13] GLOBE researchers surveyed and interviewed more than 17,000 leaders in over 950 organizations around the world. Based on their work, they identified nine cultural dimensions.

(1) *Uncertainty avoidance*—the extent to which an organization's members or society relies on established ways of doing things to avoid uncertainty. High levels of uncertainty avoidance make it difficult to tolerate situations that are unstructured or unpredictable. Singapore, Germany, and Austria were among countries scoring high in uncertainty avoidance while Hungary, Bolivia, and Venezuela scored low on this measure.

(2) *Power distance*—the degree to which members of an organization or society expect and support the centralization of power at higher levels of an organization or government. High power distance scores indicate that members do not expect equality and are accepting of the leader's position based on authority. In these studies Israel, the Netherlands, and Bolivia scored low on power distance while Morocco and Thailand were among countries scoring high. Those who score high are unlikely to challenge authority.

(3) *Institutional collectivism*—the extent to which organizations or societies encourage and reward collective action and resource distribution—

and

(4) *In-group collectivism*—the extent to which individuals express pride, loyalty, and cohesiveness in their organizations. Greeks, Swiss, and Americans are among those who tend to score lower on collectivism because of the emphasis they place on having personal needs met and personal goals realized. In contrast, as a result of the priority they give to meeting the needs of others, the Chinese, Japanese, and Eastern Europeans generally score higher on collectivism.

(5) *Gender egalitarianism*—the extent to which gender role differences are minimized and gender equality realized. Hungarians, Swedes, Russians, and Danes score high on this measure while persons from Egypt, Morocco, and India score low, indicating that in these countries men are accorded more social status and serve in more authoritative positions.

(6) *Assertiveness*—the extent to which individuals act assertively or aggressively in another's presence. People from Eastern Europe and the United States tend to be among the most assertive while persons from Sweden, Japan, and Thailand were the least assertive or confrontational because of their preference for gentleness and the low value they place on competing.

(7) *Future orientation*—the extent to which individuals spend time engaged in future-oriented activities such as planning, while delaying personal or collective gratification. People from South Africa, Malaysia, and Denmark tend to be future oriented—giving them the luxury of time to make a decision. In contrast, people from Italy, Kuwait, and Poland are among those scoring low on this dimension, preferring to emphasize short-term rewards and instant gratification.

(8) *Performance orientation*—the extent to which group member improvement and excellence are encouraged and rewarded. People in Hong Kong, Germany, and the United States are among those who value training and development in order to improve performance. In other countries in Eastern Europe and Latin America, success is more likely to be related to family background or group membership than it is to performance.

(9) *Human orientation*—the extent to which individuals are encouraged and rewarded for being caring, kind, and fair to others. People in

Ireland, India, and the Philippines score high on this measure, a result of their concern for those less fortunate. In contrast, persons from Germany, France, and Brazil score lower on this measure because of the value they give to power and material possessions.

Understanding how orientations influence the conceptualization of leadership can provide us with clues regarding how best to interact with different cultures.

THE CULTURAL DIFFERENCE EFFECT

The interactional preferences of a culture's members are affected by where their culture falls on each of the preceding dialectic scales or cultural dimensions identified by GLOBE. For example, in Asian societies, people are likely to understate personal accomplishments and successes while just the opposite is true for members of North American cultures who are taught from an early age to "claim credit where credit is due" for their personal achievements. Highly individualistic cultures are apt to use low-context communication, while highly collectivistic cultures prefer to interact more indirectly, relying more heavily on high-context communication. This explains why North Americans tend to speak directly on an issue while people from Japan, Korea, and China seek to avoid confrontation, aim to preserve harmony, and try to help others save face. Similarly, rarely will an individual from an Arab country criticize another publicly, believing that to do so would be disloyal and disrespectful. Unless we understand differences such as these, our interactions with persons from other cultures could result in misunderstandings.

Differences matter. Unless we rethink them, the stereotypes we hold can interfere with the ability to do business. For example, as Western luxury brands seek sales in China, they need to unlearn the gender stereotypes they believed to be true. Chinese women buy more whiskey and fast cars, while Chinese men purchase more face creams and bags—in part, because Chinese men perceive appearance as critical to their social and professional success and they carry so much cash.[14]

On the other hand, even when we are aware of the cultural backgrounds of others, we can still experience difficulty. For example, a U.S. leader traveled to Tokyo for an operations review. Prior to going he read a book on Japanese business customs and culture. From it he learned that typically in Japan, speakers offer an apology in their introductions. Since he wanted to build rapport with those he would be meeting with, he too began his presentation with an apology about giving such a long and detailed speech after lunch. His audience responded with laughter. When the meeting was over, he asked his Japanese counterpart why everyone laughed at his introduction. The Japanese leader told him that most of their employees had cross-cultural training and knew that Americans begin their presentations with a joke.[15] Cultural presumptions influence message reception.

Similarly, it is important to understand that the meaning our culture gives to certain behaviors is not universal. We need to understand how members of other cultures interpret behavior. For example, Yu Chen, from Taiwan, had difficulty establishing a working relationship with John, the U.S. representative of an American multinational corporation. It seems that when John became nervous, his eye blink rate increased dramatically. While blinking when another person talks is normal for North Americans, the Taiwanese consider it impolite.[16] Showing the sole of a shoe symbolizes nothing to U.S. or European observers. Because of this, when serving as delegates to a conference in Saudi Arabia, the American and European representatives thought little if anything about crossing their legs and pointing their shoes toward a conference presenter. Their behavior, however, horrified the Muslim speaker who perceived the gesture to be insulting.[17]

In like fashion, it is normal for Arabs to adopt a direct body orientation when interacting. Americans, in contrast, usually employ a less direct stance. As a result, they often perceive the communication of Arabs as aggressive and unnerving. Arabs also gesture vigorously when speaking to others, which can make the less physical Americans interpret their actions as inappropriate and unmannerly. The same holds true for the expression of feelings. In Middle Eastern cultures, people exaggerate emotional responses, while in the United States people are more likely to suppress them, and in Asian cultures, reserve and emotional restraint are the rule.

Also of note, in addition to the preceding measures we discussed, the GLOBE studies also identified six global leadership categories and situated them in the following clusters representing different regions of the world:[18]

(1) *Charismatic/value-based leadership*—emphasizing the leader's ability to inspire—common in the United States and Canada, Nordic countries, and Latin Europe

(2) *Team-oriented leadership*—emphasizing collaboration, team building, and the importance of a common purpose—common in Latin America, Confucian Asia, and Latin Europe

(3) *Participative leadership*—nonauthoritarian, emphasizing the importance of involving others in decision making and execution—common in Nordic Europe, the United States, and Canada

(4) *Humane-oriented leadership*—emphasizing the priority given to compassion, sensitivity, and supportiveness—common in sub-Saharan Africa

(5) *Autonomous leadership*—emphasizing the preference for independent leadership—common in Germanic Europe

(6) *Self-protective leadership*—emphasizing the desire to keep the leader and the group safe, ensuring their security—common in the Middle East, Confucian Asia, and Southern Europe

Understanding the leadership modes different cultures find important and desirable can facilitate the effective managing of diversity. For example, a leader who realizes that charisma and initiative work well in the United States, but could be perceived as a liability in Eastern Europe, demonstrates cultural intelligence. So does one who understands that while participatory leadership is seen as essential in German leaders, in Saudi Arabian leaders it would probably be interpreted as a weakness because the exercise of authoritative leadership is seen as a strength there.

While culture affects the leadership process, some universals do exist. Interestingly, there is great support according to GLOBE for leaders who possess interpersonal skills, are of high integrity, and are charismatic. Conversely, most agree that leaders who are asocial, ruthless, and egocentric are likely to be ineffective.[19]

WOMEN, MEN, AND LEADERSHIP

Close your eyes. Picture a leader you admire. Are you visualizing a male or a female? Was the person you pictured of the same sex as you or the opposite sex? Many people are not fully aware of our attitudes toward gender, including how it influences our feelings about leaders.

To begin developing more awareness, ask yourself these questions: (1) What qualities do you admire in leaders? (2) Who do you believe possess more of the qualities on your list, men or women? (3) What negative qualities do you associate with male leaders? (4) What negative qualities do you associate with female leaders? (5) In your opinion, are male and female leaders equally effective and equally valued?

All cultures distinguish between male and female behavior. Every culture sends its members messages regarding appropriate male and female roles and behaviors. The United States, for example, is a patriarchal culture. Despite all the advances women have made, recent news headlines testify to this. Writer Ken Auletta penned an article for *New York* titled "A Woman's Place: Can Sheryl Sandberg Upend Silicon Valley's Male-Dominated Culture?" and Sarah Lyall and Jo Becker, writing about Rebekah Wade when she was still editor of the scandal-marred British tabloid the *News of the World,* used this headline: "A Tenacious Rise to the Top in the Brutal Men's World of Tabloids."[20]

From the moment we are born, we learn gender stereotypes. Men are aggressive. Women are emotional. Men are confident. Women are cautious. Men are independent. Women are sensitive. The traits we attribute to men are those usually admired in leaders. However, companies now recognize that women bring strengths to the leadership table as well: their ability to forge personal connections, build interpersonal relationships, nurture leadership, and think before acting is being recognized as of value. Despite this, while women have made inroads into what was traditionally the male's domain, and have succeeded in increasingly occupying leadership positions, men still outnumber women in these roles (women are far less likely to head Fortune 500 companies be elected to public office, or hold others positions of power in the United States), and are paid more (women earn roughly 77 cents for every dollar a man working full time earns) for performing them.[21] What accounts for the disparity in position and income? Is it ability, style, others' perceptions and persistent stereotypes, or a combination of factors?

According to Judy Rosener, women leaders have a more inclusive leadership style; they are more apt to share power, promote involvement, and work to enhance feelings of self-worth among their followers.[22] Women leaders also are more likely to embrace a democratic and participative style of leading than men and are more likely to use transformational leadership behaviors.[23]

What expectations of their leaders do supporters have? Many expect leaders to have agentic characteristics—to be agents of change—action oriented, decisive, and direct. When it comes to women leaders, however, for too many stereotypes and sexism persist, and as a result, women have to jump hurdles that men rarely face. For example, as we noted, strength, independence, and rationality are sex typed as masculine characteristics, while emotionality, nurturing, and caring are sex typed as feminine characteristics. Even though men now share more of what were once categorized as women's responsibilities, women are still cast in primary-caregiver roles, while men are typecast as primary breadwinners. Additionally, U.S. culture gives more status to male characteristics such as decisiveness, competitiveness, and assertion. In contrast, women who violate accepted gender stereotypes, acting aggressively or too tough, run the risk of being labeled "iron maidens" or unfeminine.

Gendered expectations may bias perceptions. When they lead like men, women's efforts are devalued. To be perceived to be as good as men, women need to be viewed as better. Women, however, are less likely to self-promote than men and are also less apt to negotiate as effectively, having been conditioned to withdraw rather than be confrontational.[24] Could this be contributing to the longevity of a pay gap between men and women? Others question whether women exacerbate obstacles to their advancement. One quarter of the women surveyed by the Women at the Top project believe that women are their own worst enemies when it comes to achieving parity. However, most felt that the disparity in women occupying top leadership positions was due to other factors such as institutionalized discrimination and prejudice.[25]

When asked, Who's the better leader? their supporters judge male and female leaders to be equally effective, with the most effective leadership style reportedly combining relationship building and task and efficiency aspects. Hopefully, the leadership role will continue its evolution from what was once a masculine model into a more androgynous one.[26] This change actually was forecast decades ago and expressed in contrasting views toward the value of diversity. The *equity model,* once in vogue, viewed difference as a problem; thus, women who were viewed as different from men were apt to be perceived as inferior leaders. In contrast, the *complementary contribution model* viewed difference as a strength and asserted that eliminating difference only served to negate women's true nature and diminish the impact of their contributions.[27] Leaders benefit when they merge the best of male and female qualities into their style.

Theory Into Practice

Leadership Emergence and Exaggeration

Does gender play a role in how organizations select their leaders? When the environment is highly competitive, why are so many more men than women chosen to fill leadership positions? Could the selection of many more men be attributed to their willingness to exaggerate their abilities rather than to their inherent talents?

(Continued)

(Continued)

In a study titled "The Emergence of Male Leadership in Competitive Environments," Reuben, Rey-Biel, Sapienza, and Zingales report that a prime reason for women's underrepresentation in top corporate positions could well be that men exaggerate their achievements more than women. Unlike women, men express overconfidence when recalling past performances—a behavior resulting in their frequently being appointed leaders.[28]

To conduct the study, researchers at a number of business schools assigned MBA students to take a math quiz. Males and females taking the test performed similarly. However, a little over a year later, when asked to recall their performance on the test, male test takers inflated their scores by over 30.5% compared to only 14.4% for female test takers. Since all test takers had been told they would receive $50 for accurately recalling their results, there was no incentive for them to exaggerate.

Findings suggest that corporate boards might well be selecting as their leaders the less qualified but more boastful candidates (both real and imagined), making, in effect, suboptimal decisions. Being overconfident about abilities and being willing to lie about abilities appears to correlate with gender differences in the appointment of leaders in competitive environments.

Now that you know this, what steps are you ready to take to lessen the chances of such discriminatory and less than optimal decision making?

CAPITALIZING ON DIVERSITY

Because of the different insights and communication strengths members bring to an organization or team, it ought to be easier for an organization or team rich in diversity to achieve synergy, that is, to produce an outcome better than the sum of its parts—better than any member could produce alone. Once you use cultural awareness to discover what people from different cultures and backgrounds can contribute to one another, you also understand the rationale for promoting diversity in organizations and teams.

Diversity's Benefits

Where diversity thrives, everyone is able to contribute and benefit. But diversity does more than provide equal access or opportunity. In addition to diversity enabling organizations to recruit the best personnel, diversity also extends the

Why do you think the character in the cartoon is making such a request?

"We were hoping that you could work from work today."

Kim Warp/The New Yorker Collection/www.cartoonbank.com

organization's breadth (reach) and depth (understanding). Because people in the organization understand the needs of diverse constituencies, they enhance their ability to appeal to different cultural groups.

In addition, highly heterogeneous groups are less likely to engage in group-think. Since members have diverse backgrounds, they probably also have a variety of viewpoints, increasing the likelihood that members will be open to ideas, think in new ways, and pay greater attention to an issue's many aspects. Diversity is a strength leaders need to value and build upon.

> **Difference matters!**

Obstacles to Diversity

Diversity does not always come easy. Ethnocentrism, prejudices, and stereotypes (referred to earlier in this chapter), in addition to being the basis for unfairness and injustice in how people interact with one another, also impede many from accepting it. People who hold strong stereotypes are prone to the *fundamental attribution error.* As a result of their perceptual biases, far too many people persist in discriminating against persons if their ethnicity, race, gender, age, or other attributes differ from their own. When a member of a stigmatized or out-group causes a problem or fails, for example, those who are biased are likely to blame it on a personal defect or deficiency or other dispositional factor. However, when they or a member of their in-group experience a problem or fail, they tend to attribute it to external or situational factors, not inherent internal weaknesses.

Stereotypes create overly simple pictures of others. Those who discriminate assume members of a category are similar. Their neglect of differences results in the hardening of categories and unfair labeling of people who should be treated as individuals.

Work It Out: Alone or Together

Develop a list of obstacles facing members of the following groups: Asian Americans, Hispanic Americans, African Americans, and older men and women. What common obstacles exist? Review diversity efforts to overcome the obstacles and suggest new ones.

Surmounting the Obstacles

Leaders bring people together; their actions should not drive them further apart. The more information people have about one another, the less likely they are to engage in stereotyping or other prejudicial behavior. The more people from different cultures interact with one another, and the more they get to know one another personally, the more their discriminatory behavior declines. Thus, having an open mind and being accepting of new information helps us adjust and monitor our reactions based on a specific contextual framework.

Appreciation for diversity must start at the top and permeate every level of the organization. As with all projects, the leader communicates the value of the vision and how it serves and facilitates the enactment of the mission. Training can pave the way for acceptance. Everyone deserves the freedom to be authentic. Effective companies balance the drive for individualism and personal achievement with the drive for inclusion and group affiliation. Once diversity's lessons are taught, internalized, and practiced, the organization will reap the benefits.

Post It: Imagineering a Better Way

HSBC is a global operation. With a workforce drawn from 144 different nations, diversity is a reality of the bank's daily business.[29] The bank contends that by embracing diversity it is better able to adapt to new situations and opportunities. How does HSBC define diversity? HSBC equates diversity with a willingness to value the contributions of employees regardless of their background or lifestyle. For HSBC diversity and an attitude of open-mindedness go hand in hand. The bank focuses on all aspects of diversity. Sometimes its focus is on gender, other times on ethnicity, and still other times on disability or age. Contending that inclusiveness supports diversity, HSBC has made diversity a management practice, not an option. Thus, HSBC has a diversity committee for every one of its business units. Among the committees' responsibilities are to oversee flexible working practices that remove discrimination or disadvantages from the work place. They also provide training on diversity issues across management levels—effectively binding the HSBC group together. Stressed in their training is the importance of being open toward different ideas. HSBC also measures annually the extent to which employees believe the bank values diverse perspectives and welcomes new ideas.

   With this as background, create a diversity profile of your organization (use your class or group if you are not employed). Next, identify the leadership challenges and opportunities in building an organizational culture that creates synergy by harnessing diversity's strengths. Finally, if you do not interact regularly with persons different from you, identify steps you can take to expand your involvement as well as how such an expansion might enhance your leadership intelligence.

LOOK BACK

Reread the opening poem. What benefits can you add to a team created on the basis of diversity?

Key Terms

Cognitive diversity (238)

Collectivism (242)

Cultural relativism (239)

Culture (241)

Diversity (237)

Ethnocentrism (239)

Feminine culture (244)

Globalization (238)

Glocalization (238)

High-context communication (242)

Identity diversity (238)

Individualism (242)

Low-context communication (243)

Masculine culture (244)

Monochronic (244)

Multiculturalists (238)

Polychronic (244)

Power distance (243)

Prejudice (240)

Stereotypes (240)

Uncertainty avoidance (245)

Notes

1. Marshall McLuhan, *The Medium Is the Message* (New York: Bantam Books, 1967); Marshall McLuhan, *Understanding Media* (New York: Mentor, 1964).

2. Alicia Clegg, "Multinational People Managers," *Financial Times* (August 4, 2011): 8.

3. Jean Francois Manzoni, Paul Strebel, and Jean-Louis Barsoux, "Why Diversity Can Backfire on Company Boards," *Wall Street Journal* (January 25, 2010): R3.

4. S. Ting-Toomey, *Communicating Across Cultures* (New York: Guilford, 1999).

5. James Flanigan, "Passports Essential for These MBAs," *New York Times* (February 21, 2008): C5.

6. Katherin Hille, "Global Pioneers of China Inc.," *Financial Times* (June 28, 2011): 10.

7. See William B. Gudykunst, *Bridging Differences: Effective Intergroup Communication,* 4th ed. (Thousand Oaks, CA: Sage, 2003).

8. For more background on prejudice, see M. L. Hecht, ed., *Communicating Prejudice* (Thousand Oaks, CA: Sage, 1998).

9. E. M. Rogers and T. M. Steinfatt, *Intercultural Communication* (Long Grove, IL: Waveland Press, 1999), 79.

10. See G. Hofstede, *Culture's Consequences: Comparing Values, Behaviors, Institutions, and Organizations Across Nations,* 2nd ed. (Thousand Oaks, CA: Sage, 2001); and G. Hofstede, *Cultures and Organizations: Software of the Mind* (London: McGraw-Hill, 1991).

11. E. Hall, *Beyond Culture* (Garden City, NY: Anchor, 1977).

12. See G. Hofstede, *Cultures and Organizations.*

13. R. J. House, P. J. Hanges, M. Javidan, P. W. Dorfman, V. Gupta, et al., eds., *Culture, Leadership, and Organizations: The GLOBE Study of 62 Societies* (Thousand Oaks, CA: Sage, 2004).

14. Patti Waldmeir and Barney Jopson, "Taste for Fast Cars and Whiskey Casts China's Women in New Light," *Financial Times* (July 5, 2011): 1.

15. L. Carobolante, "Leveraging Effective Communications in Multiple-Culture Business Environments," *Mobility* (August, 2011): 52–59.

16. William B. Gudykunst, *Bridging Differences: Effective Intergroup Communication*, 4th ed. (Thousand Oaks, CA: Sage, 2004), 12–13.

17. See G. Hofstede, *Masculinity and Femininity: The Taboo Dimension of National Cultures* (Thousand Oaks, CA: Sage, 1998).

18. See R. J. House, P. J. Hanges, M. Javidan, P. W. Dorfman, V. Gupta, et al., eds., *Culture, Leadership, and Organizations: The GLOBE Study of 62 Societies* (Thousand Oaks, CA: Sage, 2004).

19. P. W. Dorfman, P. J. Hanges, and F. C. Brodbeck, "Leadership and Cultural Variation: The Identification of Culturally Endorsed Leadership Profiles," in R. J. House, P. J. Hanges, M. Javidan, P. W. Dorfman, V. Gupta, et al., eds., *Culture, Leadership, and Organizations: The GLOBE Study of 62 Societies* (Thousand Oaks, CA: Sage, 2004), 669–722.

20. The Auletta article appeared in the July 11–18, 2011, issue of the *New Yorker*; the Lyall and Becker article appeared in the July 8, 2011, issue of the *New York Times*.

21. See, for example, Julianne Malveaux, "More Female Grads, but What About Pay?" *USA Today* (May 13, 2011): 11A; "77 Cents on the Dollar Isn't Fair," *New York Times* (April 21, 2011): A26.

22. J. B. Rosener, "Ways Women Lead," *Harvard Business Review* (November-December, 1990): 119–25.

23. See, for example, M. L. Van Engen and T. M. Willemsen, "Sex and Leadership Styles: A Meta-Analysis of Research Published in the 1990s," *Psychological Reports* 94 (2004): 3–18.

24. H. R. Bowles and, K. L. McGinn, "Claiming Authority: Negotiating Challenges for Women Leaders," in D. M. Messick and R. M. Kramer, eds., *The Psychology of Leadership: New Perspectives and Research* (Mahwah, NJ: Lawrence Erlbaum, 2005), 191–208.

25. Andrew Hill, "Are Women Their Own Worst Enemies in the Boardroom?" *Financial Times* (February 16, 2011): 6.

26. See A. H. Eagly and L. L. Carli, *Through the Labyrinth: The Truth About How Women Become Leaders* (Boston: Harvard Business School Press, 2007).

27. See both C. Epstein, "Debate: Ways Men and Women Lead," *Harvard Business Review* (January-February 1991): 150–52, and J. Marshall, "Paths of Personal and Professional Development for Women Managers," *Management Education and Development* 16(2) (1985): 169–79.

28. See Ernesto Reuben, Pedro Rey-Biel, Pala Sapienza, and Luigi Zingales, "The Emergence of Male Leadership in Competitive Environments," a study conducted for the Institute for the Study of Labor, November 2010.

29. Much of the information about how HSBC approaches diversity is based on Charis Gresser, "Diversity Is Vital to Bank's Business," *Financial Times* (July 14, 2011): 21.

CHANGE, MEET RESILIENCE!

CHANGE MAKING:
PAVING THE WAY

CHANGE MANAGING: SHAPING THE PATH

CREATIVITY: THE KEY TO
UNLEASHING INNOVATION

Change

Or be changed.

It's a question of who's to be in charge.

As for me

I'd rather innovate

Than stagnate

Ending up pushed forward or out

Thank you—I'll do it with you,

But on my own.

14

INNOVATING

In 1532, Machiavelli's *The Prince* was first published. In *The Prince*, Machiavelli offered his perspective on change, writing, "There is nothing more difficult to take in hand, more perilous to conduct, or more uncertain in its success, than to take the lead in the introduction of a new order of things."[1]

A more recent work by Spencer Johnson titled *Who Moved My Cheese? An Amazing Way to Deal With Change in Your Work and in Your Life* is a story-book about acknowledging and preparing for the inevitability of change. In many ways *Who Moved My Cheese?* helped to repopularize the field of change management.[2] Johnson enabled us to appreciate that how leaders communicate the need for change determines how followers respond, whether they adapt to the change, and, ultimately, whether change will be implemented smoothly and successfully.

We credit transformational leaders with influencing followers to try new things. Transformational lead-

> **Be a role model for change.**

ers function as role models for change—in many ways they are change agents. They also serve as social architects, helping people feel better about themselves and their contributions to the organization.

Do you view change as a challenge you can master? Do you think you will be able to empower others to assume the responsibilities change requires? In other words, are you prepared to overcome resistance to change so you can make change? In this chapter, we explore the process of change making, including the nature of change, attitudes toward change, the importance of change, and its effects.

CHANGE, MEET RESILIENCE!

How do you feel about change? Have you ever felt the need to change things and then tried to enact it? Did others meet your efforts with open arms or did they express resistance to your ideas and seek to convince you that there was no need "to rock the boat," that things were fine, maybe even perfect? They knew and felt they understood current realities. They didn't know or couldn't visualize what would happen if things were changed.

Often, we are unable to see potential problems before they turn into crises because of the self-created illusionary cocoons we place ourselves in. This need not be the case. What can you as a leader do to help followers feel that change is not only possible but also desirable? One of the leader's prime responsibilities is to enable others to realize their resilience and the important roles they have to play in controlling their futures.

Resilience Is the Ability to Bounce Back. Do You Have It?

Are you positive and optimistic?

Are you goal focused?

Are you flexible?

Are you organized?

Are you proactive?

What is resilience? *Resilience* is the ability to bounce back. When resilient people experience a disruption, they don't give up. Instead, they think like optimists and adapt and grow.

What role does resilience play in the change process? Resilience helps protect people from giving in to their anxieties. Why? First, people who are resilient tend to be positive and optimistic.[3] They understand not just the complexity inherent in life, but also the opportunities. They engage their energies to meet life's challenges rather than retreating from real or imagined threats into a state of learned helplessness that causes them to become fearful of the future. Second, resilient people tend to be focused. They can clearly envision their goals. They know what they want to achieve. This enables them to direct their energies toward their valued goals rather than disperse it across too many less important efforts. Third, resilient people are flexible. Undeterred by uncertainty, they do not limit themselves to what is familiar or to how things have always been done. They open themselves to possibilities. Fourth, resilient people are organized. They develop systems to handle ambiguity or uncertainty; they develop disciplined courses of action, rather than responding off the cuff. And finally, resilient people are proactive. Rather than seeking to protect themselves from change, they excitedly seek to engage it.[4]

What can you do to strengthen resilience in yourself and others? How might the characteristics just identified benefit you in this effort?

Self-Reflection: Looking In and Out

How challenging is change for you? How have you managed your response to change? What can you learn from exploring how you and others handle change? Let's find out.

Begin by identifying a time when you faced what you perceived to be a disruptive change. For example, perhaps you had to move to a new school, survive a company merger, or cope with a change in supervisor. Explain what you learned about yourself when facing the change. For example, what thoughts did you struggle with? What, if anything, did you do to adapt? Identify personal qualities that you believe facilitated or impeded your handling of the change. For instance, did you voice "I can't do that because" statements that constrained your ability to respond positively? If you did, how many of your statements do you now believe were baseless, and how many do you still believe are true?

Next, identify someone you know who confronted and handled what could have been a personally disruptive change effectively. What qualities did the person display that enabled him or her to handle change so capably? Use the qualities of resilience identified earlier to assess the person's responses. For example, what did she or he do that communicated a positive nature or demonstrated organizational skills?

What did you learn from this review? What can you do to strengthen resilience in yourself?

CHANGE MAKING: PAVING THE WAY

For leaders to be able to innovate, they need to know how to overcome resistance to change in themselves as well as in those who work with and for them. An essential step in overcoming such resistance is to understand why people don't want change in their lives. Here are some reasons. As we introduce them, ask yourself which of these reasons you have used when facing the need to change.

First, people may not have trust in those who are asking for the change and, as a result, may insist that the change is unnecessary. Some worry that the organization's motive for implementing the change is to save money, and therefore, the change might result in the organization downsizing and perhaps eliminating their jobs. Second, people imagine that they might not be up to the change. They worry that they might lack the skills needed once the change is put into effect. Third, people wonder if the change might mean that they could suffer a loss in personal power or status because they might suddenly need to share resources or no longer be able to make decisions for themselves and therefore would not be in control of their futures. Whatever its source, people fearful of change often experience psychological stress, in large measure because they perceive change to be personally threatening.

What should you, the leader, do in the face of such resistance? The leader's role is to reframe the idea of change—so instead of its being seen as a threat, it is viewed as an opportunity. This can be done if you provide the means for those involved to learn new ways of doing things. It can be done if you help them find within themselves the desire to grow, to explore new paths, and to identify new ways to contribute creatively.[5]

In leading the transformation in thinking about change, the advice of leadership theorist John Kotter can help. Kotter suggests leaders take the following steps:

1. The leader needs to help receivers perceive an untapped opportunity as urgent. They need to believe that maintaining or preserving the status quo could, in short order, find them facing a crisis. Thus, they need to see not changing as more risky than changing.

2. The leader needs to identify a team of supporters—a guiding coalition whom others admire and respect—to partner with him or her, sharing leadership, in pursuit of the opportunity.

3. The leader needs to communicate a compelling vision—one neither complicated nor vague—capable of pushing others forward into the future, one that is very ambitious but at the same time possible to achieve. The vision clarifies the organization's purpose, its values, and its goal.

4. The leader needs to communicate the vision repeatedly. The leader's message needs to be consistent, delivered through a variety of means, and reach the various groups or stakeholders involved in ways that speak directly to them. Persistence and repetition are essential—it takes time for a message to really get through.

5. The leader needs to give those involved the power to act and take risks so that they no longer feel powerless—it's about involving the right people in doing the right things.

6. The leader needs to plan for and attain reachable goals. Small wins can be huge. In fact, small wins at the beginning make the big wins at the end easier to get. Wins help the leader create support for change.

7. The leader needs to emphasize achievements, building on them to yield more change.

8. Finally, the leader needs to institutionalize progress so that innovation becomes a habit—a continuing process and organizational pursuit.[6]

Theory Into Practice

It's Transformational

James MacGregor Burns and Bernard Bass were among the first to differentiate between leaders who exercise traditional leadership (transactional leaders) and those who practice a more potent kind of leadership labeled *transformational.*[7]

While transactional leaders focus on satisfying the basic needs of followers, transformational leaders seek to fulfill their higher needs. As a result, while transactional leaders rely on giving rewards to employees in exchange for desirable performance, transformational leaders seek to enrich workers' self-esteem and inspire them to become self-actualized. Burns, Bass, and others theorized that transformational leaders bring about big changes, making big differences in their organizations, whereas transactional leaders mostly succeed in maintaining the status quo.

The following factors are among leadership variables researchers identify as active in transformational leadership: *charisma* (the leader's ability to connect and build trust), *intellectual stimulation* (the leader's ability to foster effective problem solving and decision making), and *inspiration* (the leader's ability to motivate and communicate high expectations and performance).

What leaders are you aware of or do you know who embody these qualities? What innovation(s) have they succeeded in implementing?

CHANGE MANAGING: SHAPING THE PATH

To manage change, you must be able to harness the emotions of the people involved so that they willingly walk down the path to the new future you envision for the organization. How can you as the leader shape the environment to precipitate needed organizational change? In other words, what can you do to create an environment that is innovation friendly?

According to authors Chip and Dan Heath, the leader needs to balance reason and emotion for such an environment to exist.[8] Can you do this? Some of us are more analytical than emotional while others of us are the opposite. Most of us analyze and study issues; we fact-find and problem solve. We seek evidence in support of ideas. But that is usually not enough to get others onboard. To do that, we have to be able to offer them more than facts. We have to find ways to involve them emotionally. Engaging the emotions of receivers is equally as important as engaging them logically. In other words, making a decision and communicating it are different processes and, therefore, require different approaches.

Observation: Watch and Learn

What can you as a leader do to create an environment (1) that is conducive to change, (2) helps increase readiness to change, and (3) rewards small steps toward change in personalized and creative ways?

To answer this, identify both a real and fictional leader who enacted the preceding practices. Then, using actual examples (in the case of the real leader) and scenes from popular films (in the case of the fictional leader), describe the leader's words and actions and explain what the leader did in order to (1) encourage positive attitudes toward change, (2) encourage risk taking and learning from mistakes, and (3) recognize contributions and small victories.

To get others on your side, phrase what you want in ways that inspire—in ways that make those coalitions we spoke of earlier feasible. Inspire and excite others; do not order them. You need to help them develop resilience when facing change so their defenses don't harden, and they don't surrender to rigidity. You need to give others a sense of control over their futures thereby reinforcing their willingness to respond more positively to change.

Creativity releases innovation.

CREATIVITY: THE KEY TO UNLEASHING INNOVATION

For the leader, fostering change, innovation, and creative thinking go hand in hand. If you encourage the seeking of novelty instead of allowing people to become entrenched in thinking as they have always thought or relying on procedures to which they are accustomed, then you stand a better chance of creating a culture conducive to breakthrough thinking and the systemization of innovation.

Will this leader's comment spur creativity? What steps would you advise the leader in the cartoon take to unleash the creativity of team members?

"*Speaking of creativity, I'd like everyone to take a minute and note how Richard is using his tongue to make it look like he has three lips.*"

Zachary Kanin/The New Yorker Collection/www.cartoonbank.com

For example, breakthrough thinking and the systemization of innovation are credited for the recent growth of Proctor & Gamble (P&G). Some years back, the company created a "new growth factory" composed of business creation groups, focused project teams, and entrepreneurial guides. Constantly on the lookout for innovation opportunities, P&G believes its people are motivated by an emotional component that serves as their source of inspiration—the message that each innovation improves people's lives.[9] P&G also provides training in how to shake up embedded ways of thinking that too often function as innovation blockers. In effect, P&G's leaders devised ways to manage the collective creativity of employees. In like fashion, Intuit empowered its workers to develop their own innovations by creating a team of "innovation catalysts."[10] With a model based on coaching, hands-on participation, and practice, the grass roots of the company drove its innovation. By moving people from talking to doing, and involving them in workshops that ended with participants identifying something they would do differently as a result of having attended the session, preconceptions were shattered and a culture of continuous improvement emerged.

Types of Change	Characteristics
Evolutionary change	It's incremental, continuous.
Revolutionary change	It's a radical breakthrough, a reengineering.

The spectrum of change exists along a continuum with evolutionary change at one end and revolutionary change at the other. *Evolutionary change* is also known as incremental change or continuous improvement. Its goal is to make things better, and it is usually implemented rather quickly. In contrast, *revolutionary change* is known as a radical breakthrough or reengineering. Its goal is to make things different, and it typically takes longer to implement. Both kinds of change complement each other and work in tandem with one another. Your challenge is to be able to identify the type of change needed at any point in time. Which type of change interests you more? If you are intrigued by idea or product development, you likely prefer evolutionary change. On the other hand, if exploration excites you, revolutionary change is your likely preference. The situation, however, often dictates the kind of change called for. By asking and answering the following questions, you can identify the nature of a needed change:

1. Would it be better to build on current structures and systems, or create new ones?

2. Are incremental improvements called for, or would it be better to come up with something totally different?

3. Are there constraints you need to work within, or are the possibilities limitless?

4. Are you seeking something that works with systems currently in use, or would you benefit from introducing an entirely new approach?

5. Is the organization in need of a tweaking, or is a total transformation necessary?[11]

Change can be limited or far-reaching. Sometimes just an individual, group, or department needs change. Other times, the change is more extensive, affecting an entire product or service line. The most dramatic change involves altering the vision, purpose, mission, and values of the organization, as well as the kinds of people and processes used to accomplish the organization's work. Whatever its nature, however, change always has an impact.

Working It Out: Alone or Together

Identify a change that you believe needs to be implemented in your class, college, or community. Identify (1) the nature of the change sought, (2) the tasks to be accomplished if the change is to occur, (3) the risks involved, and (4) the actions you would need to take to prepare for the change, overcome the risks, and implement the change. Include how you would motivate or encourage others to accept the change and the impact the change would likely have on people, procedures or systems, and the environment. Finally, give a prediction of the likelihood (citing reasons) that the change you identified could be successfully completed.

Instead of imitating others, your role as a leader is to challenge the status quo and find a different and better way. Standing out from the competition is not easy. Creativity is required. Rather than trying to keep up with the competition and achieve a homogenization of the marketplace, your goal is to distinguish your organization from the competition.[12] As the leader, your responsibility is to encourage the search for innovation—you are the idea stimulator in chief. This means you will need to experiment and take risks and encourage your team to do so as well. You will learn from your mistakes and move forward, generating small and then bigger wins. You will be a catalyst, motivator, and idea factory builder. You will be the director of possibilities, and you will help others imagine the future. How will you do this?

Breaking out of comfortable mind-sets is challenging but doable. Your role as leader is to create the environment that makes that possible. People need autonomy and work that is meaningful and makes a difference. They need time as opposed to constricting deadlines. And, of course, they need to be able to share—to collaborate—because collaboration drives creativity.[13] Leadership theorists Kouzes and Posner tell of one leader who asked the organization's members to imagine they had left their jobs to join a startup whose intent it was to put their former company out of business. The leader then asked those participating to generate in a half hour as many ways to do that as they could think of. Kouzes and Posner tell of another leader who wanted to increase the number of research grants coming into the university. To do this, the leader felt that faculty had to become more involved in exchanging ideas. The leader put chalkboards on the hall walls so that faculty could engage in spontaneous scientific discussions anywhere and at any time. They tell of yet another leader of a fund-raising organization who wanted to take away the fear of failing that risk taking engendered. At the end of the fund-raising drive the leader held a "postmortem" during which all talked about lessons learned, what went well and poorly, and how they could change things the next time. The leader was the first to admit mistakes made, alleviating the fear of doing so in others.[14] Thus, the leader encouraged others to fail and then think forward. To facilitate this, you, as leader, could give "risk/failure rewards"—such as a stuffed giraffe for sticking your neck out or lottery tickets to people who take chances.[15]

Figure 14.1

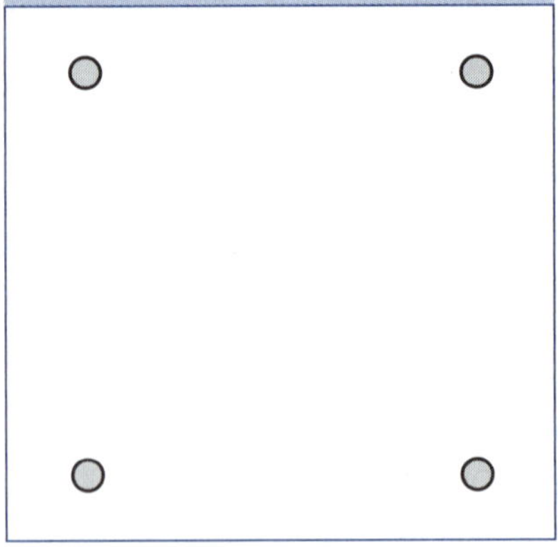

Ideas make change possible. Ideas without constraints make change more possible. With this in mind, link the points in Figure 14.1 to form a star. (See Figure 14.2 at the end of the chapter for the solution.)

If you experience difficulty, ask yourself what constraints you unconsciously placed on the problem. Then ask yourself if we imposed any of the constraints you just identified. Did we tell you that you couldn't add extra points? As with change, we build constraints where none exist, when instead we should be creating attractors that pull energies in new directions and create new forms of doing things. By challenging and changing norms and procedures, and encouraging new understandings and actions, you as the leader can help the organization grow and develop, catalyze change, and innovate.

Observation: Watch and Learn

In *Images of Organization*, Gareth Morgan writes, "The message is that, even though our actions shape and are shaped by change, we are just part of an evolving pattern."[16]

By definition, change and the status quo are opposites. Creating a new future inevitably finds you leaving the present behind. For example, we want to innovate, but we fear making mistakes. We want to think long term, but we want immediate results. We need to reduce staff, but we want to improve teamwork. We seek low costs and at the same time high quality. Your role as leader is to be a skilled manager of tensions like these. The creative manager finds ways not only of unfreezing resistance to change, but also discovers ways of integrating the competing elements and reframing them in positive ways. This requires the development of new understandings. For example, problems generate new solutions, and breakthroughs create new frontiers for new competitors, creating new problems, generating new solutions, leading to break-throughs, and so on.

To appreciate how this works, identify a change made by an organization that created new competitors for the organization, which then led to more changes.

Once you have done that, consider this. Not too long ago, the leadership of Google likely looked at Facebook and said, "We can do what Facebook is doing, only better." They came up with a new social networking site and called it Google+. First, explore how and why Google+ was able to influence the face of social networking. Once you have done that, imagine that you work for a competitor of a company such as Cisco, PepsiCo, Nike, or Whole Foods (pick a company that interests you). You have just been asked to look at your company's competitors and come up with an idea that will enable your company to take market share away from them. Work with your team to identify an innovation that will take the company into the future. After you identify such an innovation, your task is to present your idea to the rank and file (your class) and persuade them that such a change is in their best interests.

Here's the challenge: a problem you face in garnering this support is that people in your company have become too complacent with their success. Because the company is successful they see no reason to change anything. The company's members believe that they are better than they actually are. Now they believe that you and your team want to shake things up. A number of the people you are addressing are approaching retirement and fear being forced out because they lack new skills.

(Continued)

(Continued)

Other members also fear they will soon lose their jobs because the economy is in a slump, they are the newest hires, and "last in, first out" is on their minds. Still others are concerned because they view things as now "out of their hands," falsely assuming they have no power to influence your thinking or actions, and so they are depressed and demoralized.

That said, your team's next task is to help give members of the rank and file a sense of control over their destiny by helping them understand how making the change your team suggests will let them contribute more directly to the company's efforts to out-smart its competition. Develop a presentation that inspires them to get on board.

The answer to the leadership challenges of the future lies in changing the processes, behaviors, and thinking of the past. Playing it safe and avoiding the risk of changing won't work. Do you now feel better prepared to accept the change challenge? We hope so!

LOOK BACK

Reread the opening poem. In light of what you have read in this chapter, do you agree with the decision made by the poem's speaker? Who, in your opinion, should direct change, and how should changes sought be accomplished?

Figure 14.2

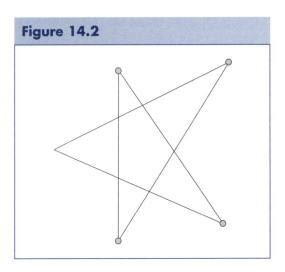

Notes

1. Niccolò Machiavelli, *The Prince* (New York: Bantam Classics, 1984).

2. Spencer Johnson, *Who Moved My Cheese? An Amazing Way to Deal With Change in Your World and In Your Life* (New York: Putnam, 1998).

3. Martin E. P. Seligman, "Building Resilience," *Harvard Business Review* (April 2011): 100–6.

4. See James M. Kouzes and Barry Z. Posner with Elaine Biech, *The Leadership Challenge Activities Book* (San Francisco: Pfeiffer, 2010).

5. See James Collins and Jerry Porras, *Built to Last* (New York: HarperCollins, 1994).

6. See, for example, John Kotter, *Leading Change* (Boston: Harvard Business Press, 1996).

7. See J. M. Burns, *Leadership* (New York: Harper & Row, 1978); and B. M. Bass, *Leadership and Performance Beyond Expectations* (New York: Free Press, 1985).

8. Chip Heath and Dan Heath, *Switch: How to Change Things When Change Is Hard* (New York: Crown Business, 2010); and Chip Heath and Dan Heath, *Made to Stick: Why Some Ideas Survive and Others Die* (New York: Random House, 2007).

9. Bruce Brown and Scott D. Anthony, "How P&G Tripled Its Innovation Success Rate," *Harvard Business Review* (June, 2011): 64–72.

10. Roger L. Martin, "The Innovation Catalysts," *Harvard Business Review* (June 2011): 82–87.

11. For a discussion of these change types, see Scott G. Isaksen, K. Brian Dorval, and Donald J. Treffinger, *Creative Approaches to Problem Solving: A Framework for Innovation and Change,* 3rd ed. (Thousand Oaks, CA: Sage, 2011), p. 201–4.

12. Youngme Moon, *Different: Escaping the Competitive Herd* (New York: Crown Business, 2010).

13. Keith Sawyer, *Group Genius: The Creative Power of Collaboration* (New York: Basic Books, 2007).

14. James M. Kouzes and Barry Z. Posner, *The Leadership Challenge Workbook* (San Francisco: Jossey-Bass, 2003), 85–86.

15. Ibid., 74.

16. Gareth Morgan, *Images of Organization,* 2nd ed. (Thousand Oaks, CA: Sage, 1997), 300.

Because I friend you
Doesn't mean I like you.
Because I follow you
Doesn't mean I approve.
Because I invite you in
Don't feel empowered
You still have to earn my trust
So don't push "Send all."

SOCIAL NETWORKING AND TECHNOLOGY

15

In the playgrounds of our lives, including nursery school and kindergarten, it is likely that we were taught to share. As we matured, however, many of us also learned to keep things to ourselves. The competing lessons of *share* and *mine* complicated our lives a bit. What should we share? What should we keep for ourselves?

Being graded on individual achievement in school initially made the idea of sharing even more difficult for us. Yet today we frequently find ourselves in groups and teams, and we are all expected to share and collaborate. Achieving balance between these two forces of sharing and keeping information to ourselves has not been easy for some of us. Every aspiring or practicing leader, however, needs to work it out. Some are having more difficulty than others accomplishing this, while recognizing that sharing and collaborating are 21st-century imperatives.

According to data from Fisheye Analytics, while online venues typically discuss company executives, too few of these executives actively use *social media*—media for social interaction—to spread their own messages. Not enough leaders are using social media strategically to build their personal brands in and out of their organizations or to engage with peers, employees, customers, and the public.[1]

> We live in a culture of sharing.

If you are like many students of leadership today, you may be ready to change that perception. Just consider your own connectedness. When you arrive in class, do you immediately turn off electronic devices disconnecting yourself from others? Do you turn off your cell or merely put it on vibrate? Do you ever text before, or maybe even after, the instructor enters and starts class? If using an iPad or laptop, do you use it only for taking notes, or do you also use it to check your Facebook or LinkedIn pages? Who, if anyone, do you follow on Twitter? How many followers, if any, do you have on Twitter? If you have followers, does that automatically make you a leader? How connected a leader do you aspire to be?

THE SHARING LEADER: HOW DO YOU FEEL ABOUT LEADING VIA ENGAGEMENT?

How do you want to lead? What tools do you see yourself using to interest and excite followers?

One focus of this chapter is on social networks internal to the organization. The fact is that tools of collaboration have multiplied, and leaders can no longer be reactive rather than proactive when it comes to social media use.[2] Another focus of this chapter is how you can use technology, specifically social media, to help redefine "sharing" and the leader-follower relationship. As Soumitra Dutta writes in "What's Your Personal Social Media Strategy?", "It's no secret that social media—global, open, transparent, non-hierarchical, and real time—are changing consumer behavior and workplace expectations."[3] Social media can be your partner in connecting you with members of your team, facilitating the nurturing of new ideas, the solving of problems, and the transformation of your organization.

Rachel Sterne embraced social media when she was named the first chief digital officer for the city of New York, one of only a few governmental officials in the country focused on transforming their organizations' relationships with stakeholders using the digital arena. Sterne, for example, was charged with reinventing how the city engages its stakeholders and chose to use

Facebook, Tumblr, Foursquare, and Twitter to reach her goal. Sterne also hopes to persuade colleagues to embrace, not fear, digital outlets. Sterne asserts that only if leaders use social media in an authentic way (posting themselves, not having assistants manage their accounts) will they succeed.[4]

Chances are that the people you are interested in reaching and rallying are already online. They likely use YouTube, Twitter, Yammer, LinkedIn, Facebook, and Google+, just to name a few social media sites. In fact, they may have participated in creating much of the content they view and share online. As we think about it, our culture could be described as a *culture of sharing*. We update our status on Facebook numerous times a day, check in at Foursquare, tweet thoughts and recommendations, and upload photos or videos to Flickr and YouTube. As a leader, you can take advantage of this. As Mark Zuckerberg, the founder and chief executive of Facebook, explained, "People want to share and stay connected with their friends and the people around them"; that if people have "control over what they share, they will want to share more"; and that "if people share more, the world will become more open and connected. And a world that's more open and connected is a better world."[5] User sharing can benefit leaders and their companies as well.

Let's see where we are. You aspire to lead, and you want others to follow. For this to happen, you need to build relationships, and technology can assist you in that effort by giving you a platform through which you and those you hope will be your partners in mission, goals, and values are able to share ideas and experiences. But first, we need to explore how you really feel about sharing when it comes to leading.

Self-Reflection: Looking In and Out

What is your SQ—sharing quotient? Using a scale of 1 to 5, with *1* representing "strongly agree" and *5* representing "strongly disagree," score your response to each of the following questions:

I prefer keeping information confidential. _____

I believe that explaining an idea to everyone takes too much of my time. _____

I believe I have no responsibility for others' understanding of how and why we make decisions. _____

(Continued)

I don't believe in using technology to foster collaboration. _____

I don't believe the leader should blog. _____

Using technology to update those in and external to the organization is PR and nothing more. _____

I cannot commit to hearing from everyone who wants to voice his or her opinions in the organization. _____

It is not my responsibility to promote the uncensored contribution of ideas. _____

I don't think it is advisable to involve everyone in innovation efforts. _____

Open technology platforms are not in a leader's best interests. _____

TOTAL _____

The higher your score, the higher your SQ. If you scored lower than you thought you should have, you may need to consider the following: how a lack of openness could impede goal achievement, what led to your viewing sharing as antithetical to leading, and what you can do to increase your comfort with sharing. On the other hand, whether you scored high or low on sharing, it is time to ask yourself what you can do to formally encourage sharing and the specific kinds of sharing you would like to implement.

We may not all feel good about sharing because we may not have had good experiences with what was shared about us in the past or fear what could be shared about us in the future. In part, Watergate became a crisis because the tapes made of former president Nixon's oval office conversations were ordered to be shared. Today, sharing occurs via the Internet. Users have "fans" and "followers" with whom they can maintain digital contact. Only communication doesn't just go in one direction, it goes in all directions—creating transparency as opposed to privacy, openness as opposed to secrecy, engagement with others as opposed to distance from them. We are getting more and more used to expressing ourselves in public and in real time. Leaders now have the opportunity, perhaps the obligation, to deal with this.

Use social media to build your personal brand.

Of what value is sharing? Why are we talking about it? Consider this: at Comcast, one executive started a Twitter account named @ComcastCares and, with that effort, succeeded in putting a more human face on the company.[6] Being open to the use of online media may enhance your ability to excite and involve people who would otherwise follow from the sidelines. People once left outside the doors where decisions are made suddenly can find themselves enticed to enter. Sharing can help you determine what people like and dislike, embrace and fear. By engaging with others, you can develop a more collaborative team because the engagement generated by sharing also fosters trust.

Use Sharing To

Excite others

Increase understanding

Foster trust and collaboration

Increase connection and support

Increase access to ideas

Accelerate involvement and innovation

Additionally, sharing can also engender connection to and support for one another. For example, the U.S. Army used a social media program, ArmyStrongStories.com, to encourage soldiers to blog about their experiences. Any rank-and-file soldier is free to post a blog. The natural allies of a company and its most believable voices are its employees.[7] When people are able to pose questions (answered by either one another or you) and comment on one another's ideas, they effectively are given a voice and shed their reluctance to voice opinions.

There are also other benefits. If they are interacting on your social network, they are less likely to be interacting on a network unrelated to the organization. And if you can use technology to cut down on unproductive travel, limit the number of poorly planned meetings, and harness the collaborative productivity of your partners and followers by forging links that improve the quality and quantity of interactions, then you can increase access to new ideas, accelerate innovation, and make sizeable leadership gains. For example, Alcatel-Lucent

What do the characters' comments reveal about how they see their leader? Based on their responses, what advice would you give the leader?

CEO Ben Verwaayen blogged on the company's internal website, asking for input from all 80,000 staff worldwide. Asserting that the blog let him get beyond "corporate speak" and dialogue directly with employees, Verwaayen credits it for increasing employee support of him and the company's strategic plan.[8]

DO YOU CARE WHAT YOU SHARE?

What is it that you can share? How will sharing facilitate leading?

First, you can share information. You can use social networks to communicate or reinforce a decision, introduce a goal, and involve your team in implementing strategy and connecting with one another so they can focus on the goal. Second, you can use a blog or another collaborative platform like Yammer to update thinking and progress. If one of the leader's tasks is to communicate the organization's mission, a blog can facilitate this effort. Third, by conversing online you can open yourself to more immediate feedback, making it easier for you to more readily identify who supports and who has problems with an idea. People can help one another with problems not by ignoring them, but by airing, addressing, and coming together to resolve them. Fourth, you can apply the creative solutions generated by crowdsourcing to help solve a specific problem. Finally, you can generate buy-in for decisions by opening up information sharing—meaning that by using collaborative technology, everyone is free to offer input, with the leader responsible for the ultimate decision.

> You can't be a secret sharer.

THE BENEFITS OF SHARING

Relationships have value. Sharing enables leaders and followers to grow, converse, help, and accomplish change together. Let us look at these outcomes in turn.

Growth

Sharing facilitates personal and organizational growth. It lets leaders enhance their understanding of supporters across multiple locations and vice versa. Leaders and supporters listen, learn about, and respond to one another's concerns, offering ideas on initiatives and generating feedback and insights that make decision making easier.

Conversation

Sharing promotes conversation, removing barriers between people, enhancing understanding, and leading to the creation of long-term focused relationships. Conversation is at the heart of every relationship. When people talk to each other, others become curious, first watching what is going on and, perhaps in time, entering the conversation as well. Dialoguing can feed itself. Adding a "share this" button facilitating the posting of content is now commonplace.

Alerts You to Problems

Monitoring online interactions can alert you to problems and potential problems, letting you answer questions and respond more quickly than you otherwise could. When you see what people comment on, you pick up on concerns and areas of weakness. Giving feedback and offering advice becomes natural, as do offers to help.

Accomplishes Change

Ask a simple question. For example, How can we be better? People want to play a role in making things better—an idea that can have a transforming effect on internal communications. If a conversation around such a question is moderated, say by the innovation director, ideas never thought of before—ideas beyond the familiar—can be handed over to developmental teams and transformed into actions leading to a culture of continuous improvement.[9]

Observation: Watch and Learn

Interview an organization's leader regarding his or her thoughts and feelings about using social networking, the kinds of online sharing occurring in the organization, the role the leader plays in the network(s), problems and benefits he or she perceives, and how the leader would like to see social networks evolve.

Every sharing activity you engage in, whether a blog, Wiki, tweet, discussion forum, or podcast, needs to have a goal. Once you formulate the goal you want to address—for example, let's say yours is to reduce turnover—then you can activate an action plan. You can learn about how people feel about the goal (why they think turnover is high), talk about it (discuss reasons for leaving the company), figure out how to support concerns (suggest alternatives to leaving), and then change what needs to be changed to reach your goal (put a retention program into effect).

LIMITING RISKS OF SHARING: COMMUNICATING AUTHENTICITY

Sharing can make you feel that you are losing or giving up control. Some companies have even blocked the use of social media—perhaps fearful that confidential company information might be disclosed. But sharing is not necessarily an uncontrollable activity. You can structure a social media policy to ensure accountability.

Establishing Ground Rules for Sharing

It is okay for you to establish limits on what your "wills" and "won'ts" are when it comes to sharing. Begin by identifying where sharing can contribute to gains. Lay out the ground rules for participation. If people use good judgment

---

Figure 15.1

The wills and won'ts of your in-house network

Do:

- Adopt systems that look and feel like popular consumer applications such as Facebook, Dropbox, and Evernote.
- Explain their purpose to employees, notably group collaboration and information sharing.
- Analyse the data emerging from the network to help manage ideas and people.

Don't:

- Let the networks become too personal. There is always Facebook for that.
- Confuse internal and external social networks, ie those for customers and those for employees.
- Be entirely hands-off. The community will eventually police itself, but needs guidance and monitoring early on.

© *The Financial Times*, August 10, 2011.

and common sense, understand the company's values, promise to act in accordance with them, are in tune with the reasons for embracing social media, and take responsibility for their posts, then the trust you place in them should be reciprocated, with all acting in accordance with understood expectations. And as trust builds, the trust you place in them and the trust they place in you, so will the value of sharing, as deep, productive relationships are forged.

There are a number of other decisions to make about sharing. Do you feel the need to know who is blogging about what topics, for example? If your answer is no, then you are okay with uncoordinated sharing. In contrast, you may decide to initiate and empower a few people to orchestrate the effort, making sharing primarily their responsibility. Which do you prefer? If you are optimistic about social media's ability to build connections and comfortable working with others to get things done, then sharing will come easily to you. On the other hand, some contend that the "good intentions" of sharing cannot possibly last—that excessive sharing actually makes surveillance of employees easier—and could potentially cause users harm down the road. Do you agree? For example, Social Intelligence Corp. provides a service that feeds to client companies every faux pas, every sarcastic comment, every line

Figure 15.2

© *The Financial Times*, August 10, 2011.

of implied prejudice, even lewd personal photographs, by scouring sites such as Facebook, Tumblr, Twitter, and LinkedIn and compiling a dossier containing findings.[10] The lesson: don't put anything online that you would not want anybody to know.

Working It Out: Alone or Together

First, you are going to work collaboratively online to develop your own social network. In order to do this, you need as a team to name the network, establish the network's form and goals, identify who the stakeholders are in the network and how you intend to ensure inclusiveness, and write scenarios depicting good and bad practices, as well as the "wills" and "won'ts" of your social network's online interaction policy. Effectively, you are establishing "best practices" guidelines for your network's users. Once this is done, create a podcast or video to share what you have developed with the class.

Acquiring Authenticity

According to an article from the *Harvard Business Review,* "Managing Authenticity: The Paradox of Great Leadership," "Authenticity is a quality that others must attribute to you. No leader can look into a mirror and say, 'I am authentic.'"[11]

When you are authentic, you are genuine—an individual, not a copy. You know who you are. People trust you because they judge you to be genuine.[12] Authentic leaders share to build trust. In like fashion, shared goals depend on trust. Authentic leaders depend on support teams to help them achieve their goals. They open themselves to different viewpoints, make themselves available to people throughout the organization, and use technology to facilitate their communication. They engender a culture of transparency, publicly admitting errors and explaining rationales for decisions.

Technology such as project blogs, video blogs, and internal Wikis facilitates sharing and helps reveal how an organization does business. Networks spread goals, help the vision permeate the organization, and explain strategy. As more and more people follow you, your leadership profile rises. However, that does not mean leaders have to share everything. In fact, sharing everything can actually contribute to others seeing you as inauthentic. If you explain your reasons, people will accept why you can't reveal more to them.

Sharing, or a culture of open leadership, can transform an organization.[13] A skillful and pragmatic social networking program can help communicate and drive home the organization's vision. However, it all starts with a leader who is willing to embody personally the culture of sharing, encourage participants to experiment, take risks that sometimes lead to failure, and resiliently move on. With technology supporting collaborative processes, and goals functioning as the catalyst, empowered participants learn to think like team members, not just individuals. Everyone becomes a stakeholder in growing the company.

Theory Into Practice

The Merging of Virtual and Real

In their book, *Infinite Realty: Avatars, Eternal Life, New Worlds, and the Dawn of the Virtual Revolution,* Jim Blascovich and Jeremy Bailenson suggest that avatars are able to make a better impression than we could ever hope to make.[14] What this means is that workplaces likely will be making a paradigm shift to three-dimensional avatar conferencing. Participants attending such conferences will feel immersed in the scene as they perceive the situation through the eyes of their avatars.

The theory is that while many don't like video conferencing because it doesn't feel like a real meeting, once users can feel like they are sitting around a table and have full view of others present, they will enjoy it more. A leader, for example, could program his or her avatar and make it appear that he or she was looking directly at you—but actually create the same illusion for all others involved in the meeting who were programmed similarly to be perfect participants. What is more, the authors report that avatars could be created with faces that actually morph with the faces of those you want to impress, enabling each person present to see a face containing some of his or her own features.

Why do you believe we are more likely to approve of someone who resembles us? In your opinion, is there anything ethically questionable about creating an avatar's face for yourself that partially morphs with the face of another?

LEADING VIRTUAL TEAMS

In today's organizations, virtual teams are responsible for much of the organization's work including marketing, strategic planning, and customer service. Empowered by collaborative technologies, virtual team members can shape the organization's course as never before.

Virtual teams draw on the expertise of employees based around the globe. Employees across multiple countries are participating in highly interactive meetings, shaping ideas in concert, and yet never leaving their desks. Team members currently create user-generated content, posting and sharing content in ways not possible a decade ago—even using crowdsourcing to access brainpower outside the organization as a means of securing creative solutions to posted problems.

E-Leadership Tools and Strategies

Leading a virtual team does not change the leader's charge of building a climate of trust, collaboration, and commitment that fosters the diversity of opinion critical for making sound decisions. However, it does complicate and energize it. The reason: for at least some of the time, the leader is decoding and encoding messages without the benefit of nonverbal cues that face-to-face communication offers. The tone of a comment, the facial expression of the person posting a comment, as well as the person's posture and demeanor are left to the leader to imagine. That said, Skype and webcams are accelerating in use, making it easier for leaders to use video conferencing to interact with employees and other stakeholders located anywhere. With leaders spending increasing amounts of time leading virtual teams, the ability to interpret emotions while fostering collaboration is critical.

It falls to the leader to provide guidelines and structure for the online group's work. The leader has to make the team's purpose absolutely clear, outline the team's operating parameters, and set contribution and performance expectations—such as consistency of participation, responding to questions and requests for input promptly, and completing tasks on time. The leader should monitor but not impede the group's work, facilitate the team's choice of media, offer comments and feedback as needed, and respond enthusiastically to the team's creative ideas and efforts. Virtual leaders need to listen, demonstrate respect for diverse opinions, and express their appreciation for the team's work.

Because online media encourage sharing and openness, the directive/authoritarian leader and the laissez-faire leader will likely be disadvantaged while the collaborative leader will excel.[15] Because sharing spreads information throughout the organization, letting others in on what the leader knows and vice versa, the leader needs to function as other than the primary information source. Instead, the leader has to be a process implementer, that is, a facilitator of the team's work.[16]

Special Challenges Facing Virtual Leaders

Increasing numbers of leaders work in offices that contain few if any other people in the same physical space. Organizations have gone global—venturing beyond the building box. They no longer are constrained by walls, meaning they no longer are limited by their physical spaces. Because their employees are geographically dispersed, their leaders lead them in virtual teams—separated by time and distance—directing their virtual projects from afar.

E–team leaders need to be ready to coordinate work accomplished globally—on a 24/7 basis—exerting leadership not only across space, but also through time. Thus, the definition of the workday has also evolved. Virtual workdays cross time zones, generating a "follow the sun" approach that depends on technology, including telecommuting, teleconferencing, and video-conferencing, to function.[17]

While still affirming traditional goals, leaders of virtual groups face a number of unique challenges, including that they may never physically meet the members of their staffs. Thus, they find ways to use technology to collaborate and bridge physical distances. They do not depend on face-to-face contact to resolve conflicts or solve problems. Instead, they use technology to communicate enthusiasm, inspire quality work, foster collaboration, and convince others who may have never met them up close and personal to trust them. While in face-to-face teams trust develops from the formation of social and emotional attachments, in virtual teams it develops more from the timely sharing of information and the keeping of team commitments.

Those who lead from a distance need to be proactive, engage team members, and display their confidence in them. They need to build systems that sustain team synergy, and to do this, they need to rely on tools that foster teamwork and feelings of connection between and among team members and the leader. Of interest is the finding that in virtual teams transformational leaders significantly improve the performance of team members.[18] Empowerment also tends to be higher in virtual teams.[19] When leaders reach out, listen and respond to, and value and respect the members of their team, they are better able to connect with them and lead.

Unfortunately, working virtually may also increase the potential for mistaken first impressions and stereotyping based on geographic and cultural differences. Such faulty perceptions work against the building of effective relationships and if left unchecked, can impede the team's operation. As a result, virtual leaders need to be person-centric, doing their best to forestall misperceptions, feelings of employee isolation, misunderstandings due to delays in responding, and confusion resulting from cultural differences or equipment troubles. Instead, they need to capitalize on the built-in diversity knowledge of the teams they lead.[20]

While in traditional teams leaders use facial expressions, office size, dress, body language, and vocal cues to exert leadership, in virtual teams they tend to use an abundance of task-oriented messages—initiating, scheduling, questioning, and taking time to ensure followers understand and can execute goals.[21]

In summary, virtual teams are just like real teams, except that team members work in geographically dispersed workplaces, possibly at different times. Like all teams, members need to share information about themselves and their task, establish trust, define goals, develop shared expectations, and work out conflicts, including individual roles and responsibilities, so they can complete their projects. When they work well, the members of virtual teams come to trust one another to behave consistently, understand each other so that they can anticipate one another's behavior, and share compatible values and goals.[22] When led effectively, virtual teams reduce costs and increase the sharing of knowledge, contributing to the growth and success of the organization.

Post It: Imagineering a Better Way

In *Open Leadership: How Social Technology Can Transform the Way You Lead,* author Charlene Li identifies five levels of engagement people have with social networking:

(1) *Watching.* Watchers passively read a site's content, reading blogs, listening to podcasts, or watching video content, for example. There is little engagement you can have with a watcher, also known as a lurker.

(2) *Sharing.* Sharers are a step up from watchers. Sharers pass on what they read or see to one or more other people.

(3) *Commenting.* Commenters add their voices to the discussion.

(4) *Producing.* Producers create content; they are not engaged intermittently, but they are engaged over time.

(5) *Curating.* Curators are highly and personally engaged as a moderator, editor, or motivator. Few people are curators; most are watchers.[23]

Here's the challenge: What can you do to get people to increase not just the amount but also the usefulness of the sharing and commenting they engage in? What can you do to encourage their full participation?

Being social is fundamental to our humanness. Being virtual is in vogue. The popularity of social media and virtual spaces demonstrate this. While you have likely used an array of social media in your private life to make connections and share with friends, using social media and leading virtual teams are now also critical leadership tools. How eager are you to embrace them?

LOOK BACK

Reread the opening poem. Of what relevance is it when considering the leader's use of social media and technology? How would you respond to the message it offers and the request it contains?

Notes

1. Soumitra Dutta, "What's Your Personal Social Media Strategy?" *Harvard Business Review* (November 2010): 127–30.

2. Philip Delves Broughton, "Brave New Networked World," *Financial Times* (July 19, 2011): 10.

3. Dutta, "What's Your Personal Social Media Strategy?" 127–30.

4. Javier C. Hernandez, "A Digital Matchmaker for the City and Its Public," *New York Times* (July 31, 2011): 1, 9.

5. Michiko Kakutani, "Company on the Verge of a Social Breakthrough," *New York Times* (June 8, 2010): C1.

6. Leslie Gaines-Ross, "Reputation Warfare," *Harvard Business Review* (December 2010): 70–76.

7. Ibid.

8. Ibid.

9. See, for example, Larry Huston and Nabil Sakkab, "Connect and Develop: Inside Proctor & Gamble's New Model for Innovation," *Harvard Business Review* (March, 2006): 58–66.

10. William D. Cohan, "From Tweets to Blogs, We're Being Watched," *Record* (July 31, 2011): 1, 4.

11. Rob Goffee and Gareth Jones, "Managing Authenticity: The Paradox of Great Leadership," *Harvard Business Review* (December, 2005): 86–94.

12. Bill George, Peter Sims, Andrew N. McLean, and Diana Mayer, "Discovering Your Authentic Leadership," *Harvard Business Review* (February, 2008): 129–38.

13. Charlene Li, *Open Leadership: How Social Technology Can Transform the Way You Lead* (San Francisco: Jossey-Bass, 2010).

14. Jim Blascovich and Jeremy Bailenson, *Avatars, Eternal Life, New Worlds, and the Dawn of the Virtual Revolution* (New York: William Morrow, 2011).

15. This was noted by K. Fisher and M. D. Fuisher, *The Distance Manager* (New York: McGraw-Hill, 2001).

16. See B. J. Avolia, *Leadership Development in Balance: Made/Born* (Mahwah, NJ: Lawrence Erlbaum, 2005).

17. D. D. Davis, "The Tao of Leadership in Virtual Teams," *Organizational Dynamics* 33(1) (2004): 47–62.

18. R. K. Purvanova and J. E. Bono, "Transformational Leadership in Context: Face-to-Face and Virtual Teams," *Leadership Quarterly* 20(3) (2009): 343, 357.

19. S. Nauman, A. M. Khan, and N. Ehsan, "Patterns of Empowerment and Leadership Style in Project Environment," *International Journal of Project Management* 28 (2009): 638–49.

20. S. V. Ryssen and S. H. Godar, "Going International Without Going International: Multinational Virtual Teams," *Journal of International Management* 6 (2000): 49–60.

21. P. L. Hunsaker and J. S. Hunsaker, "Virtual Teams: A Leader's Guide," *Team Performance Management* 14(1) (2008): 86–101.

22. S. J. Zaccaro and P. Bader, "E-Leadership and the Challenges of Leading E-Teams: Minimizing the Bad and Maximizing the Good," *Organizational Dynamics* 31(4) (2003): 377–87.

23. Charlene Li, *Open Leadership: How Social Technology Can Transform the Way You Lead* (San Francisco: Jossey-Bass, 2010), 59–63.

INDEX

ABOUT THE AUTHORS

Teri Kwal Gamble (PhD, New York University; BA and MA, Lehman College, CUNY) and Michael W. Gamble (PhD, New York University; BA and MFA, University of Oklahoma) are professional writers of education and training materials and the coauthors of numerous textbooks and trade books. Their most recent publication is the 11th edition of their bestselling text *Communication Works* (McGraw-Hill). Among their other books are *Sales Scripts That Sell* (AMACOM Books), *The Gender Communication Connection* (Houghton Mifflin), and *Public Speaking in the Age of Diversity* (Allyn & Bacon). Teri and Michael are also the cofounders of Interact Training Systems, a consulting firm that conducts seminars, workshops, and short courses for business and professional organizations across the United States.

Additionally, Michael served as an officer and taught leadership skills for the U.S. Army Infantry School during the Vietnam War. Together, Teri and Michael also produce training and marketing materials for the real estate industry.

Teri and Michael have two grown children, Matthew, a scientist at Einstein Medical School, and Lindsay, who has completed her MBA and is currently finishing law school. They share their home with twin poodles—Charlie and Lucy.

⑤SAGE research**methods**

The essential online tool for researchers from the world's leading methods publisher

Find exactly what you are looking for, from basic explanations to advanced discussion

More content and new features added this year!

"I have never really seen anything like this product before, and I think it is really valuable."

John Creswell, University of Nebraska–Lincoln

Discover **Methods Lists**— methods readings suggested by other users

Watch video interviews with leading methodologists

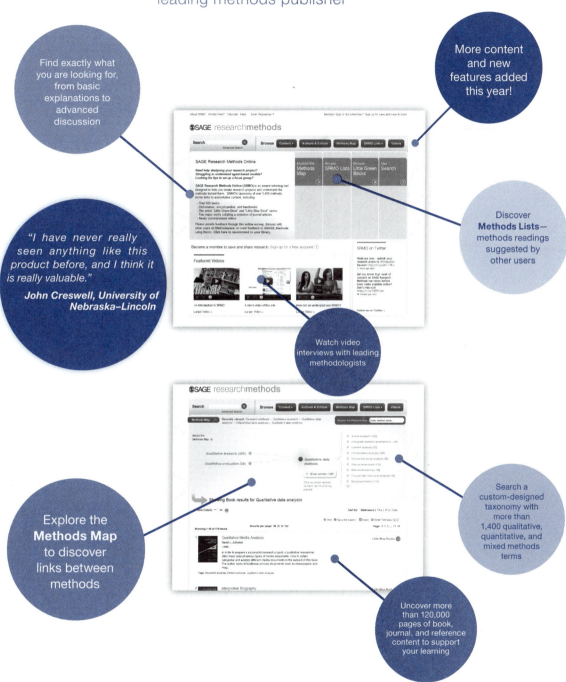

Explore the **Methods Map** to discover links between methods

Search a custom-designed taxonomy with more than 1,400 qualitative, quantitative, and mixed methods terms

Uncover more than 120,000 pages of book, journal, and reference content to support your learning

Find out more at
www.sageresearchmethods.com

Exercises

1. Use the variable `grass` from the GSS2016 dataset.

    A. Identify what the variable represents.

    B. Run a table of the variable to get the frequencies for each of the attributes.

    C. Create a new variable `grassrecode` from the existing variable.

    D. Recode new variable to remove all the Don't knows, No answers, and Not applicable responses.

    E. Run an updated table of the variable.

2. Open an Excel spreadsheet. Use the picture below to create a csv.file and save as "sample1.csv."

Name	Age	Gender	Height
Daniel	25	M	72
Cammi	24	F	61
Tammy	35	F	68
Angela	33	F	64
Shannon	30	F	0
Ben	NA	M	74
Bill	42	M	69
Elizabeth	56	F	66
Susan	28	F	62
Rick	39	M	72
Becky	63	F	67

3. Now practice bringing the sample1 dataset into R using the **read.csv** command.

    A. First, set your working directory.

    B. Next, upload the newly created .csv file.

    C. Check the data by clicking on it in the environment window.

    **Note the missing data for Ben's age and the 0 for Shannon's height.

2. For the variable `age`, fill in (impute) the missing data with the mean of the variable.

    A. Calculate the mean of the variable.

    B. Then fill in the data using the **impute** command.

    C. Now check your data again to see if the missing data has been filled in. You should see the mean for the age of Ben.

5. Create a new variable named `height1` from the existing variable of height.

6. Remove the 0 response from your data by recoding it to be missing data, or NA.

    A. Calculate the median of the variable `height1`.

    B. Fill in the missing data using the **impute** command.

    C. Now check your data to make sure that the height for Shannon has been filled in using the median for the height variable.

Supplementary Digital Content

Download datasets and R code at the companion website at https://study.sagepub.com/researchmethods/statistics/gillespie-r-for-statistics

DATA FREQUENCIES AND DISTRIBUTIONS

FREQUENCIES FOR CATEGORICAL VARIABLES

Once a hypothesis has been developed, data have been collected from a sample population, and the data have been "managed," researchers begin the process of data analysis. A preliminary step when testing a hypothesis is to examine variability in the data. Variability is the amount of variation—or heterogeneity—in a variable's scores. Variability is important because if everyone scores the same on a given measurement, it would be impossible to locate other factors that influence that variable.

For example, if a researcher is interested in examining whether individuals' marital status (`marital`) impacts their self-reported happiness (`happy`) and if all individuals in the sample are married, then there is no way to determine whether being married or not is associated with differences in individuals' self-reported happiness. For this reason, one of the first steps of statistical analysis is to look at the variation in each of the variables of interest.

Another reason that frequency tables are important is because they present a summary of a great deal of information in an easily interpretable way. Table 3.1 shows how data appears within a database for the first five variables and 20 individuals in the *General Social Survey* (Smith, Davern, Freese, & Morgan, 2019). Each row represents one individual within the data frame. The first column, `idnum`, contains a unique number that represents each respondent. In this case, the identification numbers are consecutive numbers from 1 to 20. Each additional column contains information pertaining to other measures/variables in the study.

Column 5 in this data frame contains information on the variable `marital` with arbitrary numbers representing whether a given respondent is Married (1), Widowed (2), Divorced (3), Separated (4), Never Married (5), or No Answer (9). It would be difficult to glean much information about marital status in the sample based on an at-a-glance assessment of these

TABLE 3.1 ● FIRST FIVE VARIABLES AND 20 RESPONDENTS IN THE GSS 2016 SUBSET				
Idnum	Age	Cohort	Sex	Marital
1	47	1969	1	1
2	61	1955	1	5
3	72	1944	1	1
4	43	1973	2	1
5	55	1961	2	1
6	53	1963	2	1
7	50	1966	1	1
8	23	1993	2	1
9	45	1971	1	1
10	71	1945	1	3
11	33	1983	2	5
12	86	1930	2	2
13	32	1984	1	1
14	60	1956	2	1
15	76	1940	1	3
16	33	1983	2	5
17	56	1960	1	1
18	62	1954	2	2
19	31	1985	1	5
20	43	1973	1	3

raw scores. (This would be even more difficult with a wider range of options and a larger sample size.) Therefore, in order to present and interpret the data efficiently, researchers examine frequency tables.

Absolute Frequencies

Frequency tables provide a summary of the observed scores and how they are distributed across a sample population. These tables contain information about how frequently scores occur, including information about missing values for a given variable. The code below pulls the variable for gender (sex) from the GSS2016 dataset and produces a table for the variable using the table() function. The dollar sign ($) simply indicates that the variable sex can be found within the data frame "GSS2016."

> **Tip:** Throughout the book, we use the term *gender* to denote whether an individual is male or female. However, the GSS naming convention for this variable is sex. Therefore, we use *sex* when discussing the variable itself and gender when discussing/presenting results.

First, read your data into RStudio by typing the following code into the script window (top left):

```
GSS2016 <- read.csv("C:/Users/Desktop/R/GSS2016.csv", header =
TRUE) #Load the .csv-formatted data into RStudio.
```

Be sure to include the appropriate pathname to your data, which will depend on where it is stored on your computer. Highlight the code and select "run" at the top. This will read the .csv data file into RStudio, where it can be seen listed in the workspace (top right).

> **Tip:** The "header" argument indicates that variable names are included in the top row of the data. Therefore, the variable names will not be interpreted as part of the raw data that were collected.

> **Tip:** Make sure the slashes in the output that point to the location of the data file are *forward* slashes (as above). If backslashes are copied in the file path from Windows Explorer, which is sometimes the Windows explorer default, the dataset will not load.

> **Tip:** It is often useful to work from a folder on your desktop, usually labeled something brief, like "R." Once you have a better grasp of the program, you can set a working directory (see p. 17).

> **Tip:** There are quotation marks around the file name because, unlike the data and variable, it is an object *external* to the R program. Moreover, the quotation marks should be vertical ("")—unlike quotation marks often copied from MS Office, which have curls (" ").

Then, in order to produce raw frequencies for gender (sex) with value labels, type the following code into the scripting window and run it:

> **Tip:** As an alternative to clicking the "run" button, you can also highlight the code and hit **ctrl + enter** to run the code.

```
GSS2016$sexrec <- factor(GSS2016$sex,
                levels = c(1,2),
                labels = c("Male", "Female")) #Generate value
labels for gender.
table(GSS2016$sexrec)  # Produce a basic table with raw frequencies
for gender.
```

The output in Table 3.1 is produced in the console window (bottom left).

Output: Raw frequencies for sex with value labels.

Male	Female
1276	1591

Table 3.1 presents frequencies for marital status (maritalrec) in the 2016 *General Social Survey* (Smith et al., 2019). This set of absolute frequencies presents raw counts for each attribute of the variable. In this case, there are five attributes—Married, Widowed, Divorced, Separated, and Never Married. To produce the following table in RStudio, use the "table" function. Type the following code into the scripting window:

```
GSS2016$maritalrec <- factor(GSS2016$marital,
                levels = c(1,2,3,4,5),
                labels = c("Married", "Widowed",
                "Divorced", "Separated",
                "Never Married"))# Add value labels for
                marital.
table(GSS2016$maritalrec)  # Produce a basic table with raw
frequencies for marital status.
```

Output: Raw frequencies for maritalrec with value labels.

Married	Widowed	Divorced	Separated	Never Married
1212	251	495	102	806

This produces output for the variable marital in the console/output window (bottom left). However, rather than working with the variable within the data frame, it is also possible to save the information in the table as an independent object in the workspace using the assignment operator (arrow).

```
maritalrec.tbl <- table(GSS2016$maritalrec)  # Produce a
table with raw frequencies for marital status and save the table as an
independent workspace object.
maritalrec.tbl # Call the table that was just created to the output window.
```

Tip: To view information about your data or any given variable, simply type and run the name of the object.

The assignment operator then creates a new object in the workspace environment:

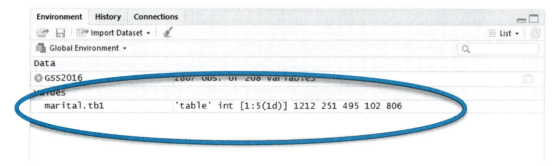

Based on the researcher's needs, the frequencies table can be modified in ways that make it easier to interpret. For example, in order to create a new frequencies table with the categories listed in descending order of their frequency, use the "sort" function. The following code uses the original table (`marital.tb1`) to generate a new table of frequencies (`marital.tb2`) that are sorted in descending order using the Boolean operator for decreasing frequency:

```
maritalrec.tb2 <- sort(maritalrec.tb1, decreasing = TRUE)
# Create the new frequencies table with the values in descending
order (from most to least) and save it as a new workspace
object.
maritalrec.tb2 # Call the new table to the output window.
```

Output: Raw frequencies for `maritalrec` (declining).

Married	Never Married	Divorced	Widowed	Separated
1212	806	495	251	102

The absolute frequencies presented in these tables indicate that there are 1,212 married individuals in the 2016 GSS sample. Since this is the `marital` category that occurs most frequently, it is also the mode. However, this information alone does not provide sufficient information to assess variability of marital status in the sample. Knowing that there are 1,212 married individuals is useful information but what if the entire sample consists of only 1,250 individuals? Here, absolute frequencies are not as informative as relative frequencies. Relative frequencies are a proportional measure of each category relative to the entire sample.

Relative Frequencies

Relative frequencies provide information about the frequency of scores in the context of the entire sample. These can be presented as proportions or percentages. The following R code produces a table of proportions for `marital` in the GSS using the function "prop.table":

```
prop.table(maritalrec.tb2)  # Produce a table with proportions.
```

Output: Relative frequencies (proportions) for `maritalrec`.

Married	Never Married	Divorced	Widowed	Separated
0.42288904	0.28122819	0.17271458	0.08757851	0.03558967

These numbers provide proportions for each marital category. However, having numbers carried out this far into the decimal spaces is likely unnecessary. These proportions can be rounded (e.g., to the nearest thousandth) by nesting the previous code within the "round" function. The number of decimal places is included after the first set of parentheses:

```
round(prop.table(maritalrec.tb2), 3)  # Round proportions to the
thousandths place.
```

Output: Relative frequencies of variable `maritalrec` rounded to the thousandths place.

Married	Never Married	Divorced	Widowed	Separated
0.423	0.281	0.173	0.088	0.036

Percentages

To facilitate interpretation, relative frequencies are often presented in the form of percentages rather than proportions. In order to convert relative frequencies into percentages, multiply the proportion by 100. Rather than calculating percentages by hand, an additional instruction can be added to the R code. The following R code creates an independent object (marital.tb3) that builds on the previous code—at the end of the code is an additional instruction to multiply the results by 100. The resulting output has percentages for each category of marital; however, take note that the results are not presented with percentage symbols (%).

```
maritalrec.tb3 <- round(prop.table(maritalrec.tb2), 3)*100
# Present frequencies as percentages (proportions multiplied
by 100).
maritalrec.tb3
```

Output: Percentages for the variable `maritalrec`.

Married	Never Married	Divorced	Widowed	Separated
42.3	28.1	17.3	8.8	3.6

Based on the results presented in the output above, we now have a better sense of how much variability exists across marital statuses in the 2016 GSS. The results indicate that 42.3% of individuals in the sample are married, 8.8% are widowed, 17.3% are divorced, 3.6% are separated, and 28.1% are classified as having never been married. The next section discusses one way that researchers can deal with "missing data," which is a common issue in social science data analysis.

Missing Values in Frequencies

However, researchers are also interested in assessing the number of missing cases for variables of interest. This occurs in survey research, for example, when a respondent refuses to answer or skips a question. Whether or not missing values are included in the frequencies can impact how the relative frequencies are presented and interpreted.

By default, R will ignore NA values when producing tables using the "table" function. This also means that the full sample (N) is not being considered when relative frequencies are presented. Thus, there is a distinction between (a) the full percent, which includes all cases in the sample, even missing values, and (b) the valid percent, which is based on a sample size that does not include missing, or null, values. An example of this distinction is discussed in Information Box 3.1.

INFORMATION BOX 3.1

Different Interpretations With Full Versus Valid Percentages

The principal of an elementary school with 100 enrolled students is interested in knowing how many of the students will be participating in a "walk-a-thon" fundraiser. During school one day, the principal asks students to report whether or not they will attend. The frequency distribution is as follows: 40 students will attend, 22 students are unsure, and 18 students will not attend—20 students were absent from school on the day the poll was taken.

The principal notes that the *full percent* of students planning to attend the fundraiser is 40% since the sample includes all 100 students, including those who were absent. However, when the sample consists only of individuals who were present on the day of the poll (N = 80), then the *valid percent* of students attending the "walk-a-thon" becomes 50%. The principal needs to decide whether to interpret the full or valid percentages. In many cases—including this case—the valid percentage is more informative because the principal does not have information about the absent students' intentions.

To review from the previous chapter, we can assess missingness in the data and present tables accordingly. The following sets of code (1) present the full percent of cases, including missing data for the variable for sexual orientation (`sexornt`) and (2) recode the variable so that missing values are not produced in the accompanying frequency table (`sexorntrec`).

Full Percent

```
sexornt.tbl <- table(GSS2016$sexornt)  # Generate table with raw
numbers, including missing values.
sexornt.tbl <- round(prop.table(sexornt.tbl), 2)*100
# Create a new table with percentages, including the percentage
missing.
sexornt.tbl  # Call the new table to the output window.
```

0	1	2	3	8	9
38	2	2	57	0	1

Valid Percent

In the above output, there are no value labels and the missing variables are still included—this provides the full percent. However, a new variable can be generated that identifies labels for the different sexual orientation classifications in the GSS codebook. As mentioned in the previous chapter, this procedure also eliminates the additional (missing) categories, leading to a valid percent. Therefore, it is important to generate a new variable (`sexorntrec`):

```
GSS2016$sexorntrec <- factor(GSS2016$sexornt,
                    levels = c(1,2,3),
                    labels = c("Gay/Lesbian", "Bisexual",
                    "Heterosexual"))  # Add value labels for
                    sexorntrec.

sexorntrec.tbl.miss <- table(GSS2016$sexorntrec)  # Generate
table with raw numbers, including missing values.

sexorntrec.tbl.miss  # Call the newly developed table.
```

Gay/Lesbian	Bisexual	Heterosexual
46	56	1641

```
sexorntrec.tb2.miss <- round(prop.table(sexorntrec.tb1.miss),
2)*100
```
\# Create a new table with percentages, including the percentage missing.
```
sexorntrec.tb2.miss
```
\# Call the new table to the output window.

Output: Valid percentages of sexual orientation.

Gay/Lesbian	Bisexual	Heterosexual
3	3	94

CUMULATIVE FREQUENCIES AND PERCENTAGES

Cumulative Frequencies

When working with variables that are measured at the ordinal or interval/ratio level, researchers often assess cumulative frequencies. Cumulative frequencies provide a "running tally" of scores on an ordered scale (e.g., from low to high). Information is presented in terms of accumulated frequencies as they exist, up to and including a given category.

The code below creates a set of cumulative frequencies for number of children (childs) with the values presented in increasing order using the "cumsum" argument to produce a cumulative summary:

```
childs.tb1 <- table(GSS2016$childs)
```
\# Create a new table object for childs.
```
cumsum.childs <- cumsum(childs.tb1)
```
\# Produce a cumulative summary for childs.
```
cumsum.childs
```

Output: Cumulative frequencies for number of children (childs).

0	1	2	3	4	5	6	7	8	9
797	1256	1989	2456	2669	2761	2812	2837	2859	2867

As mentioned, a table of cumulative frequencies is also a useful way to present ordinal-level variables. The code and output below present absolute and cumulative frequencies for individuals' highest degree obtained (degreerec) in the GSS.

```
GSS2016$degreerec <- factor(GSS2016$degree,
                    levels = c(0,1,2,3,4),
                    labels = c("LT HS", "HS", "Some
                    College", "College",
                    "Grad School"))  # Add value labels for
                    degree.
```

```
degreerec.tbl <- table(GSS2016$degreerec)# Generate a table
```
object of absolute frequencies for degree.

> **Tip:** When referencing objects within a data frame (i.e., specific variables), the "Data$Variable" approach is effective but can get tedious. You can also use the **attach()** and **detach()** commands so that R has a default location to search for a given variable. In this case, you could leave out the data frame and dollar sign altogether. However, this approach has several potential drawbacks. For these reasons, we choose to stick with the data frame and dollar sign convention.

```
degreerec.tbl
```

LT HS	HS	Some College	College	Grad School
328	1461	216	536	318

These absolute frequencies can also be presented alongside cumulative frequencies. The following code uses the "cbind" argument to affix absolute and cumulative frequencies into the same table so that it is possible to see the number of respondents with each score as the cumulative frequencies increase:

> **Tip:** The "cbind" argument combines two columns into a single table (i.e., binds them together).

```
cbind(Freq=degreerec.tbl, Cum=cumsum(degreerec.tbl))
```
Generate a table with raw frequencies and cumulative frequencies.

The absolute frequency in the output below shows that 536 individuals in the sample have a college degree. However, in order to ascertain how many individuals have a college degree *or lower*, cumulative frequencies are needed. In the second column, the cumulative frequencies show 2,541 for college degree. This means that 2,541 individuals in the sample have a college degree *at most*.

Output: Cumulative frequencies for highest degree completed (`degreerec`).

	Freq	Cum
LT HS	328	328
HS	1461	1789
Some College	216	2005
College	536	2541
Grad School	318	2859

INFORMATION BOX 3.2

No Cumulative Frequencies for Nominal Variables

Reminder: Cumulative frequencies and percentages cannot be presented for nominal-level variables. The output below provides cumulative percentages for the variable `maritalrec`.

```
maritalrec.tb1 <- table(GSS2016$maritalrec)
cbind(Freq=maritalrec.tb1, Cum=cumsum(maritalrec.tb1))  # This
```
code will run but the results are not intuitive since marital status is a factor (qualitative/nominal) variable and does not move from low to high.

Incorrect: Cumulative Frequencies for `maritalrec`

	Freq	Cum
Married	1212	1212
Widowed	251	1463
Divorced	495	1958
Separated	102	2060
Never Married	806	2866

These variables do not have a logical ordering so any interpretation of cumulative percentages for a nominal variable would be incorrect. It would not make sense to propose that 68.3% of individuals are divorced *or less* because there is no such thing as "less than divorce." The categories of marital status have no logical rank ordering.

Cumulative Percentages

Cumulative percentages, which are also known as percentile ranks, indicate where values fall within the ordered set of cumulative percentages. For example, the code and information presented in the subsequent output shows information on individuals' reported frequency of prayer (`pray`) in the GSS.

The ordered scale, which ranges from 1 to 6, is based on the following prompt: "How often do you attend religious services?" Accordingly, the response options are: Never (0), Less than once a year (1), About once or twice a year (2), Several times a year (3), About once a month (4), 2–3 times a month (5), Nearly every week (6), Every week (7), and Several times a week (8).

```
GSS2016$attendrec <- GSS2016$attend
GSS2016$attendrec[GSS2016$attendrec=="9"]=NA
attendrec.tbl <- data.frame(table(GSS2016$attendrec))
# Create a table object with raw frequencies for religious service
attendance.
attendrec.tbl$Prop <- prop.table(attendrec.tbl$Freq)
# Based on the raw frequencies, generate relative frequencies
(proportions).
attendrec.tbl$CumPct <- cumsum((attendrec.tbl$Prop)*100)
# Calculate cumulative percentages.
attendrec.tbl # Call the table to the output window.
```

Output: Cumulative percentages for `attendrec`.

	Var1	Freq	Prop	CumPct
1	0	723	0.25368421	25.36842
2	1	173	0.06070175	31.43860
3	2	385	0.13508772	44.94737
4	3	312	0.10947368	55.89474
5	4	190	0.06666667	62.56140
6	5	250	0.08771930	71.33333
7	6	126	0.04421053	75.75439
8	7	481	0.16877193	92.63158
9	8	210	0.07368421	100.00000

Tip: Percentiles tell us the value below which a certain percentage of observations can be found. Based on the code and output for religious service attendance, an individual who reports that they attend religious services "about once or twice a year" falls in the 45th percentile. That means that their religious service attendance is greater than or equal to 45% of the sample.

INFORMATION BOX 3.3

Pay Attention to How Variables Are Coded

Always understand how variables are coded before interpreting statistical analyses. Sometimes ordered categories ascend from the lowest to the highest values, such as the `attend` variable, which ranged from Never with a value of (0) to Several times a week, with a value of (8). Higher values indicate more frequent religious service attendance.

On the other hand, variables are sometimes coded with higher values corresponding to *lower* levels of the variable. In the GSS, the variable `pray` is coded to descend from Several times a day (1) to Never (6). Higher values indicate a *lower* frequency of prayer. The cumulative percentages for `pray` are presented below.

```
GSS2016$prayrec <- GSS2016$pray

GSS2016$prayrec[GSS2016$prayrec=="0"]=NA
GSS2016$prayrec[GSS2016$prayrec=="8"]=NA
GSS2016$prayrec[GSS2016$prayrec=="9"]=NA

prayrec.tb1 <- data.frame(table(GSS2016$prayrec))

prayrec.tb1$Prop <- prop.table(prayrec.tb1$Freq)

prayrec.tb1$CumPct <- cumsum((prayrec.tb1$Prop)*100)
```

`prayrec.tb1` # Produce the same table as above (for church attendance), except for how often R prays (pray). This is an example of the complications that can arise from reverse–coded items.

	Var1	Freq	Prop	CumPct
1	1	857	0.30197322	30.19732
2	2	827	0.29140240	59.33756
3	3	302	0.10641297	69.97886
4	4	171	0.06025370	76.00423
5	5	257	0.09055673	85.05990
6	6	424	0.14940099	100.00000

The cumulative percentage for "Less than once a week" is 85.1. In this case, 85% of individuals in the sample report praying "Less than once a week" *or more*. However, this interpretation would be very different if the codes were reversed so that higher values corresponded to more frequent prayer.

FREQUENCIES FOR INTERVAL/RATIO VARIABLES

Interpreting frequency distributions for quantitative data is a more difficult process because these variables often have a large number of values. One method to present more comprehensible frequency tables for interval/ratio variables is to present grouped frequencies. Grouped frequencies collapse the many quantitative values into a smaller number of groups. How the groups are collapsed depends on the researcher's needs.

The following R code collapses the variable age into three categories—young adulthood (18–35), adulthood (36–59), and older adulthood (60+) using the **cut()** function. The cut() function is used to recode the variable age into three ordered categories using the cut points 0–35, 36–59, and 60+. Since the default is to label the scores based on their range (e.g., 36–54), additional labels are added to better differentiate among the clustered age groups.

```
GSS2016$agerec <- GSS2016$age
GSS2016$agerec[GSS2016$agerec=="99"]=NA

agegroup<-cut(GSS2016$agerec, c(0,35,59,90), labels = c("Young
Adult", "Adult", "Older Adult")) #Collapse age into three
categories.
```

After collapsing age this way, the variable went from having 71 unique interval/ratio values to just three ordered categories without consistent intervals.

```
table(agegroup)
```

Young Adult	Adult	Older Adult
793	1205	859

```
agegroup.tbl <- data.frame(table(agegroup)) # Create a data
frame with the raw data from agegroup.
agegroup.tbl$Prop <- prop.table(agegroup.tbl$Freq) # Add
relative frequencies to the data frame.
agegroup.tbl$CumPct <- cumsum((agegroup.tbl$Prop)*100)
# Generate cumulative percentages for each age group.
agegroup.tbl # Produce the full table with absolute frequencies,
relative frequencies, and cumulative percentages in the output
window.
```

The code above creates the following tables (a) absolute frequencies, (b) relative frequencies as proportions, and (c) cumulative percentages for agegroup, which are presented in the following output box.

Output: Frequencies table for `agegroup`.

	agegroup	Freq	Prop	CumPct
1 Young	Adult	793	0.2775639	27.75639
2	Adult	1205	0.4217711	69.93350
3 Older	Adult	859	0.3006650	100.00000

Output: Rounded frequencies for `agegroup`.

	agegroup		Freq	Prop	CumPct
1	young	adult	793	27.76	27.76
2		adult	1205	42.18	69.94
3	older	adult	859	30.07	100.01

✔ INFORMATION BOX 3.4

Percentages

An additional command can be entered in order to round the variables and create percentages:

```
agegroup<-cut(GSS2016$agerec, c(0,35,59,90), labels = c("young
adult", "adult", "older adult"))

agegroup.tb1 <- data.frame(table(agegroup))

agegroup.tb1$Prop <- prop.table(agegroup.tb1$Freq)

agegroup.tb1$Prop <- round((agegroup.tb1$Prop), 4)*100
# This is the same code as above, except for this line,
which rounds the proportions and cumulative
percentages.

agegroup.tb1$CumPct <- cumsum(agegroup.tb1$Prop)

agegroup.tb1
```

Now that age has been collapsed into only three categories, the frequencies are much easier to interpret. Based on the relative frequencies, the sample is comprised of 27.8% young adults between the ages of 18 and 35, 42.2% adults between ages 36 and 59, and 30.1% older adults age 60 and over. Of course, these percentages would be different if the researcher were to choose different designations for the age groups (e.g., if adults were grouped as 26–59 instead of 36–59). Another way of assessing the distribution of interval/ratio-level data (without having to collapse the variable into smaller categories) is to examine the distribution in a histogram.

HISTOGRAMS

One common method for exploring variability within interval/ratio variables is to explore the distribution of values in a histogram. A histogram helps researchers assess the shape, variation, and center of interval/ratio frequency distributions. The x axis of a histogram is situated horizontally along the bottom and represents the values for a given variable (e.g., different ages for the age variable). The y axis of a histogram is the vertical axis that represents the frequencies for each value.

The basic histogram function in R is "hist." The following example produces a basic histogram for the variable agerec without the need to collapse the variable into a smaller number of categories. As with all charts and graphs, the histogram will be produced under the "Plots" tab in the lower right window:

```
hist(GSS2016$agerec)  # Generate a basic/default histogram for age.
```

FIGURE 3.1 ● DEFAULT HISTOGRAM OF agerec

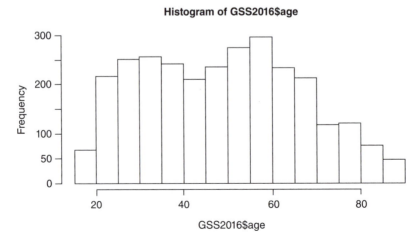

Histogram of GSS2016$age

There are a number of ways to customize histograms. The following sections will detail how to customize the bins, produce a histogram of relative frequencies, and add a main title and a label along the *x* axis.

Titles

One modification for histograms is to add a main title and an *x* axis title. The following code includes a title for the histogram (main) and a label for the *x* axis (xlab):

```
agerec.hist <- hist(GSS2016$agerec,
            main = "Histogram of Age \n in the 2016 GSS",
            xlab = "Respondent's Age") # Create a new histogram
            object using the variable age. Add a title for the histogram
            and a label for the x axis (xlab).
```

Tip: The "\n" notation enters a line break in the main title of the histogram.

Tip: With each additional line of code, always be sure to include a comma.

FIGURE 3.2 ● HISTOGRAM FOR **agerec** WITH TITLES

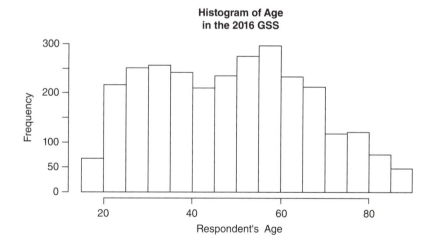

Bins

The intervals presented along the *x* axis—commonly referred to as "bins"—can also be modified to represent different intervals using "breaks." The code below produces a histogram for age with sequential ("seq") breaks every 10 units—starting at 10 and ending at 100:

FIGURE 3.3 ● HISTOGRAM WITH RECONFIGURED BINS

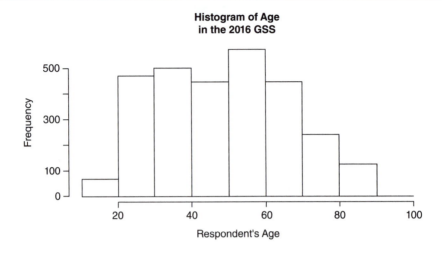

```
agerec.hist <- hist(GSS2016$agerec,
                    breaks = seq (10, 100, by = 10),
                    main = "Histogram of Age \n in the 2016 GSS",
                    xlab = "Respondent's Age")  # Change the size
                    of the bins.
```

Relative Frequencies

By default, absolute frequencies are produced for histograms in R. However, relative frequencies can be produced using the Boolean operator "freq = FALSE" in the code. Moreover, a color can also be added:

Tip: You can view some of R's extensive color library by running colors().

```
agerec.hist <- hist(GSS2016$agerec,
                    breaks = seq (10, 100, by = 10),
                    col = "lightsteelblue",
                    main = "Histogram of Age \n in the 2016 GSS",
                    xlab = "Respondent's Age",
                    freq = FALSE)  # Add color and produce relative
                    frequencies.
```

Tip: When introducing base-R colors into charts/graphs, be sure to put quotation marks around the color itself in the code. This is so R knows to use the literal color (e.g., "lightsteelblue") instead of referencing a workspace object that might have the same name.

Taken together, the resulting relative frequency histogram has clear titles, defined bins, and (blue) colored bars:

FIGURE 3.4 ● RECONFIGURED HISTOGRAM OF `agerec`

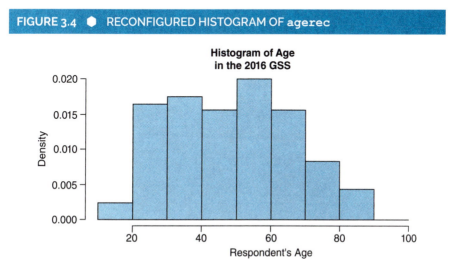

In order to compare the histogram's distribution to a theoretical model, researchers compare it to a theoretical frequency curve known as the normal distribution.

THE NORMAL DISTRIBUTION

A normal distribution is a theoretical "standard" distribution that researchers use to approximately parallel the frequency distribution of their quantitative variables. The distribution, which is used as a comparison model for an arrangement of data, has relatively more values clustered in the middle range and tapers off symmetrically toward the "tails." Researchers do not expect all observations to form a perfect normal distribution. However, the central limit theorem establishes that over time, and with more observations, most distributions will tend toward a normal curve. Thus, with the inclusion of more observations of individuals' age, the histogram shown in Figure 3.4 would more closely approximate a normal distribution (see Information Box 3.5).

When assessing a histogram to compare with the normal distribution, researchers examine a number of characteristics: the peak, the shoulders, and the tails. These characteristics are illustrated and discussed in Information Box 3.5.

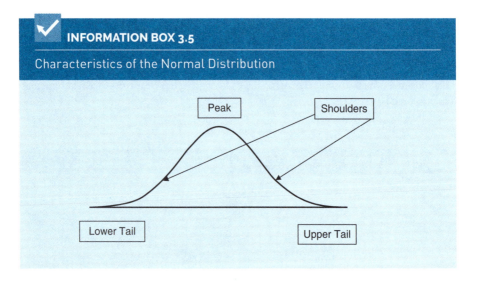

INFORMATION BOX 3.5

Characteristics of the Normal Distribution

NON-NORMAL DISTRIBUTION CHARACTERISTICS

When examining distributions for interval/ratio variables, researchers sometimes encounter aspects of the histogram that depart from the normal distribution. The next section discusses two such departures from the shape of a normal distribution—skewness and kurtosis.

Skewness

The shape of a distribution is formed, in part, by its skew, which is a feature of a distribution characterized by a directional bias to the left or right. The direction of the skew (positive or negative) depends on which side of the distribution "sticks out." When there are fewer values on the left side and the distribution is clustered toward the higher values, the distribution has a negative skew (see Figure 3.5). A positive skew occurs when there are fewer values on the right side and the scores are clustered on the lower end of the histogram (see Figure 3.5).

FIGURE 3.5

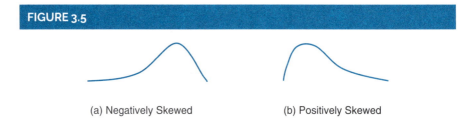

(a) Negatively Skewed   (b) Positively Skewed

A distribution's skewness is a statistical metric that points to the existence, direction, and magnitude of skew in a distribution. The metric is based on how symmetrical the distribution is—since a normal distribution is symmetric, its skewness is 0 (i.e., there is no skew in the data). When the value of skewness is positive, then the distribution is positively skewed. On the other hand, if the value of skewness is negative, then the distribution is negatively skewed.

Kurtosis

Another way of assessing a distribution is its peakedness—or how concentrated the scores are around some central value(s). A normal curve has a mesokurtic distribution. A platykurtic distribution appears flatter and a leptokurtic distribution appears pointier (i.e., there is a steeper drop in the shoulders of the curve). These non-normal distributions are illustrated in Figure 3.6.

FIGURE 3.6 ●   AN EXAMPLE OF A LEPTOKURTIC DISTRIBUTION AND A PLATYKURTIC DISTRIBUTION

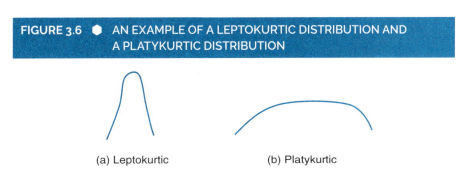

(a) Leptokurtic   (b) Platykurtic

A distribution's kurtosis is the statistical metric that identifies kurtosis when compared to the normal distribution, which has a kurtosis of 3. A value of kurtosis greater than 3 points to a leptokurtic distribution and a value less than 3 indicates that there is a platykurtic distribution.

The code below produces a histogram for the variable `tvhoursrec`. The "breaks" function sets each bin in the histogram to break at 1-unit intervals, starting with 0 hours and running through to 24 hours.

```
GSS2016$tvhoursrec <- GSS2016$tvhours
GSS2016$tvhoursrec[GSS2016$tvhoursrec=="-1"]=NA
GSS2016$tvhoursrec[GSS2016$tvhoursrec=="98"]=NA
GSS2016$tvhoursrec[GSS2016$tvhoursrec=="99"]=NA


tvhoursrec.hist <- hist(GSS2016$tvhoursrec,
                   breaks = seq(0,24, by = 1),
                   freq = FALSE,
                   main = "Hours of Television Watched
                   in the 2016 GSS",
                   xlab = "Per Day Hours of
                   Television")  # This histogram has
                   breaks defined (from 0 to 4 by 1 hour).
```

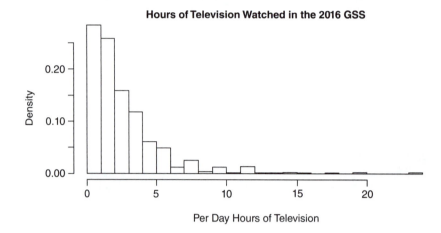

FIGURE 3.7 ● HISTOGRAM FOR WEEKLY HOURS OF TELEVISION

A visual assessment of the histogram would suggest that there is a positive skew since the scores are clustered on the lower end (i.e., watching fewer hours of television), while there is a bias to the right, with some individuals reporting that they watch many hours of television. The peak of the distribution is also very high, which would suggest a leptokurtic distribution.

A simple way of calculating skewness and kurtosis for an interval/ratio distribution is to use the package **moments**. The following code (a) calls on the package moments and (b) produces information on the skewness and kurtosis of the tvhoursrec distribution:

```
install.packages("moments")  # Install the package moments.
library("moments")  # Require the package moments from the
library.
skewness(GSS2016$tvhoursrec, na.rm = TRUE)  # Calculate skewness
for the variable tvhoursrec in the GSS data. Do not include missing values
in the calculation.
kurtosis(GSS2016$tvhoursrec, na.rm = TRUE)  # Calculate kurtosis
for the variable tvhoursrec in the GSS data. Do not include missing values
in the calculation.
```

Output: Skewness and kurtosis for tvhoursrec.

```
skewness
2.809179

kurtosis
16.05903
```

The value of skewness for `tvhoursrec` points to a positively skewed distribution. At the same time, the positive value of kurtosis indicates that the distribution for `tvhours` is a leptokurtic one.

EXPORTING TABLES

Once analysis is finished, the information from the analyses can be exported to word processing, spreadsheet, or other software applications. This section details how to export tables and figures from RStudio into Microsoft Word and Excel.

Microsoft Word

The code `write.csv()` is one way to copy information from a table into Microsoft Word. The following example details how to export information from Information Box 3.4 above into a Word document.

```
write.csv(agegroup.tb1)  #This writes the content of the table
agegroup.tb1 to a comma-separated values file (.csv).
```

First, copy the .csv formatted information and paste it into Word:

```
Console ~/
xcept for this line, which rounds the proportions and cumulative percentages.
>
> agegroup.tb1$CumPct <- cumsum(agegroup.tb1$Prop)
>
> agegroup.tb1
      agegroup Freq  Prop CumPct
1 young adult   793 27.76  27.76
2       adult  1205 42.18  69.94
3 older adult   859 30.07 100.01
>
>
>
> write.csv(agegroup.tb1) #This writes the content of the table "agegroup.tb1" to a comma-se
parated values file (.csv).
"","agegroup","Freq","Prop","CumPct"
"1","young adult",793,27.76,27.76
"2","adult",1205,42.18,69.94
"3","older adult",859,30.07,100.01
>
> |
```
Copy

Inspect

Second, in order to properly format the table, highlight the information and access the "Insert" menu in Word:

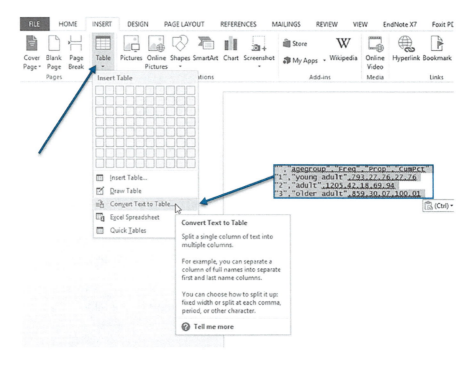

Third, select "Table" and "Convert text to table . . ." Since the information is .csv (comma-separated values), select the option for "Separate text at . . ." "Commas". Finally, select OK:

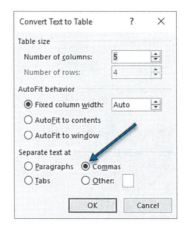

Once pasted, the table can be edited and formatted as needed:

TABLE 3.2 ● AGE BREAKDOWN OF GSS 2016

	Frequency	Percent	Cumulative %
Young adults	793	38.66	38.66
Adults	1205	58.75	97.41
Older adults	859	30.07	100.01

Microsoft Excel

One way to export information from RStudio into Microsoft Excel is to save the information on the clipboard with the code `write.table`. The following code preserves the format and structure of the information in Information Box 3.4 so that it can be pasted directly into Excel.

```
write.table(agegroup.tbl, "clipboard", sep = "\t")  # Create a table
```
(to paste into Excel) based on the information in the object agegroup.tbl. Copy the information to the clipboard and use tab-delimited formatting.

This information can then be pasted directly into Microsoft Excel using the regular paste feature.

CONCLUSION

In order to assess variability in their data, researchers look closely at frequency distributions (for categorical data), cumulative frequencies (for ordinal data), and grouped frequencies for collapsed interval/ratio variables. It is also important to focus on visual and numerical aspects of distributions for interval/ratio variables. These interpretations are based on comparison to a theoretical model, the normal distribution. In addition to the procedures in this chapter, a variety of charts and graphs allow researchers to easily interpret the distribution of scores. These data visualizations are the focus of Chapter 5.

References

Smith, T. W., Davern, M., Freese, J., & Morgan, S. L. (2019). *General Social Surveys, 1972–2018* [Machine-Readable Data File]. Chicago, IL: NORC at the University of Chicago. Retrieved from http://www.gss.norc.org/getthedata/Pages/Home.aspx

Exercises

1. For the following exercise, use the variable race in the GSS. You might need to check the GSS codebook to determine the labels for the numerical codes.

   A. Produce a frequency table for the variable `race`.

   B. Identify the (a) mode and (b) median of the distribution.

   C. If you are unable to determine either of these, explain why.

2. Create a *new* factor variable called `racerec` with three categories (White, Black, and Other). **Note**: The addition of the "rec" to the end of a variable is a way to indicate that it is a **rec**oded version of a variable. Label the three attributes accordingly.

   A. Produce a frequency table for `racerec`.

   B. Identify the mode of the distribution.

3. Describe the difference between the valid percent and full percent in a frequency distribution. (Feel free to use `race` and `racerec` as examples in your explanation.)

4. Using the variable `degreerec`, generate a new variable, `degreerec2,` that collapses "college" and "graduate school" into a single category named "College or More."

   A. Produce a table of cumulative frequencies for `degreerec2`.

   B. Identify the (a) mode and (b) median of the distribution.

Supplementary Digital Content

Download datasets and R code at the companion website at https://study.sagepub.com/ researchmethods/statistics/gillespie-r-for-statistics

CENTRAL TENDENCY AND VARIABILITY

MEASURES OF CENTRAL TENDENCY

Measures of central tendency indicate the central, average, or typical values of a distribution. Choosing the correct measure of central tendency for your data requires some knowledge about the variable(s). In particular, the level of measurement must be known, and in some cases, it would be useful to know if the distribution is skewed. These issues are discussed in Chapter 3.

The mean is a measure of central tendency suitable to calculate for variables measured at the interval or ratio level. However, when the distribution of an interval or ratio level variable is skewed, either positively or negatively, the median is likely a better reflection of the center of the distribution. For example, personal income in the United States is a variable that is positively skewed; a relatively small number of individuals make an astronomical amount of money.

In calculating the mean for personal income, the relatively few extremely large income amounts will cause the mean to be artificially high as a representation of the middle of the distribution. The median, however, locates the true middle, where 50% of the distribution lies above it and 50% of the distribution lies below it. As such, it cannot be artificially inflated or deflated by a relatively small number of outliers.

Using the *General Social Survey* 2016 data (Smith, Davern, Freese, & Morgan, 2019), we calculate the mean. The first logical step to building this command would be to write `mean(GSS2016$age)` to calculate `age`. This will work but only if there are no missing (NA) cases. If any cases are missing, then R will return the response NA. Essentially, if any of the cases have an unknown value for age (e.g., if someone refused to tell the interviewer their age), then R informs you that the mean is truly unknown, as well, since, technically, the mean truly is unknown without having the age of each and every person from the sample included in the calculation. That is very proper of R, but it does not help when you need to compute the mean for the available data! So, the solution is simple and can be programmed as follows:

```
mean(GSS2016$age, na.rm=TRUE)

GSS2016$age[GSS2016$age==99]=NA
```

Tip: The addition of the code **na.rm=TRUE** tells R to remove the unknown entries from the list that will be used to make calculations (in this case for the mean).

```
49.15576
```

As you can see the average age of the *General Social Survey* (Smith et al., 2019) respondent in 2016 was just over 49 years old.

The median is a measure of central tendency that is appropriate to calculate for variables measured at the ordinal level. There are also variables for which the median would be appropriate to calculate for some interval or ratio level variables, but typically only when those variables are either positively or negatively skewed. Also, you might be interested in calculating both the median and the mean to see if a distribution is skewed. For example, if the mean and the median are approximately equal, then the distribution is said to be symmetric. If the mean is much larger than the median, this is an indication that the distribution is positively skewed. Similarly, if the mean is much smaller than the median this would present evidence of a negatively skewed distribution.

In developing the appropriate command code to calculate the median, you must keep in mind the same issue we encountered above with the mean surrounding missing or unknown data. Failure to remind R that we are not interested in considering the unknown values will result in a swift return of NA by R. To avoid that issue, be sure to include the details in your command to remove unknown data from the list:

```
median(GSS2016$age, na.rm=TRUE)
```

```
49
```

The mode is a measure of central tendency that is appropriate for variables measured at the nominal level. There are some instances where the mode could be used for some variables measured at the ordinal level, too.

Using R to calculate the mode can create considerable frustration for users, particularly new users. Simply put, there is no function in R to calculate the mode. It seems like a simple thing, yet it is just not available. As with any programming language, if there is not a direct method to complete a task, you can create a program to take advantage of other tools to complete your work, but this involves the creation or usage of a whole new program routine just to request a very simple statistic. We recommend that you save this program so that you can call on it each time you need to compute the mode.

If we are interested in knowing the mode of age in the 2016 *General Social Survey* (Smith et al., 2019) data, we can use the following command code to produce the mode. Note that R will return the value of the mode first; then in the next row R will provide the frequency of that category, as well:

```
table_age <- table(GSS2016$age)

subset(table_age, table_age==max(table_age))
```

```
57
70
```

In this case, the mode for age within the GSS data file is 57. That is, the most frequent age that respondents reported was 57. The second row indicates that there were 70 respondents who were 57 years old.

MEASURES OF VARIABILITY

Measures of variability are appropriate tools to complement measures of central tendency. While measures of central tendency illustrate where the middle of a distribution lies, measures of variability explain how far from that middle the distribution tends to fall. Most often, these two types of measures are calculated and used together to describe a distribution. Determining which measure of variability is appropriate for your data requires understanding how the data were collected and at what level they were measured: nominally, ordinally, or on an interval or ratio basis. The following measures require at least an ordinal level of measurement.

Range

The range is a value that expresses the full variation across a variable, from the lowest value to the highest value. If we were to compute this by hand, we would take the maximum value (highest value) and subtract the minimum (lowest value) from that. This would yield the range. Another way of thinking of the range is to include both the maximum and minimum values, stating the interval that covers the variable. (One can always perform the subtraction if, for instance, the value of the range is being used in comparison with other variables' ranges.) Below, you will find the command code requesting R to produce the range. In this case, the range for respondent's age in the *General Social Survey* (Smith et al., 2016) has been requested. The result is a range from 18 to 89. In other words, the youngest respondent was 18 years of age and the oldest respondent was 89 years old. The code is shown as follows:

```
range(GSS2016$age, na.rm=TRUE)
```

```
18 89
```

While the range is useful, it is highly susceptible to the effect of outliers. If there were just one person in a sample, for instance, who is 99 years old, but the next youngest person was 65, the range would be inflated to 99 because of only one person—even if the sample contained thousands of people! As you can see, the range can very often overstate the variation in a variable. The solution to this problem brings us to the next measure to be discussed, the IQR (inter-quartile range).

IQR (Inter-Quartile Range)

The inter-quartile range (IQR) is a measure of variation for use with interval ratio variables. It could also be used with some ordinal variables. The IQR reveals the width of the middle 50% of a distribution. Since the IQR represents the middle 50% of a distribution, any outliers on either end of the distribution will not have an effect on the computed value for the IQR, making this a more valid assessment of variation for distributions with—or even without—outliers. We can define the IQR as the difference between the upper and lower quartiles (Q3 and Q1, respectively). The lower quartile (Q1) represents the 25th percentile, while the upper quartile (Q3) represents the 75th percentile.

$$IQR = Q3 - Q1$$

$$Q3 = 75\text{th percentile}$$

$$Q1 = 25\text{th percentile}$$

Now we will compute the IQR for the variable, age, in the *General Social Survey* (Smith et al., 2019) using R. You will need to utilize the following command code:

```
IQR(GSS2016$age, na.rm=TRUE)
```

```
28
```

Not surprisingly, the command to compute the IQR is **IQR**. Once again, it is important to make sure that missing data are omitted from the calculation, so na.rm=TRUE tells R to remove any instances of NA or unknown data from the calculation. The output from R after running the command yields 28. This means that there are 28 years between the age of respondents at the 75th percentile (Q3) and the age of respondents at the 25th percentile (Q1).

Variance

Variance is a measure of variation suitable for interval and ratio variables. The variance can be computed by taking the average of the squared deviations from the mean of a distribution—the result is always a positive number ranging from zero to infinity. Zero would be indicative of absolutely no variation whatsoever; all elements of the distribution would be the same on the variable being measured (e.g., all respondents having the exact same annual income would yield a variance of zero for the annual income distribution). As the computed variance begins to increase, so too does the variation within a distribution.

In order to have R compute the variance of `age` in the *General Social Survey* 2016 data (Smith et al., 2019), use the **var** command.

> **Tip:** Again, remember to include the code to remind R to exclude missing or unknown cases from the list (otherwise R will return an NA).

```
var(GSS2016$age, na.rm=TRUE)
```

```
313.0349
```

Notice that the computed variance is *much* larger than any person's age in the sample. You might be wondering how the value of the variance corresponds to the scale of the distribution of the variable, `age`. Part of the reason that the variance is not used—and instead the standard deviation has emerged as the pervasive comparable variability measure—is that the scale does not match and cannot be directly compared with the values, including the mean. It can, however, be compared with variance values from other distributions.

Standard Deviation

The standard deviation is a measure of variation for interval/ratio variables. The standard deviation is calculated simply by taking the square root of the variance. Like the variance, the standard deviation cannot be negative and can range from zero to infinity. At zero, the standard deviation would indicate that the distribution has absolutely no variation and therefore all elements of the distribution are the same (e.g., all members of the sample are exactly the same age in years). As the calculated value of the standard deviation becomes larger, the greater the indication of variation in the sample and, by extension (when using a representative sample), in the population. In order to have R compute the standard deviation of the variable `age` from the *General Social Survey* (Smith et al. 2019), you will need to use the **sd** command:

```
sd(GSS2016$age, na.rm=TRUE)
```

```
17.69279
```

Now you can see that the standard deviation seems to be in an appropriate scale with the distribution of the variable, `age`. In fact, the standard deviation provides critical information that will ultimately lead to making inferences about a population from a sample. The next step in that process is to discuss standard scores, also called *z*-scores.

THE *Z*-SCORE

A *z*-score or standard score is a value that denotes how many standard deviations away from the mean a particular raw score lies. This could be an indication of a raw score being either above or below the mean. A positive (+) *z*-score is an indicator of a raw score that is greater than the mean. A negative (−) *z*-score is an indicator of a raw score that is lower than the mean. As explained below, a *z*-score that is neither positive nor negative, but equal to zero, is an indicator that the particular raw score happens to be equal to the value of the mean.

A raw score is the value of a particular case on a variable in your dataset. So, 65 years might be the raw score for the variable, `age`, in your dataset. To compute the *z*-score for that, we need some additional information first.

It is important to remember that this work surrounding *z*-scores ultimately involves using a sample to make predictions about a population using a theoretical family of distributions (the standard normal distribution). This is called inferential statistics. As such, it is assumed that the sample is representative of the population. Later in this book (starting with Chapter 6), we will show how to use R to compute inferential statistics. It might help to consult a statistics book for assistance understanding representative sampling, such as *Using and Interpreting Statistics in the Social, Behavioral, and Health Sciences* (Wagner & Gillespie, 2018).

The normal distribution is a bell-shaped, symmetrical, theoretical distribution (see Figure 4.1). In fact, it is a family of theoretical distributions that adheres to certain principles. The mode, median, and mean are all equal, coinciding at the peak in the middle of this theoretical distribution. Frequencies decrease as you move in either direction toward the ends of the curve.

The normal distribution is an ideal distribution. Real-life empirical distributions will not perfectly mirror this ideal type. However, a great many things in life do approximate the normal distribution, and we can say that they are "normally distributed."

FIGURE 4.1 ● AN EXAMPLE OF A NORMAL DISTRIBUTION WHERE THE MEAN, MEDIAN, AND MODE ALL COINCIDE AT THE SAME POINT

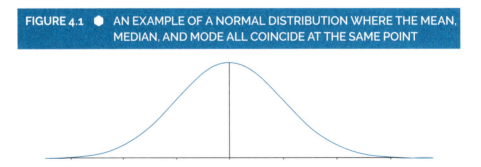

How to Calculate a *z*-Score

Let's start with a real-world scenario and some data. In Dr. Handelsman's biostatistics course, the average final score was 75/100 (75%) and the standard deviation of those scores was 10 percentage points.

We also know that the scores were approximately normally distributed. This information reveals a great deal—the middle of the distribution is at 75 and the standard deviation of 10 illustrates how steep the curve is on both sides.

To convert a raw score (your score earned in the class, for example), use the following formula:

$$z = \frac{Y - \overline{Y}}{S_y}$$

The z-score, or standard score, represents how many standard deviations away from the mean that particular raw score lies. As mentioned, when the z-score is positive, the raw (original) score lies above the mean. If the z-score is negative, the raw score is lower than the mean. If the z-score is equal to 0, that means the raw score must have been exactly equal to the mean (if your raw score is equal to the mean, there is no need to even do any calculation—the z-score is 0).

So, if your score was 80, the z-score should be positive, since it is greater than the mean (75) and therefore on the right side of the normal curve. To confirm,

z = (80-75)/10 = .5

Therefore, the z-score associated with a raw score of 80 in this distribution is .5 (one half SD above the mean). See the graph, below, for a visual representation of the location of the raw score and note that the location corresponds to a positive z-score:

FIGURE 4.2

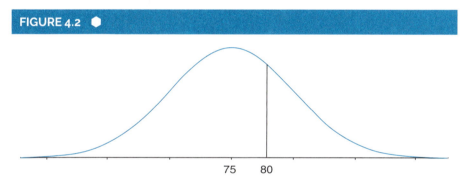

75   80

What about a raw score of 60, someone who barely passed the course with a D-? This z-score will be negative since the raw score is less than the mean of 75:

z = (60-75)/10 = -1.5

So, the z-score associated with a raw score of 60 in this distribution is -1.5, as shown in the following:

FIGURE 4.3

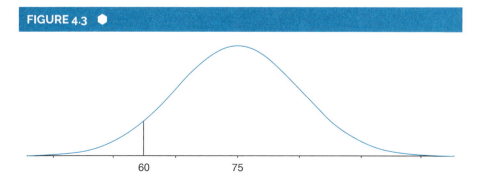

60   75

Suppose you want to convert all of the ages of the respondents in your dataset to standard scores (*z*-scores). One way to do that is to use the **scale()** command.

Since the dataset with which we are working (GSS 2016) is fairly large at over 2,800 cases or respondents, we will need to address the line limit in R. The default setting is only 1000. You can see what the setting is currently on your version of R by typing the following command:

```
getOption("max.print")
```

```
1000
```

Then, you can change this limit to a different value. To be on the safe side, you can select a number much higher than the GSS 2016 sample size. We will try 5000.

```
options(max.print=5000)
```

Now we can use the **scale** command to instruct R to return standardized scores for all of the values of respondents' ages. Below, you will find the command code, but this time we will not include the output:

```
scale(GSS2016$age, center=TRUE, scale=TRUE)
```

What you will be given is a very long table showing all 2,867 standard scores (*z*-scores).

This procedure is particularly useful for much smaller data files. When working with the GSS, it becomes a bit cumbersome.

We have already learned how to calculate the mean and the standard deviation earlier in this chapter, so in order to calculate a *z*-score in R, we simply need a raw score, the Y value. We can convert this formula to terms that R will understand in command language. Below is an example, using 72 as the case for which we would like to calculate a *z*-score. Notice that we have identified the mean of the variable age in the GSS data file and the standard deviation of the variable age in the GSS data file. We have also taken the precaution to tell R to ignore any cases that are missing or unknown while calculating both the mean and standard deviation.

```
(72 - (mean(GSS2016$age, na.rm=TRUE)))/(sd(GSS2016$age,
na.rm=TRUE))
```

```
1.291161
```

The *z*-score given is 1.29. Since this is a positive number, we know that a positive *z*-score is associated with a number larger than the mean. An age of 72 years is indeed larger than the mean that we calculated earlier in this chapter: 49.16 years of age.

SELECTING CASES FOR ANALYSIS

For certain analyses, researchers may not be interested in including all of the cases from a particular data file. There are many reasons why this might be the case—and it often is. For example, if the researcher is interested in studying only the characteristics of persons 21 years and over, then it will be necessary to remove all of the respondents under 21 years of age from the analysis.

This condition can commonly emerge when working with secondary datasets—a data file created by a third party, such as the *General Social Survey* (Smith et al., 2019) data that we examine in this book. Because the dataset was not originally custom tailored to meet your particular needs, you will likely need to select the appropriate cases or respondents (as well as possibly recode variables into new variables).

There are several available approaches for selecting cases, and the best decision is usually based on your purposes for doing so. It is possible that you may want to work with a smaller subsample of a data file and therefore might want to select a random number or fraction of cases or rows from the original data file. Alternatively, you may want to filter out respondents with certain characteristics, such as being below or over a certain age, or select men or women only. Each of these purposes requires a different sequence of command code.

Before we begin, however, we need to revisit our discussion of R packages. The package that allows us to sample and select cases is called **dplyr**. If you have installed the **tidyverse** package, then you will not need to download the package; all you need to do is enter the following command code:

```
library(dplyr)
```

Once the **dplyr** package is active, R can respond to commands related to selecting cases randomly or based on criteria, including scores on one or more variables.

First, we will begin by discussing how to create a random subsample of data. Suppose you are in need of just a very small data file to work with, one containing only five cases or respondents. We can do this by creating a new data file (data frame) in R. The command code to select five random cases from the GSS 2016 data file is as follows:

```
GSS2016random <- sample _ n(GSS2016, 5, replace = FALSE)
```

The first term, GSS2016random is the name of the new data frame (designated by "<-"). Then, as one might imagine, the **sample _ n** command selects a certain number of cases; in this case, of course, we have selected five cases.

Now, suppose instead of random case selection, you have an interest in using a variable to select cases from the main data file. If your research involves men only, then you can use the sex variable to choose only men for a subsample to analyze. The following command code will accomplish that and place the resulting cases in a data file (data frame) called GSS2016sub:

```
GSS2016sub <- subset(GSS2016, sex==1)
```

Notice that the upper right frame of the R window, we can now see the original GSS2016 dataset listed first, but now we also have two new data sets: GSS2016random and GSS-2016sub. These are the two datasets that we just created. You can save them or even export them to different files for use in other programs if need be.

FIGURE 4.4 ⬡

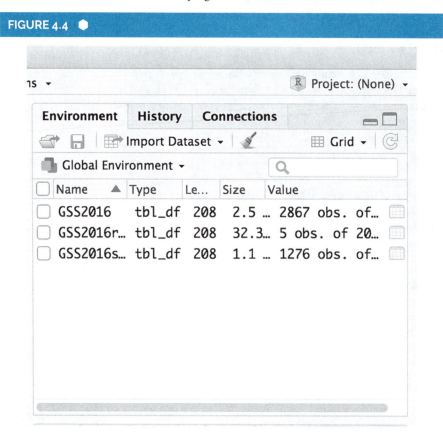

For those who prefer the point-and-click method, there is another way to accomplish this. We will review the case of selecting only the men for analysis.

In the upper left pane of the R window, you will see the data matrix. Rows represent cases and columns represent variables. If you click the word "Filter", you will see fill-in boxes appear beneath each of the variable names. There will be gray italicized printing that says "All" under each variable name.

If you click there, you will have the option to change what values are filtered. In this case, after changing the variable sex from a range from 1 to 2, to a range of 1 to 1 (just 1—just males), you can look toward the bottom of that pane to see that the number of cases in the data frame has decreased from 2867 to 1276, as a result of the filtering operation. We can also confirm that this is the same number of observations (i.e., cases) as in the newly created subsample above, GSS2016sub.

Measures of central tendency and variability showcase the basic features of a distribution. Standard scores (z-scores) allow for the raw data to be standardized (using z-scores)

FIGURE 4.5 ● SELECTING A SUBGROUP FOR ANALYSIS USING THE POINT-AND-CLICK METHOD

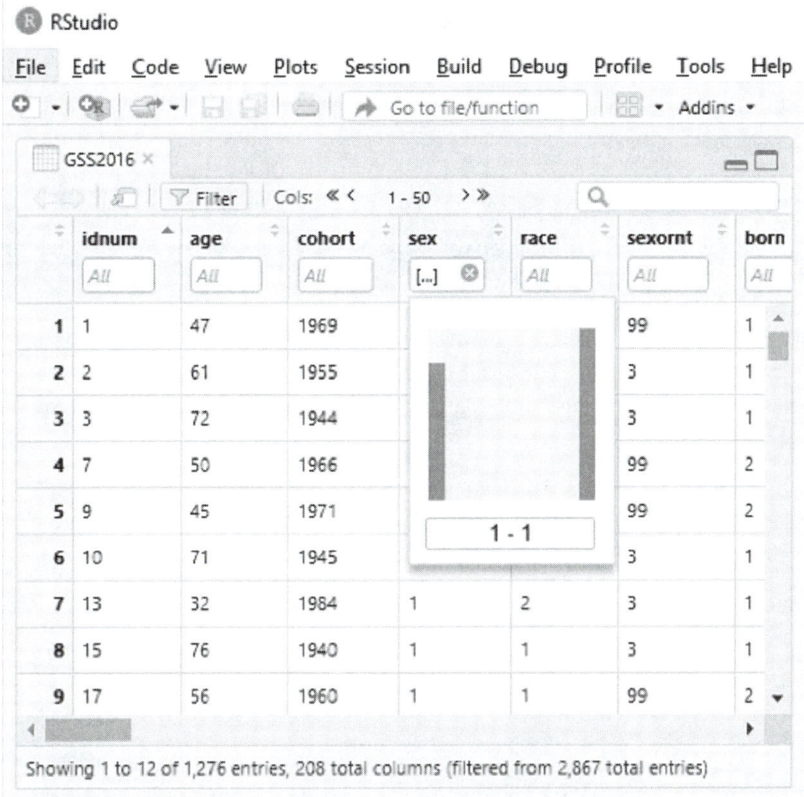

and are also important for inferential statistics, which are covered later in this book. Sampling—selecting cases for analysis—of course, plays a key role in working with subsets of populations as well as understanding sampling distributions in inferential statistics.

CONCLUSION

R allows you to compute measures of central tendency, measures of variability, and to work with standard (z-) scores. From here, it is possible to work with percentiles and probabilities within a distribution. These operations help form the foundation of univariate data analysis, to begin understanding the nature of the distribution of a single variable. (Later in this book, we will discuss bivariate and multivariate relationships.) In this chapter, we also learned how to work with the cases in a dataset, selecting cases tailored to the particular needs of the analysis. Among other things, this can be helpful for drawing samples and conducting an analysis of different segments of a population/dataset.

References

Smith, T. W., Davern, M., Freese, J., & Morgan, S. L. (2019). *General Social Surveys, 1972–2018* [Machine-Readable Data File]. Chicago, IL: NORC at the University of Chicago. Retrieved from http://www.gss.norc.org/getthedata/Pages/Home.aspx

Wagner, W. E., III, & Gillespie, B. J. (2018). *Using and interpreting statistics in the social, behavioral, and health sciences.* Thousand Oaks, CA: Sage.

Exercises

1. Using R, how would you hypothetically compute the average for a variable: number of dog walks per week (walks) in a dataset, named: `socialdogs`? In other words, what command would you type to return the mean as the result? Assume that the dataset is already open in R and remember to exclude missing cases from the calculation.

2. Using R, how would you create a subset of a data file, named `CAjobs2019`, that only includes people who were employed full time, at the time the data were collected. Assume that there is a variable called `employed` and the value for full-time employment is *1*.

3. What command would you use to compute the inter-quartile range using R?

4. Which measure of central tendency cannot be directly computed with a single command using R, and instead requires a short work-around?

Supplementary Digital Content

Download datasets and R code at the companion website at https://study.sagepub.com/researchmethods/statistics/gillespie-r-for-statistics

CREATING AND INTERPRETING UNIVARIATE AND BIVARIATE DATA VISUALIZATIONS

INTRODUCTION

Before beginning formal statistical analysis, researchers can tell a great deal about their data by interpreting charts and graphs. Like frequency tables discussed in the last chapter, data visualization is the process of taking many data points and presenting them in a way that is interpretable. This chapter discusses how to interpret some of the most common types of charts and graphs. This is important because data are sometimes presented in misleading ways (sometimes on purpose but other times because of poor understanding of the ways data can/should be presented). Therefore, we also explicitly discuss common ways that data visualizations can be misinterpreted. This is so you can (a) avoid these pitfalls in your own research and (b) assess other visualizations to determine if they are effectively displaying information that represents the data.

At the outset, a researcher must choose an appropriate way to present their data visually—this is usually based on the level of variable measurement, discussed in Chapter 2. Once a technique has been established, a researcher presenting data in visual form must establish *what they are trying to convey*. The use of graphs and charts differ based on the information being presented (the story you want to tell). Similar to the distributions discussed in Chapter 3, data visualizations vary in their usefulness depending on whether a researcher is interested in presenting data in absolute terms, relative terms, or cumulatively. In this way, charts and graphs are useful for telling a visual story about patterns in the data—based on what you want to convey. However, if there is no story to tell, then a visual will likely be an ineffective tool.

Data can be presented in visual form for a single variable (univariate visualization), two variables (bivariate visualization), or multiple variables (multivariate visualization). This chapter will focus primarily on univariate and bivariate charts and graphs. One important concept linking most of the graphs and charts in this chapter are the horizontal (*x*) and vertical (*y*) axes, which are necessary for variable placement and interpretation. First, we turn to two of the most common forms of univariate data visualization, bar charts and pie charts.

> **Tip:** For help with charts, run the following script: `?plot`

R's COLOR PALETTE

R has an extensive color palette for data visualization. For a list of many of the colors offered, you can simply google "Colors in R," which will provide you with the most up-to-date list of color offerings. You can also switch the RGB (red, green, blue) as well as list specific numbers.

You can view some of the library of available colors by running **colors()**

UNIVARIATE DATA VISUALIZATION

It bears mentioning that the package **ggplot2** has a wealth of resources for advanced data visualizations. While we use base R functions for visualizations in this book, once you become more familiar with R and start to branch out, we recommend you focus on this package, which is part of the **tidyverse**, a collection of packages that simplify the process of data management and analysis.

Bar Graphs

Bar graphs, also known as simple bar charts, are a common way of visually presenting categorical (nominal, ordinal, and dichotomous) data. These charts are useful for showing absolute frequencies across multiple independent categories of a variable. As such, the columns in the chart are presented as independent categories with appropriate labels for each. The lines do not line up against each other as they do with histograms (see Chapter 3), because histograms represent quantitative (interval/ratio) data ranges with consistent intervals along the *x* axis. Instead, bar charts show variation in the data frequencies for standalone categories. Figure 5.1 presents bar charts for marital status (marital) in the 2016 *General Social Survey* (GSS) (Smith, et al., 2019) illustrating the different frequencies across each category.

```
GSS2016 <- read.csv("C:/Users/Desktop/R/GSS2016.csv", header = TRUE)  # Open the .csv data.
```

In order to generate a bar chart, a frequency table needs to be created as an object within the workspace. To do so, run `varname <- table(dataname$varname)`—this generates an independent workspace vector with the breakdown of the variable in the dataset. The following example first defines value labels for the variable `marital` and then generates a frequencies table as a separate object in the workspace:

```
GSS2016$maritalrec <- factor(GSS2016$marital,
                  levels = c(1,2,3,4,5),
                  labels = c("Married", "Widowed",
                  "Divorced", "Separated",
                  "Never Married"))
```
 # Add value labels for marital.

```
maritalrec <- table(GSS2016$maritalrec)
```
 # Add value labels to marital and create a frequencies table as a separate object in the workspace.

Typing the name of the object will show the frequencies in the console window. Then, **barplot(varname)** creates a bar graph based on the information. The output will be produced in the output/console window (bottom left), while the graph will be produced in the "Plots" tab in the lower right window.

```
maritalrec
```

Married	Widowed	Divorced	Separated	Never Married
1212	251	495	102	806

```
barplot (maritalrec, main="Marital Status (GSS 2016)",
            xlab="Marital Status",
            ylab="Frequency")
```
 # Create a barplot based on the raw data information in the "marital" object with a main and axis titles.

Tip: When generating any graphic, you can also use the assignment operator to save it as an object for later reference: plotname ←- barplot(varname).

FIGURE 5.1 ● DEFAULT (VERTICAL) BAR CHART FOR `maritalrec`

The bar graph in Figure 5.1 is also sometimes referred to as a vertical bar chart or a column chart. The vertical length of the bar represents the frequencies for each marital status category. In order to facilitate quick interpretation, the bars are usually arranged from highest to lowest frequency unless there is some other reason to order them differently. Even the quickest glance indicates that modal category for the individuals in the sample is married, followed by never married, and then divorced. In order to avoid redundancy and reduce clutter, the raw numbers are not necessary in a bar chart—unless, of course, they are important to effectively tell your story.

To arrange the barplot by order of frequency, use the order command and indicate how you want the categories to be ordered. For example, for decreasing order (Figure 5.2),

```
barplot(maritalrec[order(maritalrec, decreasing = TRUE)],
        main="Marital Status (GSS 2016)",
        xlab="Marital Status",
        ylab="Frequency")  # Generate a bar chart for marital with
        values presented in descending order.
```

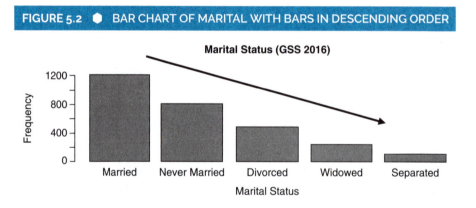

FIGURE 5.2 ● BAR CHART OF MARITAL WITH BARS IN DESCENDING ORDER

Tip: The "parameter" function (par) can be used to set the margins of the plot. With this function, you can specify the margins for the bottom, left, top, and right of the chart (in that order): par(oma = c(#, #, #, #)) changes the outside margins and par(mar = c (#, #, #, #)) changes the margins within the graph. Any changes will affect all plots created after the command is run until it is restored to the default setting.

A number of additional arguments are useful for customizing the direction (horiz), axis labels (las), color (col), borders (border), title (main), and label for the y axis (xlab).

The code for each of these arguments ends in a comma to point to the next command until the final argument. Note that the first parenthesis remains open until the very end of the command. When using titles and labels, "\n" means to include a line break. The following example presents a bar chart for gender (the variable is named sex in the GSS [Smith et al., 2019] dataset). First, value labels are added for the variable to indicate that a code of 1 is male and 2 is female:

```
GSS2016$sexrec <- factor(GSS2016$sex,
                levels = c(1,2),
                labels = c("Male", "Female")) # Add value labels
                for gender.
```

The following code first creates an independent object for the variable sex in the RStudio workspace. The subsequent code uses the barplot function to generate a horizontal bar chart for gender with specifications for the titles/labels, direction, size, color:

```
sexrec <- table(GSS2016$sex) # Move the sex vector into an
independent object.
barplot(sexrec [order (sexrec)], # Create a barplot ordered by the
frequencies in the data.
        horiz = TRUE, # Customize the direction.
        las = 1, # Customize the axis labels.
        col = c("royalblue3", "lightsteelblue"), #Add colors for
        each bar.
        border = NA, # Do not use a border.
        main = "Gender of the \n GSS 2016 Sample", # Give the
        bar chart a main title.
        xlab = "Frequency") # Add a label along the x axis.
```

This code generated an object "sex" in the workspace based on the variable sex in the dataset. Then, a titled horizontal bar chart was produced for gender frequencies (named sex in the GSS) with different colors and no border around the bars (Figure 5.3). The choice between whether the bars are presented horizontally (along the x axis) or vertically (along the y axis) is mostly a matter of personal preference—the use and interpretation is the same. Some argue that horizontal bar charts are easier to interpret since it is easier to quickly identify the endpoints. Moreover, the use of horizontal bars allows for longer names beyond the y axis—so if each category has long titles, a horizontal chart might be a more appropriate option.

FIGURE 5.3 ● HORIZONTAL BAR CHART FOR `sexrec`

Pie Charts

> **Tip:** When possible, avoid using pie charts!

Although bar graphs and pie charts are sometimes used interchangeably to represent data visually, the two serve somewhat different purposes. The primary function of a pie chart is to visually demonstrate the relative frequency or percentage of each category in its relation to the whole sample. Therefore, the most important feature of a pie chart is the relative contribution of individual sections, or "slices," to the whole pie. The area of each section determines its relative contribution to the full pie. Therefore, if one section gets bigger, others must get smaller—the composition of the pie chart depends upon the relative size of each section. In addition to the area of the pie taken up by each section, the angles for each section (where the lines intersect) provide insights into its relative contribution to the full proportion of responses.

The categories of a pie chart must total 100% of the full sample. As such, the sections of a pie chart must hold two important properties: They must be exhaustive and mutually exclusive. In order for the categories in a pie chart to be mutually exclusive, data points cannot be represented in more than one section of the pie. For example, a researcher would not be able to use a pie chart to depict individuals' report of which social media items they use. Given that individuals are able to identify *multiple* social media outlets in the GSS (e.g., someone could mark Facebook *and* Snapchat), the resulting chart is not based on mutually exclusive categories. The count totals would add up to more than 100%, which would not be an intuitive presentation of data. This type of "check all that apply" data would need a more complex design to represent the overlapping categories visually.

The sections represented in a pie chart must also be exhaustive; there must be representation for all of the attributes of a variable. Thus, in order to create a pie chart, the measure should first be converted to cumulative percentages, which was discussed in Chapter 3. The first part of this code collapses the age variable into three groups, creating the variable `agegroup`. This does not need to be redone if the variable was already recoded (from Chapter 3):

```
agegroup<-cut(GSS2016$age, c(0,35,59,90), labels = c("young
adult", "adult", "older adult"))

agegroup.tb1 <- data.frame(table(agegroup))

agegroup.tb1$Prop <- prop.table(agegroup.tb1$Freq)

agegroup.tb1$CumPct <- cumsum((agegroup.tb1$Prop)*100)
```

`agegroup.tb1` # This is from Chapter 3, which created cumulative percentages for each of the three collapsed age categories.

`pie(agegroup.tb1$CumPct)` # Create a pie chart based on the cumulative percentages with default configurations.

Since the pie chart in Figure 5.4 is not very informative when using the default specifications, there are a number of options to customize the chart, including the radius, direction, color, title, and labels. In order to produce labels for the pie chart, the classifications ("young adults," "adults," and "older adults") need to be created as independent objects within the workspace. Additional details are then added to the labels using the "paste" function. In the example below, labels for age group are defined in Step 1 (`agelbl`) and then percentages are created based on the table of proportions (Step 2) and pasted onto the labels (Step 3). The "%" is then pasted onto the labels (Step 4). The "sep=""" argument indicates that there should be no space separating the value and the percent sign in the pie chart.

Based on the added configurations, the resulting pie chart starts clockwise, uses several variations of the color blue from the R color palette, and has labels and percentages listed for each section. The additional specification for radius defines the radius of the graph and "cex.main" indicates that the main title of the chart should be 1.5 times larger than the default size.

FIGURE 5.4 ● PIE CHART FOR agegroup WITH DEFAULT CONFIGURATIONS

Age Groups

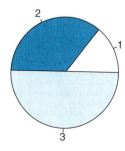

```
agelbl <- c("Young Adults", "Adults", "Older Adults")# Step 1:
    Add labels to the slices.
agepct <- round(agegroup.tbl$Prop*100)  # Step 2: Create an object
    with percentages.
agelbl <- paste(agelbl, agepct) #Step 3: Paste the percentages to
    the labels.
agelbl <- paste(agelbl,"%", sep="")  # Step 4: Paste the "%" sign to
    the labels.
pie(agegroup.tbl$CumPct, labels = agelbl, #Generate the pie chart
with the labels.
        main="Age Groups in the GSS 2016",  # Add a main title.
        radius = 1.0,  #Change the radius of the pie chart.
        clockwise = TRUE,  # Start clockwise at 12:00 (90).
        col = c("lightsteelblue", "royalblue3", "darkblue"),
        # Customize the colors.
        cex.main = 1.5)  # Resize the main title to be twice as large as
        the default.
```

FIGURE 5.5 ● CUSTOMIZED PIE CHART FOR agegroup

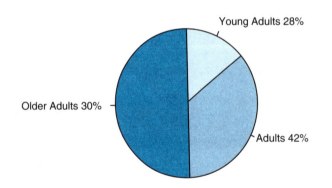

Age Groups in the GSS 2016

Bar graphs are useful for presenting absolute frequencies and percentages and pie charts can be useful to illustrate relative frequencies and percentages. However, the cumulative properties of each category are not presented in either of these types of data visualization. In order to illustrate the *cumulative* nature of data for a variable, researchers use cumulative frequency polygons.

Cumulative Frequency Polygons

Cumulative frequency polygons chart frequencies across multiple categories except they also include *all preceding frequencies* (a running total). Therefore, cumulative frequency polygons are useful for graphing ordinal-level variables or grouped frequencies for interval/ratio variables. The cumulative percent is represented along the *y* axis and trends upward to 100% as it approaches the highest category. The curvature reflects the gradual cumulative increase. Once the graph reaches the rightmost (highest) category, all individuals are represented. This graph therefore allows for some visual interpretation of percentiles and quartiles, including the median.

Figure 5.6 presents a cumulative frequency polygon for individuals' self-reported frequency of sexual activity. The measure is on a 7-point scale with 0 indicating that a person reported having *no sexual activity at all* and 6 indicating that an individual's reported a frequency of sexual activity that was *four or more times per week*. The following code produces cumulative frequencies for respondents' self-reported frequency of sexual activity on this ordered scale (sexfreq).

First, replace the missing values for sex frequency (sexfreq) using a new variable (sexfreqrec):

```
GSS2016$sexfreqrec <- GSS2016$sexfreq
GSS2016$sexfreqrec[GSS2016$sexfreqrec=="-1"]=NA
GSS2016$sexfreqrec[GSS2016$sexfreqrec=="8"]=NA
GSS2016$sexfreqrec[GSS2016$sexfreqrec=="9"]=NA
```

sexfreqrec.tbl <- table(GSS2016$sexfreqrec) # Create a new object with the variable sex frequency.
sexfreqrec.prop <-prop.table(sexfreqrec.tbl) #Generate a proportions table.
sexfreqrec.cumpct <- cumsum((sexfreqrec.prop)*100) # Produce the cumulative summary for the variable sex frequency based on the proportions table. Multiply the proportions by 100.

plot(sexfreqrec.cumpct, type = "o", # Create a line plot to illustrate the cumulative frequencies. (The letter "o" is for points plotted over a line.)
        main = "Cumulative Frequency Polygon \n for Sex Frequency",
        xlab = "Frequency of Sexual Activity (Ordered Categories)",
        ylab = "Cumulative Percent") # Additional commands allow for modifications—filling in the circles for data markers (pch), colors for data markers (col), title (main), *x* axis label (xlab), and *y* axis label (ylab).

A guideline for interpreting the quartiles of the distribution in a cumulative frequency polygon is to find the percentile on the *y* axis and trace it to the area of the line that falls in that percentile. For example, the arrow in the graph in Figure 5.6 indicates that the 50th percentile—the median—is (3) *2–3 times per month*.

FIGURE 5.6 ● CUMULATIVE FREQUENCY POLYGON FOR `sexfreqrec`

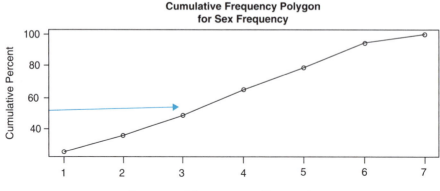

Boxplots

Boxplots, also known as box-and-whisker plots, are useful visual tools to present measures of central tendency and variability discussed in Chapter 4. As such, these graphs provide useful illustrations of the important characteristics of the distribution (i.e., distribution shape, central tendency, variability, and outliers) of interval/ratio data. There are a number of features that help a researcher interpret the distribution of a given variable.

> **Tip:** If you have a data frame with all vectors/variables on the same numeric scale, you can run the boxplot for the entire data frame: `boxplot(dataname)`. This will produce a series of boxplots for the entire set of vectors in the data frame in a single output window for comparison.

Boxplots can be presented on the horizontal (*x*) or vertical (*y*) axis but the interpretation is the same. The boxplot consists of a box (rectangle) that can be presented either vertically or horizontally. The left/lower end of the box, the lower bound, marks the first quartile of the variable's distribution. The right, upper end of the box, or the upper bound, indicates where the third quartile of the distribution lies. Therefore, the box itself represents the middle range of the data, with the median marked by a line. The whiskers are the areas that represent the range of data on either side of the quartile distribution, with end markers for the lowest and highest values.

With all of this information, you can interpret a number of features about the distribution based on four pieces of information: the range from the lowest to the highest observation, the median, and the upper and lower quartiles.

When interpreting, the distribution is symmetrical if (a) the line representing the median is in the middle of the box and (b) the whiskers are the same size. However, a distribution is skewed if the median is closer to one side or if one whisker is longer than the other.

Figure 5.7 presents a boxplot for the variable `age`. In this example, there appears to be a fair amount of variability in the data given that the upper bound and lower bound are far apart from each other. The box is approximately central in the distribution and the median is located in the middle of the box, which suggests that the distribution is approximately normal.

```
GSS2016$agerec <- GSS2016$age
GSS2016$agerec[GSS2016$agerec=="99"]=NA


boxplot(GSS2016$agerec,  # Generate a basic boxplot for age with
default configurations.
                main = "Distribution of Age",  # Add a title along
                the x axis.
                col = "blue")  # Add color.
```

FIGURE 5.7 ● ANNOTATED BOXPLOT FOR agerec

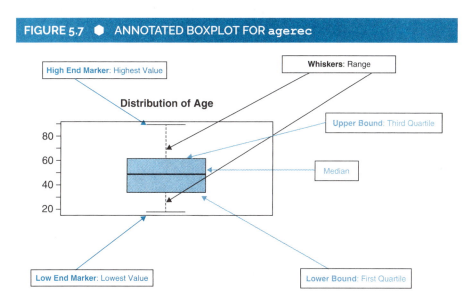

The following code produces an enlarged and customized slate gray boxplot for respondents' score on the socioeconomic index (`sei10`), which ranges from 0 to 100:

```
GSS2016$sei10rec <- GSS2016$sei10
GSS2016$sei10rec[GSS2016$sei10rec=="-1"]=NA


boxplot(GSS2016$sei10rec,  # Generate a boxplot for variable sei10.
        main = "Socioeconomic Index Score (GSS2016)",  #Add a
        main title.
```

```
horizontal = TRUE,  # Change the direction to horizontal
(default is vertical).
xlab = "SEI",  # Add a label along the x axis to identify the
variable.
col = "slategray",  # Customize the color of the
box plot.
boxwex = 1.5,  # Resize the boxplot.
whisklty = 1,  # Change the whisker line type.
staplelty = 2,  # Change the lines at the end.
outcol = "dark blue")  # Add a color for possible outliers.
```

FIGURE 5.8 ● MODIFIED BOXPLOT FOR SOCIOECONOMIC INDEX (sei10rec)

Socioeconomic Index Score (GSS2016)

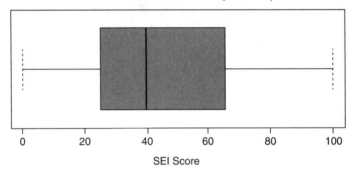

SEI Score

The resulting boxplot is horizontal and titled with a main title and variable identifier on the *x* axis. The whisker lines have been changed from dashes—the default—to a solid line. The lines at each end have been changed to dashes. Although there are no apparent outliers in the boxplot, they were configured in the code to show up as solid green dots.

Histograms Revisited

Another common way of visualizing univariate interval ratio variables is with histograms, which were discussed in Chapter 3. Here we provide an additional example of a histogram and its attendant configurations within RStudio for the variable sei10 as a reminder for the format of this data visualization technique:

```
sei10rec.hist <- hist(GSS2016$sei10rec,
          col = "blue",
          main = "Histogram of Socioeconomic Index Scores",
          xlab = "SEI Score")  # Present a histogram for sei10.
```

FIGURE 5.9 ● HISTOGRAM FOR SEI IN GSS 2016

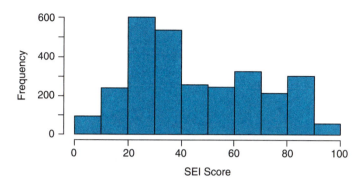

Histogram of Socioeconomic Index Scores

BIVARIATE DATA VISUALIZATION

Visualization techniques can also be used to provide visual cues about the relationship between two—or more—variables. Some of these techniques require the presentation of charts and graphs presented above (e.g., boxplot, stem and leaf plot) for multiple groups for comparison. For example, in order to compare income distributions between men and women, a researcher might present separate boxplots for men and women. Doing so would allow for examination of the income range, median, and upper and lower quartiles for men and women separately. This section will discuss a number of commonly used bivariate data visualizations: clustered and stacked bar graphs, bar chart for grouped means, grouped boxplots, and scatterplots.

Stacked Bar Graphs

Another way of presenting the breakdown of a variable across the categories of another is through the use of a stacked bar chart, which combines multiple bars (variable categories) into a single column for each category of the independent variable. Stacked bar graphs can be presented to illustrate frequencies and relative percentages.

Figure 5.10 presents a stacked bar graph for two of the variables discussed above, sex and happy. Instead of a side-by-side presentation, the categories for Very Happy (1), Pretty Happy (2), and Unhappy (3) are collapsed into a single column. The legend helps identify which stacked section represents the frequencies for each job satisfaction category.

The first step is to define value labels for each of the variables. However, value labels for sex were created earlier in the chapter so the following code adds value labels for respondents' self-reported level of happiness:

```
GSS2016$happyrec<- factor(GSS2016$happy, #Define value labels for
happiness.
```

```
                 levels = c(1,2,3),
                 labels = c("Very Happy" , "Pretty Happy" ,
                 "Not Happy"))
```

`genderhappy <- table(GSS2016$happyrec, GSS2016$sex)` # Create a bivariate table using the sex and happy variables.

`genderhappy` #Produce the bivariate table in the output window.

Output: Bivariate table of raw frequencies for `sexrec` and `happyrec`.

	Male	Female
Very Happy	364	442
Pretty Happy	718	883
Not Happy	191	261

`barplot(genderhappy,` # Generate a stacked bar chart (default) using the information from the bivariate table.

```
        main = "Happiness by Gender in the GSS 2016",
        xlab = "Self-Reported Happiness", # Add main title and x
        axis label.
        col = c("royalblue3" , "slateblue" , "lightblue"), #
        Customize colors.
        legend = rownames(genderhappy)) # Denote which
        categories will be in the legend.
```

FIGURE 5.10 ● STACKED BAR CHART FOR HAPPINESS AND GENDER (GENDER ALONG THE X AXIS AND HAPPINESS IN THE LEGEND)

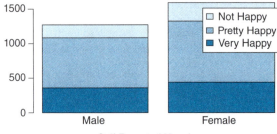

Happiness by Gender in the GSS 2016

The resulting stacked bar chart is a visual representation of the breakdown of happiness between men and women. The different classifications for "happiness" are shown in the same order as they occur in the variable (from 1 to 3) and the total value of the bar is the sum of each of the categories by gender.

Clustered Bar Graphs

Clustered bar graphs, also known as grouped bar graphs or charts, are a common way of visually presenting a relationship between two categorical (nominal, ordinal, or dichotomous) variables. Clustered bar graphs visually present the breakdown of one variable across different categories of another. For example, Figure 5.11 presents a clustered bar graph for the relationship between sex and self-reported happiness (happy), which has three categories: Very Happy (1), Pretty Happy (2), and Not Happy (3). This is the same information as was presented in Figure 5.10; however, the additional argument "beside = TRUE" signals that the resulting chart should have clustered, rather than stacked, bars.

```
barplot(genderhappy,
        main = "Happiness by Gender in the GSS 2016",
        xlab = "Self-Reported Happiness",
        col = c("royalblue3" , "slateblue" , "lightblue"),
        legend = rownames(genderhappy),  # Same code used for
        stacked bar chart above.
        beside = TRUE)  # Since the default is "stacked," this
        command clusters the bars instead.
```

FIGURE 5.11 ● CLUSTERED BAR GRAPH

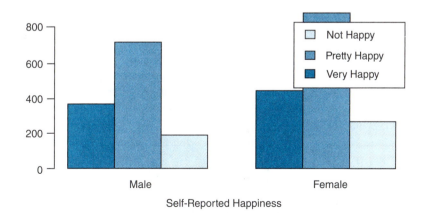

Happiness by Gender in the GSS 2016

Bar Charts for Grouped Means

Bivariate bar graphs have also been used to present measures of central tendency for interval/ratio variables across different categories of a nominal variable. Bar charts for grouped means present the means for an interval/ratio variable across different categories of a categorical variable. The following example presents a bar chart for grouped means for average number of sex partners in the last year (`partners`) across different categories of marital status (`marital`).

In order to plot the grouped means, the means must be calculated using the **aggregate** command and saved as an object in the workspace environment (Step 1):

```
GSS2016$partnersrec <- GSS2016$partners
GSS2016$partnersrec[GSS2016$partnersrec=="-1"]=NA
GSS2016$partnersrec[GSS2016$partnersrec=="98"]=NA
GSS2016$partnersrec[GSS2016$partnersrec=="99"]=NA
```

```
partnersrec<- as.numeric(GSS2016$partnersrec) #Generate a
```
numeric object for partners.

```
GSS2016$maritalrec <- factor(GSS2016$marital,
                  levels = c(1,2,3,4,5),
                  labels = c("Married", "Widowed",
                  "Divorced", "Separated",
                  "Never Married")) # Add value labels for
                  marital.
```

```
maritalrec <-(GSS2016$maritalrec) #Create an object for marital
```
status.

```
partnersmarital <- aggregate(partnersrec ~ maritalrec, FUN =
mean) # Generate a table with mean sex partners for each marital status
```
group and save it as an object.

```
partnersmarital # Call the table to the output window.
```

Output: Mean number of sex partners (partnersrec) in the last year for each marital status.

	maritalrec	partnersrec
1	Married	1.0371846
2	Widowed	0.3622047
3	Divorced	1.1461039

4	Separated	1.1481481
5	Never Married	1.3899614

The values must then be transposed using the "t" function (Step 2). This command takes the information on marital status and mean number of sex partners from the table above and presents it horizontally rather than vertically.

```
mean.partners <- t(partnersmarital [-1]) # Create a new object
and transpose the information in the table of grouped means.

mean.partners # Call the transposed object to the output window.
```

Output: Transposed mean sex partners for each marital status.

	[,1]	[,2]	[,3]	[,4]	[,5]
partners	1.037185	0.3622047	1.146104	1.148148	1.389961

Since the values for each marital status category were removed in Step 2, they can be replaced by using the **colnames** command—this uses the original variable (`partnersmarital`) to place the variable labels for marital status into the transposed table (Step 3):

```
colnames(mean.partners) <- partnersmarital [, 1] # Replace
marital status labels in the transposed table.
mean.partners # Call the group means with column names to the
output window.
```

Output: Transposed mean sex partners with column names.

	Married	Widowed	Divorced	Separated	Never Married
partners	1.037185	0.3622047	1.146104	1.148148	1.389961

```
barplot(mean.partners,
        col = "blue",
        main = "Sex Partners in the Last Year\n by Marital
        Status",
        xlab = "Marital Status",
        ylab = "Mean Number of Sex Partners") # Use the barplot
command to create a bar chart for each of the means with any additional
configurations.
```

The resulting bar chart presents means for number of sexual partners by marital status. However, outliers might be masked, which can lead to misinterpretation of the differences

FIGURE 5.12 ● BAR CHART FOR GROUPED MEANS WITH SEX PARTNERS AND MARITAL STATUS

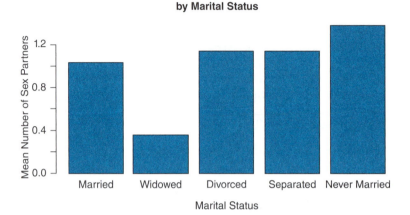

between groups. In this case, the grouped means bar chart in Figure 5.12 might be influenced by an outlier or outliers in any or all groups. As such, instead of using a clustered bar graph, a more appropriate data visualization would be to explore separate box plots, which would point to differences in the distribution *and* identify any outliers.

Grouped Boxplots

Grouped boxplots are useful when comparing several groups on the same quantitative outcomes. Similar to grouped mean bar charts, grouped boxplots assess a quantitative variable as a function (~) of a categorical variable. The interpretation is the same as the interpretation discussed above for individual boxplots. Moreover, the configurations to modify the boxplots are also the same.

The following example ties back to the previous section on grouped mean bar charts and assesses grouped boxplots for number of sex partners in the last year across different marital statuses. As noted, grouped mean bar charts can be greatly influenced by outliers so an additional configuration has been added to the code to mark outliers as solid dots (outpch) that are royal blue (outcol).

```
boxplot(GSS2016$partnersrec ~ GSS2016$maritalrec,
        bowex = .05,
        whisklty = 1,
        outpch = 16,
        main = "Number of Sex Partners in the Last Year \n
        by Marital Status",
        xlab = "Marital Status",
```

```
ylab = "Sex Partners in the Last Year",
outcol = "royalblue3")  # Add a color for possible outliers.
```

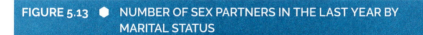
FIGURE 5.13 ● NUMBER OF SEX PARTNERS IN THE LAST YEAR BY MARITAL STATUS

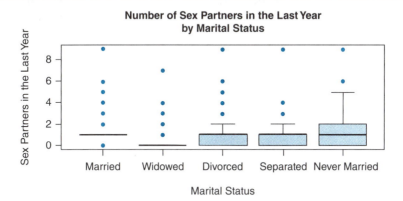

The series of boxplots indicates that there are outliers across each marital status. There-fore, the grouped mean bar charts above would not have been an appropriate way to dis-play the relationship between these two variables. Instead, the grouped boxplots identified that the distribution of the number of sex partners in the last year was skewed—with several outliers—for each of the marital status groups.

Scatterplots

Up to this point, the *y* axis has been used to represent *frequencies* in graphs. However, the *y* axis can also represent an individual number when the variables are interval/ratio level variables. Therefore, the assigned designation for the independent and dependent variables is important for interpretation. The general convention is that the independent variable is presented along the *x* axis and the dependent variable is presented along the *y* axis.

Scatterplots present the relationship between two interval/ratio variables. The data are encoded, or plotted, simultaneously on the *x* axis (IV) and *y* axis (DV) in order to indicate how two variables are related. They are read left to right, with the *y* axis markers on the left-hand side. For scatterplots, coordinates are plotted based on the value of both of the variables. The *x* axis plots a specific number and the *y* axis plots the other—thus allowing for a single plotted dot on a Cartesian plane. Since data points in quantitative variables can be negative, the axis does not always need to start at 0 for a scatterplot.

Individuals who are plotted in the upper right quadrant of the plane scored high on the independent variable (*x* axis) and high on the dependent variable (*y* axis). A plotted dot in the lower right quadrant is an individual who had a high score on the *x* axis and a low score on the *y* axis. If one were to draw a line from each plotted value, the scatterplot becomes a line graph, which plots change across each value on the *y* axis (similar to the time series plot without the consistent temporal order plotted on the *x* axis).

Figure 5.14 presents a scatterplot with values on the coordinates plotted for the weight and height in inches (height) for the 15 hypothetical individuals. The hypothetical data is presented in Table 5.1. Each individual's pair of scores is represented by a single point on the scatterplot. For example, respondent 3 (idnum) reported a weight of 217 pounds (which is located along the *y* axis) and 73 inches in height (located along the *x* axis). Therefore, the pair of scores for this individual are coordinates for the plot. The score on the *x* axis is the first value in the coordinate, followed by the score on the *y* axis: (73, 217). The location where those coordinates match is in the upper right quadrant of the graph, which corresponds to a high score on height and a high score on weight. Figure 5.14 shows a scatterplot for height (*x* axis) and weight (*y* axis) based on a small subset of hypothetical data (*n* = 15). The dashed lines point to the plot on coordinates 73, 217.

Tip: Scatterplots are often far easier to interpret when there is a reasonable *N*. That is why we use a smaller hypothetical dataset to provide the following examples.

FIGURE 5.14 ● SCATTERPLOT FOR height (*X*-AXIS) AND weight (*Y*-AXIS) BASED ON A SMALL SUBSET OF HYPOTHETICAL DATA (*n* = 15).

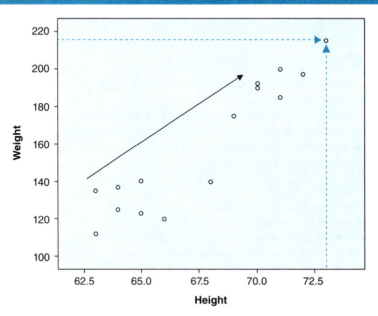

TABLE 5.1 ◆ ID NUMBERS AND DATA FOR A SMALL HYPOTHETICAL SAMPLE OF 15 INDIVIDUALS' height AND weight IN INCHES		
Id	**Height**	**Weight**
651	65	123
666	63	135
693	73	215
730	65	140
737	64	125
750	63	112
796	71	185
830	71	200
900	64	137
916	69	175
990	66	120
996	70	192
1001	70	190
1049	68	140
1121	72	197

Respondent 6 (`idnum`) reported a weight of 112 pounds—which is low on the y axis—and a height of 63 inches—which is low on the x axis. Therefore, the individual is plotted along the coordinates (63, 112), which is located in the bottom left quadrant of the graph, indicating a low score on both height and weight. Therefore, the trend between height and weight is linear and positive, with higher scores on weight corresponding to higher scores on height. This is an example of a positive correlation, which will be discussed further in Chapter 10. Higher scores on weight are associated with higher scores on height—and, conversely, lower scores on weight correspond to lower scores on height. This is represented with a black arrow on the scatterplot in Figure 5.14 that moves from the lower left to the upper right.

An example of a negative correlation is presented in Figure 5.15, which presents hypothetical data on the age an individual's first child was born (`agefirstbirth`) and

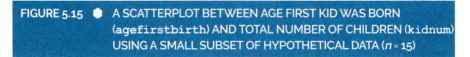

FIGURE 5.15 ● A SCATTERPLOT BETWEEN AGE FIRST KID WAS BORN (`agefirstbirth`) AND TOTAL NUMBER OF CHILDREN (`kidnum`) USING A SMALL SUBSET OF HYPOTHETICAL DATA (*n* = 15)

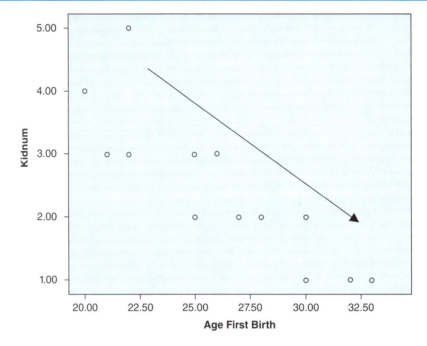

their number of children (`kidnum`) for 15 individuals. In this scatterplot, the plotted points move from the upper left quadrant to the lower right quadrant (illustrated with a black arrow), indicating that there is a negative relationship between the two variables. In other words, in this small sample, those who have their first child at a young age appear to have a higher number of children. Those who have their first child at higher ages tend to have a smaller total number of children. Additionally, a dashed line is included to represent the mean total number of children. This allows for faster processing of who lies above versus below the mean score based on where their score is on the *x* axis.

The direction of a bivariate relationship and the magnitude of the correlation between two interval/ratio variables is conveyed numerically in the form of a correlation coefficient, which is discussed further in Chapter 10. However, not all relationships between interval/ratio variables are linear, which means they form an approximate line. Researchers often encounter other types of relationships in the data, such as curvilinear shapes and accelerated change.

Scatterplots are the most common way of visualizing the relationship between quantitative, continuous variables. This is done with **plot(varname, varname)**. The following code creates a scatterplot between mother's education and father's education:

```
GSS2016$maeducrec <- GSS2016$maeduc
GSS2016$maeducrec[GSS2016$maeducrec=="97"]=NA
GSS2016$maeducrec[GSS2016$maeducrec=="98"]=NA
GSS2016$maeducrec[GSS2016$maeducrec=="99"]=NA


GSS2016$paeducrec <- GSS2016$paeduc
GSS2016$paeducrec[GSS2016$paeducrec=="97"]=NA
GSS2016$paeducrec[GSS2016$paeducrec=="98"]=NA
GSS2016$paeducrec[GSS2016$paeducrec=="99"]=NA
```

`plot(GSS2016$maeducrec, GSS2016$paeducrec)` # Generate a basic scatterplot with the default settings.

FIGURE 5.16 ● SCATTERPLOT FOR MOTHER'S/FATHER'S EDUCATION

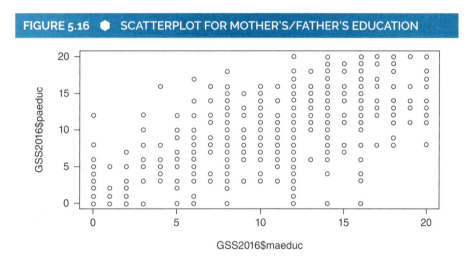

Although the scatterplot is somewhat difficult to interpret because of the large number of plotted coordinates, there seems to be a positive relationship. The following code adds some customized features to the plot, such as colored and filled dots as well as a main title and axis titles.

```
plot(GSS2016$maeducrec, GSS2016$paeducrec,
     pch = 16,
     col = "blue",
     main = "Mothers' Education and Fathers' Education",
     xlab = "Mother's Education",
     ylab = "Father's Education") # Additional commands allow
```
for modifications—filling in the circles for data markers (pch), colors for data markers (col), title (main), x axis label (xlab), and y axis label (ylab).

FIGURE 5.17 ● COLORED SCATTERPLOT WITH TITLES FOR MOTHER'S/FATHER'S EDUCATION

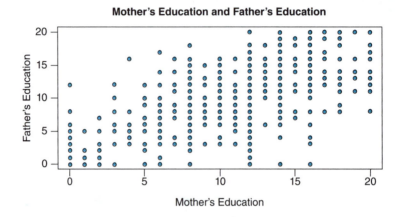

It is also possible to overlay a regression line over the scatterplot to show the linear relationship between the two variables (Figure 5.18).

```
abline(lm(GSS2016$maeducrec ~ GSS2016$paeducrec),
       col = "darkblue",
       lwd = 2)  # Other modifications add a regression line (abline) for
```
a linear model (*lm*) with a certain color (*col*) and width (*lwd*).

FIGURE 5.18 ● REGRESSION LINE SCATTERPLOT FOR MOTHER'S/FATHER'S EDUCATION

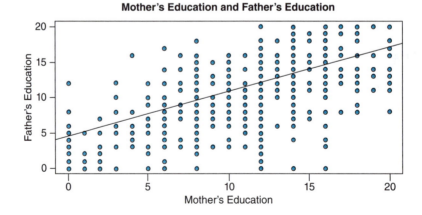

The overlay of the regression line on the scatterplot also helps to pinpoint the positive direction of the relationship between mother's education and father's education.

The scatterplot suggests that higher levels of education for mothers correspond to higher levels of education for fathers. Later chapters cover the statistical procedures used to test this relationship with statistical analyses.

EXPORTING FIGURES

When finished developing a visual, save it by going to "Export" in the output window and save the graphic as an image or PDF file:

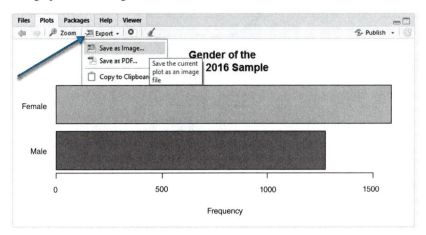

A separate window opens with options for saving the image file. This is where you specify the name of the chart/graph, the file type for saving (e.g., PNG or JPEG), and the path to the location on the drive where the figure will be saved.

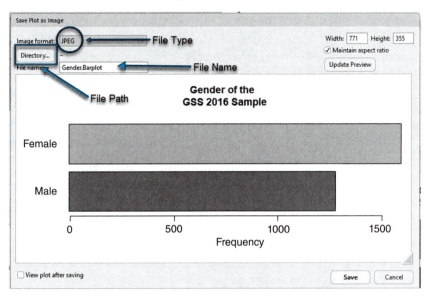

Once this information has been added, click "Save" and the file will save to the location specified in "Directory . . ." From there, the file can be dragged and dropped into a Word document or imported into a Word document or Excel spreadsheet using the "Pictures" item in the "Insert" tab:

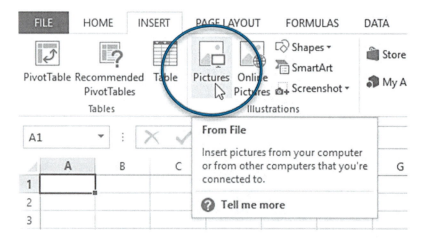

CONCLUSION

In order to effectively interpret charts and graphs, researchers must understand that interpretation is largely influenced by the way the data are presented. For example, cluttered graphs with too many colors might unnecessarily complicate the information being presented—once a visualization is chosen, consider carefully whether or not the same story can be told with fewer adornments. If so, it might ease interpretation to keep extraneous information to a minimum. For example, visualization becomes far more complex when presenting univariate and bivariate data in 3D charts because, while they do add to the visual appeal, they can lead to the distortion of data (especially when 3D charts are tilted). Therefore, some suggest avoiding the practice altogether.

The art of presenting data visually is essentially using statistics and creativity to quickly communicate a story in your data. The purpose of this chapter was to help you more effectively present and interpret data visualizations using base R commands along with RStudio. We recommend further exploration of packages in the **tidyverse**, including **ggplot2**, which has a variety of impressive features for presenting advanced charts and graphs.

References

Smith, T. W., Davern, M., Freese, J., & Morgan, S. L. (2019). *General Social Surveys, 1972–2018* [Machine-Readable Data File]. Chicago, IL: NORC at the University of Chicago. Retrieved from http://www.gss.norc.org/getthedata/Pages/Home.aspx

Exercises

1. Create a new variable called `racerec` from the variable race. Apply names for each of the attributes (White, Black, Other)—this will also transform the variable to a factor variable.

   A. Produce the default bar chart for the newly created variable of `racerec`.

   B. Create a bar chart for `racerec` with the bars in descending order.

2. Generate a new variable named `attendrec`. Recode the new variable to remove DK and NA responses. Note: You might need to search the GSS codebook to find out which numerical codes correspond to DK and NA.

   A. Produce a cumulative frequency polygon for `attendrec`.

   B. Based on this chart, identify the median of the `attendrec` distribution.

3. Based on the variable `hompop`, create a new variable named `hompoprec` for household size. Recode the new variable to remove DK and NA responses. Note: You might need to search the GSS codebook to find out which numerical codes correspond to DK and NA.

   A. Generate a default boxplot for `hompoprec`.

   B. Based on the boxplot, identify (1) the high-end and low-end markers, (2) the whiskers, (3) the upper and lower bounds, and (4) the median.

4. Generate a clustered bar chart for `sex` and `racrec`.

5. Create a bar chart for grouped means for individuals' number of sex partners (`partnersrec`) across the categories for highest degree completed (`degreerec`). **Note**: These variables were recoded in earlier chapters.

Supplementary Digital Content

Download datasets and R code at the companion website at https://study.sagepub.com/researchmethods/statistics/gillespie-r-for-statistics

6

CONCEPTUAL OVERVIEW OF HYPOTHESIS TESTING AND EFFECT SIZE

Tip: We do not use R or RStudio within this chapter. Rather, this is a transitional section, which sets the groundwork for the hypothesis tests in the chapters that follow. The information presented in this chapter is essential in order to accurately interpret the results of the statistical analyses discussed in the chapters to follow. Nevertheless, this is merely an overview of the most important concepts related to hypothesis testing and effect size—*this is not meant to be a comprehensive treatment of the topic*.

INTRODUCTION

A hypothesis is a testable statement about the relationship between variables. Based on theory and logic, researchers set up expectations about the social world. Data are then collected from a sample and statistical procedures are used to test those expectations and make inferences about larger populations. This chapter focuses on the logic of testing hypotheses and making assessments about the strength of relationships.

NULL AND ALTERNATIVE HYPOTHESES

When beginning a study, researchers first identify the hypotheses they plan to test—this includes the null and alternative hypotheses. The null hypothesis (H_0) suggests that a relationship, change, or effect *does not appear to exist* between the study's variables. In other words, the independent variable does not exert a substantial influence on the dependent variable. When the results of a statistical analysis have been reached, researchers then interpret their findings and make a statement about the null hypothesis. By making a statement about the null hypothesis, researchers provide support for their alternative hypothesis. The alternative hypothesis (H_a) is the opposite of the null hypothesis; this is a statement that there *is* a relationship between the independent variable(s) and the dependent variable. The following statements are examples of a null and alternative hypothesis.

> **Tip:** The null hypothesis is sometimes referred to as the "no change hypothesis" or the "no effect hypothesis." The alternative hypothesis is sometimes referred to as the research hypothesis, represented as H_r or H_1.

Null Hypothesis (H_0): There is *no* difference between men and women in the number of hours spent using the Internet.

This null hypothesis is essentially proposing that the difference in the amount of time spent using the Internet between men and women is 0—this is the same as saying that gender and time spent on the Internet are not related. The population mean, which is estimated based on the sample mean, for the amount of time women spent using the Internet (μ_1) is *the same* as the population mean for amount of time men spend using the Internet (μ_2). Therefore, the null hypothesis can also be stated in the following format: $\mu_1 = \mu_2$.

Non-Directional Alternative Hypothesis (H_a): There is a difference between men and women in the amount of time spent on the Internet.

This alternative hypothesis proposes that the difference in the amount of time spent online between men and women is *not* 0, which can also be presented as $\mu_1 \neq \mu_2$. In other words, some relationship *does* exist between the two variables: gender—the independent variable—is in some way related to the amount of time spent on the Internet—the dependent variable. This framing is an example of a non-directional alternative hypothesis, which is usually proposed when a researcher does not have a theoretical basis to present a more specific directional hypothesis.

If there is some reason to believe that women, on average, will spend more time using the Internet than men, then you would propose this expected difference in the following directional alternative hypothesis, which reflects that difference:

Directional Alternative Hypothesis (H_a): Women spend more time using the Internet than men ($\mu_1 > \mu_2$).

The actual procedures used to test such a hypothesis and the notation used to describe them will be covered in Chapter 8. For now, it is important to focus on the language used in the hypothesis testing process.

Determination About the Null Hypothesis

When interpreting the results of a statistical analysis, researchers *make a determination about the null hypothesis* based on their results. This is the conventional way of making a statement supporting or contradicting the alternative hypothesis. If the results show support for the alternative hypothesis, the conventional language researchers use is that they "reject the null hypothesis." Since the null hypothesis suggests that no effect exists between two variables, this notion is rejected when a relationship is present. On the other hand, if the results provide too little or no support for the alternative hypothesis, then researchers would "fail to reject the null hypothesis." This is tricky language—the expression basically states that the researcher is unable to reject the notion that no relationship exists.

Researchers are often interested in rejecting the null hypothesis, which means that a relationship *does* exist between two variables (i.e., they reject the hypothesis that no relationship exists). Using the hypothesis examples above, imagine a researcher collects and analyzes data and concludes that she "rejects the null hypothesis." This means she found that a relationship exists between gender and the amount of time individuals spend on the Internet (i.e., one gender spends more time using the Internet than the other). On the other hand, if she found that no significant difference exists, then she would then "fail to reject the null hypothesis."

It is important to remember that *there are never absolutes in scientific research*. When interpreting the results of a statistical analysis, it is crucial to avoid definitive conclusions. One common remark in student papers is "Therefore, I have *proven* my hypothesis." Instead of making such absolute determinations, researchers use hedge language to highlight how *confident* they are about their research findings. The criteria for confidently supporting an alternative hypothesis is based on statistical significance.

STATISTICAL SIGNIFICANCE

Type I and Type II Errors

Since there is no way to ever be completely confident in the results of a study, researchers accept—but try to reduce—the probability of error in their conclusions. One type of error is made when a researcher rejects the null hypothesis (i.e., states there is a relationship) but the null hypothesis is actually true (there is no relationship in real life)—this type of error is known as a Type I error. A Type I error is also referred to as a "false positive" since the data do show a relationship (+) but this conclusion is false. Another way researchers might draw an erroneous conclusion would be failing to reject the null hypothesis when the null hypothesis is false, which is known as a Type II error. Type II errors are also known as "false negative" errors since the researcher *does not* find a relationship (-) but one does exist.

These errors do not occur because of some statistical oversight or mistake made by the researcher; rather, they are errors about the applicability of the findings to real life. Therefore, it could never be definitively established whether a null or alternative hypothesis is "true" in real life. The types of error exist so that researchers can present how confident they are in their results despite the probability of error.

As shown in Table 6.1, the two types of error cannot be present at the same time. This table presents the four possible outcomes of a hypothesis test based on the decision that is made

TABLE 6.1 ● FOUR POSSIBLE OUTCOMES OF A HYPOTHESIS TEST		
	Research Conclusion:	
Reality	Reject H_0	Fail to Reject H_0
H_0 is True	(a) Type I error	(b) No error
H_0 is False	(c) No error	(d) Type II error

about the null hypothesis. In cells (b) and (c), there are no errors made. The researcher is correct in either rejecting the null hypothesis (b) or failing to reject the null hypothesis (c). On the other hand, cells (a) and (d) represent the errors that might be made. Type I error (a) is erroneously rejecting a null hypothesis that is true—a false positive. Type II error is reflected in cell (d), which is failing to reject a null hypothesis when the null hypothesis is false—a false negative.

In order to assess the probability of making a Type I error, researchers use tests of statistical significance, which is covered next. Issues surrounding Type II errors are discussed in the second half of this chapter. For the following sections, it is important to recognize the following: (a) Type I errors occur when researchers reject the null hypothesis but the null hypothesis is true and (b) Type II errors occur when researchers fail to reject the null hypothesis but the null hypothesis is false. The next section discusses the criteria researchers use to make determinations about Type I errors and draw conclusions about their null hypothesis.

Alpha

To address the possibility of a Type I error, researchers decide on the amount of probable error they are willing to handle if they reject the null hypothesis and the null hypothesis is true. This criterion is represented by the term *alpha* (α). *Alpha* is the cutoff probability a researcher allows for erroneously rejecting the null hypothesis when the null hypothesis is true. The standard levels of alpha conventionally used in social science research are .05, .01, and .001. These probabilities respectively correspond to allowing for a 5%, 1%, or .1% chance of making a Type I error (i.e., erroneously rejecting the null hypothesis).

In any given test of statistical significance, the estimated probability of making a Type I error is known as the *p*-value. If the *p*-value is lower than the alpha cutoff, a researcher can be confident that the results are statistically significant at that level. However, if the *p*-value is higher than the alpha, then the researcher has a higher chance than anticipated of being wrong if he or she rejects the null hypothesis. Therefore, researchers reject the null hypothesis if the probability of making a Type I error (*p*-value) is lower than the cut off established (alpha). In this case, the researcher can conclude that the hypothesized relationship is statistically significant at that level of alpha.

> **Tip:** When presenting the results of statistical analyses in tables, social science researchers often use the following conventions to indicate the level of statistical significance when presenting their results. A single asterisk (*) is used next to a statistic to denote that the result is significant at the .05 level of alpha. Two asterisks (**) are used to indicate that a relationship is significant at the .01 level of alpha. Three asterisks (***) are used to indicate that the result is significant at the .001 level of alpha. Additional symbols can also denote when a result is significant at higher levels of alpha (e.g., † is sometimes used to represent a relationship that is significant at the .10 level). However, this is allowing for a 10% chance of making a Type I error, which is often considered too large.

For example, the researcher testing the null hypothesis that there is *no* gender difference in the amount of time spent using the Internet sets an alpha of .05. This means he is willing to reject the null hypothesis only when there is *at most* a 5% chance of making a Type I error. If the results of his statistical analysis yield a *p*-value of .04, then he can reject the null hypothesis because *the probability of making a Type I error is less than the alpha of .05.* He can therefore conclude that there is a statistically significant relationship between gender and amount of time spent using the Internet at the .05 level of alpha. However, since the *p*-value is .04, this means there is still a 4% chance of making a Type I error. The common notation for this finding is $p < .05$, where p stands for "the probability of making a Type I error." In other words, the *probability of making a Type I error is less than the predetermined alpha level of .05.* However, in order to provide more insight into their results, some choose to sidestep this convention and present the actual *p*-value for all findings (rather than using .05, .01, and .001 cutoffs).

It is important to note that just because a result is statistically significant, it does not always have practical importance. Providing support that a relationship exists between variables should never imply that the relationship is substantively meaningful. Taking the above example, finding a statistically significant relationship between gender and amount of time spent using the Internet simply means that the difference between men and women *is not zero*. Whether or not this effect has any practical or theoretical value is a separate issue, explored later in this chapter. The next section explores the test statistic—the statistical value used to make a determination about the null hypothesis.

TEST STATISTIC DISTRIBUTIONS

In order to interpret the results of a hypothesis test, researchers draw on a test statistic, which is a numerical value that represents the relationship between variables. All test statistics have an underlying probability distribution. Researchers are most interested in finding out where a given test statistic falls within a distribution of values. The distribution is defined, in part, by the degrees of freedom. Degrees of freedom refers to the amount of independent information available in the data to estimate parameters. In other words, degrees of freedom refer to the number of scores in a dataset that are "free to vary" when calculating a test statistic. More degrees of freedom lead to more precise parameter estimates. As mentioned, degrees of freedom inform the shape of the underlying probability distribution for test statistics, which are separated into two parts, the region of rejection and the non-rejection region.

If a test statistic falls within the non-rejection region, then a researcher fails to reject the null hypothesis. If, however, the test statistic falls outside of the non-rejection region—in the region of rejection—then a researcher rejects the null hypothesis. The point where one region ends and the other begins depends on the alpha. The first panel of Figure 6.1 presents an example of these regions for a normal (z) distribution with an alpha level of .05. The regions of rejection are located in either extreme of the distribution (i.e., the upper and lower tails). If you were to use a larger alpha (e.g., .10), that would lead to a higher probability of rejecting the null hypothesis and, in turn, a larger region of rejection.

> **Tip:** The region of rejection is also sometimes referred to as the critical region.

FIGURE 6.1 ● ONE-TAILED AND TWO-TAILED DISTRIBUTION

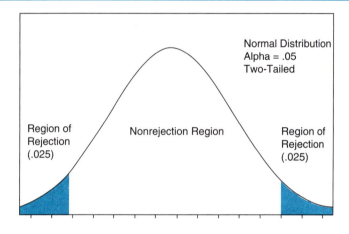

Normal Distribution
Alpha = .05
Two-Tailed

Region of Rejection (.025)   Nonrejection Region   Region of Rejection (.025)

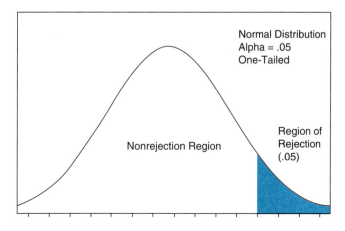

Normal Distribution
Alpha = .05
One-Tailed

Nonrejection Region   Region of Rejection (.05)

In Figure 6.1, the alpha level was set at .05, which means the regions of rejection are located in the uppermost 2.5% and the lowermost 2.5%, totaling .05 or 5%. This is an example of a two-tailed test, where a researcher is comparing the test statistic against rejection regions on both sides of the distribution. A two-tailed distribution is used to test a non-directional hypothesis (e.g., if the researcher has no reason to expect the test statistic to fall in one tail of the distribution or the other). However, not all hypothesis tests compare a test statistic against rejection regions in both tails.

When a researcher proposes a *directional* hypothesis, which can happen with a *t*-test (discussed in Chapter 8), the region of rejection will be reflected on only one side of the distribution—this is known as a one-tailed test. The tail where the region of rejection exists depends on the hypothesis. The second panel of Figure 6.1 presents an example of the region of rejection for a one-tailed test of a directional hypothesis. In this distribution, the region of rejection is located only in the right tail. Note that in this panel, which still uses a .05 alpha level, all 5% of the region of rejection is located in the uppermost tail of the distribution. In the first panel with a two-tailed test, the alpha level was distributed evenly on both sides.

CHOOSING A TEST OF STATISTICAL SIGNIFICANCE

Since, up to this point, the chapter has focused on introducing the major concepts and conventions for interpreting statistical results, some of the terms might have seemed vague. However, once hypotheses and alpha levels have been established the next step is to identify an appropriate statistical test for a hypothesis. This will ultimately lead to obtaining a test statistic, which can be compared to the test statistic's distribution.

When choosing a test of statistical significance, the most appropriate test will depend upon a number of factors, including the levels of measurement for the independent and dependent variables. Statistical procedures also rest on assumptions about the data that must be met in order to accurately interpret the results of the test. For example, if you were to interpret the mean score for gender in your study, this would be an erroneous interpretation of central tendency because it violates the assumption that a variable must be interval/ratio in order to have a meaningful mean. Doing so for a nominal variable produces an arbitrary number. Table 6.2 presents the most common hypothesis tests based on the level of measurement of the independent and dependent variables. Each of these tests will be covered in the chapters to follow—the last column of the table indicates which chapters cover a given hypothesis test.

There are two different types of statistical tests, parametric and nonparametric. The distinction between them is rooted in their assumptions about the data, particularly whether the data come from a known distribution. Parametric tests are procedures where information about a sample is used to estimate the population characteristics. Accordingly, there are strict assumptions about the distribution of the data. These tests are usually most appropriate when the data are interval/ratio level and normally distributed. On the other

TABLE 6.2 ⬡ GUIDELINES FOR CHOOSING A HYPOTHESIS TEST				
Level of Variable Measurement				
Independent Variable	*Dependent Variable*	**Null Hypothesis**	**Hypothesis Test**	**Chapter**
Nominal or Ordinal	Nominal or Ordinal	Statistical Independence	Chi-Square	7
Nominal (2 Categories)	Interval/Ratio	No Mean Difference	*t*-Test	8
Nominal (3+ Categories)	Interval/Ratio	No Mean Difference	Analysis of Variance	9
Interval/Ratio	Interval/Ratio	No Linear Relationship	Correlation and Regression	10–12

hand, nonparametric tests—also known as distribution-free statistics—do not use sample data to approximate a larger sample. As such, these procedures have fewer assumptions about the distribution. Therefore, if you have categorical (nominal, ordinal, or dichotomous) or non-normally distributed interval/ratio data, then nonparametric statistics are usually an appropriate approach, particularly with smaller samples.

When planning to test a hypothesis, make sure to take into account some of the concepts and issues introduced in the last several chapters. First, in order to get a sense of how the data are distributed, check descriptive statistics and examine data visualizations. Check frequencies to get a sense of the amount of missing data—if certain variables are missing a great deal of data, that could influence the results and interpretation.

HYPOTHESIS TESTING OVERVIEW

Hypotheses are testable statements about the relationship between variables. Additionally, tests of statistical significance allow researchers to test hypotheses and draw inferences about larger populations. When making inferences about a larger population, the first steps are to (a) establish null and alternative hypotheses, including—if applicable—choosing whether the alternative hypothesis is directional; (b) choosing the appropriate statistical analysis and calculating a test statistic; and (c) making a determination about the null hypothesis based on the test statistic, degrees of freedom, and p-value in the study.

In order to avoid poor interpretation or misrepresentation of your results, it is important to remember several important points about hypothesis testing. First, adequate information about your sample characteristics, hypotheses, and alpha levels must be provided to support your claims. This transparency is necessary in order for scientific research to remain rigorous. Second, avoid using causal language when tests are not designed to test for causality. The tests of statistical significance discussed in this chapter were designed to test for relationships (i.e., correlations) between variables. It would be misleading to suggest, for example, that not having children *causes* individuals to spend more time using the Internet since the *t*-test only shows a *correlation* between the two variables. Third, it is important not to conflate the idea of statistical significance with theoretical or practical importance. Since tests of statistical significance are influenced by sample sizes, it is equally important to focus on effect size in the interpretation of results.

EFFECT SIZE

Introduction

A Type II error occurs when a researcher fails to reject the null hypothesis but the null hypothesis is false—a false negative. The probability of making this type of error is represented by beta (β). Since the probability of making a Type I error is contingent upon *rejecting* the null hypothesis and the probability of making a Type II error is contingent upon *failing to reject the null hypothesis*, the two errors cannot be present at the same time. In fact, the reduction of one type of error makes a study more vulnerable to the other type of error.

If, for example, a researcher wants to set their alpha at .001 in order to be cautious against making a Type I error, she might be erroneous failing to reject the null hypothesis because of the strict criteria on the *p*-level. At the same time, however, relaxing the criteria for rejecting the null hypothesis by setting a higher alpha level, such as .10, to *reduce* the probability of Type II error would, in turn, increase the likelihood of making a Type I error. Researchers try to balance these errors in order to determine whether their results are identifying *actual* relationships.

Since the probability of making a Type I error (*p*-value) is largely dependent on the number of individuals in a study, the results of a study will vary based on the sample size. A small sample size can lead to the oversight of meaningful relationships because there are too few data points to detect an effect. On the other hand, a very large sample could produce significant results for even trivial relationships. For this reason, researchers should interpret their findings in light of both statistical significance and effect size. The following section focuses on post-hoc measures of effect size, which are then introduced and discussed in their respective chapters to follow. These measures are based on statistical procedures that allow researchers to make determinations about the magnitude of a relationship in *practical* terms after the data for their study have been collected.

Effect Size

In the first part of this chapter, we discussed how to establish whether or not relationships between variables are statistically significant—or how likely it is that the relationship is due to chance. However, in order to accurately interpret the findings of a study, researchers must also understand the *size of the effect*. Effect sizes help researchers determine whether their results are *meaningful*. While statistical significance tells us how precise we are in our interpretation of an effect, effect size adds the magnitude of that effect. Both are necessary in order to accurately interpret the results of scientific research. There are many different

TABLE 6.3 ● GUIDELINES FOR CHOOSING AN EFFECT SIZE MEASURE			
Level of Variable Measurement			
Independent Variable	*Dependent Variable*	**Measure of Effect Size**	**Chapter**
Nominal or Ordinal	Nominal or Ordinal	Phi and Cramer's *V*	7
Nominal (2 Categories)	Interval/Ratio	Cohen's d	8
Nominal (3+ Categories)	Interval/Ratio	Eta-Squared	9
Interval/Ratio	Interval/Ratio	Coefficient of Determination (r^2)	10–12

varieties of effect size, and the most appropriate measures depend on the data and variables under study. Several effect sizes will be introduced in the chapters to follow. Table 6.3 provides guidelines for selecting a measure of effect size based on the level of measurement for the independent and dependent variables. As with their attendant hypothesis tests, each of these effect size measures are discussed in later chapters, indicated in the final column. This table includes only the effect size measures discussed in this book; however, depending on the properties of the data (e.g., sample size, distribution), other measures might be more appropriate for your analyses.

Ellis (2010, pp. 35–42) provides a useful pneumonic to keep in mind when interpreting effect size. He identifies the "three C's of interpretation—context, contribution, and Cohen." First, even small effect sizes can hold some meaning based on their context. In other words, small effects can be meaningful if (a) they lead to important consequences, (b) increase the probability of important consequences, (c) they accumulate to lead to larger consequences, and (d) they change the way we think about relationships and effects. Second, researchers should keep in mind what a given effect size reveals in the context of previous research findings.

Understanding the magnitude and direction of an effect allows researchers to assess the value of their contribution to research on a given topic. Third, Cohen's (1988) criteria, which will be presented in each of the relevant chapters to follow, provide a useful set of cutoffs for interpretation. However, it is important to remember that these cutoffs are merely *guidelines*. The practical importance of a relationship should also be judged based on the context of the findings and their potential contribution to the literature.

Effect Size Overview

There is a tradeoff between the probability of making a Type I error versus a Type II error. Researchers try and minimize these errors by setting an appropriate alpha, and conducting studies with sample sizes amenable to finding differences if they exist. The magnitude of an effect—the effect size—provides the context for interpreting whether or not a given research finding is valuable in practical terms. Accordingly, effect size is among the most important elements of statistical interpretation. Statistical significance and effect size give you information on the meaning of your results in two ways. First, you can establish how likely the relationship is a real one (statistical significance). Second, you can establish whether or not the result is a meaningful one (effect size).

CONCLUSION

This transitional chapter provided a brief overview of hypothesis testing and effect size. Each of the chapters to follow will draw on these concepts to help you accurately interpret the results of your statistical analyses in R/RStudio.

References

Cohen, J. (1988). *Statistical power analysis for the behavioral sciences*. Hillsdale, NJ: Erlbaum.

Ellis, M. (2010). *The essential guide to effect sizes: Statistical power, meta-analysis, and the interpretation of research results*. New York, NY: Cambridge University Press.

Exercises

1. Describe the conclusion a researcher would draw about a null hypothesis if she found that no statistically significant relationship existed between two variables.

2. Provide an example of (a) a non-directional hypothesis and (b) a directional hypothesis.

3. Explain the difference between effect size and statistical significance.

4. Describe a hypothetical situation where a researcher makes a Type II error.

RELATIONSHIPS BETWEEN CATEGORICAL VARIABLES

SINGLE PROPORTION HYPOTHESIS TEST

A single proportion hypothesis test compares proportions of values from a single sample to a larger sample of the population from which the sample is drawn. A researcher looking to assess whether the number of males sampled for a survey matches the population of males in the United States would use a single proportion test (and perhaps data from the U.S. Census) in order to make this assessment. Since we need only proportions for the single proportion test, the *General Social Survey* (GSS) (Smith, Davern, Freese, & Morgan, 2019) 2016 data is not used for the following example. Instead, we use hypothetical proportions.

For example, a researcher is interested in assessing poverty in a rural school district, which enrolls students from 1,432 different households. Her null hypothesis is that the proportion of households participating in the program is not significantly different from half of the total district's student enrollment (.5). Therefore, the research hypothesis is that the proportion *is* significantly different from .5 of the district enrollment. As this is a two-tailed hypothesis, no directional difference has been proposed.

The researcher obtains files on participation in the district's Free and Reduced Price Lunch program—as a proxy for poverty—and finds that 453 households in the district participate in the program. She would use the *prop.test* function in R to test the number of "outcomes" (participation in the School Lunch Program) against the total number of "possibilities" (overall enrollment in the school district).

In the following code, the number 452 is the number of households participating in the school lunch program (outcomes)—1432 is the total number of households in the school district (possibilities). R's default proportion for comparison is .5. Therefore, the code below runs a single proportion hypothesis test (prop.test) to test whether 453 participating households is significantly different from half of the school district total.

> **Tip:** There is no need to load the GSS dataset just yet since these examples are based on hypothetical data.

To run the analysis, type the following code into the scripting window:

```
prop.test(453, 1432) # Two-tailed (default) single proportion
```
hypothesis test for two hypothetical proportions.

Output: Two-tailed single proportion hypothesis test for hypothetical data.

```
        1-sample proportions test with continuity correction

data:   453 out of 1432, null probability 0.5
X-squared = 192.48, df = 1, p-value < 2.2e-16
alternative hypothesis: true p is not equal to 0.5
95 percent confidence interval:
 0.2924317 0.3412468
sample estimates:
         p
 0.3163408
```

> **Tip:** The p-value here is reported in scientific notation—remember, if the sign and number after the "e" is negative, move the decimal point that many places *to the left*.

In this case, the researcher would reject the null hypothesis—the number of households participating in the Free or Reduced Price Lunch program in the rural school district is significantly different from 50% of the total student households in the district.

The output shows the number of households enrolled in the lunch program (453) out of the total number of student households (1,432). By default, the null (comparison) probability is .5, or 50%. The value of "X-squared" is the one-sample chi-square test, along with degrees of freedom and the probability value. The value under "sample estimates" (.32) indicates the observed probability of a household participating in the lunch program.

By default, R runs a two-tailed test; however, if the researcher has reason to believe that a directional hypothesis is in order, she could add the option to run a one-tailed test by indicating whether the research hypothesis points to greater (alt = "greater") or less than the established probability (alt = "less"). The following code tests whether participation in the lunch program is significantly *less* than half the household enrollment in the school district:

```
prop.test(453, 1432, alt = "less") # Test whether the sample
```
proportion is significantly less than half of the population.

Output: One-tailed single proportion test on hypothetical data.

```
        1-sample proportions test with continuity correction

 data: 453 out of 1432, null probability 0.5
 X-squared = 192.48, df = 1, p-value < 2.2e-16
 alternative hypothesis: true p is less than 0.5
 95 percent confidence interval:
 0.0000000 0.3372395
 sample estimates:
        p
 0.3163408
```

The results of this analysis are the same—they indicate that the researcher should again reject the null hypothesis. She can conclude that 453 participating households (31.6%) is significantly different from half of the total household enrollment in the school district.

> **Write-Up:** A single proportion hypothesis test examined whether the proportion of school district households participating in a Free and Reduced-Price Lunch program was significantly different from half of the total households in the school district. The null hypothesis stated that the proportion of participating households did not significantly differ from 50% of the total households. The results of the analysis indicate that the proportion of participating households (.31) is significantly different from .5. Therefore, we reject the null hypothesis ($\chi^2 = 192.5$, $df = 1$, $p < .001$).

GOODNESS OF FIT

The Goodness of Fit test is used for comparing observations of a categorical variable taken from a single population to some other distribution. The test assesses whether or not the observed proportions are significantly different from an expected distribution. In other words, it assesses the "goodness of fit" between observed proportions and what is otherwise expected based on theory or logic.

We use the GSS data for the following example, so type the following code into the scripting window to read the .csv file with the data into RStudio. Make sure to revise the file path (inside the quotes) so that it points to the location of the file on your drive:

```
GSS2016 <- read.csv("C:/Users/Desktop/R/GSS2016.csv", header =
TRUE) # Read the data into RStudio.
```

In order to run a Goodness of Fit test in R, the first step is to create a table of proportions for the categorical variable, which are rounded to the hundredths place, and save the table as an object in the workspace. The following example uses the variable sexual orientation (sexornt). First, value labels are defined; however, this does not need to be redone if the labels were already generated for the variable when it was used in Chapter 3:

```
GSS2016$sexorntrec <- factor(GSS2016$sexornt,
                    levels = c(1,2,3),
                    labels = c("Gay/Lesbian",
                    "Bisexual",
                    "Heterosexual")) # Add value labels for
                    sexorntrec.
sexorntrec.tbl <- table(GSS2016$sexorntrec) #Save the table as an
object in the workspace.
prop.table(sexorntrec.tbl) #Show proportions for the information in
the table.
```

Output: Proportions table for sexual orientation (sexorntrec).

Gay/Lesbian	Bisexual	Heterosexual
0.02639128	0.03212851	0.94148021

```
round(prop.table(sexorntrec.tbl), 2) # Round the proportions to
the hundredths place.
```

Output: Proportions table for sexual orientation (sexorntrec) rounded to hundredths place.

Gay/Lesbian	Bisexual	Heterosexual
0.03	0.03	0.94

Once the proportions table has been generated, it can be used for the Goodness of Fit test. Type the following code into the scripting window and run it in order to test the (default) null distribution. The default distribution is whether there are equal proportions of gay/lesbian, heterosexual, and bisexual men and women in the sample:

```
chisq.test(sexorntrec.tbl) # Use the information in the table to run
a Goodness of Fit test.
```

Output: Goodness of fit for `sexorntrec` using the default configuration (equal proportions).

Chi-squared test for given probabilities

data: sexorntrec.tb1

X-squared = 2900.9, df = 2, *p*-value < 2.2e–16

While it is not very surprising (based on the proportions above), the researcher should reject the null hypothesis. The results indicate that there are significant differences in the proportions of sexual orientation in the data (i.e., there are not equal proportions of each group).

Since the default option to assess for equal proportions is not usually of particular interest for research purposes (especially in this case), additional information about expected probabilities can be included. In 2011, the Williams Institute (Gates, 2011) estimated that 3.3% of individuals in the United States are gay/lesbian (.033), 3.6% are bisexual (.036), and—for the sake of simplicity—we assume the remaining 93.1% are heterosexual (.931). We can compare these estimates—transformed to proportions—with sexual orientation reported in the GSS 2016 sample (Smith et al., 2019). The null hypothesis is that the proportions of sexual orientation observed in the GSS 2016 are not significantly different from the expected proportions outlined by the Williams Institute:

`chisq.test(sexorntrec.tb1, p = c(.033, .036, .931))` **Goodness of Fit test for sexual orientation based on empirically-derived expectations.**

Output: Goodness of fit for `sexorntrec` with specific proportions.

Chi-squared test for given probabilities

data: sexorntrec.tb1

X-squared = 3.2382, df = 2, *p*-value = 0.1981

The results of the Goodness of Fit test indicate that we *fail to reject the null hypothesis*. There is no significant difference between the proportion of gay/lesbian, bisexual, and heterosexual men and women in the GSS 2016 sample and the estimates provided by the Williams Institute.

Write-Up: A chi-square Goodness of Fit test assessed whether the proportions of gay/lesbian, bisexuals, and heterosexuals in the 2016 *General Social Survey* significantly differ from proportions established in the scientific literature (Gates, 2011). The null hypothesis stated that there was no significant difference between the GSS observed proportions of sexual orientation and the expected proportions based on prior estimates. The results indicate that proportions of sexual orientation in the GSS do not differ significantly from those outlined in Gates (2011). Therefore, we fail to reject the null hypothesis ($\chi^2 = 3.2$, $df = 2$, $p = .20$).

The single proportion and Goodness of Fit tests are useful when comparing proportions of a single variable with other predefined proportions. However, researchers are often more interested in looking at the interrelationships between two variables in a single dataset. The next section introduces this topic, starting with a discussion of bivariate frequencies.

BIVARIATE FREQUENCIES

As Chapter 6 discussed, hypotheses are testable statements about the relationship between variables. As a first step in understanding how relationships between variables play out in data, researchers examine bivariate contingency tables—also known as crosstabulation tables or crosstabs. Contingency tables are frequencies and/or percentages of one variable tabulated separately across the different categories of a second variable. In other words, they show the breakdown of categories in one variable as they are *contingent upon* values of another variable. They are a tabular representation of the information presented in clustered and grouped bar charts discussed in Chapter 5.

An example of this would be a researcher who is interested in exploring whether there are gender differences (sex) in individuals' belief in life after death (postlife). Because both categorical variables are nominal and dichotomous, they are each represented by arbitrary numerical codes in the data. In the variable gender (named sex in the GSS), the code for *male* is "1" and the code for *female* is "2." The variable postlife is based on the GSS question "Do you believe there is a life after death?" The numerical codes assigned to the responses are "1" for *yes* and "2" for *no*. For ease of interpretation, we have left out information on those individuals who reported "Don't Know." Table 7.1 presents a contingency table with information about the relationship between these variables.

In the table, we identify sexrec as the independent variable and postliferec as the dependent variable. By convention, researchers assign the independent variable to the top of the table, where the categories are represented by columns. The dependent variable is on the left, represented in the rows. The boxes in the table that provide individual frequencies and percentages are known as cells. The cells give the value of one variable across different categories of another.

The cells that are located in the sidelines of a contingency table are known as the margins. Margins are the totals for a given category of a variable and are therefore essentially the same as exploring a frequency table for that variable. The modal response for the dependent variable is the highest frequency reported in the row total.

The following examples will use data on respondents' gender (`sexrec`) and their reported beliefs about life after death (`postliferec`). First, value labels are added to the newly recoded variables. If the value labels in sexrec have already been added based on the work from prior chapters, they do not need to be added again:

```
GSS2016$sexrec <- factor(GSS2016$sex,
                      levels = c(1,2),
                      labels = c("Male", "Female"))


GSS2016$postliferec <- factor(GSS2016$postlife,
                      levels = c(1,2),
                      labels = c("Yes", "No"))
```

Although we do not draw heavily on R packages in this book, the **gmodels** package provides an extremely efficient way to generate contingency tables. Therefore, the **gmodels** package is needed for the next section. The annotated code below details how to develop the contingency table to assess the relationship between gender and beliefs about life after death. First, install the **gmodels** package and load it from the package library:

```
install.packages("gmodels")  # Install the package to be used for the
following example.
library("gmodels")  # Attach the package to be used for the following
example.
```

In order to generate a contingency table using these two variables, use the CrossTable function, which is part of the **gmodels** package. The dependent/row variable (`postliferec`) is listed first, followed by the independent/column variable (`sexrec`).

> **Tip:** The **prop.r**, **prop.c**, and **prop.t** commands in the code denote the amount of information that will be provided in the output. They can be set to false to remove information from the output. If, for example, you want to compare column percents only, then you would add "prop.r = FALSE" to the code.

```
CrossTable(GSS2016$postliferec, GSS2016$sexrec, prop.chisq =
FALSE, prop.t = FALSE)  # Produce a full contingency table.
```

Output: Contingency table for `sexrec` and `postliferec` with row totals and column totals.

```
Cell Contents
|------------------------|
| N                      |
| N / Row Total          |
| N / Col Total          |
|------------------------|

Total Observations in Table: 2588
```

| | Sex | | |
Postlife	Male	Female	RowTotal
Yes	859	1230	2089
	0.411	0.589	0.807
	0.751	0.852	
No	285	214	499
	0.571	0.429	0.193
	0.249	0.148	
ColumnTotal	1144	1444	2588
	0.442	0.558	

In Table 7.1, the box for "Cell Contents" points to the organization of the table. Within each cell, the top number represents the number of individuals, the second number is the row total as a proportion, and the third number is the column total as a proportion. Based on the information in the table, we can say that most individuals in the sample—regardless of their gender—reported that they believe in life after death (80.7%). Since fewer individuals reported not believing in life after death ($n = 499$), the modal category for the dependent variable is belief in life after death ($n = 2,089$). Similarly, the column total indicates that the modal category for the independent variable is female ($n = 1,444$) when compared with 1,144 men. The cells inside of the margins present the crosstabulation data on `postliferec` for men and women separately.

While the raw numbers can tell us the modal response and point to some other interesting trends in the margins, the data in a contingency table *must be interpreted using percentages* in order to draw meaningful comparisons. If one were to interpret differences between men and women based on the raw numbers, the comparisons would be susceptible to different sample sizes for the groups. For example, since there are more women in the sample, then it might appear in the raw frequencies that more women than men report believing in life after death—but this might merely be a reflection of the fact that the whole sample has more women in it than men. Therefore, it is important *to make comparisons based on the percentages across each category.*

Within a contingency table, each cell presents three different proportions, which are based on their contribution to the whole sample. However, the table is read differently depending on the placement of the variable in the table. Since `sexrec` is the independent variable in this example, the contingency table present percentages for belief in life after death for men and women independently—in this case, we explore the column percentages. Column percentages identify percentages for each response in the row variable for the full sample of men and the full sample of women. Therefore, these percentages add up to 100% for men and 100% for women in the column total. In a table with column totals only, a researcher can more efficiently explore the differences in the percentages of men and women within each category of the variable `postliferec`. For instance, if the same percentages of women and men report believing in life after death, that is a strong indication that the two are pretty similar. The following code uses the **gmodels** package to present information on column totals and percentages only:

```
CrossTable(GSS2016$postliferec, GSS2016$sexrec, prop.chisq =
FALSE, prop.t = FALSE, prop.r = FALSE) # Produce a contingency
table with information on row and overall totals removed.
```

One way to quickly spot similarities and differences between two groups is to take one category as a reference and compare the other group by subtracting the percentage. For example, in Table 7.1, subtract the postlife percentage for males (75.1%) from the percentage for females (85.2%). Thus, there is a 10% difference between men and women in believing in life after death.

As with all data interpretations, a main objective is to take a complicated series of units or numbers and present a boiled-down version of the most interesting identifiable patterns. One possible interpretation based on the column percentages is (Table 7.1), "of all the women in the sample, 85.2% reported believing in life after death, compared to 75.1% of men." Put more simply, a researcher could say, "A higher percentage of women than men reported that they believe in an afterlife."

It is also possible to review and interpret only the row percentages in contingency tables. Row percentages indicate what percent each `postliferec` category consists of either males or females. These percentages *are not the same values as column percentages* because now we are exploring percentages across the `postliferec` groups rather than across gender categories.

> **Tip:** Researchers are usually more interested in interpreting differences in column percentages because they show differences between independent variable groups (e.g., comparing men and women).

TABLE 7.1 ● CONTINGENCY TABLE WITH COLUMN PERCENTAGES ONLY

```
Cell Contents
|------------------------|
| N                      |
| N / Col Total          |
|------------------------|
Total Observations in Table: 2588
```

|Sex
Postlife	Male	Female	Row Total
Yes	859	1230	2089
	0.751	0.852	
No	285	214	499
	0.249	0.148	
Column Total	1144	1444	2588
	0.442	0.558	

The following code uses the **gmodels** package to present information on row totals and percentages only:

```
CrossTable(GSS2016$postliferec, GSS2016$sexrec, prop.
chisq = FALSE, prop.t = FALSE, prop.c = FALSE) # Produce
a contingency table with information on column and overall totals
removed.
```

Interpretation of Table 7.2 is based on entirely different classifications within the table than when looking at column percents—rather than exploring *all of the women* and comparing them to *all of the men*, we are now looking at *all of the individuals who believe in life after death* and comparing them with *all of the individuals who do not*. Therefore, the frequencies and interpretation are different: "Of those who reported that they believe in life after death, 58.9% were women."

In a single crosstabulation table, a number of different questions can be answered based on (a) which variable is in the row and which is in the column and (b) whether or not the interpretation is based on column percentages or row percentages. See Information Boxes 7.1 and 7.2 for examples of row and column interpretations using Table 7.2.

TABLE 7.2 ● CONTINGENCY TABLE WITH ROW PERCENTAGES ONLY

```
Cell Contents
|------------------------|
| N                      |
| N / Row Total          |
|------------------------|
Total Observations in Table: 2588
| Sex
```

Postlife	Male	Female	Row Total
Yes	859	1230	2089
	0.411	0.589	0.807
No	285	214	499
	0.571	0.429	0.193
Column Total	1144	1444	2588

INFORMATION BOX 7.1

Interpretation of Column Percentages in Table 7.1

Column percentages are necessary in order to answer the following questions:

Question: Of all men in the sample, what percentage believe in life after death?

Answer: *75.1*

Question: Of all women in the sample, what percentage believe in life after death?

Answer: *85.2*

Question: Of all males in the sample, what percentage do not believe in life after death?

Answer: *24.9*

Question: Of all females in the sample, what percentage do not believe in life after death?

Answer: *14.8*

INFORMATION BOX 7.2

Interpretation of Row Percentages in Table 7.2

On the other hand, row percentages help to answer these fundamentally different questions:

Question: Of all individuals who believe in life after death, what percentage are male?

Answer: *41.1*

Question: Of all individuals who believe in life after death, what percentage are female?

Answer: *58.9*

Question: Of those who do not believe in life after death, what percentage are male?

Answer: *57.1*

Question: Of those who do not believe in life after death, what percentage are female?

Answer: *42.9*

Once you are finished with your analysis, you can detach the **gmodels** package from RStudio with the following code:

```
detach("package:gmodels")  # Detach the package gmodels.
```

Contingency tables form the basis for one of the most common hypothesis tests researchers use, the chi-square test of independence, which is the focus of the next section.

THE CHI-SQUARE TEST OF INDEPENDENCE (χ^2)

The chi-square test of independence, which is represented by the notation χ^2, is a test to explore the relationship between two categorical variables. The test examines whether two nominal variables are related. The tests can also be used for ordinal-level or even grouped interval/ratio-level data; however, the ordered nature of the data is not taken into account (i.e., the variables are "treated" like a nominal variable).

In the test of independence, the null hypothesis states that two variables are independent; in other words, they are unrelated and operate independently of each other. Conversely, the research hypothesis proposes that two variables are related in some way. Because the data are treated as nominal, there is no directional hypothesis. There is also no distinction between the independent variable or dependent variable.

The hypotheses for the chi-square test of independence simply state whether or not the two variables are related. For example, a researcher is interested in examining whether there is a relationship between gender and the belief in life after death. The null hypothesis is that no relationship exists between `sexrec` and `postliferec`. On the other hand, the research hypothesis is that `sexrec` and `postliferec` are related in some way.

Observed and Expected Frequencies

To test a hypothesis using the chi-square test of independence, a set of observed frequencies—the frequencies you observe in your data—are compared to a set of hypo-thetical expected frequencies, which are what you would expect if the variables were truly independent. Both sets of frequencies (observed and expected) are presented in contingency tables. Observed frequencies are contingency tables that are based on the *actual* data (e.g., gendered observations of belief in the afterlife in the GSS). They present the frequency of one variable across different categories of another. Expected frequencies, on the other hand, are calculated for each cell based on the row and column totals in the observed data. The resulting "expected model" is a hypothetical distribution that would exist *if the two variables were independent*. For example, based on the observed frequencies in Table 7.2 above, we could calculate the expected frequencies for gender and postlife. This is what the data would look like if equal percentages of men and women reported that they believed in life after death or, in other words, if gender and `postliferec` were unrelated to—or independent of—each other.

The following code presents the observed frequencies for gender (`sexrec`) and the belief in life after death (`postliferec`). Since this is what was actually observed, this is the same as the bivariate frequencies presented in Table 7.3. The code runs a chi-square analysis and stores the relevant information as a separate workspace object.

```
postlife.sex.chi <- chisq.test(GSS2016$postliferec,
GSS2016$sexrec) #Run the chi-square test and store the information
as an object in the workspace.
```

Once the information exists as a workspace object, information on observed frequencies can be pulled using the name of the object, a dollar sign ($), and which information to produce:

```
postlife.sex.chi$observed # Pull and show observed frequencies
from the chisq.test object.
```

Output: Chi-square observed frequencies for `postliferec` and `sexrec`.

	Sex	
Postlife	Male	Female
Yes	859	1230
No	285	214

The expected frequencies are calculated for each cell based on the row and column totals in the observed data. The resulting "expected model" is a hypothetical distribution that would exist *if the two variables are completely independent*. The frequencies and percentages in Table 7.3 are what the data would look like *if equal percentages of men and women reported that they believed in life after death*.

> **Tip:** Decimal places are common for expected frequencies because this is only a hypothetical distribution.

`postlife.sex.chi$expected` # Pull from the chisq.test object just created and present expected frequencies.

TABLE 7.3 ● CHI-SQUARE EXPECTED FREQUENCIES FOR `postliferec` AND `sexrec`

	Sex	
Postlife	Male	Female
Yes	923.4219	1165.5781
No	220.5781	278.4219

Chi-Square Test Statistic

The primary objective of the chi-square test of independence is to assess how closely the observed model resembles the expected model. If the observed frequencies are extremely similar to the expected frequencies, then the variables could be independent. On the other hand, if the two sets of frequencies are extremely different, the test of independence assesses (a) how different and (b) the likelihood that those differences could be based on chance. In other words, the test examines whether the difference between the observed and expected frequencies is large enough to reject the null hypothesis.

In this example, the null hypothesis is that there is no relationship between gender and belief in an afterlife. The following code produces all of the main results of the chi-square analysis (based on the object that was saved in the workspace earlier):

TABLE 7.4   ● CHI-SQUARE TEST BETWEEN `sexrec` AND `postliferec`

Pearson's Chi-squared test with Yates' continuity correction data: GSS2016$postliferec and GSS2016$sexrec X-squared = 41.13, df = 1, *p*-value = 1.424e-10

`postlife.sex.chi` #Produce a table with all of the main results of the chi-square test of independence in the output window.

The resulting statistic (41.13) is known as the *obtained value* of chi-square. Think of this numerical value as a representation of how different the observed table is from the expected table. If the chi-square test statistic value is 0.00, then the observed model is basically the same as—or at least *very close* to—the expected model. Since the expected model reflects complete independence, an obtained value of 0.00 would indicate that the observed model (based on the data) is also independent. Accordingly, greater differences between the observed and expected models means a larger obtained value. The output from this analysis indicates that there is a significant relationship between gender and belief in life after death ($\chi^2 = 41.13$, $p < .001$).

> **Write-Up**: A chi-square test of independence examined the relationship between gender and belief in life after death in the 2016 *General Social Survey*. The null hypothesis stated that the two variables are not related. Based on the analysis, we reject the null hypothesis. The results suggest that there is a significant relationship between gender and belief in an afterlife ($\chi^2 = 41.13$, $p < .001$).

A Brief Note on Degrees of Freedom and the χ^2 Critical Value

In order to determine whether or not the test statistic is larger than one might expect based on chance alone, the test statistic must be compared to a known distribution of chi-square values based on chance. The test statistic is compared to such a distribution, the chi-square distribution.

The shape of the chi-square distribution is determined largely by the number of degrees of freedom in the analysis. Degrees of freedom are the number of cells that can vary based on the row and column totals. There is a different chi-square distribution for every degree of freedom. In order to make a determination about the test statistic and the distribution, a chi-square table is used (along with the degrees of freedom and alpha) to retrieve a critical value of chi-square.

The chi-square table provides a critical value, which is where the nonrejection region ends and the region of rejection begins for different degrees of freedom (distributions) and levels of alpha. In order to make a determination about the null hypothesis, you need to compare the test statistic (obtained value) to the critical value found in this table.

For example, with one degree of freedom, the critical value of chi-square at the .05 level of alpha is 3.84. If the obtained value (i.e., chi-square test statistic) is higher than the critical value, you reject the null hypothesis. The conclusion in this case would be that there is a statistically significant relationship between the two variables. If the obtained value is smaller than the critical value, you fail to reject the null hypothesis. Since R produces this information without the need for the table, the next section ties everything together with several examples.

INFORMATION BOX 7.3

Writing Up the Results of Hypothesis Tests

When interpreting the results of the hypothesis tests discussed in this book, it is important to remember that the relationship is only *correlational*—no statements can be made about a causal relationship. Therefore, the results must *always* be framed as correlational—you would never say, "The independent variable caused a change in the dependent variable." Rather, you would simply state that there is a relationship between the two variables.

Additionally, when writing up results of any statistical analysis, it is important to *at least* include information about the null/research hypotheses, test statistic, degrees of freedom, and *p*-value (probability of making a Type I error). The format for presenting test results vary based on professional standards; be sure to check the style guide conventionally used in your discipline (e.g., ASA, APA, Chicago, MLA) before writing up results.

Additional Chi-Square Examples

Example 1: Gender and Fear of Walking Alone in Neighborhood at Night

The following example assesses whether there is a relationship between gender and fear of walking alone in one's neighborhood at night. The dependent variable was assessed with the question "Is there any area right around here—that is, within a mile—where you would be afraid to walk alone at night?" The response options were *yes* (1) and *no* (2). The null hypothesis states gender and fear of walking alone at night are unrelated, or independent of each other. The following code details the process of conducting the analysis within RStudio:

The first step is to add value labels for the variable `fear`:

```
GSS2016$fearrec <- factor(GSS2016$fear,
                    levels = c(1,2),
                    labels = c("Yes", "No"))
```

Then, generate an independent object in the workspace with information on the chi-square test of independence between gender (sexrec) and fear of walking at night in the neighborhood (fearrec). Call the information from the object to produce the results of the analysis in the output window:

```
fear.sex.chi <-chisq.test(GSS2016$fearrec, GSS2016$sexrec)
# Run the chi-square analysis and save the results as an object in the
workspace.
fear.sex.chi # Call the information from the chisq.test object into
the output window.
```

TABLE 7.5 ● CHI-SQUARE TEST OF INDEPENDENCE BETWEEN **sex** AND **fear**
Pearson's Chi-squared test with Yates' continuity correction data: GSS2016$fearrec and GSS2016$sexrec X-squared = 97.992, df = 1, *p*-value < 2.2e-16

Table 7.5 provides information about the relationship between gender and fear of walking in one's neighborhood at night.

The table shows the chi-square value of 98 with 1 degree of freedom. The *p*-value reflected in the output is less than .001, which means if we reject the null hypothesis based on the results of this analysis, there is only a slight chance we would be making a Type I error. Therefore, based on the information in the table, we reject the null hypothesis.

Write-Up: A chi-square test of independence examined the relationship between gender and whether or not an individual reported feeling afraid to walk in their neighborhood at night. The null hypothesis stated that the two variables were not related. Based on the analysis, we reject the null hypothesis. The results indicate that there is a significant relationship between gender and fear of walking in one's neighborhood at night ($\chi^2 = 97.99$, *df* = 1, *p* < .001).

Example 2: Sexual Orientation and Self-Reported Happiness

The following analysis examines whether or not there is a relationship between sexual orientation (sexorntrec) and self-reported happiness (happyrec). The null hypothesis is that sexual orientation and happiness are independent (i.e., not associated). The research hypothesis is that the two variables are related in some way (i.e., not independent).

As with the other examples above, first provide value labels for all new variables. Then, save the results of the chi-square test of independence as an object in the workspace. Finally, call on the object to produce the results of the analysis in the output window:

```
GSS2016$sexorntrec <- factor(GSS2016$sexornt,
                      levels = c(1,2,3),
                      labels = c("Gay/Lesbian",
                      "Bisexual",
                      "Heterosexual"))  # Add value
                      labels for sexorntrec.
GSS2016$happyrec<- factor(GSS2016$happy,
                      levels = c(1,2,3),
                      labels = c("Very Happy", "Pretty
                      Happy", "Not Happy"))
                      # Add value labels for happy.
happy.sexornt.chi <-chisq.test(GSS2016$happyrec,
GSS2016$sexorntrec)  #Create object with chi-square
information.
happy.sexornt.chi  # Call the results of the analysis to the
output window.
```

TABLE 7.6 ● CHI-SQUARE TEST OF INDEPENDENCE BETWEEN happyrec AND sexorntrec
Pearson's Chi-squared test data: GSS2016$happyrec and sexorntrec X-squared = 12.89, df = 4, p-value = 0.01183

Table 7.6 presents information from the chi-square test of independence. The chi-square test statistic is 12.9 with 4 degrees of freedom. The p-value listed is .011, which indicates that rejecting the null hypothesis would lead to a less than 5% chance of making a Type I error.

Write-Up: A chi-square test of independence examined whether there was a relationship between sexual orientation and self-reported level of happiness in the 2016 *General Social Survey*. The null hypothesis stated that there was no relationship between the two variables. However, based on the results of the analysis, we reject the null hypothesis. The results suggest that there is a statistically significant relationship between sexual orientation and self-reported happiness ($\chi^2 = 12.9$, $df = 4$, $p < .05$).

However, additional testing would be needed in order to ascertain other details about the relationship (e.g., which sexual orientation group reports greater happiness).

Chi-Square Overview

The chi-square test of independence is used to test the relationship between two nominal variables and make inferences about a larger population. The procedure can also be used for ordinal variables and interval/ratio variables collapsed into small groups but the test of independence treats the categories as nominal. The test statistic (obtained value of chi-square) is a numerical representation of how the observed frequencies in the contingency table differ from a set of expected frequencies that would occur if the two variables were completely independent. The chi-square distribution is defined by the degrees of freedom and the region of rejection is based on the critical value of chi-square, which is informed by the level of alpha. The obtained and critical value of chi-square are compared in order to make a determination about the null hypothesis.

There are several assumptions about the data that can lead to erroneous results when violated. First, the *expected* frequency model should not contain cells with a frequency lower than 5. This is a common problem with very small samples or with nominal variables that have many categories, leading to large contingency tables. In some cases, smaller groups can be collapsed into larger ones. At other times, auxiliary statistical procedures (e.g., Fisher's Exact test) might be employed to account for small sample sizes.

Second, one individual must not be in more than one cell or group. This might be the case in an experimental design if you are interested in whether or not arguing with one's spouse is related to stress. This could occur if you (a) asked individuals whether or not arguing causes them stress (`argue1`), then (b) observe individuals arguing with their partner, and (c) asked the same individuals to report again whether or not arguing causes them stress (`argue2`). A chi-square test would be an inappropriate procedure to examine the relationship between `argue1` and `argue2` because the same individuals are in both groups at two different times.

Despite the importance of the hypothesis test above, which details the likelihood of making a Type I error, the chi-square test of independence does not give much information about how strong the relationship is. Researchers use effect size to determine the magnitude of the relationship between two variables.

Effect Sizes for Chi-Square: φ and Cramér's V

The phi coefficient of effect size (φ) is used to assess the strength of the relationship between two variables when both variables are dichotomous (i.e., they each have only two categories, such as gender). Therefore, when conducting a chi-square analysis with a 2 x 2 table, the phi coefficient will indicate the magnitude of difference between the observed and expected frequencies. The resulting coefficient is between 0 and 1. A phi coefficient of 0 indicates that there is no association between the variables. On the other hand, a phi coefficient of 1 would indicate a perfect association between the two variables. The coefficient is symmetric, which means that the value will be the same regardless of which variable is the independent versus dependent variable. Below, we present Cohen's (1988) recommended guidelines for interpreting the phi coefficient:

TABLE 7.7 ● COHEN'S GUIDELINES FOR INTERPRETING φ AND CRAMÉR'S *V*	
Value of φ or Cramér's *V*	**Suggested Interpretation**
0.00 through 0.10	**Weak/Small** Effect
0.11 through 0.30	**Moderate/Medium** Effect
0.31+	**Strong/Large** Effect

Taking the example from Table 7.7, a chi-square test of independence tested whether gender (male/female) was associated with feeling afraid to walk alone at night in one's neighborhood. The null hypothesis was that `sexrec` and `fearrec` are independent (i.e., not associated). The information presented in the statistical output led us to *reject the null hypothesis.* The results suggested that there was a statistically significant relationship between gender and fear of walking in one's neighborhood at night ($\chi^2 = 97.99$, *df* = 1, $p < .001$).

Now that we know there is a statistically significant relationship between the two variables, we should assess whether the relationship is a meaningful one. Since both variables are dichotomous, we can assess the magnitude of the relationship with the phi coefficient of effect size. Since these are not readily available in the R output, the package **vcd** is needed for the following analysis.

```
install.packages ("vcd") # Install the vcd package.
require("vcd") # Load the vcd package.
fear.sex.tbl <- table(GSS2016$sexrec, GSS2016$fearrec) # Create
a contingency table.
```

Generate the output with effect size using the **assocstats** command, which is part of the **vcd** package:

```
assocstats(fear.sex.tbl) # Generate measures of association based
on the information in the table.
```

Output: Effect size—phi coefficient for `sexrec` and `fearrec`.

```
                     X^2 df P(> X^2)
Likelihood Ratio  101.922  1        0
Pearson            98.979  1        0
Phi-Coefficient    : 0.23
Contingency Coeff.: 0.224
Cramér's V         : 0.23
```

In this example, the value of φ is .23. Based on Cohen's guideline for assessing the magnitude of the relationship, we would conclude that there is a moderate relationship between gender and fear of walking alone in one's neighborhood at night. Therefore, in addition to being a statistically significant relationship (i.e., we have confidence that the relationship is real), the correlation is a reasonably meaningful one.

For statistical analyses with more than two groups on one or both variables (i.e., non-dichotomous categorical variables), Cramér's V provides a symmetric measure of effect size with similar guidelines for interpretation (see Chapter 6). Therefore, a value of 0 for Cramér's V indicates that there is no relationship between the variables. Smaller values indicate a weaker relationship between the two variables, while larger values point to a stronger relationship.

This final example in this chapter ties in with the previous section to assess both statistical significance and effect size for the relationship between self-reported level of happiness (happyrec) and fear of walking alone at night (fearrec). The null hypothesis is that there is no relationship between individuals' level of happiness and their fear of walking alone at night in their neighborhood. We first conduct a chi-square test of independence to assess whether or not a statistically significant relationship exists between the two variables:

```
fear.happy.chi <-chisq.test(GSS2016$fearrec, GSS2016$happyrec)
# Run the chi-square analysis and save the results as an object in
the workspace.
fear.happy.chi # Call the information from the chisq.test object into
the output window.
```

TABLE 7.8 ● CHI-SQUARE TEST OF INDEPENDENCE BETWEEN happyrec AND fearrec
Pearson's Chi-squared test data: GSS2016$fearrec and GSS2016$happyrec X-squared = 18.363, df = 2, *p*-value = 0.0001029

The results of this test indicate that we should reject the null hypothesis. There is evidence of a statistically significant relationship between fearrec and happyrec. Now, in addition to statistical significance, we will assess the practical significance of the results. Because happiness has three categories (very happy, pretty happy, and not happy), Cramér's V is an appropriate effect size to measure the magnitude of the correlation between happiness and fear of walking alone at night. Below, we present the code and output for such an analysis using the same package and technique that was used to find the phi coefficient:

```
happy.fear.tb1 <- table(GSS2016$fearrec, GSS2016$happyrec)
# Create a bivariate table with both variables in the analysis.
assocstats(happy.fear.tb1) # Generate the measures of association
based on the information in the table.
detach("package:vcd") # Detach the vcd package.
```

Output: Measures of effect size for `fearrec` and `happyrec`.

```
                        X^2  df  P(> X^2)
Likelihood Ratio  17.995   2  0.00012373
Pearson           18.363   2  0.00010292


Phi-Coefficient       : NA
Contingency Coeff.    : 0.099
Cramér's V            : 0.099
```

Although the results of our earlier analysis indicated that there was a statistically significant relationship between fear of walking alone at night and happiness (χ^2 = 18.4, df = 2, $p < .001$), the effect size, Cramér's V (.09), indicates that the relationship is a weak one. Thus, although we reject the null hypothesis, the relationship between the two variables does not appear to be a meaningful one in practical terms.

> **Write-Up:** A chi-square test of independence examined whether there was a relationship between respondents' self-reported happiness and whether they reported feeling afraid to walk around their neighborhood alone at night. The null hypothesis stated that there was no relationship between the two variables. Based on the results of the analysis, we reject the null hypothesis. The results suggest there is a statistically significant relationship between happiness and fear of walking alone at night (χ^2 = 18.4, df = 2, $p < .001$). However, based on Cramér's V effect size coefficient (V = 0.9), the magnitude of the relationship is small.

CONCLUSION

This chapter detailed several statistical procedures that researchers use to analyze and explain relationships between categorical (nominal and/or ordinal) variables. The first part of the chapter discussed hypothesis testing for population proportions. The single proportion hypothesis test assesses whether a given proportion for a categorical variable is significantly different from some hypothesized value. This was followed by a discussion of the chi-square goodness-of-fit test, which is one way to assess how closely an observed distribution "fits" an expected distribution based on theory, logic, or prior research. The chapter then shifted focus to contingency tables, a common way that researchers assess relationships between categorical variables (i.e., by breaking down the scores of one variable across the categories of another). Importantly, contingency tables are also used to represent a hypothetical model of frequencies we might expect if two variables operated independently of each other. These "expected" frequencies are then compared to observed frequencies, forming the crux of the chi-square test of independence. This test assesses whether or not there is a significant relationship between two variables based on the observed and expected frequencies. However, statistical significance provides necessary, but not sufficient, evidence for a relationship between two variables. The final part of this chapter discussed ways that researchers complement the results of their hypothesis tests with measures of effect size in order to provide details about the magnitude, or practical importance, of the relationship between two variables.

References

Gates, G. J. (2011). *How many people are lesbian, gay, bisexual, and transgender?* Los Angeles, CA: The Williams Institute. Retrieved from https://williamsinstitute.law.ucla.edu/wp-content/uploads/Gates-How-Many-People-LGBT-Apr-2011.pdf

Smith, T. W., Davern, M., Freese, J., & Morgan, S. L. (2019). *General Social Surveys, 1972–2018* [Machine-Readable Data File]. Chicago, IL: NORC at the University of Chicago. Retrieved from http://www.gss.norc.org/getthedata/Pages/Home.aspx

Exercises

1. Identify two ways someone might visually present the data in a contingency table.

2. Run a two-tailed single proportion hypothesis test to assess whether 30 students failing a midterm exam is significantly different from half of the full class size of 72. Be sure to write up your results in the same format as presented within the chapter.

3. Generate a contingency table for sex and racerec (this variable was recoded in an earlier exercise). Answer the following questions:

   A. Of all men in the sample, what percentage are Black?

   B. Of all women in the sample, what percentage are White?

   C. Of all White respondents, what percentage are women?

   D. Of all Black respondents, what percentage are men?

4. Run a chi-square test of independence for racerec and postlife. Choose and report the most appropriate measure of effect size for the analysis. Interpret and write up the results in the same format as presented within the chapter.

Supplementary Digital Content

Download datasets and R code at the companion website at https://study.sagepub.com/researchmethods/statistics/gillespie-r-for-statistics

COMPARING ONE OR TWO MEANS

INTRODUCTION

This chapter details the logic of the *t*-test and provides detailed information on how to perform several different *t*-test analyses using RStudio and the *General Social Survey* (GSS) (Smith et al., 2019) data. In the following sections, we cover three different *t*-tests (1) the one-sample *t*-test, (2) the independent samples *t*-test, and (3) the paired *t*-test. The one-sample *t*-test compares a single mean to some hypothesized value, which is usually the population mean. The independent samples *t*-test compares means between two different groups in the same population. The paired *t*-test compares means between two groups when the observations in one group are in some way associated with, or dependent upon, the observations of the other (e.g., the same person at two different points in time). See Table 8.1 for the type of comparison each of these three *t*-tests is suited to make.

One common thread across each test is that they draw on a single quantitative (interval/ratio) variable. In the case of independent samples and paired *t*-tests, the independent, or grouping, variable is dichotomous. Another common thread linking the three tests is that the hypotheses presented can be non-directional or directional. Recall from Chapter 6 that a two-tailed test is used to assess a *non-directional* hypothesis. This situation occurs when

TABLE 8.1 ● DIFFERENT TYPES OF *t*-TESTS	
Test	**Comparison**
One-Sample *t*-test	Sample Mean and a Constant Value
Independent Samples *t*-test	Independent Populations (e.g., Two Different Groups)
Paired Samples *t*-test	Related Groups (e.g., Same People at Different Times)

a researcher has no preconceived idea about the direction of the relationship (i.e., there is no reason to expect the test statistic will fall in one tail of the distribution or the other). Therefore, the null hypothesis is simply that there is no difference. On the other hand, researchers use one-tailed tests to assess *directional* hypotheses. This occurs when the researcher has some reason to believe the mean will be either smaller or larger than the other mean or hypothesized value. The region of rejection for the test statistic is reflected on only one side of the distribution. In this case, the null hypothesis states that no significant difference exists in the hypothesized direction.

ONE-SAMPLE *t*-TEST

Like the single-proportion test discussed in Chapter 7, a one-sample *t*-test uses data on a single variable in a sample to compare with a specific hypothesized value, which is usually based on theory, logic, and/or existing research. A two-tailed single-sample *t*-test assesses whether the sample mean is significantly different from the comparison value specified while a one-tailed test proposes a specific direction for the hypothesized relationship. For example, a professor interested in assessing whether the average of his final exam was significantly higher than 60 would use a one-tailed one-sample *t*-test to compare the mean final exam score with the value 60 (i.e., the lowest passing score).

To test whether the mean of a single continuous variable is significantly different from some other non-arbitrarily defined number, the one-sample *t*-test uses the **t.test** command. For the one-sample *t*-test, the default ("null") value is 0—so the default analysis tests whether or not a given mean differs significantly from 0. R's default operation is to run a two-tailed *t*-test and, as such, the research hypothesis is non-directional. Therefore, using the default specifications, we hypothesize the mean score provided is significantly different from the hypothesized value—in this case, 0.

The following example uses the variable `partnrs5`, which is the GSS 2016 measure for the number of sexual partners an individual reported having in the last 5 years. The null hypothesis for this analysis is that the number of sex partners in the last 5 years is not significantly different from 0.

First, read the data into RStudio by typing the code below into the scripting window. This will read the .csv data file into RStudio, where it will then be listed in the workspace environment.

Tip: Be sure to include the appropriate pathname to your data, which will depend on where it is stored on your computer.

```
GSS2016 <- read.csv("C:/Users/Desktop/R/GSS2016.csv", header =
TRUE))# Read the .csv-formatted data into RStudio.
```

The following code runs a one-sample hypothesis test using the default specifications in R to test if the number of sexual partners in the last 5 years is significantly different from 0.

```
GSS2016$partnrs5rec <- GSS2016$partnrs5
GSS2016$partnrs5rec[GSS2016$partnrs5rec=="-1"]=NA
GSS2016$partnrs5rec[GSS2016$partnrs5rec=="95"]=NA
GSS2016$partnrs5rec[GSS2016$partnrs5rec=="98"]=NA
GSS2016$partnrs5rec[GSS2016$partnrs5rec=="99"]=NA
t.test(GSS2016$partnrs5rec)  # Run a two-tailed one-sample
hypothesis test with the default options for number of sexual partners in
the last 5 years.
```

Output: One-sample t-test for `partnrs5rec` with default options.

```
          One Sample t-test
data: GSS2016$partnrs5rec
t = 40.307, df = 1748, p-value < 2.2e-16
alternative hypothesis: true mean is not equal to 0
95 percent confidence interval:
 1.777577 1.959416

sample estimates:
mean of x
 1.868496
```

The output provides the t-statistic, degrees of freedom, and p-value. The value under "sample estimate" is the observed mean of the variable, which is 1.87 sexual partners. The p-value for this analysis is less than .001. Therefore, we reject the null hypothesis and conclude that individuals' number of sexual partners within the last 5 years *is* significantly different from 0 ($t = 40.3$, $df = 1748$, $p < .001$).

Write-Up: A two-tailed one-sample t-test examined whether the mean number of sexual partners reported in the last 5 years was significantly different from 0. The two-tailed alternative hypothesis proposed that the number of sexual partners significantly differed from 0. The null hypothesis stated that the number of sexual partners did not differ significantly from 0. The results of the analysis indicate that the observed mean number of sexual partners (1.86) is significantly different from 0. Therefore, we reject the null hypothesis ($t = 40.3$, $df = 1748$, $p < .001$).

Tip: The p-value here is reported in scientific notation—remember, if the sign and number after the "e" is negative, move the decimal point that many places *to the left*.

Of course, using the null value of 0 is rarely theoretically meaningful. To modify the null value, use the "mu" qualifier. For example, if there is some theoretical reason to believe that five is an important number of sexual partners to have within a 5-year period, then a researcher would compare the mean of partnrs5rec to the value "5":

```
t.test(GSS2016$partnrs5rec, mu = 5)  # Run a two–tailed one–
```
sample *t*-test for a predefined value of 5.

Output: One-sample *t*-test with mean provided.

```
      One Sample t-test
data: GSS2016$partnrs5rec
t = -67.553, df = 1748, p-value < 2.2e-16
alternative hypothesis: true mean is not equal to 5
95 percent confidence interval:
 1.777577 1.959416
sample estimates:
mean of x
 1.868496
```

This analysis compares the mean number of sex partners in the past 5 years (part-nrs5rec) to the value "5," which results in a rejection of the null hypothesis. The mean number of sexual partners in the last 5 years is significantly different from 5 (t = -67.6, df = 1748, p < .001).

> **Tip:** When writing up the results of your analysis, be sure to include information about the hypothesis (and direction, if applicable), the test statistic, degrees of freedom, whether the test is one-tailed or two-tailed, and the *p*-value.

Write-Up: A two-tailed one-sample *t*-test examined whether the mean number of sexual partners reported in the last 5 years was significantly different from 5. The null hypothesis stated that the number of sexual partners did not significantly differ from 5. However, the results of the analysis indicate that the observed mean number of sexual partners (1.87) is significantly different from 5. Therefore, we reject the null hypothesis (t = 67.6, df = 1748, p < .001).

One might also choose to test a directional hypothesis when there is a proposed expectation about where (i.e., which tail) the region of rejection falls. Therefore, rather than splitting the alpha into two rejection regions, the region of rejection is only in "one tail." A one-tailed alternative hypothesis states that a given mean is significantly *greater than* (alternative = "greater") or *less than* (alternative = "less") the proposed value. The following example uses a one-tailed one-sample *t*-test to examine whether or not the mean number of sexual partners is significantly *greater* than 5:

```
t.test(GSS2016$partnrs5rec, mu = 5, alternative="greater")
# Run a one-tailed one-sample t-test for a predefined
value (5).
```

Output: One-tailed one-sample *t*-test.

```
        One Sample t-test
data: GSS2016$partnrs5rec
t = -67.553, df = 1748, p-value = 1
alternative hypothesis: true mean is greater than 5
95 percent confidence interval:
 1.792206 Inf

sample estimates:
mean of x
 1.868496
```

Tip: The upper-bound confidence interval is "infinity" because a one-tailed test was conducted.

Based on the above output, we fail to reject the null hypothesis. The mean number of sexual partners in the last 5 years is *not* significantly greater than 5 (t = -67.6, df = 1748, p = 1).

Write-Up: A one-tailed one-sample *t*-test examined whether the mean number of sexual partners reported in the last 5 years was significantly greater than the predefined value of 5. The null hypothesis stated that the number of sexual partners was not significantly greater than the predetermined value of 5. The results of the analysis indicate that the observed mean number of sexual partners (1.87) was not significantly greater than 5. Therefore, we reject the null hypothesis (t = 67.6, df = 1748, p < .001).

If the researcher wanted to test whether or not the mean number of sexual partners differs significantly from 1.9, she would change the value in the R code accordingly. The following example tests a one-tailed hypothesis for whether number of sexual partners in the last 5 years is significantly different from 1.9. An additional specification has been added to the code (conf.level = 0.99) in order to use an alpha of .01 for the analysis:

```
t.test(GSS2016$partnrs5rec, mu = 1.9, alternative="less",
conf.level = 0.99) # Run a one-tailed one-sample hypothesis
```
for whether the number of sexual partners in the last five years is
significantly less than 1.9 using an alpha of .01.

Output: One-tailed one-sample t-test with different comparison value and alpha level.

```
        One Sample t-test
data: GSS2016$partnrs5rec
t = -0.6796, df = 1748, p-value = 0.2484
alternative hypothesis: true mean is less than 1.9
99 percent confidence interval:
-Inf 1.976436

sample estimates:
mean of x
 1.868496
```

Based on the results of the previous analysis, we fail to reject the null hypothesis. The true mean of sexual partners in the last 5 years is not significantly less than 1.9 (t = -0.68, df = 1748, p = 0.25). In this instance, if we were to reject the null hypothesis, there would be a 25% chance of making a Type I error.

Write-Up: A one-tailed one-sample t-test examined whether the mean number of sexual partners reported in the last 5 years was significantly different from the predetermined hypothesized value of 1.9. The null hypothesis stated that the number of sexual partners did not significantly differ from 1.9. The results of the analysis indicate that the observed mean number of sexual partners (1.87) does not differ significantly from 1.9. Therefore, we fail to reject the null hypothesis (t = 0.68, df = 1748, p = 0.25).

While the one-sample t-test uses a single mean to compare to a fixed value, researchers are often interested in comparing the means of two groups (e.g., the mean number of sex partners between men and women). To do so, researchers use the independent samples t-test.

THE INDEPENDENT SAMPLES t-TEST

The independent samples t-test is a procedure used to assess whether or not a mean significantly differs between two independent groups. In this context, the term *independent* means that the individuals in one group do not influence the selection of individuals into the other group.

To conduct an independent samples *t*-test, the independent variable must be dichotomous (a variable with only two groups) and the dependent variable must be measured at the interval/ratio level. This type of situation is common in social science research. For example, in survey-based research, the *t*-test is often used to compare interval/ratio scores (e.g., income) between two groups (e.g., men and women). In experimental research, the *t*-test is useful when comparing the mean scores for experimental and control groups.

As a parametric test, the *t*-test has more assumptions regarding distribution and variance than the chi-square test of independence. Three of the most important assumptions are that (a) the data are normally distributed for both populations; (b) there is homogeneity of variance, which means that the standard deviations are approximately equal for both populations; and (c) there are no extreme outliers in either group, which can be examined by looking at grouped box plots (see Chapter 5). While the latter two assumptions are important, the *t*-test will produce reasonably accurate results even if they are violated, insofar as neither assumption is violated egregiously. However, if the data for either group have small sample sizes, are highly skewed, and/or there are large differences in variance, then a different (nonparametric) statistical test might be more appropriate.

Independent Samples *t*-Test Notation and Hypotheses

The alternative hypotheses for an independent samples *t*-test state whether or not there are expected differences between population means based on the sample means. While it is very likely that the two means will differ, the important part of the test states how likely it is that the differences *are based on chance*. The null hypothesis (H_0) states that there is *no* mean difference between Group 1 and Group 2—or, in other words, the difference between the two groups is 0. The μ ("mu") symbol represents the population mean; therefore, the null hypothesis can also be stated as $\mu_1 = \mu_2$. Saying much the same thing but framing it in terms of the *difference* between groups instead: $\mu_1 - \mu_2 = 0$. A non-directional (two-tailed) research hypothesis (H_a) is that the difference between the two groups is not 0, or $\mu_1 - \mu_2 \neq 0$.

As discussed above, the research hypothesis for a *t*-test can also be directional—which means that the *t*-test will be one-tailed. A directional research hypothesis can be presented in different ways depending on which group is expected to be larger. For example, if you had reason to believe that the mean for Group 1 would be greater than that of Group 2, the hypothesis would be framed as follows:

> H_a: The mean for Group 1 is greater than that of Group 2 ($\mu_1 > \mu_2$). In terms of difference between the groups, this is the same as saying that $\mu_1 - \mu_2 > 0$.

The directional hypothesis is always the opposite of the null hypothesis. Therefore, in the example previous ($\mu_1 > \mu_2$), even if Group 2 is significantly larger than Group 1, you still *fail to reject the null hypothesis* (conclude that there is *no significant difference*). This is because the region of rejection in a one-tailed test is in the opposite tail.

If the test statistic is located in the extreme of the *other* direction, it is still considered the non-rejection region and you would fail to reject the null hypothesis. This might obscure otherwise significant and interesting differences between two groups, which is why some researchers have cautioned against using one-tailed *t*-tests.

The Logic of the Independent Samples *t*-Test Statistic

The basic premise behind the *t*-test statistic is to compare distributions based on the difference between means. In the simplest terms and most convenient definitions, the logic is to calculate the *difference between means* by (a) randomly selecting a sample mean from Group 1, (b) randomly selecting a sample mean from Group 2, and (c) subtracting the sample mean from Group 2 from that of Group 1. Repeating this over and over again results in a *distribution of the differences between means*.

The *t*-statistic—which can be negative or positive—can be thought of as a numerical representation of the difference between the two means. A test statistic of 0 indicates that there is no difference in means between the two groups. The larger the absolute value of the *t*-statistic (the farther it gets from 0 on either side), the larger the difference between means, and the smaller the probability of making a Type I error.

One-Tailed and Two-Tailed *t*-Tests

Recall from Chapter 6 that the region(s) of rejection in the *t*-distribution depend upon whether the test is one-tailed or two-tailed. Two-tailed tests are associated with non-directional research hypotheses, where the research hypothesis is that the group means are *different* ($\mu_1 \neq \mu_2$). Since you can reject the null hypothesis for a two-tailed test when the *t*-statistic is positive *or* negative, the alpha and region of rejection are split evenly in the left and right tails. For example, with an alpha of .05, then .025 will be the cutoff for the region of rejection in the left tail and .025 will be the cutoff for the region of rejection in the right tail.

If the absolute value of the *t*-statistic falls within the rejection region in either the left tail or the right tail, we reject the null hypothesis and conclude that means for each group are significantly different. On the other hand, if the absolute value of the *t*-statistic lies within the central non-rejection region of the distribution, we fail to reject the null hypothesis.

A positive *t*-statistic indicates that Group 1 is larger than Group 2 ($\mu_1 > \mu_2$) and a negative statistic indicates that Group 2 is larger than Group 1 ($\mu_1 > \mu_2$). Therefore, when conducting a one-tailed test, two pieces of information tell us whether or not we can reject the null hypothesis: (1) the positive or negative sign of the *t*-statistic and (2) whether or not it lies within the rejection region of the appropriate tail.

> **Tip:** If the *t*-statistic is located in the extreme of the *opposite* direction than the one hypothesized, it would be considered the non-rejection region and you would still fail to reject the null hypothesis. This is an important precaution against the one-tailed hypothesis because it might lead a researcher to overlook otherwise significant differences between the groups.

A Brief Note on Degrees of Freedom and the *t*-Critical Value

The distribution of the *t*-test is known as the *t*-distribution. Like the chi-square distribution, the number of degrees of freedom for the t-statistic informs the shape of the distribution. The degrees of freedom for the *t*-test are based on the number of scores that can vary if information on the mean is provided. In other words, if you have the mean, you can extrapolate from the data to determine a single missing score. Therefore, the total degrees of freedom for the *t*-statistic is N − 1.

Like the chi-square table, a *t*-table presents *t*-critical values, which are based on characteristics of the study: the degrees of freedom, whether the test is one-tailed or two-tailed, and the alpha. Once you have retrieved the critical value for your study, you compare it to the obtained *t*-statistic. If the obtained value is higher than the critical value, you reject the null hypothesis. If on the other hand, the critical value is higher than the obtained value, you fail to reject the null hypothesis.

EXAMPLES

The following example tests whether or not the mean number of hours spent using the Internet each week differs between those without children and those with children. The two-tailed alternative hypothesis is that the mean number of hours spent using the Internet will be significantly different for those with children compared with those who do not have children. As such, the null hypothesis is that two groups do not significantly differ in their use of the Internet.

Since the GSS (Smith et al., 2019) data do not contain a dichotomous (0/1) variable for whether or not individuals have children, we first create a new variable `childsrec`—based on the variable for number of children (`childs`). The dichotomous variable `childsrec` indicates if someone is *child free* (0) or *has children* (1). Following the recode, summary statistics are assessed, including a histogram and grouped box plots for the number of hours spent using the Internet each week (`wwwhr`).

```
GSS2016$childsrec <- GSS2016$childs
GSS2016$childsrec[GSS2016$childsrec=="9"]=NA
GSS2016$childsrec[GSS2016$childsrec > 0] <- 1 # Recode
```
the childsrec variable so that values greater than "0" are recoded to "1." Thus, parental status is "child free" (0) and "has any children" (1).
```
GSS2016$childsrec <- factor(GSS2016$childsrec,
levels = c(0,1),
labels = c("No Kids", "Has Kids")) #Define value labels for
```
childsrec.
```
table(GSS2016$childsrec)
```

TABLE 8.2 ● FREQUENCIES FOR PARENTAL STATUS (`childsrec`)

No Kids	Has Kids
797	2062

```
GSS2016$wwwhrrec <- GSS2016$wwwhr
GSS2016$wwwhrrec[GSS2016$wwwhrrec=="-1"]=NA
GSS2016$wwwhrrec[GSS2016$wwwhrrec=="998"]=NA
GSS2016$wwwhrrec[GSS2016$wwwhrrec=="999"]=NA

hist(GSS2016$wwwhrrec,
main = "Histogram for Weekly Internet Use",
xlab = "Number of Hours on the Internet Each Week")
```
Check the histogram for the interval/ratio variable (weekly hours of Internet use).

FIGURE 8.1 ● HISTOGRAM OF INTERNET USE IN HOURS/WEEK (`wwwhrrec`)

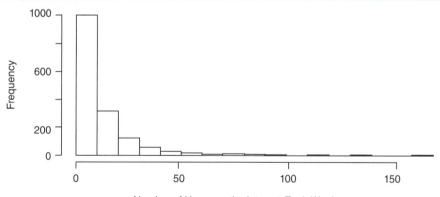

Number of Hours on the Internet Each Week

```
boxplot(GSS2016$wwwhrrec ~ GSS2016$childsrec,
horizontal = TRUE,
main = "Boxplot for Internet Use and Parental Status",
xlab = "Number of Hours/Week Spent Online")
```
Generate grouped boxplots of Internet use (wwwhrrec) by parental status (childsrec).

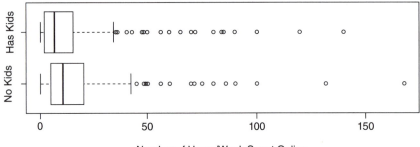

FIGURE 8.2 ● BOXPLOTS FOR INTERNET USE (wwwhrrec) BY PARENTAL STATUS (childsrec)

Boxplot for Internet Use and Parental Status

Tip: The grouped box plots in Figure 8.2 indicate that the data are positively skewed. There is also a clear outlier in the Internet use of one individual without children. This requires decisions about removing the outlier, putting a cap on the highest value (e.g., 30+ hours of Internet use), transforming the variable, or using another statistical test.

The *t*-test is run with the t.test function—first, the dependent variable is identified, followed by the dichotomous "grouping variable." The following code and output present a *t*-test with R's default configurations:

t.test(GSS2016$wwwhrrec ~ GSS2016$childsrec) # Test whether or not the difference between those with children (1) and those without (0) in hours using the Internet is significantly different from 0.

Output: Two-tailed independent samples *t*-test for weekly Internet use by parental status.

```
Welch Two Sample t-test

data: GSS2016$wwwhrrec by childsrec
t = 4.8722, df = 785.27, p-value = 1.335e-06
alternative hypothesis: true difference in means is not equal to 0
95 percent confidence interval:
 2.904452 6.823995

sample estimates:
    mean in group No Kids    mean in group Has Kids
          16.45122                  11.58700
```

The "Welch two-sample *t*-test" corrects for the difference in the variances of the two samples, which is based on the "equality of variances" assumption discussed above. The output indicates that there is a statistically significant difference in the number of hours of Internet use between those who have children and those who do not ($t = 4.9$, *df* = 785.3, $p < .001$). In other words, we reject the null hypothesis. The mean number of hours spent on the Internet among those without children is 16.5 and for those with children it is 11.6.

> **Write-Up:** A two-tailed independent-samples *t*-test examined whether the mean number of hours spent using the Internet each week was significantly different for individuals with children than for those without children. The null hypothesis stated that the mean number of hours did not significantly differ between the two groups. The results of the analysis indicate that the observed mean number of hours using the Internet is significantly different between those who have children (11.6 hours) and those who do not have children (16.5 hours). Therefore, we reject the null hypothesis ($t = 4.9$, *df* = 785.3, $p < .001$).

The next example is a follow-up to the previous example. The same variables are used; however, we now propose a directional research hypothesis (alternative = "greater"), use an alpha of .01 (conf.level = .99), and recode the variable `wwwhr` so that the highest possible value is 30.

> **Tip:** The process of recoding a variable so that scores greater than a certain value are collapsed into a lower value is called "top-coding" or "capping."

The following code changes the variable `wwwhr` so that any scores over 30 are recoded to a value of 30. This means that a score of 30 on this variable essentially represents "30+ hours."

```
wwwhr.30 <- GSS2016$wwwhrrec # Create an independent object to
recode wwwhr (wwwhr.30).
```

```
wwwhr.30[wwwhr.30 > 30] <- 30 # Recode the wwwhr variable so that
values greater than "30" are recoded to "30".
```

Now that the variable has been recoded, we can again assess the grouped boxplot for the weekly Internet use of those with children and those without:

```
boxplot(wwwhr.30 ~ GSS2016$childsrec,
        horizontal = TRUE,
        main = "Boxplot for Internet Use (Recoded) \n and
        Parental Status",
        xlab = "Number of Hours/Week Spent Online")
```

FIGURE 8.3 ● BOXPLOTS FOR RECODED INTERNET USE (wwwhr.30) BY
PARENTAL STATUS (childsrec)

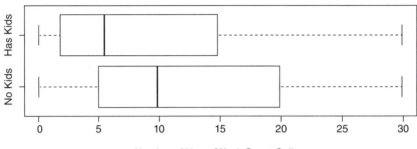

The boxplot for the recoded variables appears very different than the original boxplot
because each of the outliers have been recoded to the value "30." For the following independent samples *t*-test, the null hypothesis is that the difference in the number of hours spent
using the Internet (wwwhr.30) between those who have children and those who do not is
"0." The one-tailed research hypothesis is that the mean for Group 1 (has no children) is
"greater" than the mean for Group 2 (has children):

```
t.test(wwwhr.30 ~ GSS2016$childsrec,
alternative = "greater",
conf.level = .99)  # Run a one-tailed t-test with a revised confidence
interval.
```

Output: One-tailed *t*-test with recoded Internet use (wwwhr.30) and parental status
(childrec).

```
Welch Two Sample t-test

data: wwwhr.30 by childsrec
t = 5.7926, df = 917.61, p-value = 4.76e-09
alternative hypothesis: true difference in means is greater
than 0

99 percent confidence interval:
 1.832577 Inf
sample estimates:
    mean in group No Kids      mean in group Has Kids
    12.853659                    9.787546
```

The results of the follow-up analysis indicate that, on average, individuals who do not have a child spend significantly more time using the Internet (12.9 hours) than those who have a child (9.8 hours). Therefore, we reject the null hypothesis (t = 5.8, df = 917.6, p < .001).

> **Tip:** When interpreting and writing up the results of a t-test, keep in mind that—just as with the chi-square—the results are correlational. As such, it is important to avoid making claims about causal relationships. In the previous example, we would not propose that having children *causes* one to use the Internet less frequently. In fact, the reverse might be true—those who use the Internet less frequently might have more free time to procreate. Alas, the t-test is not equipped to assess for this type of causal relationship.

Write-Up: A one-tailed independent-samples t-test examined whether the mean number of hours spent using the Internet each week (top-coded at 30) was significantly greater for individuals without a child than for those who have a child. The null hypothesis was that the mean number of Internet hours was not greater for those without a child than those with a child. The results of the analysis indicate that, on average, individuals without children (M = 12.9) spend significantly more time using the Internet each week than individuals with children (M = 9.8). Therefore, we reject the null hypothesis (t = 5.8, df = 917.6, p < .001).

ADDITIONAL INDEPENDENT SAMPLES t-TEST EXAMPLES

Example 1: Gender and Number of Siblings (Non-Directional)

The first example assesses whether there are gender differences in individuals' number of siblings. The analysis is based on the GSS variables for gender (`sex`), the dichotomous independent variable, and number of siblings (`sibs`), the interval/ratio dependent variable. The null hypothesis states that there is no difference in mean number of siblings between men and women ($\mu_{men} \neq \mu_{women}$). There are a few reasons why men and women might have *different* numbers of siblings. However, it is less clear which group will have more siblings than the other. For this reason, we propose a non-directional research hypothesis. The research hypothesis states that there *is* a difference in the mean number of siblings for men and women ($\mu_{men} \neq \mu_{women}$).

To get a sense of how the variables are distributed, the following code (a) generates a histogram for the variable `sibsrec` and (b) produces a table of frequencies for `sexrec`.

```
GSS2016$sibsrec <- GSS2016$sibs
GSS2016$sibsrec[GSS2016$sibsrec=="-1"]=NA
GSS2016$sibsrec[GSS2016$sibsrec=="98"]=NA
```

```
GSS2016$sibsrec[GSS2016$sibsrec=="99"]=NA
```

```
hist(GSS2016$sibsrec,
       main = "Histogram for Number of Siblings",
       xlab = "Number of Siblings")
```
Generate a histogram for the dependent variable.

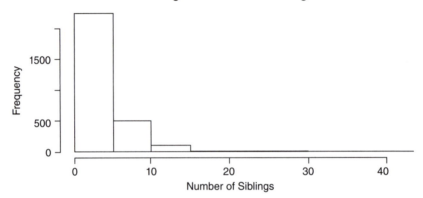

FIGURE 8.4 ● HISTOGRAM OF SIBLINGS (`sibsrec`)

```
GSS2016$sexrec <- factor(GSS2016$sex,
               levels = c(1,2),
               labels = c("Male", "Female"))
               table(GSS2016$sexrec)
```
Check frequencies for the independent dichotomous variable (sexrec).

```
boxplot(GSS2016$sibsrec ~ GSS2016$sexrec,
       horizontal = TRUE,
       main = "Number of Siblings by Sex",
       xlab = "Siblings")
```
Generate grouped boxplots for number of siblings by sex.

TABLE 8.3 ● FREQUENCIES FOR GENDER

Male	Female
1276	1591

FIGURE 8.5 ● **GROUPED BOXPLOT FOR SIBLINGS (`sibsrec`) BY `sexrec`**

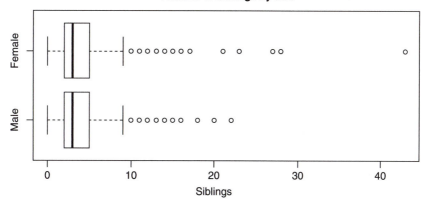

Number of Siblings by Sex

Tip: Again, the grouped boxplots indicate that the data are skewed (and there is a clear female outlier with more than 40 siblings). For the sake of understanding the process of hypothesis testing with R, we will continue with the analysis; however, this figure should certainly raise flags about the non-normality of the distribution of the dependent variable.

`t.test(GSS2016$sibsrec ~ GSS2016$sexrec)` # Run a two–tailed independent–samples *t*-test to assess whether or not the difference between men and women (`sexrec`) in number of siblings (`sibsrec`) is significantly different from 0.

Output: Two-tailed independent samples *t*-test for siblings (`sibsrec`) and `sexrec`.

```
        Welch Two Sample t-test

data: GSS2016$sibsrec by GSS2016$sexrec
t = -2.0372, df = 2801.1, p-value = 0.04173
alternative hypothesis: true difference in means is not
equal to 0
95 percent confidence interval:
 -0.478114041 -0.009133328

sample estimates:
    mean in group 1     mean in group 2
        3.583203            3.826826
```

The output provides information about siblings for both groups in the independent variable—men are in Group 1 and women are in Group 2. This table allows for a quick assessment of the individual group means (men = 3.6; women = 3.8). Thus, one can quickly compare the size of each group's means, including which group's mean is larger.

The t-statistic is -2.04 and the p-value, 0.04, points to whether or not we reject the hypothesis using an alpha level of .05. Since the p-value (0.04) is within the .05 threshold, we reject the null hypothesis. Therefore, we conclude that there is a significant difference in number of siblings between men and women (t = -2.04, df = 2801.1, p = .04). Said much the same way, the difference between men's and women's number of siblings is significantly different from 0. However, great caution should be taken when interpreting these results in any definitive way because of the issue with outliers identified earlier (Figure 8.5).

Write-Up: A two-tailed independent-samples t-test examined whether the mean number of siblings differed between men and women. The null hypothesis was that men and women did not significantly differ in their mean number of siblings. The results of the analysis indicate that men (M = 3.6) and women (3.8) differ significantly in their number of siblings (t = -2.04, df = 2801.1, p = .04). Therefore, we reject the null hypothesis.

Example 2: Children and Number of Siblings (Directional)

The second example of the independent samples t-test examines whether parental status (childsrec) is associated with differences in number of siblings (sibsrec). The null hypothesis (H_0) states that there is no difference in the number of siblings among those who do not have children and those who do ($\mu_1 \neq \mu_2$). Since individuals with children might have a preference for—and tendency toward—larger families, a directional research hypothesis is proposed. This hypothesis states that those without children will have fewer siblings than those with children ($\mu_1 < \mu_2$).

FIGURE 8.6 ● GROUPED BOXPLOTS FOR SIBLINGS (sibsrec) BY PARENTAL STATUS (childsrec)

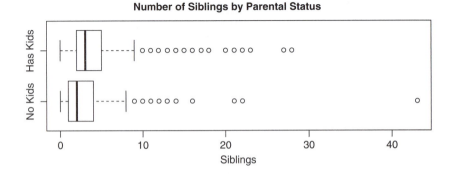

Number of Siblings by Parental Status

First, we assess grouped boxplots to assess the distribution of the dependent variable across categories of the independent variable:

```
boxplot(GSS2016$sibsrec ~ GSS2016$childsrec,
horizontal = TRUE,
main = "Number of Siblings by Parental Status",
xlab = "Siblings") # Generate grouped boxplots for number of
siblings by parental status.
```

Again, there are clear outliers present in the data. Therefore, the following code changes number of siblings (`sibsrec`) so that the topmost category is 15—all values greater than 15 are set to equal 15, which will now represent "15 or more siblings."

```
sibs.15 <- GSS2016$sibsrec #Create an independent object to recode
siblings (sibs.15).

sibs.15[sibs.15 > 15] <- 15 # Recode the sibs variable so that values
greater than "15" are recoded to "15."

boxplot(sibs.15 ~ GSS2016$childsrec,
horizontal = TRUE,
main = "Number of Siblings by Parental Status",
xlab = "Siblings") # Generate grouped boxplots for number of
siblings by parental status.
```

FIGURE 8.7 ● GROUPED BOXPLOTS FOR RECODED SIBLINGS (`sibs.15`) BY PARENTAL STATUS (`childsrec`)

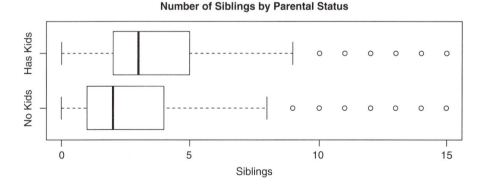

Number of Siblings by Parental Status

Once the sibling variable has been recoded, we can conduct the one-tailed indepen-dent samples *t*-test. Again, the research hypothesis states that, on average, individuals without children will have significantly fewer children than individuals with children.

```
t.test(sibs.15 ~ GSS2016$childsrec,
        alternative = "less")  # Run a one-tailed t-test with a revised
confidence interval.
```

Output: Independent samples *t*-test for recoded siblings (sibs.15) and parental status (childsrec).

```
Welch Two Sample t-test
data: sibs.15 by childsrec
t = -8.4916, df = 1692, p-value < 2.2e-16
alternative hypothesis: true difference in means is less than 0
95 percent confidence interval:
    -Inf -0.779827
sample estimates:
        mean in group No Kids    mean in group Has Kids
            2.974906                    3.942205
```

The output provides important information about characteristics of the subsamples. On average, individuals *without* children have one fewer sibling (3.0) than individuals with children (3.9). The negative *t*-statistic indicates that the mean for Group 1 is less than that for Group 2 ($\mu 1 < \mu 2$). Since the *p*-value for the test is lower than the alpha cut-off of .05, we reject the null hypothesis. Therefore, we conclude that individuals without children have significantly fewer siblings than individuals with children ($t = -8.5$, $df = 1692$, $p = < .001$).

> **Write-Up:** A one-tailed independent-samples *t*-test examined whether the mean number of siblings (top-coded at 15) differed between individuals who have children and those who do not have children. The directional research hypothesis proposed that individuals without children would have significantly fewer siblings than indi-viduals with children. Accordingly, the null hypothesis was that childfree individuals do not have significantly fewer children than parents. The results of the analysis indicate that, on average, those who do not have children have significantly fewer siblings ($M = 3.0$) than those who have children ($M = 3.9$). Therefore, we reject the null hypothesis ($t = -8.5$, $df = 1692$, $p = < .001$).

In order to provide meaningful conclusions about the relationship examined in a *t*-test, measures of effect size should also be presented in order to highlight the magnitude of the

TABLE 8.4 ● COHEN'S GUIDELINES FOR INTERPRETING EFFECT SIZE D	
Value of Cohen's d	**Suggested Interpretation**
0.2	**Weak** Effect
0.5	**Moderate** Effect
0.8	**Strong** Effect

relationship. The next section details one of the most common effect size measures for a *t*-test, Cohen's *d*.

EFFECT SIZE FOR *t*-TEST: COHEN'S *d*

Cohen's *d*—an effect size measure for the hypothesis tests for the difference between two means—is equal to the number of standard deviations of difference between the two groups being studied. Therefore, interpretation of this coefficient is straightforward. To facilitate interpretation, Table 8.4 presents Cohen's criteria for assessing the magnitude of the relationship based on effect size *d*.

For the following example, we test whether or not there is a significant and meaningful difference in number of siblings (sibs.15) between those who were born in the United States and those who were not (bornrec). The null hypothesis states that the difference in mean number of siblings between both groups is 0 ($\mu1 = \mu2$).

The first part of the code defines value labels for the variable bornrec. Then, the distribution of the variables are assessed.

```
GSS2016$bornrec <- factor(GSS2016$born,
                    levels = c(1,2),
                    labels = c("U.S.", "Non-U.S.")) # Add value
labels for nativity.
```

```
table(GSS2016$bornrec) # Check the frequencies for the
dichotomous variable (bornrec).
```

TABLE 8.5 ● FREQUENCIES FOR NATIVITY (bornrec)	
U.S.	Non-U.S.
2507	355

```
boxplot(sibs.15 ~ GSS2016$bornrec,
        horizontal = TRUE,
        main = "Number of Siblings by Nativity",
        xlab = "Siblings") # Generate grouped boxplots for siblings
(sibs.15) by nativity (bornrec).
```

FIGURE 8.8 ● GROUPED BOXPLOT FOR SIBLINGS (sibs.15) BY NATIVITY (bornrec)

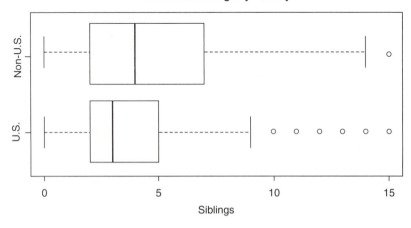

The following code conducts an independent samples *t*-test to assess the difference in mean number of siblings between native-born and foreign-born individuals:

```
t.test(sibs.15 ~ GSS2016$bornrec) # Run an independent samples
t-test.
```

Output: Independent samples *t*-test for recoded number of siblings (sibs.15) by nativity (bornrec).

```
Welch Two Sample t-test

data: sibs.15 by GSS2016$bornrec
t = -6.8171, df = 412.94, p-value = 3.307e-11
alternative hypothesis: true difference in means is not equal to 0
95 percent confidence interval:
 -1.7869116 -0.9870411
```

sample estimates:

mean in group U.S.   mean in group Non–U.S.
3.497204   4.884181

The results presented in the output indicate that we reject the null hypothesis. We conclude that mean number of siblings is significantly different between those who were born in the United States and those who were not (t = -6.8, df = 412.9, p < .001). Now, before writing up the results, we will first assess the magnitude of the relationship with the measure of effect size Cramér's V. In order to do so, the "**lsr**" package is required:

```
install.packages("lsr")  # Install the package "lsr."
require("lsr")  # Attach the package "lsr."
cohensD(sibs.15 ~ GSS2016$bornrec)  # Run the t-test with the
cohensD function.
```

Output: Effect size for recoded number of siblings (`sibs.rec`) by nativity (`bornrec`).

```
cohensD
[1] 0.02518637
```

In this example, Cohen's d, a measure of effect size for t-tests, has a value of .03. Therefore, based on Cohen's suggested cutoff points (Table 8.5), we conclude that the difference in number of siblings between those who were born in the United States and those who were not, despite being statistically significant, is a weak one.

> **Write-Up:** A two-tailed independent-samples t-test examined whether the mean number of siblings was significantly different between individuals who were born in the United States and those who were not. The null hypothesis states that the mean number of siblings did not differ significantly between the two groups. The results of the analysis indicate that there is a statistically significant difference in the number of siblings between individuals born outside the United States and individuals born in the United States. Specifically, foreign-born individuals have about 1.5 more siblings, on average, than those who were born in the United States. Therefore, we reject the null hypothesis (t = -6.8, df = 412.9, p < .001). However, assessment of effect size indicates that this relationship is a weak one (Cramér's V = 0.3).

The independent samples t-test is useful when studying unrelated independent groups. For example, in the last section we explored differences in mean number of siblings between those born within and outside of the United States, two separate groups of individuals in the same sample. However, researchers are also sometimes interested in studying groups that are matched to, or dependent upon, one another in some way (e.g., the same group of people at two different points in time). The statistical test suited to compare means in this instance is the paired t-test.

PAIRED *t*-TEST

The paired *t*-test determines whether the mean difference between two sets of *related* observations is significantly different from 0. The test is known as a paired *t*-test because one set of scores can be matched to the other in some way. As with the independent samples *t*-test, the null hypothesis for a paired *t*-test is that the difference between Group 1 and Group 2 is not significantly different from 0. The alternative hypothesis can be either one-tailed or two-tailed, meaning that a researcher can propose that the difference between the two sets of scores is either significantly greater than or less than 0.

> **Tip:** The paired *t*-test is also common in psychological experiments where measurements are taken before and after some stimulus. In this case, the paired *t*-test assesses the difference between the pretest and posttest. Since the GSS 2016 does not have a repeated measures design, we are unable to assess pretest and posttest differences.

The following example tests whether the difference between the dependent variable, mother's education (maeducrec), and the independent variable, father's education (paeducrec) is significantly different from 0 (a two-tailed test). These two interval/ratio variables are related to one another because the scores can be matched—they represent the highest number of years of education for each parent of a single GSS respondent. The null hypothesis states that the difference between mothers' mean level of education and fathers' mean level of education is 0 ($\mu_1 = \mu_2$).

To run a paired *t*-test in R, simply run a *t*-test (t.test) on the dependent and independent variables (maeducrec and paeducrec). The code includes an additional argument for "paired = TRUE":

> **Tip:** The logic behind the paired *t*-test is that it takes the mean of all of the differences between mothers' mean education and fathers' mean education and uses a one-sample *t*-test to compare that value to 0.

```
GSS2016$maeducrec <- GSS2016$maeduc
GSS2016$maeducrec[GSS2016$maeducrec=="97"]=NA
GSS2016$maeducrec[GSS2016$maeducrec=="98"]=NA
GSS2016$maeducrec[GSS2016$maeducrec=="99"]=NA
GSS2016$paeducrec <- GSS2016$paeduc
GSS2016$paeducrec[GSS2016$paeducrec=="97"]=NA
GSS2016$paeducrec[GSS2016$paeducrec=="98"]=NA
GSS2016$paeducrec[GSS2016$paeducrec=="99"]=NA
t.test(GSS2016$maeducrec, GSS2016$paeducrec, paired = TRUE)
```
Run a paired *t*–test to test the difference between mother's education (maeducrec) and father's education (paeducrec).

Output: Paired *t*-test for mother's education and father's education.

Paired *t*–test

data: GSS2016$maeducrec and GSS2016$paeducrec
t = 1.0744, *df* = 1952, *p*–value = 0.2828
alternative hypothesis: true difference in means is not equal to 0
95 percent confidence interval:
–0.06127814 0.20976764

sample estimates:
    mean of the differences
        0.07424475

In the above example, the difference between mothers' mean education and fathers' mean education is not significantly different from 0. Therefore, we fail to reject the null hypothesis ($t = 1.07$, $df = 1952$, $p = .28$). If we were to reject the null hypothesis, there would be a 28% chance that we would be making a Type I error. Even though the difference is not statistically significant, we will still go through the process of checking the magnitude of the difference with Cramér's *V* using the "**lsr**" package.

The following code (a) attaches the "**lsr**" package and (b) calculates Cohen's *d* for the paired *t*-test for the difference in means between mothers' and fathers' education:

```
require("lsr")  #Attach the package "lsr."
cohensD(x = GSS2016$paeducrec, y = GSS2016$maeducrec, method
= "paired") #Run the t-test with the cohensD function.
```

Output: Effect size for mother's education (maeducrec) and father's education (paeducrec).

---

cohensD
[1] 0.02431193

Cohen's *d* has a value of .02. Based on Cohen's suggested cutoff points (Table 8.5), we conclude that the difference between mothers' mean education and fathers' mean education is both not statistically significant and weak in magnitude.

> **Write-Up:** A two-tailed paired *t*-test examined whether mothers' mean years of education was statistically different from fathers' mean years of education. The null hypothesis stated that the mean difference between mothers' education and fathers' education is 0. The results of the analysis indicate that the mean education for

mothers is not significantly different from mean education for fathers. Therefore, we fail to reject the null hypothesis ($t = 1.1$, $df = 1952$, $p = .28$). Moreover, the effect size measure Cohen's d also indicates that the relationship between mothers' and fathers' years of education is a weak one (Cramér's $V = .02$).

CONCLUSION

This chapter discussed three different ways that researchers compare one or two means—either with some other value or another mean. First, the one-sample t-test compares a mean to some predetermined constant value based on theory, logic, or existing research. Second, the independent samples t-test compares mean scores between two independent groups of individuals in the same sample (e.g., men and women). Third, the paired t-test compares mean scores between two sets of related scores. Cohen's d, a measure of effect size, was also discussed as a way to measure the magnitude of the difference between groups.

In addition to testing differences with only one or two means, researchers are often interested in assessing mean differences across more than two groups. For example, a study might explore differences in the amount of time using the Internet among different sexual orientation groups (i.e., gay/lesbian, bisexual, and heterosexual). For this, the appropriate test is the Analysis of Variance, the focus of the next chapter.

References

Smith, T. W., Davern, M., Freese, J., & Morgan, S. L. (2019). *General Social Surveys, 1972–2018* [Machine-Readable Data File]. Chicago, IL: NORC at the University of Chicago. Retrieved from http://www.gss.norc.org/getthedata/Pages/Home.aspx

Exercises

1. Based on the variable `racerec`, generate a new variable, `racerec2`. Recode the new variable so that the "Other" category is marked as missing. The result should be a dichotomous variable with "White" and "Black" only. Then, based on the variable age, create a new variable, `agerec`, with missing (DK/NA) responses removed.

   A. Produce grouped boxplots for `agerec` across the categories of `racerec2`.

   B. Generate an independent samples t-test using `agerec` and `racerec2`.

   C. Identify the independent and dependent variables.

    D. Is this a one-tailed or two-tailed test?

    E. Interpret and report the results in the same format that was used in this chapter.

2. Create a new variable, `wwwhrrec`, that does not include missing responses (DK and NA). The information on DK/NA can be found in the GSS codebook.

    A. Identify the independent and dependent variables.

    B. Is this a one-tailed or two-tailed test?

    C. Choose and report the most appropriate effect size.

    D. Interpret and report the results.

3. List two similarities and two differences between an independent samples t-test and a paired samples test.

4. Describe a hypothetical research scenario where a paired samples t-test might be applied.

Supplementary Digital Content

Download datasets and R code at the companion website at https://study.sagepub.com/researchmethods/statistics/gillespie-r-for-statistics

COMPARING MEANS ACROSS THREE OR MORE GROUPS (ANOVA)

ANALYSIS OF VARIANCE (ANOVA)

Like the independent samples t-test, the analysis of variance, referred to as ANOVA, tests for differences in mean scores across independent groups. Unlike t-tests, however, ANOVA is suited for testing differences across *more than two groups*. Accordingly, the independent variable is a categorical variable with more than two categories and the dependent variable is an interval/ratio variable. For example, an ANOVA would be an appropriate test for whether the average number of hours spent on the Internet per week (interval/ratio dependent variable) differs across sexual orientation groups (nominal independent variable with more than two categories).

> **Tip:** Analysis of variance can also be conducted using a dichotomous independent variable but the process is more complicated than the t-test (which produces the same outcome).

ANOVA Assumptions and Notation

As with the t-test, ANOVA has a number of assumptions regarding distribution and variance. Three important assumptions are that (a) the data are normally distributed for each group, (b) the variations are the same across groups, and (c) there are no extreme outliers in any of the groups. One way to check for outliers within groups is to explore grouped boxplots (see Chapter 5). In the case of the first two assumptions, ANOVA can still produce accurate results if the assumptions are not violated too seriously.

ANOVA Hypotheses

The null hypothesis (H_0) in an ANOVA is there is no significant difference among any of the groups' means ($\mu_1 = \mu_2 = \mu_3 = \ldots \mu_g$). This notation simply states that all populations have the same mean; the letter *g* represents the total number of groups (i.e., the number of categories in the independent variable). The alternative hypothesis (H_a) is that at least two of the groups are significantly different. Although the groups are likely to differ to some extent, ANOVA tests whether those differences are either (a) so small that they could be attributed to chance or (b) large enough to be statistically significant. The ANOVA test does not make any statement about where the differences lie (i.e., between which groups). Additional tests are needed in order to make more specific determinations. Additionally, since we are drawing comparisons across multiple groups, ANOVA does not accommodate directional hypotheses.

A Brief Note on the F-Statistic and Degrees of Freedom

In ANOVA, differences in means are tested through the *analysis of their variance*. In doing so, we find out how much variance on the dependent variable is due to differences *within* groups versus between—or across—the groups. Therefore, in order to obtain the test statistic (the F-statistic), it is necessary to compare the *variation within* and *variation between* each of the groups.

The F-statistic represents *the ratio of the variation between groups and within groups*. A large value of F indicates that the variation between groups is larger than the variation within groups. Since the F-statistic is a ratio, the closer the obtained value is to 1, the smaller the between-group differences. Therefore, the larger the F-statistic, the greater the difference *between* groups—and the more likely we are to reject the null hypothesis.

In order to locate the appropriate critical value in the F-table, two values for degrees of freedom are needed. The between-group degrees of freedom are calculated by the number of groups (g) – 1. The within-group degrees of freedom are calculated by the full sample N – g (the number of groups).

As with other tests of statistical significance, the value of the F-statistic (obtained from the data) is compared to the value of F-critical (obtained in the table) in order to make a statement about the null hypothesis. If the F-statistic is higher than the F-critical, then the test statistic falls within the region of rejection and we reject the null hypothesis. In that case, we conclude that the group means are not equal—at least two of them differ significantly. On the other hand, if the value of the F-statistic is lower than the F-critical value, the test statistic lands in the non-rejection region and we fail to reject the null hypothesis.

The following examples assess differences in means across categories of a nominal variable and then use an analysis of variance to test the differences among them.

ANOVA IN R

To assess the means for a continuous variable across groups of a nominal variable, use the **aggregate** and **function** commands. In the following example, we look at the number of hours spent using the Internet (`wwwhrrec`) across the three categories of age created in Chapter 3 (i.e., young adult, midlife adult, and older adult). The null hypothesis for the following example is that there is no significant difference among any of the age groups' mean hours of Internet use ($\mu_1 = \mu_2 = \mu_3$). The research hypothesis is that at least two of the age groups are significantly different from each other.

> **Tip:** Although the age group variable is ordinal, the ANOVA test does not assess for direction. Therefore, we do not know whether, for example, higher age is associated with fewer hours of Internet use.

First, read the data into RStudio by typing the code below into the scripting window. This will read the .csv data file into RStudio, where it will then be listed in the workspace environment.

```
GSS2016 <- read.csv("C:/Users/Desktop/R/GSS2016.csv", header =
TRUE) #Read the .csv-formatted data into RStudio.
```

The following code collapses the variable age into three categories. If this has already been done based on the work in earlier chapters, it does not need to be redone.

```
GSS2016$agerec <- GSS2016$age
GSS2016$agerec[GSS2016$agerec=="99"]=NA

agegroup<-cut(GSS2016$agerec, c(0,35,59,90), labels = c("Young
Adult", "Adult", "Older Adult")) # Collapse the variable age into
three categories with labels for each.

table(agegroup)  #Check the recoding of the variable agegroup.
```

Based on the analyses in the last chapter, we know that the variable wwwhr is positively skewed so the following analyses use the recoded variable from Chapter 8 (wwwhrrec), which was top-coded so that the highest value represents "30 or more hours per week spent using the Internet." The code below should be run to top-code the variable; however, this does not need to be done again if the recoded variable already exists as a workspace object:

First, recode the missing variables to NA:

```
GSS2016$wwwhrrec <- GSS2016$wwwhr
GSS2016$wwwhrrec[GSS2016$wwwhrrec=="-1"]=NA
GSS2016$wwwhrrec[GSS2016$wwwhrrec=="998"]=NA
GSS2016$wwwhrrec[GSS2016$wwwhrrec=="999"]=NA

wwwhr.30 <- GSS2016$wwwhrrec #Create an independent object to
recode wwwhr (wwwhr.30).

wwwhr.30[wwwhr.30 > 30] <- 30 #Recode the wwwhr variable so that
values greater than "30" are recoded to "30."
```

TABLE 9.1 ● RAW FREQUENCIES FOR AGE GROUP (AGEGROUP)

Young Adult	Adult	Older Adult
793	1205	859

To get a sense of how the variable `wwwhr.30` varies across the age groups, we can assess the mean values of Internet use for each of the three groups using the aggregate function:

aggregate(wwwhr.30 ~ agegroup, FUN = mean) **#Produce a means table. Aggregate by age group and show the mean number of hours spent on the Internet per week.**

Output: Mean weekly Internet use (`wwwhr.30`) across age groups (`agegroup`).

```
      agegroup wwwhr.30
1  young adult 14.146154
2        adult 10.287834
3  older adult 6.899485
```

The grouped means indicate that there might be substantial differences in weekly Internet use across each age group. However, extreme outliers on the dependent variable would exert influence on the mean score of any group. Therefore, a more efficient and informative way to assess differences across age groups is to explore grouped boxplots for weekly Internet use (`wwwhr.30`) across the different age groups (`agegroup`):

boxplot(wwwhr.30 ~ agegroup,
        horizontal = TRUE,
        main = "Boxplots for Internet Use by Age Group",
        xlab = "Hours/Week Spent on Internet") **#Generate grouped boxplots for Internet use by age groups.**

Although the top-coding of `wwwhr.30` helped taper the highly positive skew of the data, the grouped boxplots still point to several outliers (i.e., older adults who report using the

FIGURE 9.1 ● GROUPED BOXPLOT OF INTERNET USE ACROSS AGE GROUPS

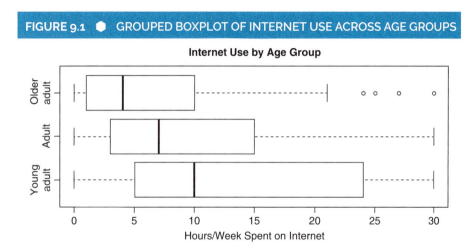

Internet relatively frequently). Here, it is up to the researcher to make additional decisions for proceeding with the analysis, removing the additional outliers, top-coding the variable at a lower value, or transforming the variable in some other way.

The **aov** command is used to test our hypothesis using one-way ANOVA. The dependent variable (wwwhr.30) is listed first, grouped by (~) the nominal independent variable (agegroup). ANOVA results should always be saved as separate objects in the workspace. The following code runs the analysis and saves the results as a workspace object:

```
age.int.aov <- aov(wwwhr.30 ~ agegroup) #Create an independent
object with information regarding an analysis of variance for Internet use
across different age groups.
```

Type the name of the object in the scripting window to produce information about the analysis, including the degrees of freedom.

```
age.int.aov #Produce the results of the ANOVA in the output
window.
```

Output: ANOVA details for Internet use (wwwhr.30) across age groups.

```
aov(formula = wwwhr.30 ~ agegroup)
Terms:
                        agegroup Residuals
Sum of Squares          11893.26 137658.13
Deg. of Freedom                2      1579

Residual standard error: 9.337054
Estimated effects may be unbalanced
1285 observations deleted due to missingness
```

To produce the results of the hypothesis test, use the summary function along with the name of the object:

```
summary(age.int.aov) #Summarize the results of the ANOVA
hypothesis test.
```

Output: ANOVA results for Internet use (wwwhr.rec) across age groups.

```
             Df Sum Sq Mean Sq F value Pr(>F)
agegroup      2  11893    5947   68.21 <2e-16 ***
Residuals  1579 137658      87
---
Signif. codes: 0 '***' 0.001 '**' 0.01 '*' 0.05 '.' 0.1 ' ' 1
1285 observations deleted due to missingness
```

The results of the ANOVA indicate that at least two of the age groups differ significantly in their weekly Internet use ($F = 68.2$; df between = 2, df within = 1579; $p < .001$). However, as mentioned above, ANOVA does not indicate *which* pairs of groups are significantly different—it could be all pairs of groups or it could be a single pair. Therefore, in the event that you reject the null hypothesis, there are several additional procedures, called post-hoc tests, which can help tease out the effects of individual pairs.

Post-Hoc Tests

When the results of the "omnibus" ANOVA test are statistically significant, post-hoc tests are used to assess which pairs of groups are significantly different from each other. One intuitive approach is to conduct multiple independent sample t-tests to examine differences between two groups at a time. While this might be useful to get a rough estimate of paired differences, there are at least two reasons this is a problematic approach. First, a series of paired t-tests is computationally inefficient (e.g., an independent variable with only four categories would require six individual t-tests). Second, and more importantly, when conducting multiple tests, each test increases the likelihood of making a Type I error. A number of post-hoc tests, which vary in their degree of flexibility and conservativeness, are designed to make pairwise comparisons that account for this issue. We do not discuss or compare the different post-hoc tests here; rather, we use one of the most common tests, Tukey's HSD (honestly significant difference) test, to assess for all pairwise differences when the results of an ANOVA are statistically significant.

In order to perform this post-hoc test, use the command **TukeyHSD** along with the name of the object that was created for the ANOVA:

```
TukeyHSD(age.int.aov)  #Run a series of pairwise tests to assess
significant differences between the age groups based on the omnibus
ANOVA test.
```

Output: Tukey's HSD for Internet use and age group.

```
    Tukey multiple comparisons of means
      95% family-wise confidence level

Fit: aov(formula = wwwhr.30 ~ agegroup)

$agegroup
                             diff       lwr       upr p adj
adult-young adult        -3.858320 -5.136797 -2.579843 0.0
older adult-young adult  -7.246669 -8.716096 -5.777243 0.0
older adult-adult        -3.388349 -4.784200 -1.992499 0.0
```

These results show the pairwise differences between each of the age groups. Based on the p-values in the last column, each of the groups differ significantly from the other ($p < .000$).

Tip: When interpreting and writing up the results of an ANOVA, keep in mind that the results are correlational. As such, it is important to avoid making claims about causal relationships. Additionally, when discussing your results, be sure to include information about the hypothesis, the value of the F-statistic, between and within-group degrees of freedom, and the p-value.

Write-Up: A one-way analysis of variance was performed to examine whether the mean number of hours of Internet use each week differed across three different age groups (young adults, adults, and older adults). The null hypothesis stated that the mean number of hours was the same across each group. The results of the analysis indicate that weekly Internet hours was significantly different between at least two of the groups. Therefore, we reject the null hypothesis ($F = 68.2$; df between = 2, df within = 1579; $p < .001$). Additional post-hoc tests (Tukey's HSD) indicated that all pairwise differences were significant ($p < .000$).

Additional ANOVA Examples

Example 1: Sexual Orientation and Ideal Number of Children

This example uses one-way ANOVA to examine whether there are differences in respondents' ideal number of children across sexual orientation groups (gay/lesbian, bisexual, and heterosexual). The dependent variable for the analysis is the ideal number of children respondents' report wanting to have. The null hypothesis states that the mean ideal number of children is the same across each of the sexual orientation groups. The alternative hypothesis is that the mean ideal number of children significantly differs between at least two of the sexual orientation categories.

```
GSS2016$sexorntrec <- factor(GSS2016$sexornt,
                      levels = c(1,2,3),
                      labels = c("Gay/Lesbian", "Bisexual",
                      "Heterosexual"))  #Add value labels for
                      sexorntrec.
table(GSS2016$sexorntrec)

GSS2016$chldidelrec <- GSS2016$chldidel
GSS2016$chldidelrec[GSS2016$chldidelrec =="-1"]=NA
GSS2016$chldidelrec[GSS2016$chldidelrec =="8"]=NA
GSS2016$chldidelrec[GSS2016$chldidelrec =="9"]=NA
```

TABLE 9.2 ● FREQUENCIES FOR SEXUAL ORIENTATION (sexorntrec)		
Gay/Lesbian	Bisexual	Heterosexual
46	56	1641

We first assess mean differences in the ideal number of children reported across each sexual orientation group using the aggregate function. The table of grouped means is saved as an independent object in the workspace (so.ideal):

```
so.ideal <- aggregate(GSS2016$chldidelrec ~ GSS2016$sexorntrec,
FUN = mean) # Check the means across each sexual orientation
group.

so.ideal
```

TABLE 9.3 ●	MEAN DIFFERENCES FOR NUMBER OF IDEAL CHILDREN BY SEXUAL ORIENTATION	
	sexorntrec	GSS2016$chldidelrec
1	Gay/Lesbian	2.333333
2	Bisexual	2.473684
3	Heterosexual	2.568182

These results can also be presented in the form of grouped mean bar charts, which were discussed and presented in Chapter 5. The following code generates grouped mean bar charts to illustrate mean differences in the ideal number of children by sexual orientation:

```
mean.so.ideal <- t(so.ideal [-1]) #Create a new object and
transpose the information in the table of grouped means created
above.

colnames(mean.so.ideal) <- so.ideal [ , 1] #Replace marital
status labels in the transposed table.

barplot(mean.so.ideal,
        col = "lightsteelblue",
        main = "Ideal Number of Children\n by Sexual Orientation",
        xlab = "Sexual Orientation",
        ylab = "Mean Ideal Number of Children") #Use the
        barplot command to create a bar chart for each of the means
        with any additional configurations.
```

At first glance, there do not appear to be substantial differences in the mean ideal number of children across sexual orientation groups. However, as noted in Chapter 5, grouped means bar charts might mask outliers that are present in any or all groups. Therefore, we should also check grouped boxplots to assess other characteristics of the distribution, including potential outliers:

```
boxplot(GSS2016$chldidelrec ~ GSS2016$sexorntrec,
        horizontal = TRUE,
        main = "Ideal Number of Children by Sexual Orientation",
        xlab = "Self-Reported Ideal Number of Children to
        Have")
```
#Generate grouped boxplots for ideal number of children by sexual orientation.

FIGURE 9.2 ● GROUPED MEAN BAR CHART FOR SEXUAL ORIENTATION (`sexorntrec`) AND IDEAL NUMBER OF CHILDREN (`chldidelrec`)

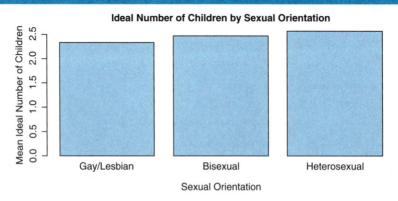

FIGURE 9.3 ● GROUPED BOXPLOTS FOR NUMBER OF IDEAL CHILDREN BY SEXUAL ORIENTATION

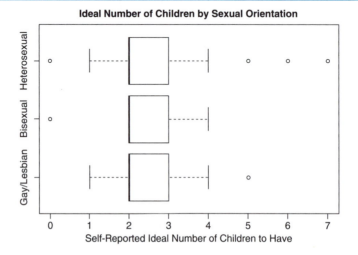

The following analysis of variance tests the alternative hypothesis that there is a significant difference in mean ideal number of children between at least two sexual orientation categories.

Tip: Remember to save the ANOVA as a separate object in the workspace.

```
so.ideal.aov <- aov(GSS2016$chldidelrec ~ GSS2016$sexorntrec)
```
Create an independent object with an ANOVA for ideal number of children across sexual orientation groups.

```
so.ideal.aov
```
Produce information about the ANOVA.

```
summary(so.ideal.aov)
```
Produce the results of the hypothesis test.

Output: ANOVA for ideal number of children by sexual orientation.

Call:
aov(formula = GSS2016$chldidelrec ~ GSS2016$sexorntrec)

Terms:
	sexornt.nomiss	Residuals
Sum of Squares	1.4194	644.7974
Deg. of Freedom	2	744

Residual standard error: 0.9309475
Estimated effects may be unbalanced
2120 observations deleted due to missingness

	Df	Sum Sq	Mean Sq	F value	Pr(>F)
sexornt.nomiss	2	1.4	0.7097	0.819	0.441
Residuals	744	644.8	0.8667		

2120 observations deleted due to missingness

The F-statistic, 0.82, is not significant at the .05 level. Therefore, we fail to reject the null hypothesis and conclude that there are no significant differences in the ideal number of children across sexual orientation groups. Given that there are no significant differences between any of the groups, a post-hoc analysis of pairwise differences is unwarranted.

Write-Up: A one-way analysis of variance was performed to examine whether the mean ideal number of children differed across sexual orientation groups (gay/lesbian, bisexual, heterosexual). The null hypothesis stated that the mean ideal number of children was the same across each sexual orientation group. The results of the analysis indicate that there were no significant differences across sexual orientation groups in the ideal number of children they would like to have. Therefore, we fail to reject the null hypothesis ($F = 0.8$; df between = 2, df within = 744; $p = .44$).

Example 2: Age Group and Number of Hours Watching Television

The next example examines differences in the mean number of hours spent watching television each day (tvhoursrec) across three different age groups (agegroup). The null hypothesis states that the mean number of hours spent watching television is the same across all three groups. The alternative hypothesis is that the mean number of hours spent watching television differs between at least two age groups.

The following code provides a table of means for TV hours across each age category (results shown in Table 9.4) as well as grouped boxplots to assess the distribution across each group (Figure 9.4):

```
GSS2016$tvhoursrec <- GSS2016$tvhours
GSS2016$tvhoursrec[GSS2016$tvhoursrec=="-1"]=NA
GSS2016$tvhoursrec[GSS2016$tvhoursrec=="98"]=NA
GSS2016$tvhoursrec[GSS2016$tvhoursrec=="99"]=NA


aggregate(GSS2016$tvhoursrec ~ agegroup, FUN = mean) #Assess
the mean number of hours of television by age group.
```

TABLE 9.4 ● GROUP MEANS FOR WEEKLY HOURS WATCHING TV (tvhoursrec) BY AGE GROUP (agegroup)

agegroup	GSS2016$tvhours.15
1 young adult	2.302583
2 adult	2.781291
3 older adult	4.053726

FIGURE 9.4 ● GROUPED BOXPLOTS FOR DAILY TV HOURS (tvhoursrec) BY AGE GROUP (agegroup)

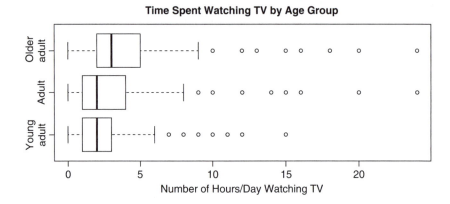

Time Spent Watching TV by Age Group

```
boxplot(GSS2016$tvhoursrec ~ agegroup,
        horizontal = TRUE,
        main = "Time Spent Watching TV by Age Group",
        xlab = "Number of Hours/Day Watching TV") # Check
```
grouped boxplots for tvhoursrec by agegroup.

Given the number of outliers—and the implausibility of watching TV, on average, for more than 15 hours per day—we will top-code the variable `tvhours` at 15. The code below generates this new variable, `tvhours.15`:

```
tvhours.15 <- GSS2016$tvhoursrec # Create an independent object
```
to recode tvhours.
```
tvhours.15[tvhours.15 > 15] <- 15 # Recode the variable so
```
that values greater than 15 are recoded to 15.

We can now assess whether the top-coding attenuated the non-normality of the `tvhours` variable with a new set of grouped boxplots:

```
boxplot(tvhours.15 ~ agegroup,
        horizontal = TRUE,
        main = "Time Spent Watching TV (Recoded) \n by Age Group",
        xlab = "Number of Hours/Day Watching TV") # Check
```
grouped boxplots for tvhours.15 by agegroup.

Now, an ANOVA tests the alternative hypothesis that the mean number of TV hours differs between at least two age groups:

FIGURE 9.5 ● GROUPED BOXPLOTS FOR DAILY TV HOURS (`tvhours.15`) BY AGE GROUP (`agegroup`)

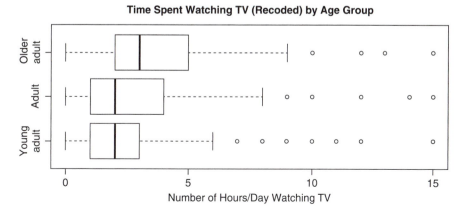

Time Spent Watching TV (Recoded) by Age Group

```
age.tv.aov <- aov(tvhours.15 ~ agegroup)  # Create an ANOVA
```
object with information regarding an analysis of variance for
number of hours of television watched across each of the different
age groups.

```
age.tv.aov
```

Output: ANOVA Information: `tvhours.15` by `agegroup`.

```
aov(formula = tvhours.15 ~ agegroup)
Terms:
                        agegroup Residuals
Sum of Squares        861.048  11657.888
Deg. of Freedom           2         1875


Residual standard error: 2.4935
Estimated effects may be unbalanced
989 observations deleted due to missingness
```

```
summary(age.tv.aov)  #Produce all of the information for the analysis of
```
variance to test for difference in the mean number of hours of television
watched across different age groups.

Output: ANOVA Information: `tvhours.15` by `agegroup`.

```
                Df Sum Sq Mean Sq  F value  Pr(>F)
agegroup         2    861   430.5   69.24   <2e-16 ***
Residuals     1875  11658     6.2
---
Signif. codes: 0 '***' 0.001 '**' 0.01 '*' 0.05 '.' 0.1 ' ' 1
989 observations deleted due to missingness
```

The F-statistic is 69.2 and the *p*-value is less than .001; therefore, we reject the null hypothesis. We conclude that at least two of the age groups differ significantly in their number of hours of television watched ($F = 69.2$; *df* between = 2, *df* within = 1875; $p < .001$). However, based on these results alone, we are not able to ascertain which groups are significantly different. Post-hoc analyses are necessary in order to make this determination. Again, we use Tukey's HSD post-hoc analysis to assess pairwise relationships based on the results of the ANOVA:

```
TukeyHSD(age.tv.aov)  # Run a series of pairwise tests to assess
```
significant differences between the age groups based on the omnibus
ANOVA results.

Output: Post-hoc analysis for TV hours and age group.

```
Tukey multiple comparisons of means
95% family–wise confidence level

Fit: aov(formula = tvhours.15 ~ agegroup)

$agegroup
                          diff       lwr        upr       p adj
adult–young adult        0.44050  0.1115914  0.7694086  0.0048594
older adult–young adult  1.67142  1.3215682  2.0212726  0.0000000
older adult–adult        1.23092  0.9078840  1.5539569  0.0000000
```

The results of the post-hoc analysis indicate that there are significant differences between each pair of age groups. The difference between adults and young adults is significant at the .01 level of alpha and the difference between older adults and young adults as well as older adults and adults is significant at the .001 level. These results indicate that, on average, older adults watch more television per day (4.1 hours) than adults (2.8 hours) and young adults (2.3 hours). Adults also watch significantly more television per day than young adults.

> **Write-Up**: A one-way analysis of variance was performed to examine whether mean hours of television per day differed across three age groups (young adult, adult, and older adult). The null hypothesis stated that the mean number of TV hours was the same across each age group. The results of the analysis indicate that at least two age groups significantly differed in the number of hours spent watching television each day. Therefore, we reject the null hypothesis ($F = 69.2$; df between = 2, df within = 1875; $p < .001$). Additional post-hoc tests (Tukey's HSD) indicated that all pairwise differences were significant at the .01 level.

There is still a bit more information about the omnibus ANOVA test that we can use to assess the relationship between the independent and dependent variable. As mentioned in previous chapters, effect size measures assess the magnitude of the relationship. Eta-squared (η^2) is the effect size coefficient commonly measured to determine the strength of mean differences across multiple groups.

Effect Size for One-Way ANOVA: η^2

A statistically significant relationship indicates that the relationship established is not likely due to chance. However, as discussed in previous chapters, researchers also rely on measures of effect size to determine the magnitude of the established relationship, or whether the relationship is meaningful in practical terms. The most common measure of effect size for a one-way analysis of variance is eta-squared (η^2).

The eta-squared coefficient has an intuitive interpretation—it is an indication of the amount of variation in the dependent variable that can be explained—or accounted for—by the

TABLE 9.5 ● COHEN'S GUIDELINES FOR INTERPRETING η^2	
Value of η^2	Suggested Interpretation
0.01	**Small** Effect
0.06	**Medium** Effect
0.14	**Large** Effect

independent variable. In other words, this effect size measure tells us how much the difference between each of the group means affects the overall grand mean. Cohen's guidelines for interpretation of this effect size are presented in Table 9.5.

In the previous example, we used one-way ANOVA to test whether or not the mean number of hours spent watching television was different across three age groups (young adult, midlife adult, and older adult). The null hypothesis was that the mean number of TV hours was the same for all three groups. The results led us to reject the null hypothesis. We concluded that at least two of the age groups differed significantly in their mean number of hours of television ($F = 69.2$; df between $= 2$, df within $= 1875$; $p < .001$). Again, this finding tells us that we can be confident that at least two of the means significantly differ and that there is a low likelihood that the differences are due to chance. However, an important piece of the puzzle remains—how meaningful is the relationship in practical terms?

This analysis uses the package **lsr** to calculate the eta-squared measure of effect size. In this case, the resulting coefficient tells us how much variation in TV watching can be accounted for by age. First, install and attach the **lsr** package:

```
install.packages("lsr")  # Install the package lsr.
require("lsr")  # Attach the package lsr.
```

Run the command **etaSquared** with the ANOVA object to obtain the effect size measure:

```
etaSquared(age.tv.aov)  # Calculate eta-squared based on the ANOVA
object.
```

The value of η^2 is .07. Based on the interpretation guidelines in Table 9.6, in addition to being statistically significant, the relationship between hours watching television and age group is a moderate one in magnitude. Seven percent of the variation in hours spent watching television each day can be explained by differences across age groups.

TABLE 9.6 ● EFFECT SIZE FOR TV WATCHING (tvhours.15) BY AGE GROUP (agegroup)		
	eta.sq	eta.sq.part
agegroup	0.06877965	0.06877965

TWO-WAY ANALYSIS OF VARIANCE

A one-way ANOVA is used when researchers are interested in examining a single independent variable (factor). However, researchers are often interested in further parsing out the effects across another level, which means a second factor is included in the analysis. A two-way, or factorial, ANOVA is a common procedure when working with two nominal independent variables and an interval/ratio dependent variable. This procedure has a more complex statistical design because it adds another independent variable to the statistical model.

Because there are two independent variables, a two-way ANOVA assesses how each variable independently affects the dependent variable (main effects) but also their interaction effect—how the effect of one factor differs across the categories of the other factor.

In the following example, we test whether there are significant differences in Internet use for gender and parental status. The interaction looks at the effect of being a man or a woman for those who have children and those who do not have children. Table 9.7 shows how the variable gender "interacts" with parental status. In the "Gender" column of this table, (0) represents a male and (1) represents female. Under "Parental Status", (0) represents individuals who do not have children and (1) represents individuals with children. The classification details how the two variables "interact."

A two-way ANOVA has the same assumptions as a one-way ANOVA—that there is a normal distribution and equal variances across each group. In a two-way ANOVA, there are two factors: Factor 1 and Factor 2, which are both nominal variables. The null hypothesis states that (a) there are no significant differences in the DV across the groups in Factor 1, (b) there are no significant differences in the DV across the groups in Factor 2, and (c) there are no significant differences in the DV at the intersection of Factors 1 and 2—the interaction term. The research hypothesis, on the other hand, states that the means are not the same across the groups in Factor 1, Factor 2, or the interaction between Factors 1 and 2.

When the interaction term is statistically significant, the main effects need not be interpreted—this means that the main effects do not operate independently—their effect depends on the other factor. On the other hand, when the interaction term is not significant, the main effects can be interpreted for their independent effect on the dependent variable.

TABLE 9.7 ● INTERACTION BETWEEN GENDER AND PARENTAL STATUS

Gender	Parental Status	Classification
0	0	Male with no children
0	1	Male with children
1	0	Female with no children
1	1	Female with children

The R command for this procedure is similar to the command for a one-way ANOVA, except it includes an interaction term between the two nominal variables. The interaction term assesses the impact of the intersection of the two groups on the dependent variable.

First, we assess the distributions of the dependent variable (wwwhr.30) across categories of each independent variable with grouped boxplots. The boxplots below show (a) the independent effect of gender on Internet use, (b) the independent effect of parental status on Internet use, and (c) the effect of the interaction between gender and parental status on Internet use:

```
GSS2016$sexrec <- factor(GSS2016$sex,
                  levels = c(1,2),
                  labels = c("Male", "Female")) # Generate value
                  labels for gender.
wwwhr.30 <- GSS2016$wwwhrrec # Create an independent object to
recode wwwhr (wwwhr.30).

wwwhr.30[wwwhr.30 > 30] <- 30 # Recode the wwwhr variable so that
values greater than "30" are recoded to "30".

boxplot (wwwhr.30 ~ GSS2016$sexrec, horizontal = TRUE,
         main = "Internet Use by Sex (Main Effects)",
         xlab = "Weekly Number of Hours on the Internet")
         #Generate a boxplot for the independent effect of gender on
         Internet use.
```

FIGURE 9.6 ● INTERNET USE (wwwhr.30) BY GENDER (sexrec)

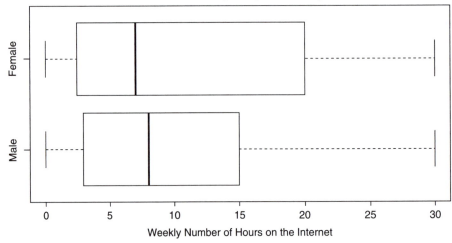

Internet Use by Sex (Main Effects)

Weekly Number of Hours on the Internet

```
GSS2016$childsrec <- GSS2016$childs
GSS2016$childsrec[GSS2016$childsrec=="9"]=NA
```

```
GSS2016$childsrec[GSS2016$childsrec > 0] <- 1
```
Recode the childsrec variable so that values greater than "0" are recoded to "1". Thus, parental status is "child free" (0) and "has any children" (1).

```
childsrec <- factor(GSS2016$childsrec,
            levels = c(0,1),
            labels = c("No Kids", "Has Kids"))
```
Define value labels for childsrec.

```
boxplot (wwwhr.30 ~ childsrec, horizontal = TRUE,
        main = "Internet Use by Parental Status (Main
        Effects)",
        xlab = "Number of Hours on the Internet Weekly")
```
Generate a boxplot for the independent effect of parental status on Internet use.

```
boxplot (wwwhr.30 ~ GSS2016$sexrec:childsrec, horizontal = TRUE,
        main = "Internet Use by Sex & Parental Status
        (Interaction)",
        xlab = "Number of Hours on the Internet Weekly")
```
Generate a boxplot for interaction effects on Internet use between gender and parental status.

FIGURE 9.7 ● INTERNET USE (`wwwhr.30`) BY PARENTAL STATUS (`childsrec`)

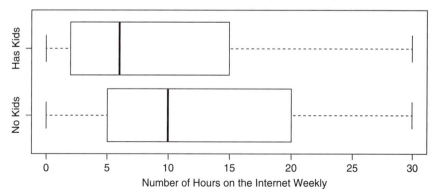

Internet Use by Parental Status (Main Effects)

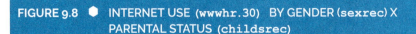

FIGURE 9.8 ● INTERNET USE (`wwwhr.30`) BY GENDER (`sexrec`) X PARENTAL STATUS (`childsrec`)

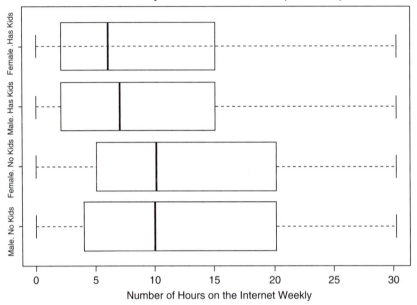

The following code and output assess whether there are differences in the number of hours spent on the Internet per week (`wwwhr.30`) based on gender (`sexrec`) and parental status (`childsrec`). Use a colon to separate the variables, which asks for an interaction term between the two variables:

```
genpar.int.aov <- aov(wwwhr.30 ~ GSS2016$sexrec + childsrec +
GSS2016$sexrec:childsrec) # Run a two-way analysis of variance using
parental status and gender (IV) and number of hours per week spent on
the Internet (DV).
```

The results of the hypothesis test can be produced with the summary function:

```
summary(genpar.int.aov) # Call the results of the two-way ANOVA
from the ANOVA object to the output window.
```

Output: Two-way analysis of variance for `wwwhr` across parental status and gender.

	Df	Sum Sq	Mean Sq	F value	Pr(>F)	
GSS2016$sexrec	1	2	2	0.024	0.8779	
childsrec	1	3215	3215	34.817	4.42e-09	***
GSS2016$sexrec:childsrec	1	510	510	5.526	0.0189	*
Residuals	1580	145905	92			

Signif. codes: 0 '***' 0.001 '**' 0.01 '*' 0.05 '.' 0.1 ' ' 1						
1283 observations deleted due to missingness						

The results of the analysis indicate that we reject the null hypothesis. The significant inter-action term indicates that the impact of gender on Internet use varies based on whether or not the male or female is a parent.

Write-Up: A two-way analysis of variance was performed to examine whether mean hours of Internet use differed across gender and parental status. The null hypotheses stated that there would be no significant difference in Internet use by (a) gender, (b) parental status, or (c) the interaction between gender and parental status. The results of the analysis indicate that there are significant gender differences in Internet use when the effects are considered by parental status. Therefore, we reject the null hypothesis ($F = 5.5$; df between $= 1$, df within $= 1580$; $p < .05$).

CONCLUSION

The concepts and techniques presented in this chapter built on the previous chapter on t-tests by exploring the statistical procedure commonly used to study mean differences across more than two groups—analysis of variance. ANOVA tests for overall differences across categories of a categorical variable. To further explore these relationships, post-hoc tests assess pairwise differences. The magnitude of the relationship is assessed with eta-squared. We also conducted a two-way analysis of variance, which includes an additional factor into the ANOVA model.

Exercises

1. Describe at least one way that a one-way analysis of variance (ANOVA) is different from an independent samples t-test.

2. Create a new variable named `chldidelrec` with missing responses (DK and NA) recoded to missing. Note: In the codebook, you will notice that one possible response is "as many as I want"; however, this is not a valid numerical response and we therefore recommend coding this as missing

along with the DK and NA responses. Also, generate a new variable, `racerec`, with three categories (White, Black, and Other):

   A.   Generate a bar chart for grouped means using `chldidelrec` and `racerec`.

   B.   Perform a one-way analysis of variance to examine potential differences in the ideal number of children across each of the three race classifications.

   C.   Propose the null and alternative hypotheses.

   D.   Identify the independent and dependent variables.

   E.   Interpret and present based on the write-up format presented in the chapter.

3.   Create a new variable named `sexorntrec` based on the variable `sexornt`. Generate a new variable named `wwwhrrec` from the `wwwhr` variable. For each new variable, remove non-responses (DK and NA).

   A.   Generate grouped boxplots for `wwwhrrec` across `sexorntrec` categories.

   B.   Perform a one-way analysis of variance to examine if there is a difference in the number of hours spent on the Internet across sexual orientation categories.

   C.   Propose the null and alternative hypotheses.

   D.   Identify the independent and dependent variables.

   E.   Choose and report the most appropriate effect size.

   F.   Interpret and write up the results based on how it is presented in the chapter.

4.   Name one primary difference between a one-way and a two-way analysis of variance.

5.   Recode marital into a dichotomous variable named `marstatrec2` (0 = not married, 1 = married).

   A.   Create a 2x2 table to describe the "interaction" (based on Table 9.7).

   B.   Run a two-way analysis of variance for `wwwhrrec` between `marstatrec` and `childsrec`.

   C.   Interpret and write up the results.

Supplementary Digital Content

Download datasets and R code at the companion website at https://study.sagepub.com/ researchmethods/statistics/gillespie-r-for-statistics

CORRELATION AND
BIVARIATE REGRESSION

REVIEW OF SCATTERPLOTS

As discussed in Chapter 5, charts, graphs, and figures provide visual depictions and representations of data. Scatterplots are often used with continuous (i.e., interval/ratio) data and sometimes accompany correlation and regression analysis. They help us determine whether a relationship exists between two variables as well as its direction and strength.

Scatterplots help us get a sense of three features of a relationship: strength, direction, and shape. You might find it useful to compare the data points in a scatterplot to a cigar. The strength—which identifies how strongly the two variables are related to one another—can be assessed based on how wide the shape becomes. The direction of the relationship—positive or negative—depends on how the data points cluster. Clustering from the lower left to the upper right quadrants indicates that the relationship is positive. On the other hand, if the data appear to create a cigar shape from the upper left to the lower right, then the relationship seems to be negative. If the shape is not a cigar shape at all (e.g., maybe more of a circle or a curved/bent cigar), then a linear relationship is unlikely. Figure 10.1 shows examples of different patterns (shapes) that could exist in a scatterplot and their relative approximate *r*-value.

We will use the variables educ (highest year of school completed) and tvhours (number of hours watching tv per day) to generate a simple scatterplot. The main title, the *x* and *y* axis labels, and the color of the data points can be added (Figure 10.2). Keep in mind that we need to recode our variables to NA for any missing values (i.e., don't know, no answer, or not applicable). For this chapter, we will recode all missing values *within the original variable*. First, before we remove the missing data (which will change the variables), we will run the scatterplot that includes all of the data, including the missing responses (Figure 10.3).

FIGURE 10.1 ● SCATTERPLOT EXAMPLES

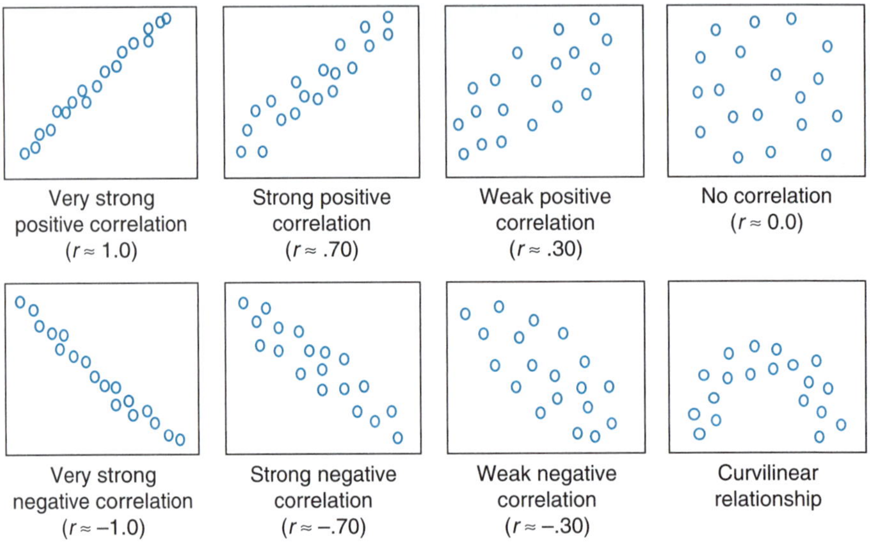

Very strong
positive correlation
($r \approx 1.0$)

Strong positive
correlation
($r \approx .70$)

Weak positive
correlation
($r \approx .30$)

No correlation
($r \approx 0.0$)

Very strong
negative correlation
($r \approx -1.0$)

Strong negative
correlation
($r \approx -.70$)

Weak negative
correlation
($r \approx -.30$)

Curvilinear
relationship

```
plot(GSS2016$educ, GSS2016$tvhours,
    pch = 16,
    col = "Dodgerblue3",
    main = "Scatterplot for Education Level and TV Watching
    Habits",
    xlab = "Highest Year of School Completed",
    ylab = "TV Hours Watched/Day") # Run a scatterplot
before recoding our variables.

GSS2016$educ[GSS2016$educ==98]=NA
GSS2016$educ[GSS2016$educ==99]=NA

GSS2016$tvhours[GSS2016$tvhours==-1]=NA
GSS2016$tvhours[GSS2016$tvhours==98]=NA
GSS2016$tvhours[GSS2016$tvhours==99]=NA

plot(GSS2016$educ, GSS2016$tvhours,
    pch = 16,
    col = "Dodgerblue3",
    main = "Scatterplot for Education Level and TV Watching
    Habits",
    xlab = "Highest Year of School Completed",
    ylab = "TV Hours Watched/Day") # Make a scatterplot of
data points for participants' highest year of education
and participants' mothers' highest year of education.
```

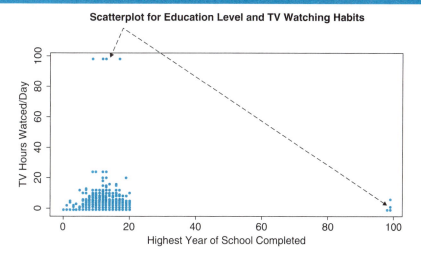

Scatterplot for Education Level and TV Watching Habits

Note: If we had not recoded the values, our scatterplot would have looked like this. This figure helps to understand how much the missing codes, especially large values like 98 and 99, can skew our results if we do not remove them properly (Figure 10.3).

Scatterplot for Education Level and TV Watching Habits

CORRELATIONS

Correlation analysis assesses the relationship, or association, between two or more variables. Typically, correlation analysis examines the direction (positive or negative) and strength of the relationship between two variables regardless of which is the independent or dependent

TABLE 10.1 ⬢ POSSIBLE CORRELATION ANALYSES

Correlation	Variable 1	Variable 2
Pearson	Continuous	Continuous
Point-Biserial	Continuous	Dichotomous (2-level nominal)
Spearman's Rho	Ordinal or Continuous	Ordinal or Continuous
Kendall's Tau (tau-b)	Ordinal or Continuous (small N)	Ordinal or Continuous (small N)
Correlation Matrix	Multiple Continuous	Multiple Continuous

variable. There are several types of correlation analyses. The one that applies to your situation will depend upon the type of variables in your study (Table 10.1); we focus mainly on Pearson's correlation coefficient and correlation matrices in this chapter.

PEARSON'S CORRELATION COEFFICIENT

The Pearson correlation coefficient (Pearson's product-moment correlation) offers insight into the existence, strength, and direction of a linear relationship between two continuous variables. There are some assumptions about the data that need to be considered prior to interpreting the coefficient:

1. The variables are both continuous (if not, there are other tests to run instead).

2. The variables are normally distributed.

3. The data have a linear relationship.

4. The data should have homoscedasticity (relatively equal variances along the fit line).

If the variables are not continuous, a separate test for correlation (e.g., Spearman's rank or Kendall rank) can be run instead. One way to check for a linear relationship, which is one of the assumptions above, is to assess the correlation visually with a scatterplot.

In order to understand the difference between a positive and negative relationship, imagine two variables: variable X and variable Y. A positive relationship exists when X and Y move in the *same* direction—if X increases, Y increases; and when X decreases, Y decreases. For example, consider the relationship between study time (in hours) and grade point average (GPA). More study hours correspond to a higher GPA. At the same time, fewer study hours correspond to a lower GPA. This is a positive relationship.

A negative relationship exists when X and Y operate in *opposing* directions. If X increases, Y decreases; and if X decreases, Y increases. For example, consider the relationship between number of hours spent watching movies and GPA. More hours spent watching movies might correspond to a lower GPA; or, fewer hours watching movies might correspond to a higher GPA.

The strength and the direction of the relationship are determined by the correlation coefficient *r*. The correlation coefficient *r* will range from −1.0 to 1.0. The sign of the correlation coefficient (positive or negative) indicates whether the relationship is a positive or a negative one (Figure 10.4). The absolute value of the coefficient (ranging between 0 and 1) denotes the strength of the relationship (Table 10.2). Values closer to -1 indicate a stronger negative relationship and those closer to 1 point to a stronger positive relationship.

There can be a significant result (a *p*-value that is below the alpha level set by the researcher) with an extremely low correlation coefficient *r*-value. In these cases, the researcher must determine and report on the substantive importance of the findings.

> **Tip:** Always remember that correlation does not mean causation. It is crucial not to infer causation when there is only proof of a correlation between variables.

> **Tip:** Correlation coefficients can be influenced by outliers. Be sure to know your data and check for outliers prior to analysis.

To run a Pearson's correlation test, use the following code: `cor.test(var1, var2)`. In R/RStudio, the default test for a correlation is the Pearson correlation. However, we discuss a few other options later in the chapter.

FIGURE 10.4 ● DIRECTION OF AN *r*-COEFFICIENT

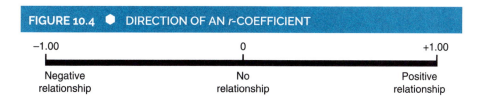

TABLE 10.2 ● STRENGTH OF AN *r*-COEFFICIENT

Interpretation of the *r*-Coefficient	Size of the *r*-Coefficient
Very strong relationship	.81 to 1.0
Strong relationship	.61 to .8
Moderate relationship	.41 to .6
Weak relationship	.21 to .4
Very weak relationship	.01 to .2

Because there appeared to be a possible correlation when examining the scatterplot, we should continue to explore the possible relationship between educ and tvhours. As with any inferential statistic, it is important first to run descriptive statistics. If you have continuous (i.e., interval/ratio) data, a simple way to run descriptive statistics is to use the **stat.desc** command in the **pastecs** library. Be sure to use the recoded variables from the beginning of the chapter. If you are starting in the middle of the chapter, you will want to be sure to recode these variables prior to running the correlation (revisit the beginning of this chapter).

```
library(pastecs) # Open the library for pastecs.
stat.desc(GSS2016$tvhours) # Run descriptive statistics.
stat.desc(GSS2016$educ)
```

Output: Descriptive statistics educ and tvhours.

```
> stat.desc(GSS2016$tvhours)
nbr.val          nbr.null       nbr.na         min            max            range
1.883000e+03 1.620000e+02 9.840000e+02 0.000000e+00 2.400000e+01 2.400000e+01
sum              median         mean           SE.mean        CI.mean.0.95   var
5.708000e+03 2.000000e+00 3.031333e+00 6.477075e-02 1.270300e-01 7.899655e+00
std.dev          coef.var
2.810633e+00 9.271936e-01
> stat.desc(GSS2016$educ)
nbr.val          nbr.null       nbr.na         min            max            range
2.858000e+03 2.000000e+00 9.000000e+00 0.000000e+00 2.000000e+01 2.000000e+01
sum              median         mean           SE.mean        CI.mean.0.95   var
3.926100e+04 1.300000e+01 1.373723e+01 5.544091e-02 1.087082e-01 8.784620e+00
std.dev          coef.var
2.963886e+00 2.157557e-01
```

Then, run the Pearson correlation coefficient for the two variables:

```
cor.test(GSS2016$educ, GSS2016$tvhours) # Pearson correlation
analysis for a relationship between the two variables.
```

Tip: you can also add the argument for "pearson" if you feel more comfortable (cor.test(GSS2016$educ, GSS2016$tvhours, method = "pearson"), but this is not necessary since it is already the default test. However, if you want to run a Spearman's rho or Kendall tau, you will need to add the argument to the code.

Output: Pearson's product-moment correlation coefficient for `educ` and `tvhours`.

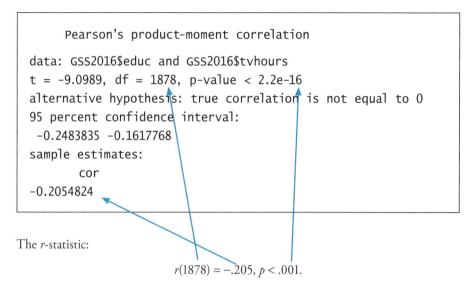

```
       Pearson's product-moment correlation

data: GSS2016$educ and GSS2016$tvhours
t = -9.0989, df = 1878, p-value < 2.2e-16
alternative hypothesis: true correlation is not equal to 0
95 percent confidence interval:
 -0.2483835 -0.1617768
sample estimates:
       cor
-0.2054824
```

The *r*-statistic:

$$r(1878) = -.205, p < .001.$$

As with other tests, in order to write up the results correctly, be sure to (1) state which analysis was run, (2) inform the readers which variables were analyzed, and (3) state the statistical significance, if applicable, as well as the direction and strength of the relationship.

Write-Up: A Pearson's correlation examined whether there was a relationship between individuals' highest level of school completed (N = 2858, M = 13.73, SD = 2.96) and the number of hours of television watched per day, on average (N = 1883, M = 3.03, SD = 2.81). The results indicated there was a significant and negative, yet weak relationship between the two [$r(1878)$ = -.205, p < .001].

COEFFICIENT OF DETERMINATION

The coefficient of determination (*r*-squared, R^2, or r^2) is a vital and informative statistical measure that is used with correlation and regression analysis. When the *r*-value is squared the outcome is the r^2 ($r \bullet r = r^2$)—multiplying this number by 100 will explain the proportional amount of covariation between the independent and dependent variables. Specifically, the proportion of the variation in the dependent variable that is explained by variation in the independent variable. Conceptually, this is the amount of change in one variable as the value of the other variable changes. For example, if our correlation results are as follows: $r(df)$ = .368, p < .001, then the r^2 is .135. The effect size is, therefore, 13.5%; meaning, 13.5% of the variation in Y can be accounted for by variation in X. To illustrate, Table 10.3 describes a few different *r*-values along with their corresponding r^2 and proportion of variance explained.

TABLE 10.3 ● COEFFICIENT OF DETERMINATION TABLE

r-value	*r²*-value	*Proportion*
10	1.	100%
9	.81	81%
7	.49	49%
5	.25	25%
3	.09	9%
1	.01	1%
0	0	None

CORRELATION TESTS FOR ORDINAL VARIABLES

Other correlation tests can be run when the variables have an ordinal—rather than continuous (i.e., interval/ratio)—level of measurement. Spearman's rank correlation coefficient (Spearman's rho), or Kendall rank correlation coefficient (Kendall's tau correlation) are two possible tests that help researchers assess the association between ordinal variables. Spearman's rho and Kendall's tau both measure for monotonic relationships instead of linear relationships (see Information Box 10.1).

Tip: Spearman's rho can be denoted by rs or the Greek letter ρ, pronounced rho.

INFORMATION BOX 10.1

Monotonic Relationships

A "monotonic" relationship between two variables means that as one varies, the second variable will vary in relation to the first variable's changes—since the changes are ranked, we are able to see if higher rankings on one variable correspond to lower rankings on the other. For example, if one variable increases the other variable will increase or vice-versa (positive monotonic relationship), or if one variable increases the other variable will decrease or vice versa (negative monotonic relationship).

You may have heard the statement "money can't buy happiness," but what if we wanted to explore if money and happiness have a relationship? The next example explores the relationship between financial satisfaction and overall satisfaction. For the first measure, use the variable happy which comes from the GSS question, *"Taken all together, how would you say things are these days—would you say that you are very happy, pretty happy, or not too happy?"* The possible responses are:

1 = Very happy	8 = Don't know
2 = Pretty happy	9 = No answer
3 = Not too happy	0 = Not applicable

As the second variable, use satfin which comes from the question, *"So far as you and your family are concerned, would you say that you are pretty well satisfied with your present financial situation, more or less satisfied, or not satisfied at all?"* The possible responses are:

1 = Pretty well satisfied	8 = Don't know
2 = More or less satisfied	9 = No answer
3 = Not satisfied at all	0 = Not applicable

Since both variables are ordinal, a Spearman's rho will determine if there is a monotonic relationship between the two. Start by viewing frequency tables for the two variables, recode the variables, and run frequencies to check that the values have been recoded properly. Then, run the Spearman's rho analysis. In order to have all the necessary information to write up the results, produce a frequency table of the paired variables.

```
table(GSS2016$satfin)
```

Output: Frequency table for financial satisfaction (satfin) before recoding.

```
  1     2     3    8   9
816   1255   785   5   6
```

```
table(GSS2016$happy)
```

Output: Frequency table for general happiness (happy) before recoding.

```
  1     2     3    8   9
806   1601   452   3   5
```

```
GSS2016$satfin[GSS2016$satfin==0]=NA # Recoding the variables.
GSS2016$satfin[GSS2016$satfin==8]=NA
GSS2016$satfin[GSS2016$satfin==9]=NA

GSS2016$happy[GSS2016$happy==0]=NA
GSS2016$happy[GSS2016$happy==8]=NA
GSS2016$happy[GSS2016$happy==9]=NA
```

```
table(GSS2016$satfin) # Produce frequencies to double check
                       the recoding of the variables.
table(GSS2016$happy)
```

Output: Frequency table for financial satisfaction (satfin) after recoding.

```
   1     2     3
 816  1255   785
```

Output: Frequency table for general happiness (happy) after recoding.

```
   1     2     3
 806  1601   452
```

```
cor.test(GSS2016$happy, GSS2016$satfin,
    method = "spearman",
    use = "pairwise.complete.obs",
    exact = FALSE) # Add which test to run ("spearman")
    and use the pairwise complete observations command for
    missing values.
```

Output: Results of the Spearman's rho run with happy and satfin.

```
data: GSS2016$happy and GSS2016$satfin
S = 2757500000, p-value < 2.2e-16
alternative hypothesis: true rho is not equal to 0
sample estimates:
      rho
0.2852914
```

the rho coefficient (effect size)   &   the *p*-value

In order to obtain the degrees of freedom, run a table of the frequencies of the pairs and subtract 2 (the number of variables).

$$df = \Sigma(\text{x-y pairs}) - (\#var)$$
$$df = 2850 - 2$$
$$df = 2848$$
$$r_s(2848) = -.285, p < .001$$

```
table(GSS2016$happy, GSS2016$satfin)
```

Output: All pairs for the correlation.

	1	2	3
1	340	341	120
2	417	761	419
3	58	151	243

Write-up: A Spearman's rho correlation assessed whether there was a relationship between participants' general level of happiness (a 3-level order which ranged from very happy to not too happy with a modal response of pretty happy), and their financial satisfaction (a 3-level order from pretty well satisfied to not satisfied at all, with a modal response of more or less satisfied). The results pointed to a significant and negative, yet weak relationship between the two variables [$r_s(2848) = -.285$, $p < .001$]. The negative relationship indicates that the two variables operate in opposite directions, such that as overall happiness increases, financial satisfaction decreases and vice versa.

THE CORRELATION MATRIX

A correlation matrix is a matrix that contains bivariate correlation coefficients between multiple sets of variables (Table 10.4). Each individual cell of the matrix shows a correlation between two variables. Correlation matrices are practical when assessing bivariate

TABLE 10.4 ● CONCEPTUAL CORRELATION MATRIX

	Variable 1	Variable 2	Variable 3	Variable 4	Variable 5
Variable 1	1				
Variable 2	.xx	1			
Variable 3	.xx	.xx	1		
Variable 4	.xx	.xx	.xx	1	
Variable 5	.xx	. xx	.xx	.xx	1

Note that variable 1 on the top row and variable 1 on the top of the first column are the same variable. This will result in a perfect correlation coefficient of 1. This will always happen in any cell of a correlation matrix that has a variable testing for correlation with itself.

This cell would be the result of the correlation between variable 2 (on the top row) and variable 3 in the first column. Each cell that has a result is the correlation coefficient of the two variables that meet in that cell.

Sometimes people choose to fill all the cells in with the results and other times people choose to only fill the results that are not duplications. Because it is a matrix there will be duplications of all partnerships. For example, these cells would both have the result from the variable 3 and variable 4 correlation coefficient.

relationships among multiple variables but also when performing multivariate regression analysis, which is discussed in the next chapter.

When running a correlation matrix, the package **Hmisc** must be installed. Go to the lower right quadrant in RStudio and click on the tab that says "Install." A new window will open that should have a default setting for "Install from: window of Repository, (CRAN, CRANextra)." The second window is for "Packages," where you can type **Hmisc**. RStudio will likely autocomplete the selection or you can continue to type it out. Next, select the install button and allow for the installation to take place. Finally, the library should be run to use the package. You will also want to do the same thing for the package **corrplot**, which will be used to plot the results of the correlation matrix.

```
library(Hmisc)
library(corrplot)
```

Now that the packages are installed and loaded, run a correlation matrix to assess the relationships. First, recode the missing data for the variables (we might have done some of the recoding in previous parts of the chapter but it is fine to run the code again). Second, create an independent object with the relevant variables. For the next example, use the highest year of school completed by the participants, their mothers, their fathers, and the numbers of hours of television watched per day, on average—i.e., educ, maeduc, paeduc, and tvhours respectively (Figure 10.5). Using the **head()** command, we can get a quick view of the dataset's top two rows to make sure it looks accurate. Run the correlation matrix command: **rcorr(as.matrix(dataframe))**.

> **Tip:** It is possible to double check the results by running each bivariate correlation individually to see if the results match the correlation matrix. This is not necessary all the time but it is a good way to become familiar and comfortable with the process.

```
GSS2016$educ[GSS2016$educ==98]=NA # Recode the missing responses.
GSS2016$educ[GSS2016$educ==99]=NA

GSS2016$maeduc[GSS2016$maeduc==97]=NA
GSS2016$maeduc[GSS2016$maeduc==98]=NA
GSS2016$maeduc[GSS2016$maeduc==99]=NA

GSS2016$paeduc[GSS2016$paeduc==97]=NA
GSS2016$paeduc[GSS2016$paeduc==98]=NA
GSS2016$paeduc[GSS2016$paeduc==99]=NA

GSS2016$tvhours[GSS2016$tvhours=='-1']=NA
GSS2016$tvhours[GSS2016$tvhours==98]=NA

MatrixData<-GSS2016[, c("educ", "maeduc", "paeduc","tvhours")]
# Create a separate object with the variables in the matrix.
```

FIGURE 10.5 ● SCREENSHOT OF THE ENVIRONMENT WINDOW SHOWING THE DATA FRAME THAT WAS CREATED

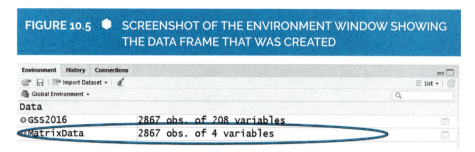

```
head(MatrixData, 4) # View first 4 rows of data.
head(MatrixData, 25) # View first 25 rows of data.
```

Output: Top four rows of data for new dataset MatrixData.

	educ	maeduc	paeduc	tvhours
1	16	13	18	1
2	12	12	8	1
3	16	8	12	NA
4	12	12	NA	1

After running the correlation matrix using rcorr(as.matrix(dataset)), there are three output matrices produced in the output window. The first is the matrix of the *r*-coefficients, the second is the matrix of the counts, and the third is the matrix for the *p*-value.

```
rcorr(as.matrix(MatrixData))
```

Output: Simple outputs for correlation matrix of maeduc, paeduc, educ, and tvhours for the *r*-coefficient, the count (*N*), and the *p*-values.

	educ	maeduc	paeduc	tvhours
educ	1.00	0.38	0.42	−0.21
maeduc	0.38	1.00	0.69	−0.14
paeduc	0.42	0.69	1.00	−0.19
tvhours	−0.21	−0.14	−0.19	1.00

n

	educ	maeduc	paeduc	tvhours
educ	2858	2577	2089	1880
maeduc	2577	2581	1953	1705
paeduc	2089	1953	2092	1370
tvhours	1880	1705	1370	1883

```
P
          educ    maeduc    paeduc    tvhours
educ                0         0         0
maeduc      0                 0         0
paeduc      0         0                 0
tvhours     0         0         0
```

More detailed outputs can be obtained by creating a data object of the correlation matrix and then extracting the specific data for the *r*-coefficient, or the *p*-values (Figure 10.6). First, save the information from the matrix as an independent object ("EdMat"):

```
EdMat<-rcorr(as.matrix(MatrixData)) # Create an object of the
correlation matrix.
```

FIGURE 10.6 ● SCREENSHOT OF THE ENVIRONMENT WINDOW SHOWING THE DATA FRAME FOR EDUCATION MATRIX

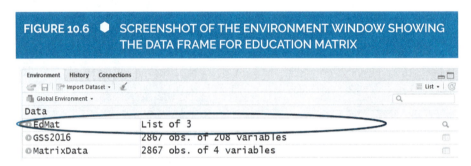

Then, call on the appropriate information from the new object:

```
EdMat$r # Extract the correlation coefficients.
EdMat$P # Extract p-values.
```

Output: More detailed results extracted from the correlation matrix for the *r*- and *p*-values.

	educ	maeduc	paeduc	tvhours
educ	1.0000000	0.3806361	0.4207906	-0.2054824
maeduc	0.3806361	1.0000000	0.6885154	-0.1419937
paeduc	0.4207906	0.6885154	1.0000000	-0.1855644
tvhours	-0.2054824	-0.1419937	-0.1855644	1.0000000

	educ	maeduc	paeduc	tvhours
educ	NA	0.000000e+00	0.00000e+00	0.000000e+00
maeduc	0	NA	0.00000e+00	3.892108e-09
paeduc	0	0.000000e+00	NA	4.442890e-12
tvhours	0	3.892108e-09	4.44289e-12	NA

Tip: When running an analysis, it is always a good idea to double-check the work.

This is each individual correlation being run in the correlation matrix—it is just a simple way to double-check the work.

```
cor.test(GSS2016$educ, GSS2016$maeduc)
cor.test(GSS2016$paeduc, GSS2016$educ)
cor.test(GSS2016$paeduc, GSS2016$maeduc)
cor.test(GSS2016$educ, GSS2016$tvhours)
cor.test(GSS2016$maeduc, GSS2016$tvhours)
cor.test(GSS2016$paeduc, GSS2016$tvhours)
```

Output: Correlation matrix coefficients compared to individual correlation results:

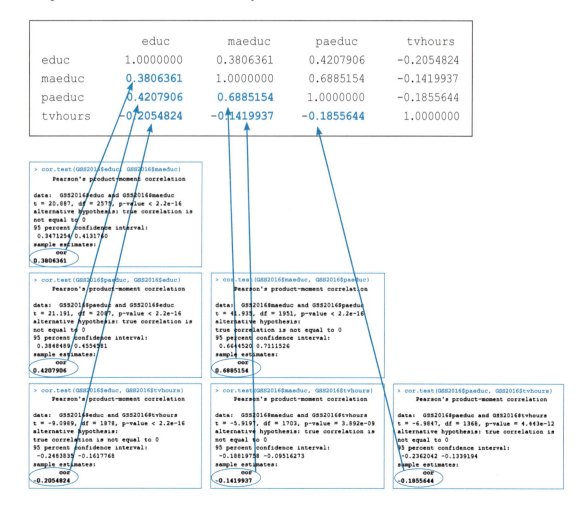

Based on the results presented in the correlation matrix, it is clear that correlational rela-tionships do exist between individuals' level of educational attainment, their parents' educa-tional attainment, and the amount of time the individual spends viewing television per day on average. Some of the relationships are positive (i.e., between maternal education attain-ment and participant education attainment, or between paternal education attainment and participant education attainment), and some are negative (all relationships with hours spent watching television are negative). We also get a sense of the strength of the relationships. For example, the relationship between a participant's level of education and their father's education is a moderate, positive, and significant relationship ($r = .42$, $p < .001$). Moreover, the r^2 is .17, which means that 17% of the variation in participants' education level can be explained by the variation in the education level of the participants' fathers.

A final step for analysis and reporting of a correlation matrix can be to present a visual depiction of the results (Figure 10.7).

```
library(corrplot)
```

> **Tip:** If you get an error message when trying to run code, make sure you have loaded all of the appropriate packages.

```
corrplot(EdMat$r, type="upper", order="hclust", tl.col = "black",
         p.mat = EdMat$P, sig.level = 0.01, insig = "blank")
```

In this analysis, all p-values are less than the alpha level of .05; therefore, all correlation coefficients are significant. The second item we want to address is the correlation coeffi-cients or r-values. If we are only interested in identifying the strength and direction of the relationships, the r-values provide that information.

FIGURE 10.7 ● GRAPHIC OF THE CORRELATION MATRIX OF educ, maeduc, paeduc, AND tvhours

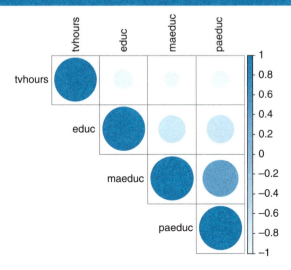

BIVARIATE LINEAR REGRESSION

A bivariate linear regression is also known as a *simple linear regression* or *linear regression* and is an example of an ordinary least squares (OLS) regression. A simple bivariate regression is a linear statistical model between two continuous variables to test if the existing correlational relationship between the two variables is a *predictive* relationship as well. A regression seeks to answer if the outcome of the DV (Y) can be predicted due to the value of the IV (X). Conceptually speaking, the information we have from the sample population allows us to calculate (predict) future outcomes of the dependent variable given new values for the independent variable. We do so by applying our data to the linear equation. In a regression, we are quantifying the relationship between the explanatory, or independent, variable (X) and the outcome, or dependent, variable (Y). Another way to say it: *for a given value of X, there is a value for Y that fits on the regression line.*

FIGURE 10.8 ● OLS REGRESSION LINE WITH THE LEAST DISTANCE (TOP) AND WITH PREDICTION LINE (BOTTOM)

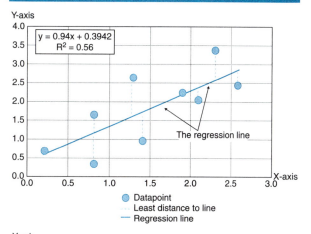

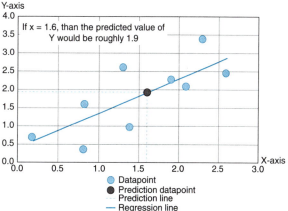

Regression Equation

$$\hat{Y}_i = b_0 + b_1(X_i)$$

$\hat{Y}_i$ = Y-hat—Predicted value of Y (DV) for observation i

b_0 = Estimate of the intercept (or constant) of the regression line

b_1 = Estimate of the slope of regression line

X_i = Value of X (IV) for observation i

The regression line is also known as the *least squares regression line*, or the *best fit regression line*. The line is calculated to have the least amount of value between the data points and the line. From the regression line we can use the intercept and the slope to predict the dependent variable given a value for the independent variable (Figure 10.8).

Tip: In statistics, the hat symbol (^), also referred to as the caret, represents an estimation or prediction of something. In the case of a regression, the "hat" is over the dependent variable, because we can "predict" the dependent variable from the independent variable(s) using the linear equation.

This chapter proceeds with an example of a linear regression between mothers' education level (maeduc) and participants' education level (educ), both of which are continuous variables that measure education level as the highest year of school completed. The first and second steps of running a regression include creating visual outputs of the data. First, produce histograms of each variable to observe the data visually. This allows you to determine if either variable has any extreme outliers, or non-linear distributions. Then, create a scatterplot of the data (Figure 10.9).

```
hist(GSS2016$maeduc)
hist(GSS2016$educ)
```

Output: Histograms of educ and maeduc.

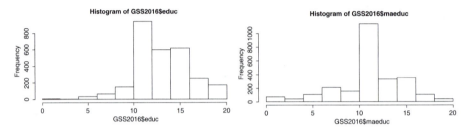

```
plot(GSS2016$maeduc,GSS2016$educ,
     pch = 8,
     col = "blue2",
     main = "Scatterplot for Education Level of Participants
             and Participants' Mothers",
     xlab = "Mother's Education",
     ylab = "Participant Education")
```

FIGURE 10.9 ● SCATTERPLOT FOR educ AND maeduc WITH A REGRESSION LINE

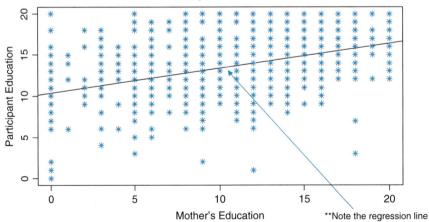

```
abline(lm(GSS2016$educ~GSS2016$maeduc)) # Then add the
regression line.
```

After viewing the scatterplot, run descriptive statistics for each variable in the regression.

```
library(pastecs) # When running stat.desc, remember to add
the library for pastecs.
stat.desc(GSS2016$maeduc)
stat.desc(GSS2016$educ) # Descriptive statistics for the 2
variables.
```

Outputs: Descriptive statistics for `maeduc` and `educ`.

```
stat.desc(GSS2016$maeduc)
nbr.val        nbr.null      nbr.na        min           max           range
2.581000e+03 5.900000e+01 2.860000e+02 0.000000e+00 2.000000e+01 2.000000e+01
sum            median        mean          SE.mean       CI.mean.0.95  var
3.061100e+04 1.200000e+01 1.186013e+01 7.252407e-02 1.422113e-01 1.357539e+01
std.dev        coef.var
3.684480e+00 3.106609e-01
```

```
stat.desc(GSS2016$educ)
nbr.val        nbr.null      nbr.na        min           max           range
2.858000e+03 2.000000e+00 9.000000e+00 0.000000e+00 2.000000e+01 2.000000e+01
sum            median        mean          SE.mean       CI.mean.0.95  var
3.926100e+04 1.300000e+01 1.373723e+01 5.544091e-02 1.087082e-01 8.784620e+00
std.dev        coef.var
2.963886e+00 2.157557e-01
```

After the descriptive statistics have been run, the simple linear regression can be run using the lm function (linear model) in a basic linear regression: `dataname <- lm(DV~IV)`. When running a linear model regression, nothing will appear automatically in the output window. In order to see the results, save the regression as an independent object that will appear in the environment window. Save the regression as `reg.ed` and then you can choose which results you want to see from the `reg.ed` model such as the actual regression, a summary which will include the *t*-value, *p*-value, residuals, and r^2 (summary(reg.ed)), or we can produce the predicted values from the regression equation (`predict(reg.ed)`).

```
reg.ed<-lm(GSS2016$educ~GSS2016$maeduc) # Run the linear
model (lm) regression of mother's education on participant's
education and save the regression as an object.
```

Tip: Since it makes logical sense to think that mothers' education will influence their child's education (and not the other way around), we use `maeduc` as the independent variable (X) and `educ` as the dependent variable (Y) in the regression.

FIGURE 10.10 ● THE SAVED OBJECT (`reg.ed`) FOR THE LINEAR REGRESSION

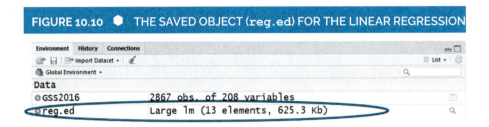

```
reg.ed
```

Output: Linear regression results for `maeduc` on `educ`.

```
Call:
lm(formula = GSS2016$educ ~ GSS2016$maeduc)
Coefficients:
   (Intercept)        GSS2016$maeduc
      10.3512              0.3014
```

Tip: If you are interested in more detailed results, including the significance, residuals, r-squared, etc., then run the summary of the regression object rather than calling the object itself.

```
summary(reg.ed) # See the results.
```

Output: Summary of linear regression results for `maeduc` on `educ`.

```
Call:
lm(formula = GSS2016$educ ~ GSS2016$maeduc)
Residuals:
    Min       1Q    Median      3Q      Max
 -12.9685  -1.9685  -0.1598   2.0315   9.6488
```

```
Coefficients:
            Estimate Std.    Error t    value     Pr(>|t|)
(Intercept)       10.35119    0.17927    57.74    <2e-16 ***
GSS2016$maeduc     0.30144    0.01443    20.89    <2e-16 ***
---
Signif. codes:  0 '***' 0.001 '**' 0.01 '*' 0.05 '.' 0.1 ' ' 1
Residual standard error: 2.697 on 2575 degrees of freedom
  (290 observations deleted due to missingness)
Multiple R-squared:  0.1449,      Adjusted R-squared:  0.1446
F-statistic: 436.3 on 1 and 2575 DF, p-value: < 2.2e-16
```

The Regression Equation

$$\hat{Y}_i = b_0 + b_1(X_i)$$

Predicted education level $= b_0 + b_1(X_i)$

Predicted education level $= b_0 + b_1$(mother's education level)

Predicted education level $= 10.35 + b_1$(mother's education level)

Predicted education level $= 10.35 + .30$ (mother's education level)

Tip: The p-value of the slope is the best indicator for significance of association and prediction.

Tip: In order to calculate the dependent variable, plug the appropriate values into the regression equation and calculate:

If mother's education (maeduc) is 12 (high school graduate), then,

$$\hat{Y} = 10.35 + (.30*12)$$
$$\hat{Y} = 13.95$$

If maeduc is Grade 16 (college graduate), then,

$$\hat{Y} = 10.35 + (.30*16)$$
$$\hat{Y} = 15.15$$

For confidence intervals, use the "confint" call.

```
confint(reg.ed)
```

Output: Confidence interval for `maeduc`.

(Intercept)	9.9996604	10.7027126
GSS2016$maeduc	0.2731433	0.3297411

Confidence intervals indicate that we can be 95% confident that the coefficient will fall within the lower and upper limits shown. For the above example, the lower and upper limits for both the highest year of school completed by the individuals and their mothers are significant and positive. In the output above, the confidence interval bands do not overlap with 0, which indicates that the value is significantly different from 0.

> **Tip:** When writing a thorough interpretation of bivariate regression results, it is useful to include the regression equation, the significance of the coefficient(s), and descriptive statistics for the relevant variables.

Write-Up: A bivariate regression analysis was run with highest year of school completed by participants as the dependent variable (N = 2558, M = 13.73, SD = 2.96) and highest year of school completed by participants' mothers as the independent variable (N = 2581, M = 11.86, SD = 3.68). The regression equation [Predicted participant education level = 10.35 +.30 (mother's education level)] points to a significant and positive relationship [B = .30, $t(2575)$ = 20.9, $p < .001$]. Mothers' education is significantly associated with participants' education [r^2 = .145 $F(1, 2575)$ = 436.3, $p < .001$]. The r^2 indicates the mother's education level predicts 14.5% of the variance in participants' education level.

The results suggest that the independent variable (`maeduc`—mothers' highest year of school completed) is a significant predictor of the outcome (`educ`—participants' highest year of school completed).

In R/RStudio, it is possible to predict outcomes of individuals' highest year of school completed based on random assigned values for the highest year of school completed by the mothers using the **predict()** command. And finally, it is possible to produce confidence intervals for respondents' predicted highest years of education.

```
predict(reg.ed) # Predict the highest year of school
completed by the participant based on created values for the
mothers' highest years of school completed.
```

Output: Screenshot of partial table of predicted values for `educ`.

1	2	3	4	5	6	7	8	9
14.26994	13.96849	12.76272	13.96849	13.96849	13.96849	13.96849	11.85840	12.76272
10	11	17	19	20	21	22	23	24
14.87282	14.26994	12.76272	14.57138	15.17426	13.96849	13.96849	12.76272	13.36561
27	28	29	31	32	33	34	35	36
13.96849	13.96849	13.96849	13.96849	13.96849	13.96849	15.17426	13.96849	13.96849
37	38	39	41	42	43	44	46	47
13.96849	15.17426	15.17426	15.17426	12.76272	15.17426	15.47570	15.17426	13.96849
48	49	50	51	52	53	54	55	56
13.96849	15.77715	15.77715	15.17426	13.96849	15.17426	13.96849	13.96849	13.96849
57	58	59	60	61	63	64	65	66

Table Note: A selection of the first 45 results offers a visual representation of the output.

```
predict(reg.ed, interval = "predict") # Produce confidence
interval for highest year of school.
```

Output: Partial output table of predicted values for `educ` including the lower and upper confidence intervals.

	fit	lwr	upr
1	14.26994	8.980073	19.55980
2	13.96849	8.678727	19.25826
3	12.76272	7.471829	18.05362
4	13.96849	8.678727	19.25826
5	13.96849	8.678727	19.25826
6	13.96849	8.678727	19.25826
7	13.96849	8.678727	19.25826
8	11.85840	6.565068	17.15173
9	12.76272	7.471829	18.05362
10	14.87282	9.582310	20.16333
11	14.26994	8.980073	19.55980
17	12.76272	7.471829	18.05362
19	14.57138	9.281267	19.86149
20	15.17426	9.883202	20.46532

Table Note: A selection of the first 14 results offers a visual representation of the output.

Thus, if the highest year of school for the participant (`educ`) was predicted to be 15.17, we can say with 95% confidence that the lowest it would be is 9.88 and the highest it would be is 20.47.

LOGISTIC REGRESSION

A regression can also have a binary, or dichotomous, dependent variable. In this case, we run an analysis known as logistic regression. With a logistic regression, the independent variable can be either categorical or continuous.

> **Tip:** For space reasons, we left out a great deal of important information regarding logistic regression. If this is your primary method of analysis, we recommend you explore the many options in R/RStudio as well as a more detailed discussion of how to calculate and interpret the analyses.

A logistic regression tells us the probability of having a specific value of the dependent variable.

$$P = 1/1 + e\text{-}y$$

We run a logistic regression in R/RStudio using the **glm** function.

First, take the variable satisfaction with financial situation (satfin) which has three categories and turn it into a binary variable. Currently the variable attributes include the following:

1 = Pretty well satisfied

2 = More or less satisfied

3 = Not satisfied at all

We create a new variable called satfinBi and combine "pretty well satisfied" and "more or less satisfied" and recode them into a category of satisfied (1). And we will recode the attribute "not satisfied at all" into category not satisfied (0). Also, make sure that the variable is a factor variable. We can do this by checking the current structure of the variable using the structure command. Change the variable to factor if needed.

```
GSS2016$satfinBi[GSS2016$satfin==1]=1

GSS2016$satfinBi[GSS2016$satfin==2]=1

GSS2016$satfinBi[GSS2016$satfin==3]=0

table(GSS2016$satfinBi)


str(GSS2016$satfinBi)

GSS2016$satfinBi <-as.factor(GSS2016$satfinBi)

str(GSS2016$satfinBi)
```

Output: Structure of the `satfinBi` variable showing it to be "numeric".

```
> str(GSS2016$satfinBi)
num [1:2867] 1 0 1 1 1 1 0 1 0 1 …
> GSS2016$satfinBi<-as.factor(GSS2016$satfinBi)
> str(GSS2016$satfinBi)
Factor w/ 2 levels "0","1": 2 1 2 2 2 2 1 2 1 2 …
```

```
logistic<-glm(GSS2016$satfinBi ~ GSS2016$educ, family = binomial)
summary(logistic)
```

Tip: The code for logistic regression can also be written with the dataset separated from the variables:

```
logistic2 <-glm(satfinBi ~ educ, data = GSS2016, family = binomial)
summary (logistic2)
```

Output: Results of logistic regression with `satfinBi` (DV) and `educ` (IV).

```
Call:
glm(formula = GSS2016$satfinBi2 ~ GSS2016$educ, family = binomial)
Deviance Residuals:
    Min      1Q     Median      3Q       Max
 -1.8755  -1.4592    0.7261    0.8517    1.3011
Coefficients:
              Estimate Std.  Error   z value    Pr(>|z|)
(Intercept)    -0.28608     0.19770   -1.447      0.148
GSS2016$educ    0.09278     0.01442    6.433     1.25e-10  ***
---
Signif. codes: 0 '***' 0.001 '**' 0.01 '*' 0.05 '.' 0.1 ' ' 1
(Dispersion parameter for binomial family taken to be 1)
```

Based on the results, we can determine the probability of individuals' reports of financial satisfaction based on their educational attainment. We can also use the results of this logistic regression model to predict the likelihood of financial satisfaction across different years of education. In the following, we use (a) 16 years of education and (b) 11 years of education. These calculations can be done by hand or in R/RStudio:

$$Y = -0.28608 + 0.09278 * \text{years of school}$$
$$Y = -0.28608 + 0.09278 * 16 = 1.1984$$
$$\text{Probability of answering satisfied} = 1/ 1+\exp (-(1.1984)) = .76824 = \textbf{76.82\%}$$
$$Y = -0.28608 + 0.09278 * \text{years of school}$$
$$Y = -0.28608 + 0.09278 * 11 = 0.7345$$
$$\text{Probability of answering satisfied} = 1/ 1+\exp (-(0.7345)) = .675792 = \textbf{67.58\%}$$

```
-0.28608+0.09278*16
1/(1+exp(-1.1984))
-0.28608+0.09278*11
1/(1+exp(-.7345))
```

CONCLUSION

The primary focus of this chapter was correlation and bivariate linear regression analysis. We discussed the essentials for producing Pearson's correlation coefficient (r) in R/RStudio, including the interpretation of direction and magnitude. As a natural extension, we developed and interpreted a correlation matrix in RStudio using the GSS data. The final part of the chapter provided directions for readers to conduct simple linear regression, which included the effect size (r^2). The next chapter focuses on using more than two variables in regression.

References

Smith, T. W., Davern, M., Freese, J., & Morgan, S. L. (2019). *General Social Surveys, 1972–2018* [Machine-Readable Data File]. Chicago, IL: NORC at the University of Chicago. Retrieved from http://www.gss.norc.org/getthedata/Pages/Home.aspx

Exercises

1. Recode the variables for respondent's 2016 income (`rincom16`), frequency of sex for 2016 (`sexfreq`), number of sexual partners in 2016 (`partners`), and average number of hours of television watched per day (`tvhours`) to remove all of the non-value answers.

2. Generate a correlation matrix to see if there are significant relationships between any or some of the variables. Produce a correlation matrix plot to give a visual depiction of the r-coefficient value results.

3. Run a simple linear regression to determine if number of sexual partners a person has in a year can predict the income of the person for the year.

Supplementary Digital Content

Download datasets and R code at the companion website at https://study.sagepub.com/researchmethods/statistics/gillespie-r-for-statistics

MULTIPLE REGRESSION

In this chapter, we discuss more advanced regression models than the bivariate regressions introduced in Chapter 10. In particular, this chapter explores the use of multiple variables in a single regression model, which is known as multiple regression. Table 11.1 highlights several different types of regression and some criteria for why we might choose those models.

TABLE 11.1 ● REGRESSION MODELS AND THEIR CRITERIA		
Regression Type	**Outcome Variable or DV**	**Predictor Variable(s) or IV(s)**
Simple Linear Regression	Continuous	Continuous
Multiple Regression	Continuous	2+ Continuous or Categorical
Logistic Regression	Categorical (2 groups)	1+ Continuous or Categorical
Multinomial Logistic	Nominal (3+ groups)	1+ Continuous or Categorical
Ordered Logit	Categorical (3+ ordered groups)	1+ Continuous or Categorical

When working with regressions, there are times when researchers will recode a variable with several categories into a dichotomous variable (i.e., with just two mutually exclusive categories). One example of such a case is if a researcher recoded a variable with information on individuals' marital status—married, single, divorced, widowed, separated, and never married—into a binary variable that indicates 0 = not coupled and 1 = coupled.

At its simplest, a multiple regression is a linear regression that has more variables. There is still only one dependent variable (also referred to as the DV, Y variable, or outcome variable), but there is more than one independent variable (i.e., the IV, X variable, or predictor variable). In other words, multiple regression is a linear model that tests to see if more than one IV can predict the outcome of the DV.

In addition to the dependent variable and the primary independent variable(s), multiple regression also incorporates *control variables*. Control variables—sometimes referred to as covariates—are not the actual focus of the study (i.e., they are not part of the formal hypothesis) but have some unignorable effect on the dependent variable. Therefore, we include them in the multiple regression model with the other independent variable(s) to "control" or "hold constant" their effect on the relationship between the independent and dependent variables. Ignoring a variable with a known impact on the DV could lead to an inaccurate estimate of the relationship.

As with all statistical procedures, there are several assumptions for a multiple regression:

1. The outcome (DV) is a continuous variable.
2. There is more than one predictor variable (IV).
3. The predictor variables are independent of each other.
4. There is no multicollinearity (extremely high correlations among IVs).
5. There should not be extreme outliers in the data.
6. The residuals should be normally distributed.
7. The data should have homoscedasticity (relatively equal variances along fit line).
8. There should be individual linear relationships between the DV and each of the IVs.

Multicollinearity occurs when variables provide information that is too closely related. For example, if one were trying to decipher what influences a person's motivation for losing weight, variables of interest might include being healthy, finding romance, feeling good, comfort in a swimsuit, or spending time at the beach or pool. The last two variables, comfort in a swimsuit and spending time at the beach or pool, might be too similar to run in the same multiple regression model because there is such a great overlap between the two. Granted, there are times at a winter resort when people might wear a swimsuit in the jacuzzi after a day on the slopes, but the practice of wearing a swimsuit is often coupled with the activity of going to the beach or pool. High multicollinearity between two variables can lead to problematic estimates in multiple regression.

In the next example, we examine which variables predict participants' level of education. Our hypothesis is that parents' years of education will be significantly associated with individuals' own years of education controlling for (or holding constant) the number of hours spent watching TV, amount of time spent using the Internet, and number of siblings. Therefore, the regression includes the following variables:

educ	highest year of school completed by the participant (DV)
maeduc	highest year of school completed by the participant's mother (IV)
paeduc	highest year of school completed by the participant's father (IV)
tvhours	number of hours per day that participant watches TV (control)
sibs	respondent's number of siblings (control)
wwwhr	number of hours per week spent on the Internet (control)

A useful place to start is by recoding values to NA to remove missing data for each of the variables that will be in the multiple regression. Make sure to open the library **Hmisc** and library **corrplot** since we will need the packages for the correlation matrix.

```
library(Hmisc)
library(corrplot)
```

#Recode the variables for education, maternal education, paternal education, hours of tv watched/day, number of siblings, and hours on the Internet/week

```
GSS2016$educ[GSS2016$educ==98]=NA
GSS2016$educ[GSS2016$educ==99]=NA

GSS2016$maeduc[GSS2016$maeduc==97]=NA
GSS2016$maeduc[GSS2016$maeduc==98]=NA
GSS2016$maeduc[GSS2016$maeduc==99]=NA

GSS2016$paeduc[GSS2016$paeduc==97]=NA
GSS2016$paeduc[GSS2016$paeduc==98]=NA
GSS2016$paeduc[GSS2016$paeduc==99]=NA

GSS2016$tvhours[GSS2016$tvhours=='-1']=NA
GSS2016$tvhours[GSS2016$tvhours==98]=NA

GSS2016$sibs[GSS2016$sibs==98]=NA
GSS2016$sibs[GSS2016$sibs==99]=NA

GSS2016$wwwhr[GSS2016$wwwhr=='-1']=NA
GSS2016$wwwhr[GSS2016$wwwhr==998]=NA
GSS2016$wwwhr[GSS2016$wwwhr==999]=NA
```

> **Tip:** We are using the "casewise deletion" approach, which drops the cases with missing data. However, there are other alternatives to recoding the missing variables for multiple regression analysis. For example, a researcher might decide to collapse all of a variable's non-values into a single code (e.g., 9) and run the regression model with the "missing" category intact.

Next, run frequency tables for each of the variables to confirm that all non-value (i.e., missing or NA) data have been recoded.

```
table(GSS2016$educ)
table(GSS2016$maeduc)
table(GSS2016$paeduc)
table(GSS2016$tvhours)
table(GSS2016$sibs)
table(GSS2016$wwwhr)
```

Output: Frequency tables for variables after recoding (educ, maeduc, paeduc, tvhours, sibs, wwwhr).

```
table(GSS2016$educ)
   0    1    2    3    4    5    6    7    8    9   10   11   12   13   14   15   16
   2    3    3    3    2    4   31   18   48   59   90  118  824  242  359  137  485

  17   18   19   20
 108  149   63  110
```

```
table(GSS2016$maeduc)
   0    1    2    3    4    5    6    7    8    9   10   11   12   13
  59    5   11   27   16   32   77   29  182   61   98   86 1055  100

  14   15   16   17   18   19   20
 236   53  302   20   89   10   33
```

```
table(GSS2016$paeduc)
   0    1    2    3    4    5    6    7    8    9   10   11   12   13   14   15   16
  43    8   11   40   26   24   80   32  157   60   74   65  774   72  147   35  274

  17   18   19   20
  28   67   16   59
```

```
table(GSS2016$tvhours)
   0    1    2    3    4    5    6    7    8    9   10   11   12   13   14   15   16
 162  370  486  297  221  113   92   22   46    6   23    1   25    1    1    4    2

  18   20   24
   1    5    5
```

```
table(GSS2016$sibs)
   0    1    2    3    4    5    6    7    8    9   10   11   12   13   14   15   16
 130  550  596  452  319  206  161  128   90   72   39   39   27   23    7    2    3

  17   18   20   21   22   23   27   28   43
   4    3    2    3    2    1    1    1    1
```

```
table(GSS2016$wwwhr)

  0    1    2    3    4    5    6    7    8    9   10   11   12   13   14   15   16
137  143  115   92   73  111   44   76   51    5  159    3   34    2   49   97    5

 17   18   20   21   24   25   27   28   30   33   34   35   36   37   38   40   42
  3    3  117   23   12   37    2    9   42    1    1   16    3    1    1   34    2

 43   45   47   48   49   50   56   60   65   70   72   75   80   84   85   86   90
  1    3    1    3    1   20    3   13    1    8    3    1   11    2    1    1    3

100  120  132  140  168
  2    3    1    1    1
```

Once you are confident the data have been "cleaned" (e.g., checked for outliers, missing values, and recoded), you can assess multicollinearity between the variables with a correlation matrix. The first step is to create a data frame object in the workspace that contains each of the relevant variables, which we can name cm (correlation matrix) for simplicity. However, in practice you should choose a more descriptive name for objects you create so that you can tell the difference between them later.

```
cm<-GSS2016[, c("educ" , "maeduc" , "paeduc" , "tvhours" ,
"sibs" , "wwwhr")]
```

FIGURE 11.1 ● SCREENSHOT OF THE ENVIRONMENT WINDOW SHOWING THE DATA FRAME cm THAT WAS CREATED

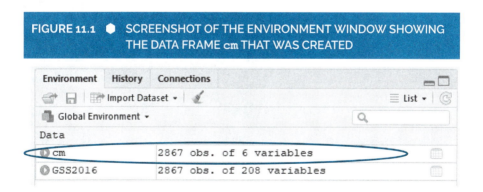

```
head(cm, 10) #Review the first ten rows of the new data frame.
```

Output: First 10 participants' responses for the selected variables in data frame `cm`.

	educ	maeduc	paeduc	tvhours	sibs	wwwhr
1	16	13	18	1	2	15
2	12	12	8	1	3	5
3	16	8	12	NA	3	NA
4	12	12	NA	1	3	7
5	18	12	16	NA	2	NA
6	14	12	11	1	2	2
7	14	12	12	2	2	5
8	11	5	5	NA	6	NA
9	12	8	8	2	5	7
10	14	15	14	NA	1	NA

```
rcorr(as.matrix(cm))
```

Output: Outputs for correlation matrix of `educ`, `maeduc`, `paeduc`, `tv hours`, `sibs`, and `wwwhr` for the *r*-coefficient, the count (*N*), and the *p*-values.

	educ	maeduc	paeduc	tvhours	sibs	wwwhr
educ	1.00	0.38	0.42	-0.21	-0.28	0.07
maeduc	0.38	1.00	0.69	-0.14	-0.32	0.13
paeduc	0.42	0.69	1.00	-0.19	-0.34	0.08
tvhours	-0.21	-0.14	-0.19	1.00	0.09	0.01
sibs	-0.28	-0.32	-0.34	0.09	1.00	-0.03
wwwhr	0.07	0.13	0.08	0.01	-0.03	1.00

n

	educ	maeduc	paeduc	tvhours	sibs	wwwhr
educ	2858	2577	2089	1880	2855	1586
maeduc	2577	2581	1953	1705	2579	1468
paeduc	2089	1953	2092	1370	2090	1180
tvhours	1880	1705	1370	1883	1880	1586
sibs	2855	2579	2090	1880	2862	1584
wwwhr	1586	1468	1180	1586	1584	1587

P

	educ	maeduc	paeduc	tvhours	sibs	wwwhr
educ		0.0000	0.0000	0.0000	0.0000	0.0030
maeduc	0.0000		0.0000	0.0000	0.0000	0.0000
paeduc	0.0000	0.0000		0.0000	0.0000	0.0036
tvhours	0.0000	0.0000	0.0000		0.0001	0.7263
sibs	0.0000	0.0000	0.0000	0.0001		0.2161
wwhr	0.0030	0.0000	0.0036	0.7263	0.2161	

The output provides Pearson correlation coefficients and p-values for all pairs of variables in the correlation matrix. Based on the p-values, there is not a statistically significant relationship between hours spent on the Internet and hours spent watching ($p = .726$). The relationship between hours spent on the Internet and number of siblings is also not statistically significant ($p = .216$). However, the remainder of the relationships are statistically significant, with p-values below the conventional alpha level of .05.

Next, review the correlation coefficients (r-values) found in the top section of the output. If there are relationships with a correlation coefficient over .7, we run the risk of multicollinearity and should remove one or more of the variables from the regression model.

```
cmED<-rcorr(as.matrix(cm))  # Data frame of extracted data for the
plot.
cmED$r  # Extract the correlation coefficients.
cmED$P # Extract p-values.
```

> **Tip:** In correlation matrices, coefficients with a value of 1.0 indicate that there is a perfect correlation—this almost always means that a variable is correlated with itself.

The first correlation matrix plot we saw in Chapter 10 said `type ="upper"` in the script, and we saw that a plot was formed consisting of the upper half of the matrix. Now, the scripts specify `type="full"` and `type="lower"`, and plots are formed with both halves (full) or with the lower half of the matrix, respectively. The color scheme for the plot in Chapter 10 was the default color scheme, but with this first plot (Figure 11.2), we have changed the color scheme of the data to a two-color black and white with a plot background of `lightblue`. Figure 11.3 combines five different shades of blue and specifies a background color of `lightgrey`.

The sizes of the circles in the correlation matrices represent the magnitude of the correlation coefficient; the higher the r-value, the larger the circle. All three plots have colors that indicate whether the relationship is positive or negative. Additionally, all three plots have a circle if the correlation is statistically significant at the .05 level and an empty space if it is not.

```
corrplot(cmED$r, type="full", order="hclust", tl.col = "black",
         col = c("black", "white"), bg = "lightblue",
         p.mat = cmED$P, sig.level = 0.05, insig="blank")
```

```
# Combine five shades of blue to create your own color palette of blues for next
matrix.
# Change type to "lower" and background (bg =) to light grey.
```

```
corrplot(cmED$r, type="lower", order="hclust", tl.col = "black",
         col = c("aliceblue", "lightblue", "cornflowerblue", "blue",
         "darkblue"), bg = "lightgrey", p.mat = cmED$P, sig.
         level = 0.05, insig="blank")
```

FIGURE 11.2 ● GRAPHIC OF THE CORRELATION MATRIX OF educ, maeduc, paeduc, tvhours, sibs, AND wwwhr

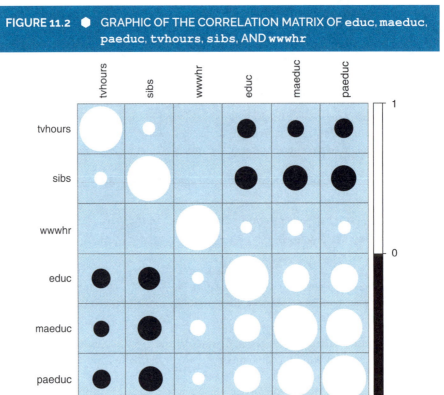

Between the output (the highlighted *r*-value of .69) and the plots, there is evidence of borderline multicollinearity between the mother's highest year of school completed and the father's highest year of school completed. In order to reduce the risk of producing unreliable estimates in our regression model, we should make some changes to the model. For example, we could remove one of the parent's highest years of school completed, take the average of the two, or compute a new variable based on the sum of mothers' *and* fathers' education, just as we did in Chapter 2. For this exercise we will do the latter. However, keep in mind that new issues might arise regarding missing data if either the mother's or father's education is missing.

Compute the new variable using the following script:

```
GSS2016$mpeduc<-(GSS2016$maeduc+GSS2016$paeduc)
table(GSS2016$mpeduc)
```

Create a new data frame object (cm2 instead of cm) and run a correlation matrix:

```
cm2<-GSS2016[, c("educ", "mpeduc" , "tvhours" , "sibs" , "wwwhr")]
rcorr(as.matrix(cm2))
```

FIGURE 11.3 ⬡ **SECOND GRAPHIC OF SAME CORRELATION MATRIX WITH DIFFERENT AESTHETICS**

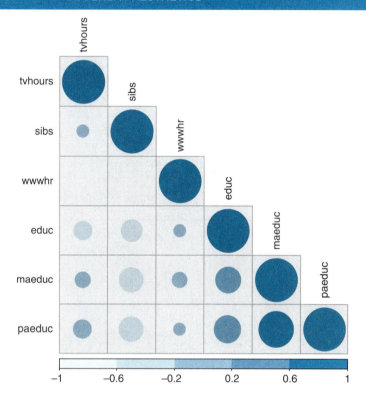

Output: Outputs for correlation matrix of educ, mpeduc, tv hours, sibs, and wwwhr for the *r*-coefficient, the count (*N*), and the *p*-values.

	educ	mpeduc	tvhours	sibs	wwwhr
educ	1.00	0.45	-0.21	-0.28	0.07
mpeduc	0.45	1.00	-0.20	-0.39	0.12
tvhours	-0.21	-0.20	1.00	0.09	0.01
sibs	-0.28	-0.39	0.09	1.00	-0.03
wwwhr	0.07	0.12	0.01	-0.03	1.00

n

	educ	mpeduc	tvhours	sibs	wwwhr
educ	2858	1950	1880	2855	1586
mpeduc	1950	1953	1285	1951	1114
tvhours	1880	1285	1883	1880	1586
sibs	2855	1951	1880	2862	1584
wwwhr	1586	1114	1586	1584	1587

```
P
            educ    mpeduc  tvhours   sibs     wwwhr
educ                0.0000  0.0000   0.0000   0.0030
mpeduc   0.0000             0.0000   0.0000   0.0000
tvhours  0.0000   0.0000             0.0001   0.7263
sibs     0.0000   0.0000   0.0001             0.2161
wwwhr    0.0030   0.0000   0.7263   0.2161
```

Create a new data frame object for the extracted *p*-values and *r*-values (cm2ED instead of cmED). With this information, create plots that include the new variable, mpeduc, instead of the two variables maeduc and paeduc (Figure 11.4).

```
cm2ED<-rcorr(as.matrix(cm2))  # Data frame of extracted data for the
plot.
cm2ED$r  # Extract the correlation coefficients.
cm2ED$P  # Extract p-values.

corrplot(cm2ED$r, type="full", order="hclust", tl.col = "black",
        col = c("black", "white"), bg = "lightblue",
        p.mat = cmED$P, sig.level = 0.05, insig="blank")

corrplot(cm2ED$r, type="lower", order="hclust", col = tl.col = "black",
        col = c("aliceblue", "lightblue", "cornflowerblue",
        "blue", "darkblue"), bg = "lightgrey", p.mat = cmED$P,
        sig.level = 0.05, insig="blank")
```

Based on the revised correlation matrix, using the sum of both parents' education creates fewer problems in the multiple regression model. Now, the regression model can be run. Below, we present the differences in code for the regression model in Chapter 10 and the multiple regression model:

Bivariate Regression (Chapter 10): `dataname <- lm(DV~IV)`

Multiple Regression (Chapter 11):   `dataname <- lm(DV~IV1 + IV2 + IV3 + IV4 …)`

> **Tip:** The tilde (~) means the DV is "a function of" or "predicted by" everything that follows it.

The best way to run a linear regression in R/RStudio, regardless of the type, is to save the regression as a new object in the workspace by assigning it a name. For this example, we run the same multiple regression twice. The first has script using the data$variable format (reg1) and the second has the variables without the data$ preceding them and a call for the data= at the end of all variables (reg2) (see Figure 11.5).

FIGURE 11.4 ⬡ PLOTS OF THE MATRIX WITH THE VARIABLE mpeduc INSTEAD OF maeduc AND paeduc

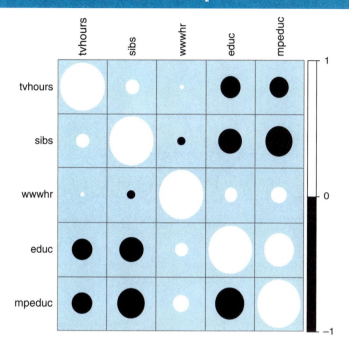

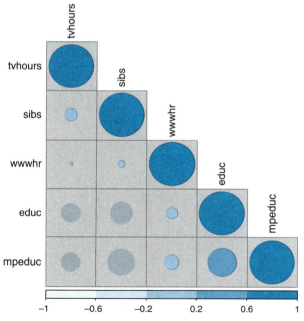

FIGURE 11.5 ● SCREENSHOT OF reg1 AND reg2

Environment	History	Connections		
Import Dataset ▾				List ▾
Global Environment ▾				
Data				
cm		2867 obs. of 6 variables		
cm2		2867 obs. of 5 variables		
cm2ED		List of 3		
cmED		List of 3		
GSS2016		2867 obs. of 210 variables		
mED		List of 3		
newOMIT		13 obs. of 4 variables		
NOT		16 obs. of 7 variables		
reg1		Large lm (13 elements, 522.4 Kb)		
reg2		Large lm (13 elements, 512.6 Kb)		
Values				
colscheme		chr [1:8] "#660000" "red" "#FF9900" "FFF333" "#66FF33" ...		

After choosing the linear model function (lm), the first variable is the predicted outcome variable (the dependent variable) followed by a tilde (~) and the independent variables separated by a plus sign (+) instead of a comma. Save the regression results as an object and call on the object in order to view the results.

```
reg1<-lm(cm2$educ~ cm2$mpeduc + cm2$tvhours + cm2$sibs +
cm2$wwwhr) # With the data name attached to each variable.
```

Tip: Writing the code with the dataset name attached to each individual variable would be a useful approach when pulling data from different sources/datasets.

```
reg2<-lm(educ~ mpeduc + tvhours + sibs + wwwhr, data = cm2)
# Code with data for all variables at the end.

reg1  # Open the results for the linear model.
reg2
```

Output: Linear regression model for multiple regression reg1.

```
Call:
lm(formula = cm2$educ ~ cm2$mpeduc + cm2$tvhours + cm2$sibs +
    cm2$wwwhr)

Coefficients:
 (Intercept)  cm2$mpeduc   cm2$tvhours   cm2$sibs   cm2$wwwhr
   12.286786    0.119117     -0.168274  -0.136684    0.007353
```

Output: Linear regression model for multiple regression reg2.

```
Call:
lm(formula = educ ~ mpeduc + tvhours + sibs + wwwhr, data = cm2)

Coefficients:
(Intercept)        mpeduc          tvhours          sibs            wwwhr
  12.286786       0.119117       -0.168274       -0.136684        0.007353
```

Since the results are exactly the same (only the code was different), use the **reg1** script for the remainder of this example.

```
summary(reg1)
```

Output: Summary of multiple linear regression results for prediction on educ.

```
Call:
lm(formula = cm2$educ ~ cm2$mpeduc + cm2$tvhours + cm2$sibs +
     cm2$wwwhr)    # Formula

Residuals:
   Min        1Q     Median        3Q       Max
-10.399    -1.912    -0.100     1.444     9.251
```

                                      The constant (or intercept)
```
Coefficients:
              Estimate     Std.Error    t value      Pr(>|t|)
(Intercept)  12.286786(b₀)  0.374872    32.776      < 2e-16  ***
cm2$mpeduc    0.119117(b₁)  0.012634     9.428      < 2e-16  ***
cm2$tvhours  -0.168274(b₂)  0.033285    -5.056      5.02e-07 ***
cm2$sibs     -0.136684(b₃)  0.028171    -4.852      1.40e-06 ***
cm2$wwwhr     0.007353(b₄)  0.004886     1.505        0.133
---
Signif. codes:   0 '***' 0.001 '**' 0.01 '*' 0.05 '.' 0.1 ' ' 1

Residual standard error: 2.478 on 1108 degrees of freedom
   (1754 observations deleted due to missingness)
Multiple R-squared:  0.1559,     Adjusted R-squared:  0.1528
F-statistic: 51.15 on 4 and 1108 DF,   p-value: < 2.2e-16
```

The p-values indicate that the first 3 predictor variables—parents' education, tv hours, and siblings—are significant; however, hours on the Internet (wwwhr) is not a statistically significant predictor of individuals' highest level of education ($p = .133$).

THE MULTIPLE REGRESSION EQUATION

$$\hat{Y}_i = b_0 + b_1(X_1) + b_2(X_2) + b_3(X_3) + b_4(X_4)$$

$\hat{Y}_i$ = Y-hat – Predicted value of Y (DV) for observation i

b_0 = Estimate of the intercept (or constant) of the regression line

b_1 = Estimate of the slope of regression line for the first IV

b_2 = Estimate of the slope of regression line for the second IV

b_3 = Estimate of the slope of regression line for the third IV

b_4 = Estimate of the slope of regression line for the fourth IV

X_1 = Value of the first IV explaining change in Y

X_2 = Value of the second IV explaining change in Y

X_3 = Value of the third IV explaining change in Y

X_4 = Value of the fourth IV explaining change in Y

The first three predictor (IV) variables: parental highest years of school completed (mpeduc), number of hours of television watched per day (tvhours), and number of siblings (sibs) were all statistically significant predictors of individuals' education at the .001 level. The results indicate that the statistically significant relationships between tvhours and educ and between sibs and educ are both negative. This means the two variables operate in opposite directions. So, more years of education are associated with fewer hours of TV per day and vice-versa. Similarly, having more siblings is significantly associated with fewer years of education. The relationship between the parental education and the participant education is a positive one, meaning they both operate in the same direction. That is, individuals with more educated parents have a higher education, on average, than those with less educated parents.

Considering the model as a whole, the value for the adjusted R^2 (.153) indicates that with this model, we can predict roughly 16% of the variation in participants' highest year of school completed (educ). However, one thing we have not considered in this model is the potential for interaction effects.

> **Write-up**: A multiple linear regression tested the association between individuals' highest years of education and their parents' education, controlling for number of hours spent watching TV, number of siblings, and number of hours spent using the Internet. The results point to a significant regression equation ($F(4, 1108) = 51.15$, $p < .001$), with an R^2 of .156. Participants' predicted highest year of education completed is equal to 12.29 years + .12 (mpeduc) + (-.17)(tvhours) + (-.14)(sibs) + .007 (wwwhr). Parents' education was significantly and positively associated with participants' education ($p < .001$) when controlling for number of hours spent watching TV, using the Internet, and number of siblings. Thus, we show support for our hypothesis.

INTERACTION EFFECTS AND INTERPRETATION

Interaction effects occur when the effect of an independent variable on the outcome depends on the value of a different independent variable. Consider a regression with plant size (DV) as the outcome when testing for the effect of hours of sunlight (IV_1) and amount of water (IV_2). Also included in the regression model will be the interaction term sunlight*water (IV_3).

$$\text{Plant growth}^\wedge = \text{constant} + X_1(\text{sunlight}) + X_2(\text{water}) + X_3(\text{sunlight*water})$$

If the interaction term X_3 is significant, it identifies a relationship where the coefficient (or effect) of IV_2 would vary depending upon the value of IV_1 or vice-versa. A significant interaction will inform us that these relationship(s) exist but the magnitude and direction must be interpreted based on the model coefficients.

Considering the previous example, an interaction effect between the watering and sunlight may be such that more sunlight increases growth of plants that were watered an average amount, but has no effect on growth of plants that were over- or underwatered. If you fit a model that did not include the interaction term, you might fail to detect any effect of sunlight on plant growth because it only occurs for plants with average water treatment. Considering the two variables together (the interaction term) elicits results that offer a more in-depth consideration of the interrelationships in the regression model.

Below, we add interaction terms to the original regression example in order to determine if there are interaction effects on the outcome variable (educ). We will focus our interpretation on the interactions between parental education and the control variables. Create the interaction term by using the multiplication (*) character between the two variables in the interaction.

```
reg3<-lm(formula = educ ~ mpeduc + tvhours + sibs + mpeduc *
tvhours + mpeduc * sibs + tvhours * sibs, data = cm2) # The
```
interaction objects are added to the original call.

```
reg3
```

Output: Linear regression model for multiple regression reg3, including interaction effects.

```
Call:
lm(formula = educ ~ mpeduc + tvhours + sibs + mpeduc * tvhours +
    mpeduc * sibs + tvhours * sibs, data = cm2)
Coefficients:
    (Intercept)            mpeduc              tvhours             sibs
       11.855057           0.137335           -0.083926        -0.280517
  mpeduc:tvhours      mpeduc:sibs         tvhours:sibs
      -0.005050           0.004473            0.015631
```

```
summary(reg3)
```

Output: Summary of multiple linear regression results for prediction on `educ`.

```
Call:
lm(formula = educ ~ mpeduc + tvhours + sibs + mpeduc * tvhours +
    mpeduc * sibs + tvhours * sibs, data = cm2)

Residuals:
    Min       1Q    Median       3Q      Max
-10.3303  -1.8606   -0.1208   1.5231  10.5561
```

The constant (or intercept)

The p-values

```
Coefficients:
                  Estimate   Std. Error   t value   Pr(>|t|)
(Intercept)      11.855057    0.564152    21.014    < 2e-16  ***
mpeduc            0.137335    0.020933     6.561    7.77e-11 ***
tvhours          -0.083926    0.086305    -0.972    0.331015
sibs             -0.280517    0.079779    -3.516    0.000453 ***
mpeduc:tvhours   -0.005050    0.003179    -1.588    0.112479
mpeduc:sibs       0.004473    0.003180     1.407    0.159771
tvhours:sibs      0.015631    0.007190     2.174    0.029898 *
```

The interactions

```
---
Signif. codes:  0 '***' 0.001 '**' 0.01 '*' 0.05 '.' 0.1 ' ' 1

Residual standard error: 2.54 on 1275 degrees of freedom
  (1585 observations deleted due to missingness)
```
Multiple R-squared: 0.2105,   Adjusted R-squared: 0.2068
F-statistic: 56.67 on 6 and 1275 DF, p-value: < 2.2e-16

When it comes to interpreting an output for a regression that includes interaction effects, we treat the interaction terms just as we would the original variables, such that a *p*-value below the alpha (typically .05) indicates the interaction effect is significant. The value of the coefficient, however, is not as easy to interpret as a main effect. The value of the interaction term coefficient is the amount of change in the DV for each unit of the first IV multiplied by a unit of the second IV. If we think back to the example of plant growth, the interaction coefficient is water multiplied by sunlight. The interaction coefficient reflects the amount of change in the DV due to the specific relationship between the two IVs.

If you are interested in more information and diagnostic details of the regression, you can produce confidence intervals for the coefficients (`confint`) and residuals for the regression (`resid`). It is also possible to ensure that the residuals are distributed normally with a histogram. These additional, more advanced, procedures are shown below:

```
confint(reg3)
```

Output: Confidence intervals for the coefficients of the multiple linear regression (`reg3`).

	2.5 %	97.5 %
(Intercept)	10.748288863	12.961825279
mpeduc	0.096268012	0.178401784
tvhours	-0.253241143	0.085388594
sibs	-0.437029904	-0.124003449
mpeduc:tvhours	-0.011287268	0.001187779
mpeduc:sibs	-0.001765385	0.010711574
tvhours:sibs	0.001524722	0.029737523

```
resid(reg3)  # Calling for the residuals from the multiple regression.
hist (resid(reg3))  # Getting a histogram of residuals. ## This will help
to check for normal distribution of residuals.
```

Output: The residuals from the regression equation `reg3`.

1	2	6	7	9
0.380468694	-1.890562874	-0.489680566	-0.457054013	-0.834546467
11	19	20	21	28
-2.466026866	3.086625406	-2.513219519	-2.409465159	-1.151094623
29	31	35	37	43
2.957241045	-2.457054013	-2.740854342	1.542945987	0.652392757
47	48	51	52	53
1.826746317	0.454835816	-0.156025676	-2.598954177	-2.440391388
55	56	57	58	64
1.714717424	1.137628815	1.171219831	1.181130007	-0.273043778
71	72	75	77	78

```
hist (resid(reg3), col="cornflowerblue")  # Added the color
"cornflowerblue" to the script for the fill.
```

Output: Histogram of the residuals for `reg3`.

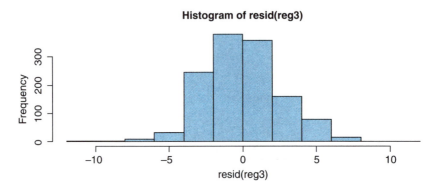

Histogram of resid(reg3)

Earlier in the chapter, we generated a correlation matrix to check for multicollinearity before running our multiple regression. An additional way of assessing whether or not there are issues with multicollinearity is by checking variance inflation factors (VIF). The VIF identifies the strength of multicollinearity that exists within the model for each variable. When checking for VIF, be sure to remove the interaction terms, otherwise there will likely be multicollinearity because the variables are in there multiple times—as direct effects and interactions. A value of 1 represents that there is no evidence of multicollinearity between the variables. As the value increases, the correlation among the independent variables increases as does the risk for multicollinearity. An average VIF value of 10 or above indicates that there might be issues with multicollinearity.

`vif(reg1)` # Checking the VIF on the regression model without the interaction terms.

Output: VIF values for the predictor (independent) variables in the regression (`reg1`).

cm2$mpeduc	cm2$tvhours	cm2$sibs	cm2$wwwhr
1.129923	1.020422	1.092505	1.015755

Upon viewing the histogram, it appears there is a normal distribution for the residuals, which indicates that this assumption was not violated.

In the interaction model, the direct effect for parents' highest year of education is still significantly and positively associated with participant's education level ($p < .001$) when controlling for all other variables. The main effect from hours spent watching television each day was no longer a significant predictor ($p = .133$). Neither the interaction between parental education and hours watching TV nor the interaction between parental education and siblings had a significant interaction effect on highest year of education completed; however, the interaction between number of hours of TV watched and the number of siblings did have a significant impact on the highest years of school completed by the participant ($p < .05$).

Write-Up: A multiple linear regression tested whether there was a significant relationship between individuals' years of completed education (educ) and their parents' education (mpeduc) while controlling for number of hours spent watching TV (tvhours), number of siblings (sibs), and number of hours spent on the Internet (wwwhr). The results point to a significant regression equation: $F(6, 1275) = 56.67$, $p < .001$ with an R^2 of .2105. Thus, participants predicted highest grade of school completed is equal to $11.86 + .137$ (mpeduc) $- .083$ (tvhours) $- .281$ (sibs), $- .005$ (mpeduc:tvhours) $+ .004$ (mpeduc:sibs) $+ .015$ (tvhours:sibs). Moreover, the interaction between number of siblings and number of TV hours (tvhours:sibs) was significant ($p = .03$). This changes the interpretation of the main effect from number of siblings to now indicate that the effect of siblings differs depending on the number of hours of TV watched.

This regression model also identifies a main effect from parental education (mpeduc) on participant education (educ) with a coefficient of .014 years increase in participants' education for each year increase in parental education. An adjusted R^2 of .201 indicates that with this model, we can predict roughly 20% of the variation in participants' highest year of school completed (educ).

We can compare the first regression model run without the interaction terms (Adj. $R^2 = .153$) and the second model run which included the interaction terms (Adj. $R^2 = .201$). Because the second model has a higher R^2, we can determine that adding the interaction terms led to an improvement in the model fit.

LOGISTIC REGRESSION

The basis of multiple regression is that the dependent variable is based on continuous (interval/ratio) data. In the event that we have a binary, or dichotomous, dependent variable we instead use a logistic regression, which was introduced in the last chapter. The next example builds on the last chapter by adding an additional (control) variable so that the logistic regression becomes a multivariate model. The following multiple *logistic* regression examines whether gender (sex) and/or age (age) are linked to homeownership (dwelown). First, recode the variable dwelown so that the non-values are recoded as NA. Then, recode the variable dwelown into a binary/dichotomous variable (dwelBi) with 0 = "pays rent and other" and 1 = "owns or is buying". Recode the variable sex into a 0/1 binary variable (sexrec)—with 0 the code for "Female" and 1 the code for "Male"—originally, male was 1 and female was 2.

> **Tip:** Recoding dichotomous variable to 0/1 values often helps with interpretation of the results.

```
GSS2016$dwelBi[GSS2016$dwelown==8]=NA
GSS2016$dwelBi[GSS2016$dwelown==9]=NA
GSS2016$dwelBi[GSS2016$dwelown==0]=NA  # Remove missing values
from dwelown.
```

```
GSS2016$dwelBi[GSS2016$dwelown==1]=1
GSS2016$dwelBi[GSS2016$dwelown==2]=0
GSS2016$dwelBi[GSS2016$dwelown==3]=0 # Recode dwelown into binary
```
variable (0,1) where own = 1 and does not own = 0.

```
table(GSS2016$dwelown)
table(GSS2016$dwelBi)
```

Output: Frequencies for original variable of `dwelown`.

0	1	2	3	9
981	1127	724	30	5

```
table(GSS2016$dwelBi)
```

Output: Frequencies for the new binary variable of `dwel`.

0	1
754	1127

Based on the output above, the original `dwelown` had 981 responses that were coded as zero. In this case, the zero for `dwelown` represented "not applicable". We changed these zero codes to NA along with five responses that were marked "no answer". Instead, codes 2 (pays rent) and 3 (other) were recoded to zero in the new variable, `dwelBi`, leading to 754 codes marked as zero. Thus, we created a binary (0 and 1) variable with 0 for "does not own" and 1 for "owns or is buying".

> **Tip:** When creating any binary variable (i.e., a dichotomous variable with codes 0 and 1), be sure to clear out the original 0s prior to recoding other values to 0. Otherwise, non-missing information will be collapsed into the same category as missing information.

Recode the variable for gender in order to remove non-values and change the codes from 1 and 2 to 1 and 0. This can be done by changing the code of 2 for female to a 0 and leaving the male code of 1 as it already is. Then, recode the non-values for the age variable.

```
table(GSS2016$sex)
GSS2016$sexrec[GSS2016$sex==1]=1
GSS2016$sexrec[GSS2016$sex==2]=0
table(GSS2016$sexrec) # Recode sex into a newly recoded variable
```
sexrec and change the code for female from 2 to 0.

Output: Frequencies for original variable of sex.

```
     1         2
  1276      1591
```

Output: Frequencies for the new binary variable of sexrec.

```
     0         1
  1591      1276
```

```
table(GSS2016$age)
GSS2016$age[GSS2016$age==99]=NA
table(GSS2016$age)
```

Run a general linear model for a binomial outcome variable and name the model LogistRegresA followed by a summary call for the model.

```
LogistRegresA<-glm(formula = dwelBi~sexrec + age, data = GSS2016,
       family = "binomial")
```

```
summary(LogistRegresA)
```

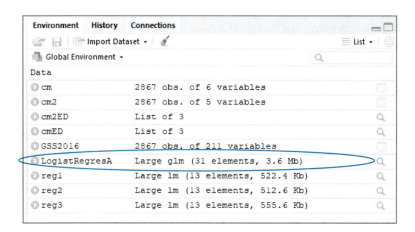

Output: Summary of the binary logistic regression (`LogistRegresA`).

```
Call:
glm(formula = dwelBi ~ sexrec + age, family = "binomial",
data = GSS2016)

Deviance Residuals:
    Min      1Q   Median      3Q     Max
-2.0811 -1.1330   0.7147  0.9760  1.5352

Coefficients:
              Estimate    Std. Error   z value     Pr(>|z|)
(Intercept)  -1.445179     0.152640    -9.468     < 2e-16 ***
sexrec        0.350688     0.099746     3.516     0.000438 ***
age           0.035261     0.002898    12.167     < 2e-16 ***
---
Signif. codes:  0 '***' 0.001 '**' 0.01 '*' 0.05 '.' 0.1 ' ' 1
(Dispersion parameter for binomial family taken to be 1)
    Null deviance: 2529.1  on 1876  degrees of freedom
Residual deviance: 2355.0  on 1874  degrees of freedom
    (990 observations deleted due to missingness)
AIC: 2361
Number of Fisher Scoring iterations: 4
```

INTERPRETATION AND PRESENTATION OF LOGISTIC REGRESSION RESULTS

The variables age and sex are both significantly associated with the outcome, homeownership. However, the output above gives the coefficient estimates in a log-likelihood scale. It is often useful to transform the coefficients to a more interpretable metric, the odds ratio. We do this by using the exponential function (`exp`) call.

```
exp(LogistRegresA$coefficients)
```

Output: Transforming coefficients from log-likelihood to likelihood scale: the odds ratio.

```
(Intercept)     sexrec         age
  0.2357039   1.4200437   1.0358898      <-log-likelihood
                                         estimates transformed
                                         into odds ratios
```

```
exp(confint(LogistRegresA))
```

Output: The 95% confidence intervals for the OR.

	2.5%	97.5%
(Intercept)	0.1743598	0.3172524
sexrec	1.1683869	1.7275893
age	1.0300782	1.0418514

An odds ratio (OR) determines or explains the relationship between two events. It is the likelihood that an event will occur given a particular "exposure" or outcome. The closer to 1 that an OR is, the more independent the two variables are from each other. When an OR is greater than 1, this means an increase in the odds of occurrence when the predictor variable is present. And when the OR is negative, this indicates a decrease in the odds of occurrence when the predictor variable is present.

The coefficient for gender (`sexrec`) is positive, indicating that there is a greater likelihood of owning a home among males.

The logistic regression equation can be written as follows:

$$\ln[Y / (1-Y)] = a + b_1X_1 + b_2X_2]$$
$$\ln[Y / (1-Y)] = 1.45 + .35(\text{sex}) + .04(\text{age})]$$

Write-Up: We examined whether gender (male, female) or age was associated with homeownership using a logistic regression. Homeownership is the dependent binary variable, coded 0 for "does not own" and 1 for "owns or is buying." Gender is a binary variable coded 0 for female and 1 for male. Age is a continuous variable in units of years. The results indicate that men are about 40% more likely than women to be homeowners (OR = 1.42, p = .001). Older individuals are also somewhat more likely to own a home than younger individuals in the sample (OR = 1.04, p < .001).

CONCLUSION

In addition to multiple linear and logistic regression, this chapter briefly discussed interaction effects and how to produce the interaction terms in multiple regression models. We also explored how to make dummy variables for running logistic regressions with a binary outcome variable. There are many more regressions that RStudio is capable of performing. Be sure to look to the Internet as a resource for additional R packages and script for different analyses you can practice on your data.

Exercises

1. Recode the variables for respondent's 2016 income (`rincom16`), highest grade completed for education (`educ`), and average number of hours of television watched per day (`tvhours`) to remove all of the non-value answers.

   A. Use the GSS Codebook to determine what values (codes) represent the attributes that need to be recoded.

   B. Be sure to run a table of the variable before and after to check that you have recoded properly.

2. Generate a correlation matrix to determine if there are significant relationships between the variables. Produce a correlation matrix plot to give a visual depiction of the r-coefficient value results. (**Note**: Be sure to check for potential multicollinearity—r-values of .7 or above).

3. Run a multiple regression to determine if education level, number of hours of television, or the interaction of education level and the number of hours watching television, is associated with individuals' annual income.

Supplementary Digital Content

Download datasets and R code at the companion website at https://study.sagepub.com/researchmethods/statistics/gillespie-r-for-statistics

ADVANCED REGRESSION TOPICS

ADVANCED REGRESSION TOPICS

In this chapter, we touch on some topics that may venture beyond the scope of what one might need for basic or intermediate statistical analyses. We do not provide much in-depth theoretical or conceptual background for the procedures we cover; rather, this chapter is for those who would like to know how to perform additional, more advanced statistical functions in RStudio.

One issue that researchers sometimes encounter is skewed data. This occurs when continuous data are not distributed evenly around a measure of central tendency—instead, they are predominant in one direction or another. A positive, or right, skew occurs when the tail is long on the right side and the data are concentrated on the left. A negative, or left, skew occurs when the tail is spread out on the left side, with the data concentrated primarily on the right side (Figure 12.1).

Many of the most common statistical procedures are rooted in assumptions that the data are distributed normally. When data are skewed, researchers must perform data transformations, or calculations, that bring the distribution closer to normal. Therefore, when you have an extremely skewed distribution, the next step is to decide the best way to transform the data. The most common data transformations are changing raw data into z-scores; scaling data; or using polynomials or logarithms to transform data.

The next several examples use the variable sei10 to perform some common transformations on data that are not normally distributed. The GSS variable sei10 is a socioeconomic index comprised of several measures, including income, occupation, and education.

As discussed in Chapter 3, researchers use statistical metrics to assess the normality of given distributions. These values also provide some indication about the direction of a nonnormal variable distribution. The value for skewness indicates the distribution's symmetry, with the baseline symmetry of a normal distribution represented as zero. When interpreting the coefficient for skewness, any deviation from zero describes the direction and magnitude of asymmetry, or skewness. If the value of skewness is positive, then the distribution is positively skewed; if the value is negative, then the data are negatively skewed.

FIGURE 12.1 ● DEPICTIONS OF SKEWNESS POSSIBILITIES

Positive skew (Right-skewed)

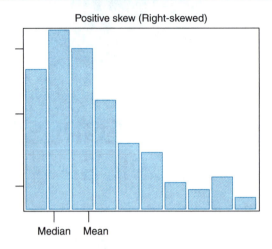

Negative skew (Left-skewed)

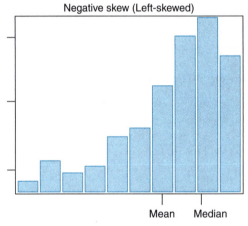

Closer to normal distribution

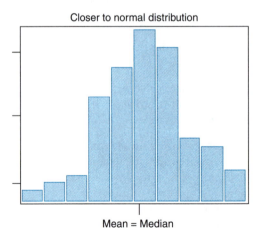

First, install the package **moments** and load it from the library. Then, recode the variable to remove the missing (i.e., not applicable) data and recode it as "NA." Confirm that the recode was successful and follow up with a call for the skewness using the **skewness()** command. It is often useful to create a histogram of the data to have a visual of the skewness (see Figure 12.2).

```
library(moments)
GSS2016$sei10[GSS2016$sei10=='-1']=NA # Recode the missing data to NA.

table(round(GSS2016$sei10, digits = 2)) # Check the recode (rounding numbers to 2 decimal places).
```

Output: Frequency table* of sei10 with the "-1" code removed after the recoding.

0	9	10.6	12.4	12.6	13.2	13.3	13.6	14	14.6	14.8	15.8	17
92	1	7	5	34	6	5	49	30	5	5	3	4
17.1	17.5	18.6	18.8	19.2	19.6	19.7	20	20.1	20.5	20.7	20.8	20.9
7	4	22	6	1	37	7	2	38	6	49	8	10

Table Note: This selection offers a visual representation of the output.

```
skewness(GSS2016$sei10)
```

```
[1] 0.2749163
```

```
hist(GSS2016$sei10, col="grey90")
```

FIGURE 12.2 ● HISTOGRAM OF sei10 DATA

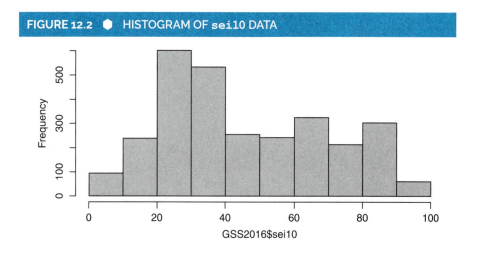

When generating histograms, it is possible to use the default configurations (Figure 12.2) or add arguments for the minimum, maximum, and number of breaks and/or add labels for the *x* axis, the *y* axis, and a main title (Figure 12.3).

```
hist(GSS2016$sei10, breaks=seq(min(GSS2016$sei10), max(GSS2016$sei10),
          length=18), col="grey70")
hist(GSS2016$sei10, breaks=seq(min(GSS2016$sei10),
          max(GSS2016$sei10),    length=30), xlab = "SEI10",
          ylab = "Frequency", main="Histogram of
          Frequencies of SEI10 Results", col="grey50")
```

Tip: Boxplots—discussed in Chapter 5—are also useful tools to assess skewness. When interpreting, the distribution is symmetrical if (a) the line representing the median is in the middle of the box and (b) the whiskers are the same size. However, a distribution is skewed if the median is closer to one side or if one whisker is longer than the other.

FIGURE 12.3 ●   HISTOGRAMS OF `sei10` DATA WITH BREAKS (18/30), COLOR CHANGES, AND APPROPRIATE LABELS

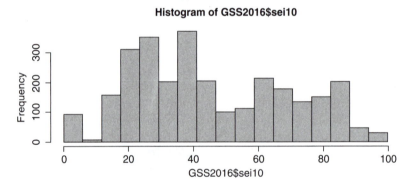

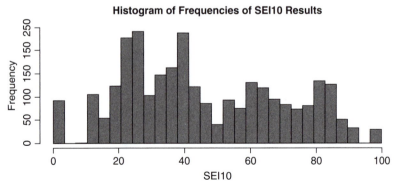

POLYNOMIALS

Even though (based on the output and graphs above) there does not seem to be a problem with skewness, we use the sei10 variable as an example to illustrate transforming the data–that is, taking the square, cube, and square root of the original variable (Figure 12.4).

```
# Transform sei10 data by squaring it, cubing it, and taking the square
root.
sei10squared<-(GSS2016$sei10^2)
sei10cubed<-(GSS2016$sei10^3)
sei10root<-sqrt(GSS2016$sei10)
```

FIGURE 12.4 ● SCREENSHOT OF NEWLY TRANSFORMED sei10 DATA WITH POLYNOMIALS

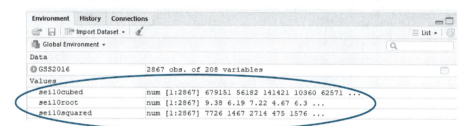

```
# Run the command for skewness for the original, and the three
transformed indices.
skewness(GSS2016$sei10)
skewness(sei10squared)
skewness(sei10cubed)
skewness(sei10root)
```

Outputs: Transformed sei10 data skewness (original, squared, cubed, square root).

```
skewness(GSS2016$sei10)
[1]  0.2749163

skewness(sei10squared)
[1]  0.934464

skewness(sei10cubed)
[1]  1.424207

skewness(sei10root)
[1]  -0.7388763
```

Histogram of SEI10

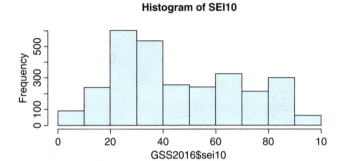

Histogram of SEI10 Squared

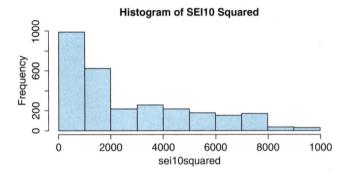

Histogram of SEI10 Cubed

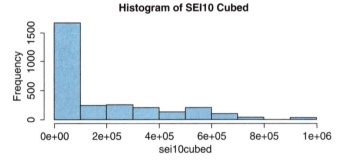

Histogram of Square Root of SEI10

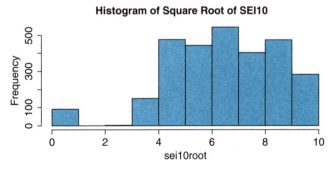

Histograms help illustrate these changes (Figure 12.5).

```
# Create histograms of original and polynomial transformed data.
hist(GSS2016$sei10, col="lightblue1", main = "Histogram of
SEI10")
hist(sei10squared, col="skyblue1", main = "Histogram of SEI10
Squared")
hist(sei10cubed, col=" skyblue3", main = "Histogram of SEI10
Cubed")
hist(sei10root, col=" skyblue4", main = "Histogram of Square
Root of SEI10")
```

Overall, polynomials and square roots transform the data and alter its distribution. However, after assessing the skewness and histograms, it seems that the original data were actually the least skewed. When using polynomials, the distribution of the data shift to the left. Therefore, these transformations are most helpful when the data are negatively skewed.

LOGARITHMS

Transforming data with logarithms can help when the data are widely distributed (i.e., overdistributed)—this means that the data have a spread that can be orders of magnitude wide. Logarithms help minimize the far-reaching tails. To illustrate the changes that transforming with logarithms can make, we again use the sei10 variable (Figure 12.6). Use the **log()** function:

```
sei10natlog<-log(GSS2016$sei10)  # Create new indices (variables) for
each log calculation.
sei10log2<-log2(GSS2016$sei10)
sei10log10<-log10(GSS2016$sei10)
```

FIGURE 12.6 ● SCREENSHOT OF TRANSFORMED sei10 DATA WITH LOGARITHMS

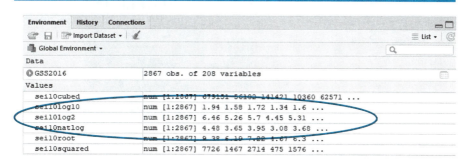

FIGURE 12.7 ● SCREENSHOTS OF TRANSFORMED `sei10` DATA WITH LOGARITHMS (ORIGINAL, NATURAL LOG, LOG2, LOG10).

Histogram of SEI10

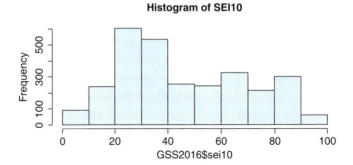

Histogram of SEI10 Natural Log

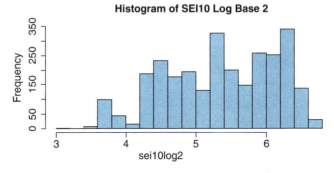

Histogram of SEI10 Log Base 2

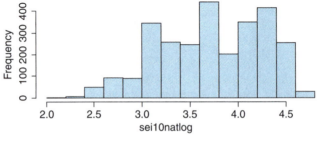

Histogram of Square Root of Log Base 10

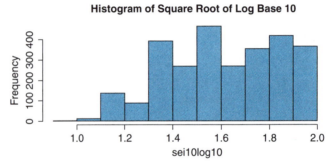

Histograms for each of the `sei10` log transformations (original, natural log, log$_2$, log$_{10}$).

```
hist(GSS2016$sei10, col="lightskyblue", main = "Histogram of
SEI10")

hist(sei10natlog, col="dodgerblue1", main = "Histogram of
SEI10 Natural Log")

hist(sei10log2, col="royalblue1", main = "Histogram of SEI10
Log Base 2")

hist(sei10log10, col = "blue2", main = "Histogram of
    Square Root of Log Base 10")
```

Based on the histograms, we see that the log transformations cause the data distribution to shift to the right. That is why log transformations are ideal for data that are positively skewed.

Other problems researchers encounter have to do with the statistical model. One such problem is dealing with multiple variables that are scaled very differently from one another. A second common issue researchers face is the problem of multicollinearity. Both topics are discussed in more detail here.

SCALING DATA

The **scale** command changes the scale of a variable without changing the distribution of the data. Researchers rescale a variable's values in order to make the scales more manageable with other measures in their statistical model (Figure 12.8). The following code rescales the variable `sei10` and rounds the values to two digits. To illustrate the change, the example also includes histograms for the original variable as well as the rescaled version.

```
sei10scale<-round(scale(GSS2016$sei10), digits=2)  # Create
sei10scale from sei10.
```

Run histograms and skewness for `sei10` and `sei10scale` variables.
```
hist(GSS2016$sei10, col="grey80", main = "Histogram of
SEI10")

hist(sei10scale, col="grey40", main = "Histogram of SEI10
Scaled")

skewness(GSS2016$sei10)

skewness(sei10scale)
```

FIGURE 12.8 ● SCREENSHOTS OF ORIGINAL AND SCALED `sei10` DATA

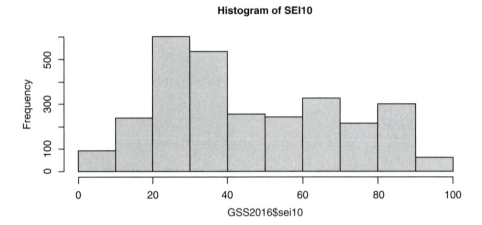

Histogram of SEI10

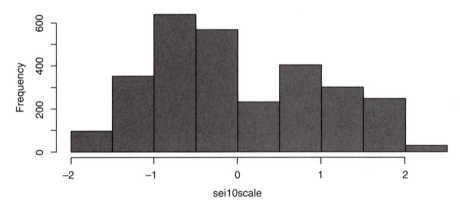

Histogram of SEI10 Scaled

Outputs: Results for **skewness** command for `sei10` and `sei10scale`.

skewness(GSS2016$sei10)
[1] 0.2749163

skewness(sei10scale)
[1] 0.2763263

The following screenshot is a comparison of the first few lines of `sei10scale` and `sei10` data values.

	sei10scale	sei10
1	1.75	87.9
2	-0.30	38.3
3	0.27	52.1
4	-0.98	21.8
5	-0.24	39.7
6	-0.04	44.6
7	1.45	80.7
8	-1.05	20.1
9	-1.05	20.1
10	-0.56	32.0

Based on the histogram and skewness results, it is clear that there has been no change to the overall data distribution. However, the *x* axis labels for the sei10scale variable (ranging from -2 to 2) show how the scale itself has changed.

MULTICOLLINEARITY

Multicollinearity occurs when the relationship(s) between variables is so strong that they should not be considered independent enough to both be run in a multiple regression. This is commonly assessed using a correlation matrix. The next example will examine the relationships among the following: general happiness (happy), income (income16), job satisfaction (satjob), financial status satisfaction (satfin), highest grade completed (educ), frequency of religious services (attend), political viewpoint (polviews), and frequency of sex (sexfreq).

As always, check the variables and recode any missing data to NA:

```
GSS2016$happy[GSS2016$happy==8]=NA
GSS2016$happy[GSS2016$happy==9]=NA
GSS2016$income16[GSS2016$income16==27]=NA
GSS2016$income16[GSS2016$income16==98]=NA
GSS2016$satjob[GSS2016$satjob==0]=NA
GSS2016$satjob[GSS2016$satjob==8]=NA
GSS2016$satjob[GSS2016$satjob==9]=NA
GSS2016$satfin[GSS2016$satfin==0]=NA
```

```
GSS2016$satfin[GSS2016$satfin==8]=NA
GSS2016$satfin[GSS2016$satfin==9]=NA
GSS2016$educ[GSS2016$educ==98]=NA
GSS2016$educ[GSS2016$educ==99]=NA
GSS2016$attend[GSS2016$attend==9]=NA
GSS2016$polviews[GSS2016$polviews==8]=NA
GSS2016$polviews[GSS2016$polviews==9]=NA
GSS2016$polviews[GSS2016$polviews==0]=NA
GSS2016$sexfreq[GSS2016$sexfreq==8]=NA
GSS2016$sexfreq[GSS2016$sexfreq==9]=NA
GSS2016$sexfreq[GSS2016$sexfreq=="-1"]=NA
```

Once the data have been recoded, run frequency tables to ensure the recoding was completed accurately. Then, create a new data frame object for the combined variables that will be in the correlation matrix. We need the **Hmisc** package loaded into the library in order to produce the correlation matrix:

```
library(Hmisc)

cm<-GSS2016[, c("income16","satjob", "satfin", "happy", "educ",
"attend", "sexfreq", "polviews")]
```

Once the results are produced, we can create a data frame for the correlation matrix. This will be used for creating a plot of the correlation matrix (Figure 12.9).

```
rcorr(as.matrix(cm2))
head(cm2,8)
```

Tip: It is always useful to check that recoded variables are appearing as you would expect.

Output: First eight rows of data for the selected variables in the correlation matrix.

	income16	satjob	satfin	happy	educ	attend	sexfreq	polviews
1	26	2	1	2	16	0	NA	4
2	19	1	3	2	12	0	2	2
3	21	NA	2	1	16	7	NA	6
4	26	1	1	2	12	6	NA	4
5	26	2	1	1	18	0	4	3
6	20	1	2	1	14	0	5	3
7	26	2	3	2	14	1	NA	3
8	16	1	2	1	11	5	NA	5

`CM2<-rcorr(as.matrix(cm2))` # Assign the correlation matrix to a data frame.

`CM2$r` # Extract the *r*– and *p*–values to be used in the correlation matrix plot.

`CM2$P`

FIGURE 12.9 ● SCREENSHOT OF NEW DATA FRAMES cm2 AND CM2 CREATED

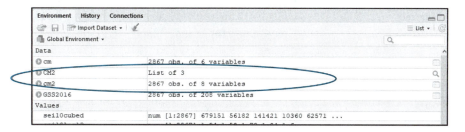

Output: Correlation matrix output including the *r*-coefficient, the count (*N*), and the *p*-values.

	income16	satjob	satfin	happy	educ	attend	sexfreq	polviews
income16	1.00	-0.16	-0.33	-0.28	0.37	0.00	0.15	-0.01
satjob	-0.16	1.00	0.26	0.28	-0.06	-0.10	0.00	-0.01
satfin	-0.33	0.26	1.00	0.29	-0.16	-0.05	0.04	-0.04
happy	-0.28	0.28	0.29	1.00	-0.11	-0.09	-0.12	-0.01
educ	0.37	-0.06	-0.16	-0.11	1.00	-0.02	0.02	-0.12
attend	0.00	-0.10	-0.05	-0.09	-0.02	1.00	-0.08	0.22
sexfreq	0.15	0.00	0.04	-0.12	0.02	-0.08	1.00	0.01
polviews	-0.01	-0.01	-0.04	-0.01	-0.12	0.22	0.01	1.00

n

	income16	satjob	satfin	happy	educ	attend	sexfreq	polviews
income16	2596	1647	2594	2591	2592	2589	1593	2521
satjob	1647	1777	1774	1773	1774	1768	1282	1713
satfin	2594	1774	2856	2850	2849	2842	1710	2749
happy	2591	1773	2850	2859	2853	2846	1709	2752
educ	2592	1774	2849	2853	2858	2845	1710	2752
attend	2589	1768	2842	2846	2845	2850	1704	2748
sexfreq	1593	1282	1710	1709	1710	1704	1712	1667
polviews	2521	1713	2749	2752	2752	2748	1667	2756

P	income16	satjob	satfin	happy	educ	attend	sexfreq	polviews
income16		0.0000	0.0000	0.0000	0.0000	0.9242	0.0000	0.5861
satjob	0.0000		0.0000	0.0000	0.0074	0.0000	0.9763	0.8090
satfin	0.0000	0.0000		0.0000	0.0000	0.0092	0.0694	0.0654
happy	0.0000	0.0000	0.0000		0.0000	0.0000	0.0000	0.7505
educ	0.0000	0.0074	0.0000	0.0000		0.3542	0.4411	0.0000
attend	0.9242	0.0000	0.0092	0.0000	0.3542		0.0005	0.0000
sexfreq	0.0000	0.9763	0.0694	0.0000	0.4411	0.0005		0.8130
polviews	0.5861	0.8090	0.0654	0.7505	0.0000	0.0000	0.8130	

When interpreting the correlation matrix we need to look at the r-values. Recall from Chapter 10 that the r-values tell us the strength and direction (positive or negative) of the realtionship. As a rule of thumb, if two variables have a correlation coefficient above $|.70|$, the relationship is likely to be too strong to include both variables in the model. For the correlation matrix we just ran, the largest correlations (in absolute values) are .37 and -.33. Therefore, multicollinearity would not be a concern in a multiple regression model using all of these variables. It is also possible to create a figure based on the correlation matrix in order to view the same results (Figure 12.10).

```
# Create a color ramp of blue colors to be used in the correlation matrix plot.
blues<-colorRampPalette(c("lightblue1","darkblue"))

# Open the library corrplot to run the multiple correlation plot.
library(corrplot)
corrplot(CM2$r, type="full", order="hclust", addrect = 3,
    col = blues(100), bg = "white",
    p.mat = CM2$P, sig.level = 0.05, insig="pch",
    tl.col = "black", tl.srt = 45)
```

The next section revisits a problem discussed in earlier chapters—missing data. One advanced approach researchers use to handle missing data is multiple imputation.

MULTIPLE IMPUTATION

This section is meant to introduce you to the topic of multiple data imputation and point to some procedures in R/RStudio. Importantly, the section was designed only to provide a loose introduction to the topic, as it has a long theoretical, conceptual, and methodological

FIGURE 12.10 ● GRAPHIC OF THE CORRELATION MATRIX

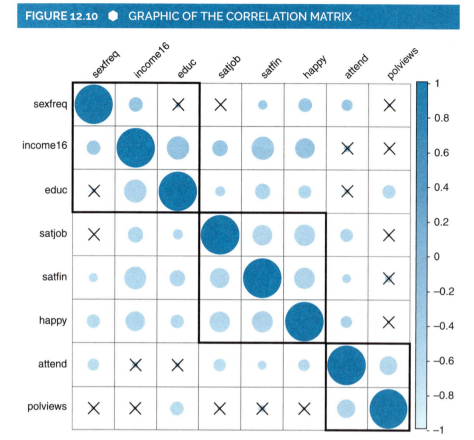

basis. We strongly recommend reading more on the topic prior to conducting any type of multiple imputation analyses for your research projects.

Multiple imputation is an iterative process by which missing data are assigned a value after several steps. The first and very important step is to decipher if the missing data are missing at random—which is necessary—or for some other reason. The second and third step are to create multiple copies of the dataset that can then all be imputed with estimated values for the missing data based on existing values and control variables. The first two steps are repeated several times allowing for a variation of the multiple estimated values, which will ultimately be averaged in order to create a single value.

Multiple imputation can be done with the library **mice** (multiple imputation by chained equations) for the calculations and the library **VIM** for some of the graphics. Using the script below, you can practice multiple imputation. As an example, we will be running a linear regression to determine if age (age) or financial satisfaction (satfin) can predict income level (`income16`). But first, we will impute the missing data for the variables age and financial satisfaction.

```
library(mice)  # Be sure to add the libraries for the multiple imputation.
library(VIM)

GSS2016$age[GSS2016$age==99]=NA  # Recode the non-value data to
missing data.
GSS2016$satfin[GSS2016$satfin==0]=NA
GSS2016$satfin[GSS2016$satfin==8]=NA
GSS2016$satfin[GSS2016$satfin==9]=NA


Group2<-GSS2016[, c("income16", "age", "satfin")]  # Assign the
variables you are working with to a small group data frame.


table(GSS2016$income16)  # Run tables to check that data was recoded.
table(GSS2016$age)
table(GSS2016$satfin)


md.pattern(Group2)  # Looking at pattern of missing data by variable
(Figure 12.11 is also produced).
```

Output: Matrix of missing observations by variable in Group2.

```
        age  satfin  income16
2587     1     1        1      0 -> 2587 out of 2867 are complete
259      1     1        0      1 -> 259 are missing data for
                                     income16
2        1     0        1      1 -> 2 are missing data for
                                     satfin
9        1     0        0      2 -> 9 are missing data for
                                     satfin & income16
7        0     1        1      1 -> 7 are missing data for age
3        0     1        0      2 -> 3 are missing data for age
                                     and income16
        10    11      271    292
```

FIGURE 12.11 ● MATRIX OF MISSING OBSERVATIONS BY VARIABLE IN GROUP2

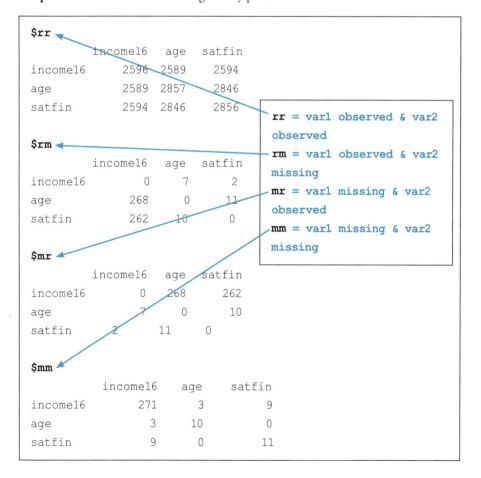

`md.pairs(Group2)` # Create individual matrices of missing/observed data for pairs within the regression model.

Output: Four matrices of the missing data by pairs.

```
$rr
           income16   age    satfin
income16      2596    2589     2594
age           2589    2857     2846
satfin        2594    2846     2856


$rm
           income16   age    satfin
income16         0     7       2
age            268     0      11
satfin         262    10       0


$mr
           income16   age    satfin
income16         0   268     262
age              7     0      10
satfin           2    11       0


$mm
           income16   age    satfin
income16       271     3       9
age              3    10       0
satfin           9     0      11
```

rr = var1 observed & var2 observed

rm = var1 observed & var2 missing

mr = var1 missing & var2 observed

mm = var1 missing & var2 missing

`IMP2<-mice(Group2)` # Running the multiple imputation and assigning it to IMP2.

In the following screenshot, the `Group 2` and the `IMP2` datasets have been created.

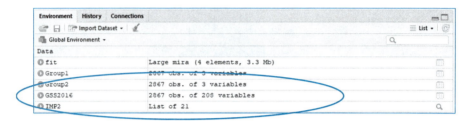

`summary(lm(income16~age+satfin, data=Group2))` # Running a linear regression and including the summary call for it.

Output: Regression for `age` and `satfin` predicting `income16`, before multiple imputation.

Call:
lm(formula = income16 ~ age + satfin, data = Group2)

Residuals:
Min	1Q	Median	3Q	Max
-19.258	-3.069	1.001	3.871	11.384

Coefficients:

	Estimate	Std. Error	t value	Pr(>|t|)
(Intercept)	23.143639	0.468506	49.399	<2e-16 ***
age	-0.011669	0.006326	-1.844	0.0652 .
satfin	-2.617021	0.146569	-17.855	<2e-16 ***

Signif. codes: 0 '***' 0.001 '**' 0.01 '*' 0.05 '.' 0.1 ' ' 1

Residual standard error: 5.501 on 2584 degrees of freedom
  (280 observations deleted due to missingness)
Multiple R-squared: 0.1101,   Adjusted R-squared: 0.1094
F-statistic: 159.8 on 2 and 2584 DF, *p*-value: < 2.2e-16

```
fit<-with(IMP2, lm(income16~age+satfin)); pool(fit)
```
 # Imputing the data that has been pooled from the multiple imputations.

```
summary(pool(fit))
```

Output: The regression for `age` and `satfin` predicting `income16`, after multiple imputation.

	est	se	t	df	Pr(>|t|)
(Intercept)	23.2296357	0.503622633	46.125083	72.22160	0.0000000
age	–0.0112156	0.008174807	–1.371972	17.02953	0.1878768
satfin	–2.6704079	0.157814751	–16.921155	76.95090	0.00000000

Now that you are familiar with the basic concept and process behind multiple imputation, you can compare the two statistical models. There are some changes in the significance of the variables in the statistical models as well as the model fit.

To summarize, we had roughly 292 missing values out of 8600 possible, which is just over 3%. Even when we impute a small percentage of data, we can see changes in our results— but, again—proceed with great caution if you plan to use this procedure in practice. *There is a great deal more to learn.*

FURTHER EXPLORATION

This book has used R/RStudio and the General Social Survey to cover a variety of descriptive and inferential staistical analyses that are commonly used in quantitative analysis. These tests, which include *t*-tests, ANOVA, chi-square, correlation, and regression offer a foundation into statistics that can be built upon for years to come. As large as the scope and potential of quantitative social science research is, the same can be said about the breadth of possibilities using R and RStudio.

There are several advanced statistical models that are beyond the scope of this book, yet might be some of the next logical considerations for researchers (e.g., multilevel models and multinomial logistic regression). Multilevel models (e.g., heirarchical linear models, nested models, mixed models, random effects models) are statistical models that deal with units of analysis across multiple levels. As an example, we would consider using a multilevel model if we wanted to analyze individuals' self-reported health data but also community level data for public health awareness programs and public health policy. Another example is the nested model, in which, data on individual levels are also nested within aggregate data at a higher level (e.g., family, census block, city, etc.).

As a refresher, logistic regression is when we have a dichotomous outcome (DV) variable instead of a continuous outcome variable, and one or more continuous or categorical predictor variables (IVs). A multinomial logistic regression also has a discreet outcome variable, but instead of it being a dichotomous (two-group) variable, a multinomial logistic regression has an outcome variable that has three or more groups that are in no particular order (nominal). The predictor variables remain to be one or more continuous or categorical variables.

CONCLUSION

This final chapter discussed some more advanced topics encountered in regression analysis, including skewed data and multicollinearity. We covered common data transformations (i.e., polynomials and log transformations) to correct for issues associated with the non-normal distribution of data. We also touched very briefly on multiple imputation. Additional advanced topics (i.e., multilevel models and multinomial logistic regression) received barely more than a mention. These are for you to explore going forward.

Exercises

1. Use the GSS codebook to read what the variable `cohort` represents and what the non-value answers are.

2. Recode the variable to remove the non-value (NA) data (i.e., Don't know, No answer, and Not applicable).

3. Create an object for each of the following transformations of the data: squared, cubed, square root.

4. Run a histogram for each of the newly transformed objects. Try a different color for each histogram and add a title (main) to each histogram.

Supplementary Digital Content

Download datasets and R code at the companion website at https://study.sagepub.com/researchmethods/statistics/gillespie-r-for-statistics

INDEX